Keeping the Ancient Way
Aspects of the Life and Work of Henry Vaughan (1621–1695)

ENGLISH ASSOCIATION STUDIES, 7

English Association Monographs: English at the Interface

Series Editors
Claire Jowitt, University of East Anglia
Jennifer Richards, Newcastle University

Editorial Board
Martin Eve, Birkbeck, University of London
Clare Lees, King's College, London
Gail Marshall, University of Reading
Anshuman Mondal, University of East Anglia
Sinead Morrissey, Newcastle University
Rick Rylance, Director, School of Advanced Studies, University of London
Lyndsey Stonebridge, University of Birmingham
Greg Walker, University of Edinburgh

Established in 1906, The English Association is the oldest established association in the UK for all those interested in English at all levels, from primary to higher education. Its aim is to further knowledge, understanding and enjoyment of the English language and its literatures and to foster good practice in its teaching and learning at all levels. In 2006, the English Association launched a new series – *English Association Monographs*, which is now published by Liverpool University Press.

English Association Monographs invites submissions that explore or represent English Studies at the interface with other languages, cultures, professions and disciplines from the medieval period to the present day. It also welcomes submissions that reflect on or contribute to interdisciplinary conversations, or which are the product of thinking across disciplines or across sectors, or which explore the intersections between English Studies, Digital Humanities, and the new technologies of any period. The General Editors and the Editorial Board will work with authors to produce books that are written clearly and eloquently, and represent the best and most exciting new work in English Language and Literature.

Also in this series:
John Keats' Medical Notebook: Text, Context, and Poems
by Hrileena Ghosh

Tyranny and Usurpation: The New Prince and Lawmaking Violence in Early Modern Drama by Doyeeta Majumder

Writing Life: Early Twentieth-Century Autobiographies of the Artist-Hero
by Mhairi Pooler

The Historical Jesus and the Literary Imagination 1860–1920
by Jennifer Stevens

ROBERT WILCHER

Keeping the Ancient Way

Aspects of the Life and Work
of Henry Vaughan (1621–1695)

LIVERPOOL UNIVERSITY PRESS
THE ENGLISH ASSOCIATION

First published 2021 by
Liverpool University Press
4 Cambridge Street
Liverpool
L69 7ZU

This paperback edition published 2024

Copyright © 2024 Robert Wilcher

The right of Robert Wilcher to be identified as the author of this book has been asserted by him in accordance with the Copyright, Design and Patents Act 1988.

All rights reserved. No part of this book may be reproduced, stored in a retrieval system, or transmitted, in any form or by any means, electronic, mechanical, photocopying, recording, or otherwise, without the prior written permission of the publisher.

British Library Cataloguing-in-Publication data
A British Library CIP record is available

ISBN 978 1 80085 974 6 (hardback)
ISBN 978 1 80207 484 0 (paperback)

Typeset by Carnegie Book Production, Lancaster
Printed and bound by CPI Group (UK) Ltd, Croydon CR0 4YY

In memory of Anne Cluysenaar and Peter Thomas

Because my people hath forgotten mee, they haue burnt incense to vanitie, and they haue caused them to stumble in their waies from the ancient paths.

(Jeremiah 18:15)

Then keep the antient way!
　　　　Spit out their phlegm
And fill thy brest with home; think on thy dream:
　　　　A calm, bright day!
A Land of flowers and spices! the word given,
　If these be fair, O what is Heaven!
　　　　　　　(Henry Vaughan, 'The Proffer',
　　　　　　　　　Silex Scintillans, 1655)

Contents

Acknowledgements — xi
List of Abbreviations — xiii
Introduction — 1

Part One: Biographical and Historical Contexts

1 Henry Vaughan and Breconshire — 11
2 Henry Vaughan and Thomas Vaughan — 37
3 Henry Vaughan and the Civil Wars — 77
4 Henry Vaughan and the Interregnum — 103
5 Henry Vaughan and the Church — 141

Part Two: Literary Practices

6 Henry Vaughan and the Art of Allusion — 171
7 Henry Vaughan and George Herbert — 193
8 Henry Vaughan and the Scriptures — 225
9 Henry Vaughan and the Book of Nature — 259
10 Henry Vaughan and the Practice of Poetry — 289

Epilogue — 327

Bibliography — 333
Index of Vaughan's Works — 351
General Index — 355

Acknowledgements

The debts I have incurred over the years that I have been writing about Henry Vaughan are many and varied. The most long-standing and deeply rooted is the one to Elsie Duncan-Jones, the supervisor of my University of Birmingham Ph.D., in which I engaged with the use of natural details in the poetry of Henry Vaughan and his contemporaries. Her example and advice shaped my approach to literary scholarship throughout my academic career. Like any toiler in this particular vineyard, I gratefully acknowledge the pioneering work of Louise Imogen Guiney and Gwenllian E.F. Morgan and the vital contribution of F.E. Hutchinson, whose *Henry Vaughan: A Life and Interpretation* (1947) incorporated and augmented the fruits of their research. Many fine studies of Vaughan have been built on these foundations and have played their part in the evolution of this book. More recently, the Vaughan Association, founded as the Usk Valley Vaughan Association by the late Anne Cluysenaar and Peter Thomas, has provided a major impetus to the development of Vaughan studies through its annual colloquium. I am personally indebted to Anne and Peter for their encouragement and to the many participants who have made the colloquium such an inspiring event. Among the latter, Jonathan Nauman, Helen and Allan Wilcox, Jeremy Hooker, Joe Sterrett, Donald Dickson, Tony Brown, Hilary Davies and Elizabeth Siberry have contributed more than they know through their stimulating papers and conversations. I am also grateful for the kindness and efficiency of the staff in the Main Library of the University of Birmingham, the Shakespeare Institute Library in Stratford-upon-Avon, the Bodleian Library in Oxford, the British Library in London and the National Library of Wales in Aberystwyth.

I have incorporated material from the following papers that were previously published in *Scintilla*, the annual volume produced by the Vaughan Association: 'Henry Vaughan and the Church' (1998) in Chapter Five; '"Feathering Some Slower Hours": Henry Vaughan's Verse Translations' (2000) in Chapters One, Two, and Three; 'The Darkened Scribe and the Blessed Man: Changing Uses of Allusion in the Work of Henry Vaughan' (2005) in Chapters Six and Seven; 'Henry Vaughan, Jeremy Taylor, Edward Sparke, and the Preservation of the Anglican Communion' (2008) in Chapter Five; 'Henry Vaughan and the Poetry of Trees' (2010) in Chapter Nine; 'Exile in Breconshire: The Double Displacement of Henry Vaughan' (2011) in Chapter One; '"Thalia" and the "Father of Lights": Nature and God in the Works of Henry Vaughan and Thomas Vaughan' (2012) in Chapter Two; and 'Henry Vaughan's Borrowings in the Secular Poems: Plagiarism, Imitation, Allusion' (2013) in Chapter Six. Part of Chapter Seven was published under the title '"The Present Times are Not / To Snudge In": Henry Vaughan, *The Temple*, and the Pressure of History', in *George Herbert: Sacred and Profane* (1995), edited by Helen Wilcox and Richard Todd, and is reproduced by kind permission of VU University Press, Amsterdam. Chapter Four had its distant origins in an article entitled '"Then Keep the Ancient Way": A Study of Henry Vaughan's *Silex Scintillans*', which appeared in the now discontinued *Durham University Journal* (1983).

I am grateful to Helen Wilcox, Jonathan Nauman, and the late Peter Thomas for their helpful comments on some of the draft chapters. My thanks are also due to Christabel Scaife, Senior Commissioning Editor at Liverpool University Press, for her generous support of the project, and to the anonymous Reader for a scrutiny of the whole typescript and valuable suggestions for its improvement. My greatest debt of gratitude, as always, is to my wife and daughters and the rest of my long-suffering family, especially during the past decade or so when Henry Vaughan has consumed so much of my retirement.

Robert Wilcher
August 2020

Abbreviations

HV Works   *The Works of Henry Vaughan*, ed. Donald R. Dickson, Alan Rudrum, and Robert Wilcher, 3 vols. (Oxford: Oxford University Press, 2018)
Life   F.E. Hutchinson, *Henry Vaughan: A Life and Interpretation* (Oxford: Clarendon Press, 1947)
OED   *Oxford English Dictionary*
TV Works   *The Works of Thomas Vaughan*, ed. Alan Rudrum (Oxford: Clarendon Press, 1984)

Except for the epigraphs to poems printed in *Silex Scintillans*, biblical quotations from the King James/Authorized Version of the Holy Bible are from the 400th anniversary edition published by Oxford University Press in 2010.

Quotations from the poetry and prose of Henry Vaughan are from the 2018 Oxford University Press edition of Vaughan's works. Only page numbers are given, since the three volumes are continuously paginated.

All italics in quoted extracts are original unless otherwise indicated.

Introduction

I

On 10 June 1673, John Aubrey wrote to his distant kinsman Henry Vaughan soliciting information for Anthony Wood, who was compiling a history of the University of Oxford.[1] Replying from the county town of Brecon on 15 June, Vaughan provided a few details about the lives of himself and his twin brother, Thomas, together with lists of their respective published works. He notes as an afterthought that his cousin might add – should he 'thinke it fitt' – 'Thalia Rediviva, a peece now ready for the presse, with the Remaines of my brothers Latine Poems (for many of them are lost,)'.[2] Since neither of the twins had ventured into print since 1657, it is not surprising that he concludes his letter with an expression of thanks to his 'Honour'd Cousin' for seeking him out in his provincial obscurity: 'Deare S^r. I am highly obliged to you that you would be

---

1 Although Vaughan and Aubrey address each other as 'cousin', the exact nature of their relationship is not known. Aubrey, whose manuscript collection of biographical information about his contemporaries was later published in various editions under the title *Brief Lives*, was in error when he claimed that the grandmother of the Vaughan brothers was an Aubrey, but there was certainly a connection by marriage, since both Charles Walbeoffe, the twins' first cousin, and his son took their wives from among the Aubrey clan. (See F.E. Hutchinson, *Henry Vaughan: A Life and Interpretation* (Oxford: Clarendon Press, 1947), pp. 206–07.)
2 *The Works of Henry Vaughan*, ed. Donald R. Dickson, Alan Rudrum, and Robert Wilcher, 3 vols. (Oxford: Oxford University Press, 2018), pp. 800–02. *Thalia Rediviva: The Pass-Times and Diversions of a Countrey-Muse* was not published for another five years and contained mostly poems composed in the 1640s and 1650s.

pleased to remember, & reflect vpon such low & forgotten thinges, as my brother & my selfe. I shalbe ever ready to acknowledge the honour you have done vs.'³ This note was struck again when he wrote to Aubrey on 9 December 1675, after some of the material he had supplied about himself and Thomas had made its way into Wood's *Historia et Antiquitates Universitatis Oxoniensis* (1674):

> That my dear brothers name (& mine) are revived, & shine in the *Historie of the Vniversitie*; is an honour we owe vnto your Care & kindnes: & realie (dear Cousin!) I am verie sensible of it.⁴

The word 'revived', which echoes the Latin epithet applied to Thalia in the title of his last volume, is indicative of Vaughan's feeling that a kind of death had swallowed up the literary activities of the twins and erased them from the public memory.

Despite his gratitude to Aubrey for acting as go-between, however, he evidently considered that Wood had failed to do justice to the Vaughan twins *as authors* and this resentment continued to rankle. When, some fifteen years later, the antiquarian wrote to him directly from Oxford with an enquiry about several prominent residents of South Wales, Vaughan seized the opportunity to register his sense of grievance: 'If you intend a second Edition of the Oxford-historie, I must give you a better account of my brothers books & mine; wch are in the first much mistaken, & many omitted.'⁵ He must have been even more disgruntled if Wood's later biographical dictionary of Oxford graduates, *Athenae Oxonienses* (1691–92), ever came his way. In this repository of information about Oxford-educated writers and clergymen, Henry is not accorded a separate entry but gets passing notice in connection with Thomas's Latin verses, the Welsh grammarian John David Rhys, and the commendatory poem he had supplied for the collected works of William Cartwright in 1651.⁶ Some amends were made in the second edition of *Athenae*

---

3 *HV Works*, p. 802.
4 *HV Works*, p. 805.
5 Letter to Anthony Wood, dated 25 March 1689, *HV Works*, p. 807. Apparently, Aubrey had already passed on Wood's request, but sickness had prevented Vaughan from replying.
6 Vaughan had supplied information about Rhys in his correspondence with Wood in 1689.

Oxonienses (1721), which drew upon manuscript material left by Wood at his death in 1695 and contained more facts than had been transmitted by Vaughan himself. Since this became the main source for subsequent accounts of the life and career of Henry Vaughan, it is worth quoting more or less in full:

> Henry Vaughan, called the *Silurist* from that part of Wales whose inhabitants were in ancient times called Silures, brother twin (but elder) to Eugenius Philalethes, alias Tho. Vaughan [...] was born at Newton S. Briget, lying on the river Isca, commonly called Uske, in Brecknockshire, educated in grammar learning in his own country for six years under one Matthew Herbert, a noted schoolmaster of his time, made his first entry into Jesus College in Mich. Term 1638, aged 17 years; where spending two years or more in logicals under a noted tutor, was taken thence and designed by his father for the obtaining of some knowledge in the municipal laws at London. But soon after the civil war beginning, to the horror of all good men, he was sent for home, followed the pleasant paths of poetry and philology, became noted for his ingenuity, and published several specimens thereof, of which his *Olor Iscanus* was most valued. Afterwards applying his mind to the study of physic, became at length eminent in his own country for the practice thereof, and was esteemed by scholars an ingenious person, but proud and humorous. [Vaughan's published works are then listed.] He died in the latter end of April (about the 29th day) in sixteen hundred ninety and five, and was buried in the parish church of Llansenfreid, about two miles distant from Brecknock, in Brecknockshire.[7]

II

The fact that this biographical information about Henry Vaughan was at last available in print did not prevent his literary works from descending deeper into the oblivion that had begun to overtake

---

7 The passage is quoted from Bliss's edition of 1813–20 (vol. IV, p. 425), since this is the main source upon which writers of the life of Vaughan relied in the nineteenth century. In his original letter to Aubrey, Vaughan had given the date of his birth as 1621 and noted that he did not stay in Oxford to take a degree.

them during his own lifetime. None of his nine published volumes was reprinted. Even the *Olor Iscanus* that appeared in 1679 was a reissue, not a reprint, of the 1651 edition, and in the augmented *Silex Scintillans*, published in 1655, the first part consisted of unsold sheets from the edition of 1650. Edward Phillips included him as the author of *Olor Iscanus* in *Theatrum Poetarum* (1675), but William Winstanley left him out of *The Lives of the Most Famous English Poets* (1687), so that before he died his name had slipped from the nation's cultural consciousness.[8] It was not until the beginning of the nineteenth century that Vaughan's work began to emerge from almost total eclipse. In the second edition of *Specimens of the Early English Poets* (1801), George Ellis reprinted from *Olor Iscanus* three stanzas of a poem celebrating a marriage or betrothal, 'To the best, and most accomplish'd Couple—'. During the same decade, his name and verse also made a brief appearance in *A History of the County of Brecknock* (1805–09) by Theophilus Jones, which contains a wealth of information about the topography, inhabitants, history, buildings, religion, laws, and customs of the region. The second volume is devoted to genealogies of leading families and descriptions of each of the parishes, including lists of patrons and incumbents. In his account of the parish of Llansantffraed, with its church dedicated to Sancta Freda or St Bridget, Jones has occasion to mention 'two brothers, of the name of Vaughan, of very eccentric characters', who lived in a farm house called Newton that 'was of some celebrity in the seventeenth century'.[9] Having given an account of Thomas's life and works derived largely from Anthony Wood, he turns his attention to Henry, 'a doctor of physic' with no qualification from 'either of the universities', who – unlike his alchemist brother – did not 'profess any regard for magic or the muses'. He later prints an extract from 'To the River Isca' and all but the opening couplet of 'The

---

8 The almost complete disappearance of Vaughan's name from the public record has been traced by E.L. Marilla in 'The Significance of Henry Vaughan's Literary Reputation', *Modern Language Quarterly*, 5 (1944), 155–62. Louise Guiney reported that Carew Hazlitt had discovered 'the advertisement of an eighteenth-century Vaughan reprint', but such a volume has never come to light. (See 'Henry Vaughan the Silurist', *The Atlantic Monthly*, 73 (May 1894), 687.)

9 Quotations are from *A History of the County of Brecknock in Two Volumes*, reprinted from the edition of 1805–09 (Brecon: Edwin Davies, 1898), pp. 435–36.

Charnel-house', the first two poems in *Olor Iscanus*, which he seems to attribute to Thomas Vaughan. Indeed, his garbled introduction to this act of retrieval suggests that he had not read the entry on the elder twin in the 1721 edition of *Athenae Oxonienses* and had little or no direct acquaintance with his works. Whatever the limitations and errors in his knowledge of Henry's literary output, however, Jones did bring two of his poems back into print and added a little to the sum of historical information: the 'eccentric' brothers who occupied Newton in the seventeenth century were related to the Vaughans of Tretower and the Somersets, who were earls of Worcester, and when he died in 1695, Henry was survived by children from two marriages.

Poems from *Silex Scintillans* made their first appearance in print since the seventeenth century in Thomas Campbell's *Specimens of the British Poets* (1819), which found room for 'The Wreath', eighteen lines from 'The Rain-bow', and the first two stanzas of 'The Timber'. A slightly larger selection from *Silex Scintillans* was made by John Mitford for *Sacred Specimens Selected from the Early English Poets* (1827); Richard Cattermole included thirteen of Vaughan's religious poems in *Sacred Poetry of the Seventeenth Century* (1836); and several items were admitted to Edward Farr's *Gems of Sacred Poetry* (1841?). In 1839, 'The Retreat' had caught the attention of Robert Willmott for expressing an aspiration towards childhood innocence that 'will find an echo in many bosoms'.[10] This was the state of knowledge up to 1847, when the Reverend Henry Lyte inaugurated modern Vaughan scholarship and criticism with his edition of *Silex Scintillans*, to which he added the religious poems and 'Daphnis. An Elegiac Eclogue' from *Thalia Rediviva*. Although most of the material in his biographical introduction was derived from Wood, Lyte had made 'what enquiries he could both at Oxford and in the neighbourhood where Vaughan lived and died', as well as 'carefully looking through' Vaughan's published volumes.[11] Some of the conclusions he drew from this latter activity are now regarded as simplistic and the texts of several poems were marred

10 Quoted from R.E.A. Willmott, *Lives of the Sacred Poets* (1834), p. 293 by Helen N. McMaster, 'Vaughan and Wordsworth', *Review of English Studies*, 11 (1935), 315. Information in this paragraph is derived from McMaster's article and from Marilla, 'The Significance of Henry Vaughan's Literary Reputation'.

11 Silex Scintillans: *Sacred Poems and Private Ejaculations by Henry Vaughan*, ed. Rev. H.F. Lyte (London: Pickering, 1847), p. xiii.

by misguided and unacknowledged editorial 'improvements', but his work constitutes the first serious attempt to revive interest in Vaughan and to place the central achievement of *Silex Scintillans* in the broader context of his life and writing. The inclusion of 'The Retreat' in *The Golden Treasury of the Best Songs and Lyrical Poems in the English Language*, selected by Francis Palgrave in 1863, was a further step in the gradual acceptance of Vaughan into the popular canon of English poets.

All the verse and prose was collected for the first time by the Reverend Alexander B. Grosart in the Fuller Worthies' Library edition of 1871; in 1896 the complete poetry was edited for the Muses' Library by E.K. Chambers; and in 1914, L.C. Martin produced what became the standard scholarly edition of the complete works for more than a century. Chambers's list of acknowledgements had concluded with a particular tribute to Miss G.E.F. Morgan of Brecon, 'whose knowledge of local genealogy and antiquities has been invaluable'.[12] Gwenllian Morgan went on, in collaboration with the American poet and critic Louise I. Guiney, to gather a mass of new information about Henry Vaughan with the object of producing a biography. The two women had begun to correspond in 1895 and it was announced more than once over the next forty years that an edition of Vaughan's poetry with a biographical introduction was being prepared, but the project was never completed. Louise Guiney edited *The Mount of Olives* as well as publishing various critical and historical essays on Vaughan before her death in 1920.[13] When Gwenllian Morgan died in 1939, her accumulated research on Vaughan was passed to Canon F.E. Hutchinson in the form of 'many notebooks, files, genealogies, copies of legal documents, magazine articles, and hundreds of letters that had passed between the two ladies during the twenty-four years of their collaboration'. Hutchinson explained that, since he could find 'nothing in it ready for printing', he decided to 'preserve all that was of value in the collection' in a book of his 'own planning', which

---

12 *The Poems of Henry Vaughan Silurist*, ed. E.K Chambers, 2 vols., The Muses' Library (London: George Routledge & Sons, 1896), Vol. II, p. lvi.
13 *The Mount of Olives and Primitive Holiness set forth in the Life of Paulinus Bishop of Nola*, ed. L.I. Guiney (London: Henry Frowde, 1902). For information about this pioneer of Vaughan scholarship and criticism, see Jonathan Nauman's article, 'Louise Imogen Guiney and Henry Vaughan', *Brycheiniog*, 48 (2017), 98–121.

would also 'incorporate the results' of his own researches.[14] The facts thus shaped into *Henry Vaughan: A Life and Interpretation* (1947) have remained the primary source for subsequent accounts of the poet's career, including Alan Rudrum's contribution to the 'Writers of Wales' series and the more substantial biography by Stevie Davies published in 1995. Since then, Rudrum has supplied the article on Henry Vaughan in the *Oxford Dictionary of National Biography*, and *Scintilla*, the annual publication of the Vaughan Association, has published a sequence of papers on various aspects of Vaughan's life by the Welsh poet and critic, Roland Mathias, originally designed as chapters for a book that was left unfinished at his death in 2007.[15]

While he was working on the material inherited from Morgan and Guiney, Hutchinson had transcribed many of their textual and explanatory notes on the poems and added 'his own observations'. This material was subsequently made available to L.C. Martin and a selection from it incorporated into the revised Commentary for a second edition of the complete works published by Clarendon Press in 1957.[16] Martin's original Oxford edition of 1914, which marked the culmination of the first phase of the recovery of Vaughan's writings from oblivion, had contributed to a growing interest in the poet that was manifested in periodical articles and the earliest (although brief) book-length studies: Edmund Blunden's *On the Poems of Henry Vaughan: Characteristics and Intimations*, published in 1927, to which were appended his own translations from Vaughan's Latin poems; and Elizabeth Holmes's *Henry Vaughan and the Hermetic Philosophy*, published in 1932, which explored Henry's debt to the occult and alchemical tradition embraced by his twin brother. After the Second World War, in the wake of Hutchinson's biography and Martin's second edition, articles and books proliferated. At first,

14 *Life*, p. v. The impact that Hutchinson's lack of sympathy with the religious and political views of Guiney and Morgan had on his interpretation of their pioneering work is discussed by Jonathan Nauman in 'F.E. Hutchinson, Louise Guiney, and Henry Vaughan', *Scintilla*, 6 (2002), 135–47. Nauman describes Hutchinson's book as 'a careful articulation of the current state of biographical research on Vaughan, punctuated by brief evaluative remarks on the poems' (136).
15 See the appreciation of Mathias and his work by Jeremy Hooker, 'For Roland Mathias: Tribute and Apology', *Scintilla*, 13 (2009), 95–100.
16 See the preface to *The Works of Henry Vaughan*, ed. L.C. Martin, 2nd edn. (Oxford: Clarendon Press, 1957), p. iii.

academic critics had chosen to focus almost exclusively on the devotional or mystical aspects of Vaughan's oeuvre. The books by Ross Garner, E.C. Pettet, and R.A Durr are representative of this concentration on *Silex Scintillans*. The cause of the secular poems had been championed by E.L. Marilla during the 1940s, however, and was taken up by James D. Simmonds in *Masques of God: Form and Theme in the Poetry of Henry Vaughan*, published in 1972.[17] Editions of the complete poetry by French Fogle in 1965 and Alan Rudrum in 1976 complemented Martin's *Works* in providing a firm textual foundation for Kenneth Friedenreich's volume in the Twayne's English Authors series, for later studies by Thomas O. Calhoun, Jonathan F.S. Post, Noel Kennedy Thomas, and Philip West and for the many articles and chapters by various hands that have carried forward the knowledge and appreciation of Henry Vaughan into the twenty-first century.[18] The twentieth-century editions were superseded by *The Works of Henry Vaughan* in three volumes, published by Oxford University Press in 2018.

This collection of essays brings together some of my own published contributions to Vaughan studies going back to 1974, revised and augmented in the light of developments in scholarship and criticism over the past forty-five years and supplemented by entirely new material. The focus is on aspects of Vaughan's life, beliefs, and art that remain areas of ongoing debate. Each chapter contains a relatively free-standing treatment of a single topic, supplying where appropriate a brief history of the development of critical interest in it, but the two groups of chapters have been organized into a structure that progressively opens up biographical, contextual, intellectual, and literary features of the man and his work. Those in the first part of the volume are concerned mainly with biographical and historical matters; those in the second part take up more literary aspects of Vaughan's writing.

17 E.L. Marilla's work culminated in his edition, *The Secular Poems of Henry Vaughan* (Uppsala: A.-B. Lundequistska Bokhandeln, 1958).
18 For a survey of the critical responses to Vaughan since the early nineteenth century, see 'A History of Vaughan Scholarship and Criticism', *HV Works*, pp. lviii–lxxxvi.

PART ONE

Biographical and Historical Contexts

CHAPTER ONE

Henry Vaughan and Breconshire

I

'Wales gave me birth,' declared Henry Vaughan in the Latin poem with which he prefaced *Olor Iscanus* (1651), 'in the place where Father Usk launches down from the windswept mountains to wander in broad valleys'.[1] From the earliest years of his infancy through his childhood and adolescence, he had lived within sight of the River Usk as it wound its way along the valley below Newton, the farmhouse in which he was born and reared, to Llangattock, where it flowed past the rectory of his tutor, the Reverend Matthew Herbert, with whom Henry and his twin Thomas boarded for six years before going to Oxford. Newton was just north of the turnpike road between Brecon (some six miles to the north-west) and Crickhowell (some nine miles to the south-east) and a little less than a mile to the east of the village of Scethrog. From a probate inventory of the Newton estate taken when Thomas Vaughan senior died in 1658, it is possible to form some idea of the proportions of the farmhouse during the seventeenth century. There was a wainscoted hall, furnished with a table, benches, and chairs, which would have been the family's main living-room; a good-sized kitchen; a buttery; and a room designated 'the study', which contained a 'little bed' and was also probably on the ground floor. Above the kitchen were two chambers and 'over the entry' a 'little chamber'. There must have been space for other bedrooms on the first floor and there was also a 'Garrett'. In addition to various furnishings, cooking and eating utensils, clothes, and such

[1] *'Ad Posteros'*, translation quoted from *HV Works*, p. 164.

farmhouse equipment as cheese vats, a 'small flax wheele', and an 'old churning tub', the inventory lists four sheep, one ram, two lambs, half a bushel of 'oaten mault', a peck of 'barley mault', and eight acres 'of hard corn growing in the field called y Llaworth y Ty'.[2] According to a survey of houses in the Brecon district undertaken during the early 1960s, the Vaughan family home was considerably altered and enlarged in the following centuries.[3] The farmhouse now standing on the site contains 'conspicuously large and ancient timbers' that may have been reused from the original building.[4]

Rising northwards behind the present Newton is Allt yr Esgair, which means 'steep wooded slope of the ridge'. Like much of the surrounding countryside, this would have been more abundantly covered in woods and copses of oak and alder than it is today.[5] Theophilus Jones described the prospects from the top of this ridge at the beginning of the nineteenth century:

> [O]n the south is the vale of Usk, westward of Bwlch with the river Usk, here perfectly *serpentine*, meandring through the middle of it; towards the west is a distant view of the town of Brecon and the adjacent country terminated by Bwlch Aberbrân; northward we catch a glimpse of Pontywal, Trephilip and the country about Talgarth, and in the back ground the Radnorshire hills; but contracting the view to the foot of the hill and the neighbourhood, that beautiful sheet of water the lake of Llynsavaddan presents itself to the eye, surrounded by the picturesque village of Llanfihangel tallyn, the churches of Llangasty and Cathedine, the ruins of Blanllyfni and the church and village of Llangorse.[6]

---

2 Quoted from the full text of the inventory given by Hutchinson in *Life*, pp. 16–17.
3 See S.R. Jones and J.T. Smith, 'The Houses of Breconshire: Part III. The Brecon District', *Brycheiniog*, 11 (1965), 44–47.
4 Stevie Davies cites private correspondence with the current owner in June 1994. See *Henry Vaughan*, Border Lines Series (Bridgend: Seren, Poetry of Wales Press, 1995), p. 31.
5 Davies, *Henry Vaughan*, pp. 144–45.
6 Theophilus Jones, *A History of the County of Brecknock in Two Volumes*, reprinted from the edition of 1805–09 (Brecon: Edwin Davies, 1898), p. 437. Today the 'sheet of water' is known as Llangorse Lake.

When Stevie Davies was preparing her tercentenary biography of Vaughan, she looked across the valley from Newton and described the view 'over the Usk plain' as 'not precisely one of grandeur', but of 'bosomy rising ground, patchworked with fields many shades of green, sparsely populated and with a rhythm of dense timbering', where 'alternations of light and shadow chase over the Beacons, turning the tender green of Talybont Forest to the sombrest black, and back again'.[7]

As well as the wide sweep of the landscape, there were particular features of the natural setting in which the Vaughan twins grew up that would have been more intimately meshed into their daily experiences. Many years later, Thomas made a note of a dream in which he was lying 'under the shelter of the great Oake, which growes before the Court yard of my fathers house'.[8] In one of the poems published in *Thalia Rediviva*, Henry recalled the time they had spent further down the Usk valley at Llangattock, where there was also an oak tree, 'whose stately height and shade / Projected far, a goodly shelter made'. Matthew Herbert used to teach his 'beauteous Flock' in its shade by day, and later, 'when the careless world did sleep', he would regale them beneath its branches with the 'visions of our black, but brightest Bard'.[9] The great yew tree that still looks out over the front wall of the churchyard at Llansantffraed would have been yet another familiar sight.[10]

The parish church of St Bridget's, fashioned out of red sandstone on the site of the seventeenth-century church in 1884, is a mile's walk from Newton along the main road towards Bwlch, Crickhowell, and Llangattock. The building frequented by Vaughan was probably the same one patronizingly described by Theophilus Jones in the early nineteenth century: 'The steeple or tower or whatever it may be

---

7 Davies, *Henry Vaughan*, p. 31.
8 *Thomas and Rebecca Vaughan's* Aqua Vitae: Non Vitis, ed. and trans. Donald R. Dickson, *Medieval and Renaissance Texts and Studies*, Vol. 217 (Tempe, AZ: Arizona Center for Medieval and Renaissance Studies, 2001), p. 239. Thomas recorded his dream in 1658.
9 'Daphnis. An Elegiac Eclogue', *HV Works*, p. 787. L.C. Martin notes Louise Guiney's suggestion that the Welsh bard was Myrddin Emrys (Merlin Ambrosius). See the note on 787:61, *HV Works*, p. 1379.
10 This tree, unlike the less ancient yew that overlooks Vaughan's grave behind the church, is some 800 or 900 years old (Davies, *Henry Vaughan*, p. 9).

called, containing one bell only, has rather a grotesque appearance, and resembles a beehive, or the bottom of a pot turned upwards.'[11] The historian of Brecknockshire believed that this church replaced an older structure that had been demolished in 1690, but Roland Mathias cites evidence that the 'curious low structure with a cupola, whitewashed and primitive', of which four water-colour likenesses still exist, dated from 1626 and survived until 1884.[12] Not far from St Bridget's was Buckland, one of the most substantial houses in the vicinity and the seat during Vaughan's lifetime of members of the local Games and Jones clans. Built in the sixteenth century by Meredith Games, it first came into the hands of the Jones family when Elizabeth Games, a great-granddaughter of Meredith, married William Jones of Ty mawr, who died there in 1661.[13] The other significant mansion in the immediate neighbourhood of Newton was Scethrog House, which passed in 1684 into the possession of Charles Vaughan, senior surviving member of the Tretower branch of the family.[14] Tretower Court, the ancestral home of the twins' father, was situated north of the turnpike road just over half way from Newton to Llangattock. Whether he was living with his parents or with Matthew Herbert, therefore, Henry was within easy reach of his closest Vaughan relatives, whose impressive late medieval residence, with its gatehouse, courtyard, and great hall – not forgetting the nearby ruined castle

11 Jones, *A History of the County of Brecknock*, p. 432.
12 Roland Mathias, 'Man on those Hills of Myrrh and Flowres', *Dock Leaves*, 3:7 (1952), 21. During the 1950s, Mathias had been shown a rubbing with the date 1626 taken from one of the windows of the church that was replaced in 1884. Water-colour paintings of the original church are reproduced in *HV Works*, p. xlii (in black and white) and in *Henry Vaughan and the Usk Valley*, ed. Elizabeth Siberry and Robert Wilcher (Little Logaston Woonton Almeley: Logaston Press, 2016), pp. 30, 33, 46, 87 (in colour).
13 See Jones, *A History of the County of Brecknock*, p. 435. The present Buckland Hall dates from the nineteenth century.
14 See *Life*, pp. 203–04. In an account of Scethrog House, Ithiel Vaughan Poppy cites Hutchinson's book (wrongly attributing it to Gwenllian Morgan and Louise Guiney), but misreads what he says and relies upon 'a copy of the Tretower branch of the Vaughan family tree from a cousin living in Africa' to argue erroneously that 'Dr Henry Vaughan M.D.' was living in Scethrog House until 1658, when he inherited Newton from his father and left Scethrog House to his eldest son Thomas ('The Homes of the Vaughans: Part II', *Brycheiniog*, 19 (1980–81), 96).

of Norman origin – must have been among the more striking components of the personal topography of his boyhood.[15]

II

During the years spent in Llangattock with their tutor, Matthew Herbert, the Vaughan twins would have received enough grounding in Latin language and literature to fit them for a university education. Jesus College, Oxford, where they were sent in 1638, had been founded on the initiative of a Brecon man, Hugh Price, in 1571, which did not prevent the title of founder from being bestowed upon Queen Elizabeth for granting it the site and buildings of the former White Hall.[16] Brigid Allen, the Archivist of the college, provides valuable information about its membership and character in the years before the Civil War. It had been almost entirely rebuilt during the seventeenth century, 'largely as the result of systematic fund-raising in Wales and the border counties'. Since 1630, its principal had been Dr Francis Mansell from Carmarthenshire, and by the early 1640s it had become 'a finishing-school for sons of the Welsh landed gentry, with the secondary function of preparing clever, often poorer boys to become clergymen or senior members of the University'. Consequently, as many as a third of its undergraduates did not matriculate and left without taking a degree. For example, Charles Walbeoffe, Vaughan's cousin from Llanhamlach, the parish adjacent to Llansantffraed, was admitted to the college in 1636 and had moved on by December 1637, having spent 'only a year or so at Jesus, acquiring friends and some superficial educational polish'.[17]

Nothing is known of Henry's activities during his time in Oxford, but he must have become acquainted, if only from a distance, with the

---

15 Descriptions of Tretower are given by C.A. Ralegh Radford, 'Tretower: The Castle and Court', *Brycheiniog*, 6 (1960), 22–50; and a photograph of Tretower Court is reproduced in *HV Works*, p. xxxix.

16 See G. Williams, 'Hugh Price, Founder of Jesus College, Oxford', *Brycheiniog*, 25 (1992–93), 57–66. I am indebted to the late Peter Thomas for alerting me to this particular link between Jesus College and Brecon. A depiction of the college in the seventeenth century is reproduced in *HV Works*, p. xxxix.

17 Brigid Allen, 'The Vaughans at Jesus College, Oxford, 1638–48', *Scintilla*, 4 (2000), 71–72.

'knot of the choicest Oxford Wits' surrounding William Cartwright, the university's leading poet and dramatist.[18] Alan Rudrum cites references to Cartwright, a popular member of the teaching faculty as well as a writer, to corroborate the belief that Henry went up to the university later than Thomas and did not stay there long.[19] Thomas evidently attended his lectures – 'When he did read, how we did flock to hear!' – but Henry, not a formally matriculated student, noted years later – in a phrase that honours Cartwright's memory by echoing Ovid's similar remark about not being one of Virgil's inner circle – that he was only acquainted with the illustrious teacher at a distance: 'I did but *see* thee!'[20]

While Thomas continued to study for his degree, Henry was soon dispatched to London, 'beinge then designed by my father', as he informed Aubrey, 'for the study of the Law'.[21] There is no documentary evidence that he became a member of one of the Inns of Court, but one of his London poems, 'A Rhapsodie', describes gatherings in the Globe Tavern, where 'royall, witty Sacke, the Poets soule' was imbibed and 'honest mirth' among friends was followed by 'dreames Poeticall'. In the middle section, Vaughan invites his drinking companions to wander the city and observe the 'Catchpoles, whores, & Carts' that infest 'ev'ry street', particularly along 'Fleet street, & the Strand' when 'the soft stirs / Of bawdy Silks, turne night to day', and in the vicinity of 'Tower wharfe' where 'the tyr'd footman reeles / 'Twixt chaire-men, torches, & the hackny wheels'.[22] This satiric vein occurs again in 'To Lysimachus, the Authour being with him in London'. The date of the poem and the identity of Lysimachus are obscure, but the opening lines cast the poet and his friend as plain countrymen strolling through the city with the same sardonic attitude as the literary comrades from the Globe:

18 For Cartwright's circle and the phrase quoted from David Lloyd's *Memoires* (1688), see P.W. Thomas, *Sir John Berkenhead 1617–1679: A Royalist Career in Politics and Polemics* (Oxford: Clarendon Press, 1969), pp. 25–26.
19 *Oxford Dictionary of National Biography* (Oxford: Oxford University Press, 2004).
20 'Upon the Poems and Playes of the ever memorable Mr. William Cartwright' (one of many commendatory poems prefixed to the 1651 edition of Cartwright's works), *HV Works*, p. 191. See Ovid, *Tristia*, 4:10:51: 'Vergilium vidi tantum' [Virgil I only saw].
21 Letter to Aubrey, *HV Works*, p. 800.
22 *HV Works*, pp. 19–21.

> Saw not, *Lysimachus*, last day, when wee
> Took the pure Air in its simplicity,
> And our own too: how the trim'd *Gallants* went
> Cringing, & past each step some Complement? [...]
> How did they point at us, and boldly call,
> As if we had been Vassals to them all,
> Their poor *Men-mules* sent thither by hard fate
> To yoke our selves for their *Sedans* and State?[23]

A related poem in the 1678 volume – 'FIDA: Or The Country-beauty: to Lysimachus' – is a conventional exercise that 'reflects an early interest in the light Cavalier vein'.[24]

From various hints in the poetry, Roland Mathias has constructed a plausible case for Vaughan's presence among the group of young wits in London that were united by their admiration for Cartwright and their attendance at assemblies hosted by John Fowler, a cloth merchant, at his house in Bucklersbury.[25] The centre of attraction in this household was the precocious talent of Fowler's daughter, Katherine, who later married James Philips of Cardigan. The 'young *Goddess*' praised by Vaughan in a poem written in 1667, three years after her death, was eleven years old in 1642.[26] In an earlier tribute, soon after she became Katherine Philips in 1647, he recalled how '*Pilgrims*' had flocked 'in Courtship' to the child prodigy and how he himself had diffidently worshipped 'at distance', when he 'first did see / New miracles in Poetrie' and his own 'weaker *Genius* … / Slept in a silent admiration'.[27] Among those drawn to Bucklersbury were some of the leading members of Cartwright's Oxford entourage, notably John Berkenhead, a protégé of Archbishop Laud. Also present was John Jeffreys, a gentleman's son from Abercynrig in Breconshire, a

---

23 *HV Works*, p. 738. Hutchinson guessed that Lysimachus was 'his brother Thomas or a friend' and saw the poem as an early one (*Life*, p. 88); E.L. Marilla considered that Lysimachus was 'a wholly imaginative creation' and suggested that the poem was a late one, reflecting Vaughan's 'disgust with one of the many indulgences in frivolity that flourished under the Restoration' (*The Secular Poems of Henry Vaughan*, ed. E.L. Marilla (Uppsala: A.-B. Lundequistska Bokhandeln, 1958), pp. 294–95).
24 *Secular Poems*, ed. Marilla, p. 318.
25 See Roland Mathias, 'The Making of a Royalist', *Scintilla,* 3 (1999), 112–16.
26 'To the Editor of the matchless Orinda', *HV Works*, pp. 748–49.
27 'To the most Excellently accomplish'd, Mrs. K. Philips', *HV Works*, p. 198.

few miles from Newton, who may have given his countryman an *entrée* to these gatherings.

After four years in the great world beyond the Usk valley, Henry Vaughan was beginning to make a place and an identity for himself as one of the bright young men who were soon to become prominent supporters of the king in the military and literary campaigns of the 1640s. As he stood on the threshold of an exciting future near the centre of the country's intellectual and artistic life, however, both his legal studies and his poetic ambitions were, in his own words, 'wholie frustrated' by 'the sudden Eruption of our late civil warres'.[28] Thomas was permitted to continue his studies at Oxford, but as the elder brother and heir to the family property, Henry was recalled to Breconshire, perhaps (as Mathias suggests in another article) because his father 'feared what his extremism might lead him to commit himself to'.[29]

III

Little is known of Henry Vaughan's activities between the autumn of 1642 and his participation in the Battle of Rowton Heath, near Chester, in September 1645.[30] His legal training, although abruptly terminated, apparently secured him a post as clerk to Sir Marmaduke Lloyd, Chief Justice of the Great Sessions for the counties of Brecon, Radnor, and Glamorgan, which would have involved travelling widely through South Wales when the judge went on circuit.[31] This occupation cannot have continued beyond 1645, when he himself was

28 Letter to Aubrey, *HV Works*, p. 800.
29 Roland Mathias, 'Reasons, Reasons', *Scintilla*, 4 (2000), 120.
30 In the prefatory note to her fictional account of the life of Henry Vaughan, written nearly a decade before the publication of Hutchinson's *Life and Interpretation*, Helen Ashton claimed to have followed Gwenllian Morgan's 'discovery that Henry Vaughan enlisted in Sir Herbert Price's regiment at the outbreak of the Civil War and served throughout with this regiment' (*The Swan of Usk: A Historical Novel* (London: Collins, 1940), p. 7). Consequently, the second part – 'The Swan Flying' – is devoted to the military exploits of the Vaughan twins from the Battle of Edgehill in 1642 until their return home after the surrender of Beeston Castle in 1645. No evidence has ever been produced to support Miss Morgan's 'discovery' and the novelist's fictions.
31 John Aubrey noted that 'he was a Clarke sometime to Judge Sir Marmaduke

under arms during the autumn and Lloyd was dismissed from office following his capture at the siege of Hereford in December. In 1646, he brought out the volume entitled *Poems, with the tenth Satyre of Iuvenal Englished*, in which the translation of the Roman poet's verses was partly a vehicle for reflecting upon the political events that he had witnessed during his residence in the capital. The remark in his prefatory epistle that the satire *'was of purpose borrowed, to feather some slower Houres'* not only suggests that he worked on the translation after his recall from the hurly-burly of the metropolis, but also reveals his dissatisfaction with the quiet provincial life to which he was condemned after 1642.[32] For although he was not one to disobey a father's commands, there are other indications that the twenty-one-year-old Vaughan did not relish this enforced return to the pastoral landscapes of his boyhood.

Soon after the publication of *Poems*, he had another collection ready for the press, for which he composed a dedicatory letter, dating it from *'Newton by Usk*, this 17. of *Decemb.* 1647'.[33] The latter part of the poetic section of *Olor Iscanus*, as the volume was called when it was belatedly published in 1651, is given over to English versions of Latin poems.[34] Harold Walley long ago asserted that those from Ovid's *Tristia* and *Epistulae ex Ponto* were 'unquestionably the earliest' and added the astute observation that these 'laments of the poet in exile, cut off from the congenial society of his fellow poets' are particularly appropriate 'to the early years following Vaughan's return to Wales'.[35] It is also obvious that the four poems by Ovid – two from each of the collections of poetry written after his banishment from Rome to the shores of the Black Sea – were carefully chosen to form a sequence that mirrored (in general terms) the translator's own experience.[36] 'To

  Lloyd' (*Aubrey's Brief Lives*, ed. Oliver Lawson Dick (Harmondsworth: Penguin Books, 1972), p. 463).
32 'To All Ingenious Lovers of Poesie', *HV Works*, p. 11.
33 *HV Works*, p. 169.
34 The second half of *Olor Iscanus* consists of prose translations.
35 Harold R. Walley, 'The Strange Case of *Olor Iscanus*', *Review of English Studies*, 18 (1942), 32.
36 The four translations, in the order in which they are printed in *Olor Iscanus*, are *Tristia*, V, iii; *Ex Ponto*, III, vii; *Ex Ponto*, IV, iii; and *Tristia*, III, iii. They are quoted from *HV Works*, pp. 201–08, with line references given in the text. Longer passages are accompanied by literal translations from *Ovid:*

his fellow-Poets at Rome, upon the birth-day of Bacchus' (his title for the first translation, in contrast to the Loeb edition's 'An Appeal to Bacchus', which better reflects the Latin poem's contents) signals the prominence Vaughan will give to the exile's loss of personal contact with the literary community in Rome. Ovid's 'loyal throng' of poets become 'my trusty friends' in Vaughan's English text and the key word 'friend' is again inserted into the question the poet imagines his former boon companions asking – '*O! Where is* Ovid *now our banish'd friend?*' (l. 54). Vaughan's feeling of resentment at being called away from a fellowship in which his own poetic talent was beginning to flourish and be recognized reverberates through the opening address to Bacchus, who is transformed into a patron of wine-inspired Cavalier merriment by the added parenthesis in the first line:

> This is the day (blith god of *Sack*) which wee
> If I mistake not, Consecrate to thee,
> When the soft *Rose* wee marry to the *Bayes*,
> And warm'd with thy own wine reherse thy praise,
> 'Mongst whom (while to thy *Poet* fate gave way)
> I have been held no small part of the day,
> But now, dull'd with the Cold *Bears* frozen seat,
> *Sarmatia* holds me, and the warlike *Gete*.
> My former life, unlike to this my last,
> With *Romes* best wits of thy full Cup did tast. (ll. 1–10)

[This is the day, if only I do not mistake the time, on which poets are wont to praise thee, Bacchus, binding their brows with sweet-scented garlands, and singing thy praises over thine own wine. Among them, I remember, whilst my fate allowed, oft did I play a part not distasteful to thee, but now I lie beneath the stars of the Cynosurian Bear, in the grip of the Sarmatian shore, close to the

Tristia and Ex Ponto, trans. Arthur Leslie Wheeler, Loeb Classical Library (London: William Heinemann, 1924), pp. 220–23, 415–17, 430–35, 108–15. The Ovid translations have been interpreted by Robert Wilcher, '"Feathering some slower hours": Henry Vaughan's Verse Translations', *Scintilla*, 4 (2000), 151–56 and by Paul Davis, *Translation and the Poet's Life: The Ethics of Translating in English Culture, 1646–1726* (Oxford: Oxford University Press, 2008), pp. 59–65.

uncivilized Gete. I who before led a life of ease, toil-free, amid studies in the band of the Pierans.]

The first-person plural pronouns introduced by Vaughan at the start insist upon his own inclusion among the poetic revellers. Another small change foregrounds his significant participation in the festivities (rather than the god's approval, as in the source) – ''Mongst whom [...] / I have been held no small part of the day'. In the last two lines, Ovid's nostalgia for a life of cultured leisure is replaced by a longing for the kind of intellectual and artistic stimulation only a capital city can supply. That longing is again emphasized in an appeal to Bacchus to use his influence on the authority figure (a father in Vaughan's personal subtext) who has removed him from the centre of cultural life: 'try then / If *Caesar* will restore me *Rome* agen' (ll. 45–46). At the end, Vaughan turns directly to 'the Jollie Crew / Of careless *Poets*!' (ll. 47–48), a phrasing that echoes the mood of some of the earlier London poetry, and adjures them not to forget him as they pursue the course that has been denied him by banishment from the city: 'And may your happier wits grow lowd with fame / As you (my best of friends!) preserve my name' (ll. 59–60).

The rest of the poems in the Ovidian group trace a growing sense of bitterness and isolation, as the poet rebukes his erstwhile companions for neglecting him and sinks into despair. Vaughan furnishes the second one, like the first, with a title to indicate the theme in the Latin source that his imagination has seized upon: 'To his friends (after his many sollicitations) refusing to petition *Caesar* for his releasement'. There is no need to look for any direct biographical parallel to Ovid's complaint that his friends in Rome have been ignoring his requests to intercede with the emperor on his behalf; it is enough that the poem expresses Vaughan's impression of having been forsaken by the companions of his London days. This time, his minor adjustments of detail have the effect of establishing the 'malice' (l. 24), and the 'base, low soules' (l. 51) of his 'degen'rate friends' (l. 55) in the city and highlighting his own psychological condition: his angry contempt at their indifference – 'my pen / Incens'd with begging scorns to write agen' (ll. 1–2), 'I scorn [Fate's] spite and yours' (l. 23) – and his desperate embrace of Fortune's enmity in lines that transform Ovid's Stoical acceptance into a reckless defiance:

> I can delight in vain hopes, and desire
> That state more then her *Change* and *Smiles*, then high'r
> I hugge a strong *despaire*, and think it brave
> To *baffle* faith, and give those hopes a *grave*. (ll. 31–34)

['Tis good to embrace a hope – though it bring no good and be ever vain – and whatever you long for that you may deem will happen. The next stage is utterly to give up hope of salvation, or to know once and for all with full assurance that one is lost.]

But perhaps the most telling moment is that in which he turns his back on the illusory dreams he has been nursing in another adaptation of Ovid's sentiments:

> And now I must forget
> Those pleas'd *Idea's* I did frame and set
> Unto my selfe, with many fancyed *Springs*
> And *Groves*, whose only losse new sorrow brings.
> (ll. 45–48)

[Was it thus that I had come to know my fate? Lo! my torture is all the worse, and the repeated description of this place but renews and freshens the harshness of my exile.]

The poem ends with a veiled allusion to Vaughan's unwilling transplantation from the banks of the Thames to the banks of the Usk (*Isca*) as Ovid's 'Euxine sea' is replaced by the name of the river that flows into it: 'I / At *Ister* [Danube] dare as well as *Tyber* dye' (ll. 57–58).

The third poem narrows the focus to one unnamed companion from happier days, whose neglect is felt all the more sharply because of their former intimacy. In the fourth, Ovid informs his wife in Rome that he is sick and alone, and – in an expression not found in the original – 'hopeless of all Comforts, but to dye' (l. 4). The Roman poet's growing desolation chimed with Vaughan's own mood as he contemplated through another's experience of exile the end of his personal involvement with the coterie of 'friends' who had sustained his first attempt at self-fashioning as a poet:

> Unpittied, and unmourn'd for, my sad head
> In a strange Land goes friendless to the dead. (ll. 51–52)

[but without funeral rites, without the honour of a tomb, this head shall lie unmourned in a barbarian land!]

Reluctantly resigning himself to death in 'a strange Land', he sinks into a despondency that colours his perception of his surroundings:

> What heart (think'st thou?) have I in this sad seat
> Tormented 'twixt the *Sauromate* and *Gete*?
> Nor *aire* nor *water* please; their very *skie*
> Looks strange and unaccustom'd to my Eye,
> I scarce dare breath it, and I know not how
> The Earth that bears me shewes unpleasant now. (ll. 5–10)

[What spirit can you think is now mine, lying sick in a hideous land among Sauromatae and Getae? The climate I cannot endure, and I have not become used to such water, and, even the land, I know not why, pleases me not.]

It is one of the ironies of Vaughan's development as an artist that the very Breconshire countryside from which he felt alienated (not a foreign outpost, like Ovid's Euxine shore, but the familiar landscapes of his youth now grown 'strange and unaccustom'd' by contrast with the public world he yearned for) would eventually become his refuge and consolation, when events in the public world drove him into a deeper political and spiritual exile.

IV

Vaughan's sense of alienation was exacerbated by the experience of being dispossessed not merely of the 'fancyed *Springs* / And *Groves*' of an imagined future as a poet but of the sustaining beliefs and practices of a remembered past. Having been displaced geographically and culturally, like Ovid, from the centre to the periphery, he had yet to be subjected to the more radical displacement that accompanied military defeat and political oppression. He had witnessed disorders personally in London during the winter of 1640–41 and they had advanced ever nearer to the borders of his immediate locality since Charles I had raised his standard at Nottingham in August 1642. In September, the king moved his headquarters to Shrewsbury and set up another base at Chester. Meanwhile, his eldest son had been sent to Raglan to raise troops in South Wales. A skirmish between royalist and parliamentarian forces had taken place at Powicke Bridge near Worcester on 23 September and three weeks later the king had marched from Shrewsbury to fight the first full-scale battle of the Civil War at Edgehill on 23 October. In November, another royalist army led by the Marquess of Hertford had been defeated at Tewkesbury in Gloucestershire. A handful of Vaughan's neighbours had been active in the king's cause since the beginning of hostilities – among them Sir Herbert Price and John Jeffreys of Abercynrig, both of whom commanded regiments, and Edward Games – but the local gentry largely kept their heads down in the hope that the conflict would soon be over.[37] In the wake of the disastrous defeat at Naseby in June 1645, however, Charles I had come recruiting in South Wales and stayed overnight at the Priory in Brecon. Vaughan volunteered for active service, probably for the first time, and was present at the Battle of Rowton Heath in September and the surrender of Beeston Castle in November.[38] When a parliamentary force marched unopposed towards Brecon, the inhabitants dismantled the town's defences in order to avoid being drawn into the conflict on either side. Smarting from direct experiences of defeat and loss – one of his close friends was killed at Rowton Heath – the returning soldier must have felt even more like an exile among his own people, as he tried once again to accommodate himself to the *'slower Houres'* of life in his native locality. In one of the most striking poems in *Olor Iscanus*, which seems to have been written during the winter following his military service – 'the slow Isicle hangs / At the stiffe thatch' – he reverts to the witty stance and style of the London poems that cast a satiric eye on the urban scene. 'To his retired friend, an Invitation to Brecknock'[39] chides its recipient – perhaps a former comrade in Herbert's troop of cavalry – for shutting himself away from social contact:

> Since last wee met, thou and thy horse (my dear,)
> Have not so much as drunk, or litter'd here […].
> What ever 'tis, a sober cause't must be
> That thus long bars us of thy Companie.

37 See Mathias, 'Reasons, Reasons', 114–16.
38 For the Civil War in Wales and Vaughan's part in it, see Chapter 3.
39 *HV Works*, pp. 180–82.

Vaughan places himself in a community of likeminded Cavaliers coping with their situation by means of conviviality and scorn for the new dispensation exemplified by the county town, where 'new fine *Worships*' have scrambled into posts once occupied by staunch royalists like his former employer, Marmaduke Lloyd, and puritans strut about in 'brotherly Ruffs and Beards'. Distaste for the rude society to which he has been consigned by a father's will and the fortunes of war is compounded with political antagonism in his call to flout the new masters of 'our *Metropolis*' by rekindling with wine the 'precious Witt' and 'mirth' that now constitute both a refuge from and defiance of the 'sullen state' (of mind and politics) his friend has fallen into.

The 'Invitation to Brecknock' reads like the work of a disillusioned bachelor kicking his heels at home after the disastrous royalist campaign in North Wales. Although it was published in 1651 in *Olor Iscanus*, it may well have been written earlier than the poem that Vaughan chose as the climax of the collection of original verse in his first volume – 'Upon the Priorie Grove, His usuall Retyrement' – which celebrates his betrothal to Catherine Wise. Since he had a second collection ready by December 1647, only fifteen months after *Poems* was registered for publication on 15 September 1646, it is likely that he selected for both volumes from a body of verse already written during the earlier 1640s, to which new material was being added. 'Upon the Priorie Grove' rounds off a series of amatory verses addressed to 'Amoret' – much as Spenser's *Amoretti* sonnets are concluded by an epithalamion marking his marriage in 1594 – and it is generally agreed that Vaughan's more modest tribute relates to his own courtship. This may well have taken place during the spring and summer of 1646, after 'Winters frosty pangs' had released their grip on the Brecon to which he had invited his friend and before the registration of *Poems* in September.

The Priory and its adjacent grove were owned by Sir Herbert Price, in whose regiment Vaughan had served during the autumn of 1645, and it was probably through him that he met his future bride. Price had married Goditha Arden from Park Hill in Castle Bromwich, a few miles from the Wise family home at Gylston Manor near Coleshill, Warwickshire. He was a close friend of George Digby, whose relatives owned Coleshill Manor, and Mathias argues that Vaughan may have accompanied him on visits there and entered the society of 'a web of families' in the English Midlands that included the Digbys, the Ardens, and the Wises.⁴⁰ It was this connection that led the poet to dedicate his planned second volume of poetry in 1647 to the youthful Lord Kildare Digby, who had been brought up at Coleshill Manor and was head of the elder branch of the Digby family. References in the dedicatory letter to 'the most *Endearing obligations*' and 'those *numerous* favours, and *kind Influences* receiv'd sometimes from your Lordship'⁴¹ led Mathias to believe that the poet 'had been a guest at Coleshill Manor', probably 'as an attendant upon Sir Herbert Price', and that 'it was through Lord Kildare Digby that [he] first found himself in the company of the Wise sisters'.⁴²

The relationship with Catherine evidently developed further while she was a guest of the Prices at the Priory. Most of the 'Amoret' poems are highly derivative; some may even have been composed as fashionable exercises while Vaughan was still moving in Cavalier literary circles in the capital and only later grafted into a more personal sequence.⁴³ 'Upon the Priorie Grove, His usuall Retyrement' is one of the few works in which Vaughan invokes a Breconshire location by name, but his poetic treatment of the secluded woodland walks next to Colonel Price's home does not venture beyond the idealizing descriptive conventions of Caroline poetry that he had encountered in Oxford and London. Opening with an invocation of the 'sacred shades! coole, leavie House!' where he courted his future wife, it closes with a vision of a 'fresh Grove in th' Elysian Land' where the couple will be reunited in their 'first Innocence, and Love'.⁴⁴

V

Vaughan's courtship and subsequent marriage to Catherine Wise must have provided a bright interlude in a darkening world. By the

---

40 Roland Mathias, 'The Midlands: Introductions and Identifications', *Scintilla*, 5 (2001), 98.
41 *HV Works*, p. 169.
42 Mathias, 'The Midlands', 96, 97.
43 As well as supplying the title of Spenser's sonnet cycle, Amoret was one of the heroines of *The Faeirie Queene* and the name was used in later poems by William Browne, Richard Lovelace, and Edmund Waller.
44 *HV Works*, pp. 24–25.

time *Olor Iscanus* was published, the poem with which it opened was no longer in harmony with the bulk of its contents. 'To the River Isca'⁴⁵ reads as if it had been written at a time when he was still nursing hopes of making a name for himself in the literary milieu centred on London and the Court. The burden of the poem is the immortality he will confer upon the stream that runs through his native valley:

> When I am layd to *rest* hard by thy *streams*,
> And my *Sun sets*, where first it *sprang* in beams,
> I'le leave behind me such a *large, kind light*,
> As shall *redeem* thee from *oblivious night*.

That this was among the poetic fruits of his return to the banks of the Usk is confirmed by the incantatory passage with which it ends. Having called for a blessing upon the river and its environs, he looks outwards to 'those *lowd, anxious Cares*' that Fate is imposing 'else-where' and prays that they will 'ne'er break thy *Peace*, nor make / Thy *repos'd Armes* to a new warre *awake*!' In the very last lines, he utters what Peter Thomas calls a 'final encircling benediction', which transfers the 'quasi-magical, sacerdotal, ritual mode' of the Caroline masque 'to Vaughan's corner of the kingdom':

> But *Freedome, safety, Joy and blisse*
> *United* in one loving *kisse*
> *Surround* thee quite, and *stile* thy borders
> *The Land redeem'd from all disorders*!

Was this benediction meant for Wales, wonders Thomas, 'Or for his Usk Valley alone?'⁴⁶

Although there was no fighting in Breconshire itself, the literary culture that had fostered what Peter Thomas calls the 'ceremonial song and oracular prophecy' of 'To the River *Isca*' was being rendered obsolete by history – and the rest of the original poetry in

---

45 *HV Works*, pp. 173–75.
46 Peter Thomas, 'Henry Vaughan, Orpheus, and the Empowerment of Poetry', in *Of Paradise and Light: Essays on Henry Vaughan and John Milton in Honor of Alan Rudrum*, ed. Donald R. Dickson and Holly Faith Nelson (Newark, DE: University of Delaware Press, 2004), pp. 224–25.

the 1651 volume might be mistaken for 'bits and pieces desperately shored against ruin'.[47] The very next item, 'The Charnel-house', contains a shocking evocation of the effects of mortality on the human body – 'Fragments of men, Rags of Anatomie' – and also an acknowledgement that the poet's 'shoreless thoughts, vast tenter'd hope, / Ambitious dreams' of conferring immortality through verse are now out of place.[48] Among other reminders of the new circumstances in which he completed the collection that would become *Olor Iscanus*, there are a semi-jesting account of the shelter afforded by a voluminous borrowed cloak 'when wee / Left craggie *Biston*, and the fatall *Dee* / [...] beaten with fresh storms, and late mishap',[49] the satire on the town of Brecknock, elegies for royalists lost in the Civil War, an epitaph for the late king's second daughter, and tributes to writers who flourished when the nation was not yet split 'into *Schismes*' nor starved with '*dearth* of wit' and when poetry had a less melancholy role than to 'teach *Posterity* our present *griefe* / And their own *losse*, but never give *reliefe*'.[50]

The title of *Olor Iscanus* serves to focus attention on the poet's native river and highlights a significant quality of the book that Jonathan Post considers 'in some ways the most "regional" of his writings'.[51] Cambria is identified as the site of his birth and education in the opening Latin address to posterity; some lines adapted from Virgil's *Georgics* furnish a motto for the volume – 'O who will set me down in the cool valleys of the Usk and protect me with the generous shadow of the mighty branches!'[52] ['*O quis me gelidis in vallibus ISCÆ / Sistat, & Ingenti ramorum protegat umbrâ!*']; the River Usk and the county town of Brecon are named in the titles of two English poems; the substitution of 'Ister' for 'the Euxine shore' in one of the Ovid translations marks the valley of the

---

47 'Henry Vaughan, Orpheus, and the Empowerment of Poetry', pp. 224, 228. Thomas goes on to argue that 'there is a design' in which 'love and literature are explored and tested by absence, enmity, and loss' (p. 228).
48 *HV Works*, p. 175.
49 'Upon a Cloke lent him by Mr. J. Ridsley', *HV Works*, p. 187.
50 'Upon Mr. Fletchers Playes, published, 1647' and 'Upon the Poems and Playes of the ever memorable Mr. William Cartwright', *HV Works*, pp. 190, 191.
51 Jonathan F.S. Post, *Henry Vaughan: The Unfolding Vision* (Princeton, NJ: Princeton University Press, 1982), p. 26.
52 Translation quoted from *HV Works*, p. 980.

Isca as a place of exile during a particular phase of the translator's experience; and the soldier-poet's later travails at Rowton Heath and Beeston figure in another set of English verses. Furthermore, as Peter Thomas has pointed out, the collection ends as it began with personal statements in Latin.[53] A second poem to the River Usk – 'Ad Fluvium Iscam' – supplies the descriptive and affective elements absent from its English counterpart:

> Usk, father of flowers, foaming from your quiet spring, you lap the golden pebbles, and with your moist murmurings soothe the sorrowful hyacinths and the flora on the colourful rock; and while the months run on to engulf new moons, and heaven wears down mortal men, you number your days with the sun, and last out every age, an unfailing stream. What comfort you bring to the remote woods and the silent grove, and with what a murmurous whisper![54]

A tribute to Matthew Herbert acknowledges the role of the rector of Llangattock in bestowing an immortality that will outlive the mortal life Henry derived from Thomas Vaughan senior: 'Divide the life of your pupil in two: let this brief and fleeting part redound to my father's credit; to yours, my existence beyond the grave.'[55] A third Latin poem compliments his close friend and neighbour, Thomas Powell, for his book on optics. The collection is rounded off with a poem 'Ad Echum', which picks up the forest setting of the volume's Virgilian motto:

> O nymph, you fly through the pleasant lairs of the leafy woods, and wander talking through the deep grove, deity of the age-old woodland, voice of the sacred glade which likes to answer only your last-spoken words [...]. I beseech you: give me the means by which I may discover the unfelled bypaths of the remote woods, the doubtful windings and recesses of the place.[56]

---

53 See Thomas, 'Henry Vaughan, Orpheus, and the Empowerment of Poetry', pp. 234–35.
54 Translation quoted from *HV Works*, p. 230.
55 *HV Works*, p. 230.
56 *HV Works*, p. 232.

Peter Thomas reads 'a hermetic epiphany of regeneration' in these lines, but they also have the simpler function of placing the poet firmly in the wooded landscape of his native valley.[57]

VI

Before *Olor Iscanus* was published in 1651, two more groups of verse translations were added to Ovid's poems of exile, selected from short metrical passages in *The Consolation of Philosophy* by Boethius and the Latin odes and epodes of Casimire Sarbiewski to form a coherent sequence. They seem to belong to the period after the defeat of the royalist cause, since they allude to political oppression and the loss of a crown; and they reflect – or perhaps were instrumental in effecting – a gradual process of psychological adjustment on Vaughan's part to the prospect of life in a rural backwater. Boethius, in prison awaiting execution for treason in the early sixth century AD, found solace amid the vagaries of Fortune and the horrors of human discord in contemplating the order of the created universe:

> All this frame of *things* that *be*,
> Love which rules *Heaven*, *Land*, and *Sea*,
> Chains, keeps, orders as we see.[58]

The work of Casimir, a Polish Jesuit whose Horatian imitations were published in 1625 and 1628, goes beyond this philosophical consolation to find contentment in the simple routines of life in the country – 'Where his *old parents* bred him up' – and to take positive pleasure in the sights and sounds of the natural world: the '*fair Oke* hung with Mast', 'shadie *Lakes* with *Rivers* deep', the 'Choice *Musick*' of blackbird, thrush, and nightingale.[59] Whatever peace of mind Vaughan had begun to derive from translating these versions of the Horatian good life, however, was shattered in the years leading

---

57 Thomas, 'Henry Vaughan, Orpheus, and the Empowerment of Poetry', p. 238.
58 Boethius, Liber II, Metrum 7, *HV Works*, p. 222.
59 Casimirus, Odes IV, xv; Epodes iii ('The Praise of a Religious life by Mathias Casimirus. In Answer to that Ode of Horace, *Beatus Ille qui procul negotiis*, &c.'), *HV Works*, pp. 226, 228.

up to 1651 by national events that had serious repercussions in Breconshire.

In May 1648, open revolt had broken out in South Wales and it may have been at the battle between Welsh royalists and a parliamentary force at St Fagans, near Llandaff, that the twins' younger brother, William, received the wounds or contracted the illness from which he later died. In January 1649, Charles I had been brought to trial and executed. On 22 February 1650, an Act for the Better Propagation and Preaching of the Gospel in Wales had been passed at Westminster and a wholesale purging of the Welsh clergy set in train. This accumulation of circumstances coincided with a spiritual awakening in Vaughan himself, whose religious faith and poetry henceforth acquired a new sense of purpose. The Breconshire countryside in which his 'conversion' took place informs the lyric poetry he began writing at the end of the 1640s with an intensity of religious experience that goes far deeper than the Stoicism and Christian Horatianism of the translations from Boethius and Casimir.

While the rural context is integral to many of the poems published in *Silex Scintillans* (1650, 1655), however, there is little descriptive detail. For Alan Rudrum, the volume 'is suffused with the atmosphere of the Usk Valley', but it evokes 'the sound of running water, the quality of light over the hills, and the rapid succession of sunshine, cloud and shower' rather than depicting specific landmarks.[60] Nevertheless, Edmund Blunden thought that 'the inhabitants of his native vale' would have been able to 'recognise the geography of it' in his poems and E.C. Pettet considered the landscape to be so 'unmistakably the Usk valley below the Brecon Beacons and Alt yr Esgair' that it 'must be set among the most important influences that went to the making of *Silex Scintillans*'.[61] The different ways in which Vaughan's imagination processed features of the natural world in which he passed his everyday life – deriving them from the classics, teasing out their emblematic significances, transforming them into what

---

60 Alan Rudrum, *Henry Vaughan*, Writers of Wales (Cardiff: University of Wales Press on behalf of the Welsh Arts Council, 1981), p. 16.
61 Edmund Blunden, *On the Poems of Henry Vaughan: Characteristics and Intimations* (London: Richard Cobden-Sanderson, 1927), p. 40; E.C. Pettet, *Of Paradise and Light: A Study of Vaughan's* Silex Scintillans (Cambridge: Cambridge University Press, 1960), pp. 87–88.

Eluned Brown has aptly termed a 'baptized Breconshire'[62] – will be explored in Chapter 9. For the purposes of the present chapter, it is enough to note that a symbol for the more occult secrets of nature in 'Vanity of Spirit' may have been furnished by some ancient lettering at the so-called hermitage of Ty Illtid on the summit of a hill in the neighbouring parish of Llanhamlach.[63] Vaughan describes how he came upon a 'peece of much antiquity', which was cast by 'in a nook' and '[w]ith Hyerogliphicks quite dismembred, / And broken letters scarce remembred'.[64] Theophilus Jones speaks of his disappointment at finding this *'venerable relique of antiquity*, so renowned in topography' to be no more than 'a very small cromlech'.[65] There were, however, other ancient stones bearing worn inscriptions in the vicinity of Scethrog and Tretower that may have supplied Vaughan with this striking image of his misguided quest for hidden knowledge.[66]

VII

The few poems by Henry Vaughan that can be dated later than March 1655, when the augmented *Silex Scintillans* was registered for publication, were occasioned by events in the family or the local community: the marriage of John Morgan of Wenallt, a neighbour and kinsman; the death of his twin brother in 1666, whose burial is recorded in 'Daphnis' (ll. 113–18); the death of Arthur Trevers, Puisne Judge of the Brecon circuit, in 1667.[67] Some notion of his professional duties as a physician and his leisure activities in these

---

62 Eluned Brown, 'Henry Vaughan's Biblical Landscape', *Essays and Studies*, new series, 30 (1977), 51.
63 See *Life*, p. 24.
64 'Vanity of Spirit', *HV Works*, p. 81.
65 See Jones, *A History of the County of Brecknock*, p. 452.
66 Jones, *A History of the County of Brecknock*, pp. 433, 416. Peter Thomas suggested that it was 'probably the nearby Scethrog Early Christian monument now in the Brecon Museum'. See 'The "Desert Sanctified": Henry Vaughan's Church in the Wilderness', in *Sacred Text–Sacred Space: Architectural, Spiritual; and Literary Convergences in England and Wales*, ed. Joseph Sterrett and Peter Thomas (Leiden and Boston, MA: Brill, 2011), p. 186, note 56.
67 *HV Works*, pp. 743–44, 789, 749.

later years can be gathered from references to his attendance on patients in Brecon, Crickhowell, and as far afield as Glamorganshire (in letters dating from 1673, 1693, and 1675) and from a Latin poem written to accompany the gift of a salmon – 'caught in the rushing weir' with 'a fly made of feathers' – to his friend Thomas Powell of Cantref.[68] During the 1670s, he became interested in contributing an account of Breconshire to a natural history of England and Wales contemplated by Dr Robert Plot, the Keeper of the Ashmolean Museum in Oxford. In spite of his readiness 'to assist him with a short account of natures Dispensatorie heer', however, there was a long delay in acquiring further information about the project through his intermediary, John Aubrey, and it eventually lapsed.[69] Evidence has recently come to light, however, of at least one report from Vaughan about the frequent lightning 'on the mountaines in Wales', which leads the most recent editor of his letters to speculate that 'it is not unlikely' that some of Vaughan's correspondence with Aubrey has 'gone missing'.[70] On 28 June 1680, he excused his tardiness in replying to another letter on the grounds that he was 'a great way from home' when it arrived, which may be evidence of occasional visits beyond South Wales – perhaps to his wife's relatives in Warwickshire.[71]

Towards the end of his life, by an indenture dated 28 January 1689, Vaughan conveyed the Newton estate to his elder son and renovated the cottage known as 'Holly Bush' in Scethrog, where he and his second wife lived until his death in 1695.[72] Among the verses collected in *Thalia Rediviva* was a translation of the well-known lines by Claudian about an old man of Verona. It is to be hoped that, in spite of the litigation that troubled the latter part of his life, there were times in his declining years when they reflected his contentment with the geographical bounds that had circumscribed so much of his own span on earth:

68 See *HV Works*, pp. 800, 809, 804–05, 778–79.
69 See *Life*, pp. 212–13 and the letter to Aubrey dated 9 December 1675, in *HV Works*, p. 805.
70 For information about the possible continuation of Vaughan's involvement with the Plot project, see the note on 805:12 in *HV Works*, p. 1390.
71 *HV Works*, p. 805.
72 See *Life*, pp. 228–29. There is a photograph of the cottage as it was early in the twentieth century in *HV Works*, p. xl.

> Most happy man! who in his own sweet *fields*
> Spent all his time, to whom one *Cottage* yields
> In *age* and *youth* a lodging: who grown *old*
> Walks with his *staff* on the same *soil* and *mold*
> Where he did creep an *infant*, and can tell
> Many fair years spent in one quiet *Cell*![73]

Indeed, the evidence assembled in this chapter tends to support John Kerrigan's recent view that Vaughan was essentially local in his response to the natural and political worlds he inhabited. In Kerrigan's own words, 'his knowledge of the country [i.e. Wales] was patchy', his religion did not encourage him to 'develop an apprehension of the Welsh people as a whole', and his '"ancient way" of custom and hierarchy' reached back not into the Welsh past but to 'the Old Testament patriarchs'.[74]

The bonds that tied him to the natural surroundings of his own locality and to the family that had put down its roots among them can be seen in the fact that he was buried in the open air, not far from the great yew tree, rather than inside the church as was the custom for members of the gentry; and in the shield engraved on his tombstone, which displayed three boys' heads with snakes entwined about their necks, divided by a chevron.[75] Breconshire's historian traced the coat-of-arms of the Tretower Vaughans back to a first cousin of the ancestor of their house in the twelfth century. Tradition had it that this man, known as Moreiddig Warwyn, had been born 'with a snake round his neck' and 'from this supposed event his posterity took their arms'.[76] When the church was rebuilt in 1896, a memorial tablet, inscribed with the coat-of-arms, was placed on the wall in tribute to the poet and physician who had worshipped on the site for so many years: 'In late but reverent remembrance of a sweet Psalmist of Israel HENRY VAUGHAN M.D. (Known as the Silurist) of Newton-by

---

73 *HV Works*, p. 762. The late Peter Thomas pointed out to me that Vaughan was drawn more and more towards the ideal of a hermit, living alone with his God and the natural world in a 'cell'.

74 See John Kerrigan, *Archipelagic English: Literature, History, and Politics 1603–1707* (Oxford: Oxford University Press, 2008), p. 207.

75 See *Life*, pp. 239–41. There is a photograph of the gravestone in *HV Works*, p. xli.

76 Jones, *A History of the County of Brecknock*, pp. 261–62.

Usk in this Parish who died April 23ʳᵈ A.D. 1695 Aged 73 Years and was buried in this Churchyard. He that hath left life's vain joys and vain care / Hath got an house where many mansions are. Silex Scintillans.'

CHAPTER TWO

Henry Vaughan and Thomas Vaughan

I

When Henry Vaughan employed the name of the ancient Greek muse of pastoral in the title of *Thalia Rediviva* (1678) and quoted from Virgil's sixth eclogue on its title-page – *Nec erubuit sylvas habitare Thalia* [Thalia blushed not to dwell in the woods] – it was a modest acknowledgement that he had been living the quiet life of a country doctor and had not ventured into print for more than twenty years. But Thalia had held a more particular significance for Henry's deceased twin brother, some of whose Latin poems were included in the volume. Thomas Vaughan's *Lumen de Lumine* (1651) opened with a dream in which the author found himself in the Temple of Nature, from which he was led by 'a most exquisit, divine Beautie' clad in a green garment of *'thin loose silks'* into a valley, where the stars 'stood *glimmering* [...] on the *Tops* of high *Hills*'. His guide addressed him by the pseudonym under which he had already published several treatises on hermetic philosophy: '*Eugenius* said she *I have many Names, but my best and dearest is* Thalia: *for I am alwaies* green, *and I shall never* wither.'[1] For Thomas, she was much more than the muse of pastoral poetry: in the continuation of the dream, she is the instructress who reveals secrets of the natural world that he was dedicated to investigating as an alchemist and an occult philosopher.[2]

---

1 *TV Works*, pp. 304–06. Michael Srigley discusses the significance of Thalia for the Vaughan brothers in 'Thomas Vaughan, the Hartlib Circle and the Rosicrucians', *Scintilla*, 6 (2002), 51–52.
2 In a detailed analysis of this episode, Alan Rudrum has found similarities between Thomas Vaughan's Thalia and the medieval goddess of Nature of

'Cock-crowing', a poem by Henry Vaughan that shares much of the language and thought of the Hermetic tradition mediated through his brother's works, opens with an apostrophe to the 'Father of lights!' Thomas used the same phrase in defining the function of the *'Anima Mundi,* or the universall *spirit* of Nature', who, 'though in some sence active', is not so 'essentially, but a meer *Instrumentall Agent,* For she is guided in her Operations by a *Spirituall Metaphysicall Graine,* a Seed or Glance of *Light,* simple, and without any Mixture, descending from the *first Father of Lights'*.[3] Although Henry had this passage in mind when he was composing 'Cock-crowing', he was also – like his brother – alluding to a verse from the Epistle of St James: 'Euery good gift, and euery perfect gift is from aboue, & commeth downe from the Father of lights' (James 1:17). This chapter will attempt to determine what was distinctive in their individual beliefs about Thalia's world of nature and the divine author of that world from whom 'euery perfect gift' descends.

II

As a prelude to this task, it will be helpful to be reminded of certain symmetries and divergences in the lives of the Vaughan brothers. According to some verses by Thomas Powell, they were identical twins: 'What *Planet* rul'd your *birth*? what *wittie star*? / That you so like in *Souls* as *Bodies* are!'[4] The fact of their twinship was thought worthy of note by others during their lifetime: the 'J.W.' who wrote a dedicatory epistle for *Thalia Rediviva* – thought to be John Williams of Jesus College, who was appointed Prebendary of St David's in 1678 – hoped that he would 'not much displease' Henry Somerset, third Marquess and seventh Earl of Worcester, 'by

---

Alanus de Insulis and Chaucer's *Parlement of Foules*. See 'Thomas Vaughan's *Lumen de Lumine*: An Interpretation of Thalia', in *Literature and the Occult: Essays in Comparative Literature*, ed. Luanne Frank (Arlington, TX: The University of Texas at Arlington, 1977), pp. 234–43.

3 *Anima Magica Abscondita, TV Works,* pp. 109, 111. For 'Cock-crowing', see *HV Works,* pp. 572–73.

4 'Vpon the most Ingenious pair of Twins, Eugenius Philalethes, and the Authour of these Poems', *HV Works,* p. 171.

putting these 'Twin Poets' into his hands; and John Aubrey began his account of them with the remark, 'There were two Vaughans (Twinnes) both very ingeniose, and writers'.[5] In Helen Ashton's novel *The Swan of Usk* the new-born brothers are 'as like as two kittens, blinking and mewing side by side on the silken pillow'; but she imagines them developing along different lines during their childhood, so that there was 'no question now of mistaking the heir for his brother' – Tom the more robust of the two, 'very lively and quarrelsome, always in mischief, often in disgrace'; and Henry a 'sickly frightened fellow, mooning about, book in hand'. By the time they are eighteen and at home on vacation from Oxford, Ashton's Tom has become 'a bold ruffling fellow, full of loud talk and tales'; Henry, by contrast, is portrayed as 'gentle and retiring', laughed at by the young men and teased by the girls 'for an arrant scholar and an ill-bred awkward bookworm'.[6] Stevie Davies, writing a biography rather than a novel, offers a more informed account of twinship. Allowing that their contemporaries 'did not possess the science to make the distinction between monozygotic and dizygotic twins', she suggests that the evidence places them firmly in the former category. Products of 'a single fertilised ovum', identical twins are 'genetic replications of one another in every detail, and always of the same sex'. In their formative years, they know 'little of the aloneness of the singleton' and 'the halving of parental attention tends to be compensated by sibling-closeness'. The Vaughans seem to have been temperamentally very similar, both being 'manifestly insecure and volatile, prodigiously intelligent, complex, eccentric, quick to anger, impetuous and ardent'.[7]

Their early mutual dependence, which continued when they left the parental home at the age of eleven to be formally educated by Matthew Herbert, rector of Llangattock, may be reflected in the third of Vaughan's translations from Ovid's Black Sea poems, in which one of the exiled Roman's forfeited companions is singled out:

5 *HV Works*, p. 722 and headnote, p. 1317; *Aubrey's Brief Lives*, ed. Oliver Lawson Dick (Harmondsworth: Penguin Books, 1972), p. 463.
6 Helen Ashton, *The Swan of Usk: A Historical Novel* (London: Collins, 1940), pp. 16, 26, 67.
7 Stevie Davies, *Henry Vaughan*, Border Lines Series (Bridgend: Seren, Poetry Wales Press, 1995), p. 35.

> I am he
> Whose *years* and *love* had the same *Infancie*
> With thine, Thy *deep familiar*, that did share
> *Soules* with thee, and partake thy *Joyes* or *Care*,
> Whom the same *Roofe* lodg'd, and my *Muse* those nights
> So solemnly endear'd to her delights.[8]

> ['Tis I [...] who have been united to you in friendship almost boy with boy; 'tis I who used first to hear your serious thoughts, first to listen to your pleasant jests; 'tis I who lived in close union with you in the same household; 'tis I who in your judgment was the one and only Muse.][9]

There is nothing in Ovid's Latin that is quite equivalent to 'thy *deep familiar*' or to the sharing of '*Soules*'; lodged under 'the same *Roofe*' has a greater ring of intimacy than 'in the same household'; and, most strikingly, the opening claim implies a much closer connection than Ovid's 'united ... in friendship almost boy with boy' – the sharing not only of '*love*' but also '*years*' and 'the same *Infancie*' sounds like a description of twinship. Furthermore, the delight taken in the writer's adolescent verses – secretly divulged, perhaps, on 'those nights' – suggests how important such encouragement was for the self-confidence of the youthful poet.

Thomas left the Usk Valley for Oxford in the spring of 1638 and made steady progress at the university: he matriculated on 14 December 1638, was awarded a scholarship in May 1640, and graduated as a Bachelor of Arts on 18 February 1642. The Senior Bursars' Accounts of Jesus College for 1638–42 show that he was regularly in residence during term time, his weekly 'battels' (sums incurred for provisions) being recorded in the Buttery Books. His studies were disrupted by the outbreak of Civil War and Charles I's subsequent establishment of his court and military headquarters in Oxford, but he received a portion of his yearly graduate stipend from the college until 1648, which indicates that he continued to reside

---

8 *HV Works*, p. 205.
9 Ovid, *Ex Ponto*, 4. 3 , ll. 10–16, in *Ovid: Tristia and Ex Ponto*, trans. Arthur Leslie Wheeler, Loeb Classical Library (London: William Heinemann, 1924), p. 431.

there intermittently.¹⁰ Henry's later educational career is less securely documented. There is no record of his admission or matriculation, but according to the 1721 *Athenae Oxonienses*, he entered Jesus College in the autumn of 1638 and studied there for two years. We have his own testimony that he spent some time at Oxford without taking a degree and was then sent to London by his father to study law, only to be called home when hostilities between king and parliament began in 1642.¹¹

Back in Breconshire, during Henry's time as a legal clerk to Judge Sir Marmaduke Lloyd, his brother was 'ordayned minister by bishop Mainwaringe & presented to the Rectorie of Sᵗ. Brigets by his kinsman Sʳ. George Vaughan'.¹² Henry's letter to Aubrey does not indicate when these events took place, but it must have been after his brother's graduation in 1642 and the death of the previous rector in 1643 or 1644. Donald Dickson speculates that Thomas may have begun to study divinity at Oxford in anticipation of a career in the church, but points out that he would not have been able to take up his post as rector at Llansantffraed until he reached the canonical age for ordination in 1645. Since he continued to spend time in Oxford, he may have hired a curate to care for his parishioners during his absences.¹³ Furthermore, both Henry and Thomas were under arms for the king in Wales through the autumn months of 1645: Thomas Vaughan was listed among the captains in Sir Herbert Price's regiment of horse who were taken prisoner after the battle on Rowton Heath near Chester in September; and there is evidence in Henry's poems that he participated in the same disastrous engagement, being among those who later sought refuge in Beeston Castle and surrendered it to a parliamentary force in November.¹⁴ The only thing known for certain about the public activities of Henry in the years immediately following his military service, while Thomas was

---

10 For details of Thomas's career at Oxford, see the introduction to *Thomas and Rebecca Vaughan's* Aqua Vitae: Non Vitis, ed. and trans. Donald R. Dickson, Medieval and Renaissance Texts and Studies. Vol. 217 (Tempe, AZ: Arizona Center for Medieval and Renaissance Studies, 2001), pp. xi–xii. Cited hereafter as *Aqua Vitae*.
11 See Letter 2, *HV Works*, p. 800.
12 Letter 2, *HV Works*, p. 801.
13 See the introduction to *Aqua Vitae*, pp. xii–xiii.
14 See *Life*, pp. 60–65.

presumably dividing his time between his parish and his college, is that he prepared two volumes of secular poetry for the press in September 1646 and December 1647.[15]

The year 1648 was a transitional one for both the twins. In the spring there was a royalist uprising in South Wales and their younger brother, William, died in July as a result of what Thomas would later call a *'glorious imployment'*.[16] At the time, Thomas was busy with *Anthroposophia Theomagica*, which was composed 'in *Haste* and in my *Dayes* of *Mourning*, on the *sad Occurrence* of a *Brother's Death*'.[17] This treatise, with a dedication to the Brethren of the Rosy Cross dated 'Oxonii 48', was eventually printed in 1650 along with *Anima Magica Abscondita*. The last record of his residence at Jesus College is in the Buttery Books for late February 1648 and by the end of the year he had made a decisive move from Oxford to London.[18] In 1650, he was lodging with Thomas Henshaw and conducting alchemical experiments at his house in Kensington. *Magia Adamica*, which incorporated a fourth hermetic text, *Coelum Terrae*, was published during that year. He became involved in a public controversy with the Cambridge Platonist, Henry More, over his first Hermetic works, but went on to publish further books on alchemy and occult philosophy – *Lumen de Lumine* (1651), *Aula Lucis* (1652), and *Euphrates, or, The Waters of the East* (1655). His two ill-tempered replies to More's attacks in print were *The Man–Mouse Taken in a Trap* (1650) and *The Second Wash: or, The Moor Scour'd once more* (1651).[19] During the period of his residence in Kensington, probably from 1648 to 1651, he helped

---

15 *Poems, with the tenth Satyre of Iuvenal Englished* was registered for publication on 15 September 1646 and the dedicatory epistle for *Olor Iscanus* was dated 17 December 1647. For a discussion of the delay in publishing the second of these volumes until 1651, see the introduction to *Olor Iscanus* in *HV Works*, pp. 151–53.
16 *The Man–Mouse Taken in a Trap* (1650), *TV Works*, p. 281. Hutchinson cites evidence discovered by Gwenllian Morgan that Thomas Vaughan senior purchased a shroud for his son William on 14 July 1648 (*Life*, pp. 95–96).
17 *TV Works*, p. 94.
18 See Dickson, introduction to *Aqua Vitae*, p. xiv.
19 For the quarrel with More, see Frederic B. Burnham, 'The More–Vaughan Controversy: The Revolt Against Philosophical Enthusiasm', *Journal of the History of Ideas*, 35 (1974), 33–49; Noel L. Brann, 'The Conflict between Reason and Magic in Seventeenth-Century England: A Case Study of the Vaughan–More Debate', *Huntington Library Quarterly*, 43 (1979–80), 103–26;

Henshaw to found a Christian Learned Society, otherwise known as the Chymical Club, which aimed to make available philosophical works in the Hermetic tradition and to promote practical research. He also became acquainted with the alchemist Dr Robert Child and other members of the intellectual circle surrounding Samuel Hartlib, one of whom – George Starkey, a well-known alchemist from the New World, who had been educated at Harvard College – was reported by no less a person than Robert Boyle to be 'about to refute Vaughan'.[20] His full-time commitment to these activities was reinforced by his formal ejection from the living at Llansantffraed in 1650 on charges of 'being a common drunkard, a common swearer, no preacher, a whoremast^r, & in armes personally against the Parliament'.[21]

Henry, meanwhile, deeply affected by the death of William and the defeat of the royalist cause, had composed the religious lyrics that comprise the first part of *Silex Scintillans*, published in 1650; and while his brother was establishing himself in the nascent scientific community in London, was producing *The Mount of Olives* (1652), the various translations of devotional works gathered together under the title *Flores Solitudinis* (1654), the augmented edition of *Silex Scintillans* (1655), and two translations of medical works, *Hermetical Physick* (1655) and *The Chymists Key* (1657). Thereafter, Henry pursued a career as a country doctor and Thomas devoted himself to chemical research in London.[22] Dickson has argued that

    Arlene Miller Guinsburg, 'Henry More, Thomas Vaughan and the Late Renaissance Magical Tradition', *Ambix*, 27:1 (1980), 36–58.

20 See Donald R. Dickson, *The Tessera of Antilia: Utopian Brotherhoods & Secret Societies in the Early Seventeenth Century* (Leiden: Brill, 1998), pp. 186–94 and the introduction to *Aqua Vitae*, pp. xiv–xvii. Nothing came of the threatened refutation by Starkey. For further information about the scientific circles in which Thomas Vaughan was moving in London during the 1650s, see Ronald Sterne Wilkinson, 'The Hartlib Papers and Seventeenth-Century Chemistry', *Ambix*, 17:2 (1970), 85–110; J. Andrew Mendelsohn, 'Alchemy and Politics in England 1649–1665', *Past and Present*, 135 (1992), 30–78.

21 See *Life*, p. 93. The charge of drunkenness is confirmed by Thomas's own admission that he had 'in former times revell'd away many yeares in drinking' (*Aqua Vitae*, p. 234).

22 In 1673, Henry informed John Aubrey that while his twin brother's employment had been 'in physic & Chymistrie', his own profession was simply in 'physic', which he had 'practised now for many years with good successe', Letter 2, *HV Works*, p. 801.

Thomas's scientific methods were consistent with those of 'the other researchers of his age' and that he contributed to 'the most important development in medicine in a millennium, the advent of chemical medicaments'.[23] There is no evidence that Thomas was involved in the scientific 'club' founded by John Wilkins, who was described by John Aubrey as 'the principall reviver of experimentall philosophy' in Oxford. Since this 'new style of scientific practice' cannot have been introduced 'much earlier than 1650' and since Thomas had decamped to London during 1648, it is unlikely that his practical laboratory researches began in earnest before he joined Henshaw in Kensington.[24] Henry does not appear to have qualified formally for his new profession, and scrutiny of a collection of his medical and scientific books, some of them annotated in his own hand, convinced Dickson that his 'training must have been far more traditional than Paracelsian' and that he made no use of 'any of the medical alchemy upon which Thomas labored'.[25]

The domestic lives of the twins took very different courses. On 28 September 1651, while still living at Henshaw's, Thomas married Rebecca Archer. They were apparently childless, but enjoyed what Dickson calls 'a truly companionate marriage', in which Rebecca both encouraged and assisted her husband in his laboratory work.[26] After she died in 1658, Thomas continued to enter details of the

---

23 Donald R. Dickson, 'Thomas Vaughan and the Iatrochemical Revolution', *The Seventeenth Century*, 15 (2000), 20, 21. Dickson points out that alchemy had become 'an intellectually respectable, if controversial, branch of natural philosophy that had little to do with gold-making' by the early seventeenth century. Many fellows of the Royal Society, including Robert Boyle and Sir Isaac Newton, maintained an interest in it, and knowledge of 'such basic compounds as alcohol, ammonia, nitric acid, and hydrochloric acid' came from alchemical laboratories (Introduction to *Aqua Vitae*, p. xxxiv).

24 For the source of this information about Wilkins and his 'club' and for general developments in natural philosophy in mid-seventeenth-century Oxford, see Mordechai Feingold, 'The Mathematical Sciences and New Philosophies', in *The History of the University of Oxford: Volume IV*, ed. Nicholas Tyacke (Oxford: Clarendon Press, 1997), pp. 426–48.

25 Donald R. Dickson, 'Henry Vaughan's Medical Library', *Scintilla*, 9 (2005), 207, 209. The collection of books was discovered in the 1950s 'among the treasures of the Library Company of Philadelphia' (189).

26 Donald R. Dickson, 'The Alchemistical Wife: The Identity of Thomas Vaughan's "Rebecca"', *The Seventeenth Century*, 13 (1998), 44.

experiments they had undertaken together in a notebook entitled *Aqua Vitae: Non Vitis*. He also included accounts of dreams, one of which associates Rebecca with the figure of Thalia described in *Lumen de Lumine*: 'shee appeared to mee in greene silks down to the ground, and much taller, and slenderer then shee was in her life time, but in her face there was so much glorie, and beautie, that noe Angell in Heaven can have more'.[27] At some time before the end of 1646, Henry married Catherine Wise, who bore him four children before she died, probably in 1653. His subsequent marriage to her sister, Elizabeth, resulted in a further four children.[28] Stevie Davies remarks on the contrasting records of their marriages in the writings of the twin brothers.[29] Thomas's manuscript journal – which he rededicated after Rebecca's death on 17 April 1658 to acknowledge her contribution to his experimental investigations – is littered with references to 'my dear wife', 'my dearest wife', 'my sweetest wife' and with the often repeated mantra, 'Whom God has joined, who will separate?' In one poignant variation on this formula, he writes at the foot of a page, 'T.V.R. Withered away and weak, I live unhappily, More than half of me separated. How long, O Lord!'[30] He comments on experiments they undertook together, 'these God gave me with you in a wedding portion'; he beseeches God to reward her 'for all the Happiness and Content shee affoorded mee'; more than once, he looks forward to meeting her again in heaven, 'whither shee is gone before mee, and with her my Heart'; and in a dream, sent in answer to 'earnest prayers, and teares', he introduces her as his bride to 'some of my friends': 'When I had thus sayd, I thought, wee were both alone, and calling her to mee, I tooke her into my Arms, and shee presently embraced mee, and kissed mee.'[31] And once, in a distressing prologue to her glorious visionary appearance 'in greene silks', he regrets 'som small unkindnesses I had used towards my deare wife in her life time'.[32] In contrast,

27 *Aqua Vitae*, p. 234.
28 For Henry Vaughan's connections with the Wise family of Coleshill in Warwickshire, see Roland Mathias, 'The Midlands: Introductions and Identifications', *Scintilla*, 5 (2001), 93–103.
29 See Davies, *Henry Vaughan*, pp. 66–68.
30 *Aqua Vitae*, p. 237.
31 *Aqua Vitae*, pp. 139, 240, 243, 239.
32 *Aqua Vitae*, p. 234.

Henry's first wife, Catherine, was (in the words of Stevie Davies) 'written in invisible ink'.[33] She left a tiny trace of her activities during a visit to London in Thomas Vaughan's reference to 'a great glass full of eye-water, made att the Pinner of Wakefield, by my deare wife, and my sister Vaughan, who are both now with god'.[34] In her husband's work, she figures as the virtually anonymous Amoret of the early derivative poems of courtship and in two of the untitled elegies in *Silex Scintillans*. In the first, which begins 'As time one day by me did pass', the poet laments the loss of 'A beauty far more bright / Then the noons cloudless light' and the description of her passing from this life to the next 'through thick pangs, high agonies' suggests the possibility that she died in childbirth.[35] The other recalls her spiritual influence, which was resisted for too long and is appreciated only when it is too late:

> Fair and yong light! my guide to holy
> Grief and soul-curing melancholy;
> Whom living here I did still shun
> As sullen night-ravens do the Sun,
> And lead by my own foolish fire
> Wandred through darkness, dens and mire.
> How am I now in love with all
> That I term'd then meer bonds and thrall,
> And to thy name, which still I keep,
> Like a surviving turtle, weep![36]

Alan Rudrum has argued that the tone of guilt in these opening lines bears witness to more than neglect or a failure to recognize the true value of Catherine. References to the 'foolish fire' that enticed him away from her 'light' into 'darkness, dens and mire' and to 'the subtilties of vice' and 'false looks', together with an allusion to Adam's spurning of 'chaste fire' to become a 'slave to lustful Elements', support Rudrum's conclusion that 'the poet may have been remembering both an act of infidelity and disease occasioned

---

33 Davies, *Henry Vaughan*, p. 66.
34 *Aqua Vitae*, p. 244. The Pinner (or Pinder) of Wakefield was an inn in Gray's Inn Lane in the parish of St Pancras (*Life*, pp. 196–97).
35 *HV Works*, pp. 600–01.
36 *HV Works*, pp. 601–02.

by it'.³⁷ Catherine's younger sister, Elizabeth Wise, who became Henry's second wife probably in 1655, survives only in reports of acrimonious court cases involving the purchase of a horse and squabbles over property among the children of Vaughan's two marriages.³⁸

After the restoration of Charles II, Thomas enjoyed the patronage of Sir Robert Moray, a founding member of the Royal Society, who had been conducting chemical research while in exile in Europe and was instrumental in setting up a royal laboratory at Whitehall. During the plague of 1665, Moray withdrew from London into Oxfordshire and it was there that Thomas died on 27 February 1666 while experimenting with mercury. He left his books and manuscripts to his patron, who paid for his burial at Albury.³⁹ Henry Vaughan lived on until 23 April 1695 and was buried in the churchyard at Llansantffraed.⁴⁰

III

The places in which they were buried are symptomatic of a crucial difference that Davies discerns in their adult strategies for coping with the experience of twinship as a social rather than a purely genetic phenomenon. When Henry emerged from the womb, he entered 'a system which rewarded elder brothers with the rewards of primogeniture'; Thomas, emerging perhaps only minutes afterwards as a younger brother, was 'condemned to find [his] own way in the world'.⁴¹ The social consequences of this distinction would not have made much intrusion upon their infancy and childhood, but would probably have influenced their father's decision to send Thomas to university before Henry, since he would need qualifications for a

---

37 Alan Rudrum, 'Henry Vaughan's Poems of Mourning', in *Of Paradise and Light: Essays on Henry Vaughan and John Milton in Honor of Alan Rudrum*, ed. Donald R. Dickson and Holly Faith Nelson (Newark, DE: University of Delaware Press, 2004), pp. 319–21.
38 See *Life*, pp. 197, 225–29; see also Letter 8 and the commentary on it in *HV Works*, pp. 809, 1395–400.
39 See Srigley, 'Thomas Vaughan, the Hartlib Circle and the Rosicrucians', 49–51.
40 See *Life*, pp. 238–39.
41 Davies, *Henry Vaughan*, p. 36.

profession in later life. With his promotion to the status of scholar, his graduate stipend from Jesus College and his annual income as rector of St Bridget's, he gradually became financially independent. Perhaps, like many a younger son in the period, he was marked out for a career in the Church of England from an early age. Being the heir to the family estate, Henry had no need of a degree; but a little intellectual polish and a smattering of law acquired at Oxford and the Inns of Court would be useful when he came into his inheritance. And when political events began to divide the nation, there was good reason for Thomas Vaughan the elder to recall him from the dangerous environment of the capital to where his local duty lay as the future head of a gentry family. Social pressure as well as differences of temperament, therefore, may have contributed to the divergent courses that the brothers followed in adult life.

Opinions have differed over the closeness of the relationship between Thomas and Henry once the latter had returned permanently to Breconshire and the former was set upon the path of Hermetic study and chemical experiment that led him from Oxford to London. On the one hand, Davies's conclusion that 'they were seldom together' after 1642 best fits the current state of knowledge.[42] On the other hand, Hutchinson points out that it is not 'improbable' that Thomas would have 'gone home during the lifetime of his father and mother', or that his brother would have visited him in London.[43] Most of the indications that the close emotional and intellectual ties of childhood and adolescence did not continue into the adult lives of the twins are of a negative kind. As far as we know, Henry did not attend his brother's marriage or funeral, although one scholar has suggested that the epithalamion entitled 'To the best, and most accomplish'd Couple', published in *Olor Iscanus*, may have been written to mark the engagement of Thomas and Rebecca, who were married less than five months after the volume was registered.[44] In response to Aubrey's request for information in 1673, Henry could only surmise that Thomas had become 'noe lesse than M^r. of Arts'

---

42 Davies, *Henry Vaughan*, p. 36.
43 *Life*, p. 146.
44 See *The Secular Poems of Henry Vaughan*, ed. E.L. Marilla (Uppsala: A.-B. Lundequistska Bokhandeln, 1958), p. 225. Hutchinson, however, thinks it likely that the poem celebrates the marriage of Katherine Fowler and James Philips in 1648 (*Life*, p. 81).

and was unable to provide the name of the village 'within 5 or 6 miles of Oxford' where he had died seven years before; and when he inserted lines about Thomas's final resting place into 'Daphnis', he mistakenly situated it on the river that flows through Oxford: 'the *Isis* and the prouder *Thames* / Can shew his reliques lodg'd hard by their streams'.[45] In fact, Thomas was buried at Albury, which is about ten miles from Oxford by the River Thame. This vagueness and apparent lack of interest is in striking contrast to the series of moving elegies on his younger brother, William, published in *Silex Scintillans*. Furthermore, he wrote no commendatory verses for Thomas's various publications and supplied no introductory epistles; and it is remarkable that there is no direct mention of his twin brother, beyond the few lines in 'Daphnis', in the poetry of a writer who addressed so many of his verses to specific individuals, often gracing them with the title of 'friend'.[46]

An oblique hint at an estrangement between the twins may be found in the third of the translations from Ovid, in which Henry seems to be alluding to their closeness in infancy and childhood. He keeps quite close to the original throughout much of the text, but when he evokes the time of early intimacy with the figure he describes in the title as 'his Inconstant friend', the expansion and the intensification of feeling suggest that the source poem has opened up an especially personal and painful area of experience in the translator:

> But now since angry heav'n with Clouds and night
> Stifled those *Sun*-beams, thou hast ta'ne thy flight,
> Thou know'st I want thee, and art meerly gone
> To shun that rescue, I rely'd upon;
> Nay, thou dissemblest too, and doest disclame
> Not only my *Acquaintance*, but my name;
> Yet know (though deafe to this) that I am he
> Whose *years* and *love* had the same *Infancie*
> With thine …

---

45 *HV Works*, pp. 800, 789. In a subsequent letter to Aubrey, Vaughan gave the dates of Thomas's death and burial as 'the 27th. of februarie, in the yeare 1666' and 'the first of March', Letter 3, *HV* Works, p. 803.

46 See, for example, 'To my Ingenuous Friend, R.W.', the James of 'To His Friend —', the elegies on 'Mr R.W.' 'Mr R. Hall', and 'C.W. Esquire', his 'worthy friend, Master T. Lewes', and his 'Learned Friend, Mr T. Powell'.

> But now, perfidious traitor, I am grown
> The *Abject* of thy brest, not to be known
> In that *false Closet* more; Nay, thou wilt not
> So much as let me know, I am forgot.⁴⁷

[Now that Fortune has frowned you withdraw upon discovering that your assistance is needed. You play the dissembler, too, and wish not to be thought to know me; when you hear the name you ask who Naso is! [...] 'tis I of whom you know not, traitor, whether I am now alive, about whom you have been at no pains to inquire.]

Much more is implied in the bitter and emotional words of the translation than Ovid's resentment at the failure of a friend to intervene on his behalf with the emperor. What he needs from this close companion of his childhood is far deeper than the Roman poet's desire for 'assistance'. Cast out from the breast of this 'perfidious traitor' and cut off from all communication, he feels completely forgotten. Could it be that Henry, 'a bonded but bereft twin', found in Ovid's poem of exile and betrayal a vehicle for the anguished experience of abandonment that overtook him when he found himself back in his boyhood home without the support of the more self-sufficient brother upon whom he had always depended for a secure sense of his own identity?⁴⁸

To set against such negative and speculative indications of a more than geographical distance between the twins after Henry's return to Wales is the more positive evidence that they took an interest in each other's later ventures into authorship. In a letter of 15 June 1673, Henry was able to list his brother's published works with details of the stationers and the location of their shops, which must have been taken from title-pages of books in his possession.⁴⁹ He had also kept manuscript copies of the poems by Thomas that were printed along with the gleanings from his own early poetic output in *Thalia Rediviva*; and in two letters to Anthony Wood in 1689, he is

---

47 *HV Works*, pp. 204–05. Ovid is quoted from the Loeb translation: see Note 9.
48 See Davies, *Henry Vaughan*, pp. 7 and 32–34. See also the discussion by Paul Davis in *Translation and the Poet's Life: The Ethics of Translating in English Culture, 1646–1726* (Oxford: Oxford University Press, 2008), pp. 55–57.
49 *HV Works*, pp. 801–02.

anxious that an adequate account of his brother's publications should be given in a second edition of *Historia et Antiquitates Vniversitatis Oxoniensis* (1674).[50] On Thomas's side, the record is even clearer. Based on an examination of the stationers employed in the production of the works of both brothers, William Parker made a convincing case that Thomas arranged for the publication of most of Henry's volumes of poetry and prose from the end of the 1640s, when he was living in London and getting his own books into print. *Poems* came out in 1646, when Thomas was still in Oxford, and was published by George Badger. But Henry's second collection of poetry, *Silex Scintillans*, registered on 28 March 1650, was published by Humphrey Blunden, the stationer who had issued Thomas Vaughan's *Anthroposophia Theomagica*, *Magia Adamica*, and *Lumen de Lumine*, registered respectively on 24 December 1649, 2 October 1650, and 23 April 1651. Badger was still in business late in 1650, so the switch to Blunden for *Silex Scintillans* was almost certainly because Thomas made the arrangements for its publication.[51] He not only acted as his brother's agent in London during the 1650s, but also wrote the epistle to the reader and some commendatory verses for *Olor Iscanus* (1651) and identified himself under his pseudonym, Eugenius Philolethes, as both publisher of *The Chymists Key* (1657) and author of an introductory letter to the reader.[52] It seems, therefore, that any estrangement must have been partially resolved by the end of the 1640s. It may

50 Letters 6 and 7, *HV Works*, pp. 807–08.
51 See William R. Parker, 'Henry Vaughan and His Publishers', *The Library*, 4th series, 20 (1940), 401–11.
52 Parker's conclusion that Thomas Powell was the 'friend' who negotiated the publication of *Olor Iscanus* in 1651 with the stationer Humphrey Moseley was once widely accepted by modern scholars. This was challenged by Thomas Willard, who reverted to an earlier view (going right back to Henry Lyte in 1847) that Thomas Vaughan was instrumental in getting the volume into print and that he, not Humphrey Moseley, was the author of 'The Publisher to the Reader', with its assertion that he did not have *'the Author's* Approbation *to the* Fact' (*HV Works*, p. 170) (see Willard, 'The Publisher of *Olor Iscanus*', *Bibliographical Society of America, Papers*, 75 (1981), 174–79). This argument was developed further by Jonathan Nauman, 'Toward a Herbertian Poetic: Vaughan's Rigorism and "The Publisher to the Reader" of *Olor Iscanus*', *George Herbert Journal*, 23 (1999), 80–104. For a summary of the debate about the circumstances of the publication of *Olor Iscanus*, see the introduction to the volume in *HV Works*, pp. 149–53.

be that William's death in 1648 and the final collapse of the royalist cause with the execution of the king in 1649 helped to heal the rift between them. Nevertheless, the early intimacy was never recovered and negative feelings towards Henry may be read into a curious passage in Thomas's manuscript book dated 9 April 1659: 'I dreamed I was in some obscure, large house, where there was a tumultuous rayling people, amongst whom I knew not any, but my Brother H.'[53] However much their personal relationship meant or ceased to mean to them as their lives unfolded, together and then apart, it is from their published works that insights are to be gained into the coincidences and divergences of their beliefs about the physical and metaphysical dimensions of the world that became the main subject of their poetry and prose and that will occupy the rest of this chapter.

IV

A few glimpses of an idyllic boyhood in the Usk valley, gleaned from the later writings of both brothers, look forward to their more mature experiences and beliefs. Both wrote Latin tributes to Matthew Herbert, honouring him as a distinguished classical scholar. There is a pastoral evocation in Henry's 'Daphnis' of the years spent at Llangattock, when they listened to ancient Welsh 'visions' recited by their tutor.[54] Thomas looked back to this time in *Euphrates* (1655) and traced his interest in Hermetic science and philosophy to an early fascination with the action of fire upon water: 'This *Speculation* (I know not how) surpris'd my first youth, long before I saw the University, and certainly *Nature*, whose pupill I was, had even then awaken'd many *Notions* in me, which I met with afterwards, in the *Platonick Philosophie*.'[55] Whereas one twin remembered his tutor's recitation of bardic verses, the other recalled the effect of natural phenomena on his inquisitive mind. Their future lines of development were already being mapped out during these formative years.

In one of the notes in *Aqua Vitae*, Thomas reveals that his childhood observations of nature led him from speculation to the

---

53 *Aqua Vitae*, p. 234.
54 See *HV Works*, p. 787.
55 *TV Works*, p. 521.

experiments in which his wife assisted him: 'I employ'd my self all her life time in the Acquisition of some naturall secrets, to which I had been disposed from my youth up.'⁵⁶ He also insisted that he had no *'private ends'* in mind when he first put his thoughts on paper, being 'drawn, and forc'd to it by a *strong Admiration* of the *Mysterie* and *Majestie* of *Nature*'.⁵⁷ Both the elder twin's youthful love of poetry and the younger twin's early curiosity about the natural world were encouraged by the learned rector of Llangattock, to whom Thomas dedicated *Aula Lucis* in 1651:

> Our *Acquaintance* began with my *Child-hood*, and now you see what a *Peere* you have purchased. I can partly refer my *inclinations* to your self, and *those* onely which I derive from the *contemplative* Order, for the *rest* are besides your *influence*. I here present you with the *fruits* of them.⁵⁸

The reservation about the extent of his tutor's influence implies that it was responsible for Thomas's interest in the philosophical dimension of the Hermetic tradition, but not for his later involvement in experimental alchemy.

It can be inferred that Henry absorbed the same Hermetic teaching as well as a love of poetry during his time at Llangattock. Indeed, traces of it can be seen in the love poems printed in his 1646 volume. One likens the 'predestin'd sympathie' between Amoret and the poet to the natural force linking stars with creatures upon the earth, an attraction between the higher and lower spheres that Thomas Vaughan explains in *Magia Adamica* as a consequence of the process of Creation: 'To speak plainly, *Heaven* it self was *originally extracted* from *Inferiors*, yet not so *intirely*, but some *portion* of the *Heavenly Natures* remained still *below*, and are the *very same* in *Essence* and *Substance* with the *separated starrs* and *skies*'.⁵⁹ Similarly, the effects of sunset on streams and flowers described in another of the Amoret poems are said to be the result of 'the loose tye of influence' that operates even on creatures 'that have no

---

56 *Aqua Vitae*, p. 240.
57 *Lumen de Lumine* (1651), *TV Works*, p. 302.
58 *TV Works*, p. 453.
59 'To Amoret, Walking in a Starry Evening', *HV Works*, pp. 16–17; *TV Works*, p. 190.

sence'.⁶⁰ In 'Upon the Priorie Grove, His usuall Retyrement', Henry imagines the translation of the trees – when 'the consuming yeares, / Shall these greene curles bring to decay' – to 'th' Elysian Land' of an idyllic afterlife.⁶¹ Although this fancy is classical in origin, it reflects a strong temperamental yearning for a transcendent realm beyond the strife and corruption of this world that would manifest itself in both Hermetic and Scriptural terms in Henry's later poetry.

The poetic reflections of the two brothers on the river that ran through their home valley reveal the same contrasting dispositions as their memories of childhood. 'To the River Isca' invokes the *'bubling Springs* and *gliding streams,* / And *happy banks'* of rivers that have been hallowed by poets of the past; and, as the Swan of Usk, Henry promises to keep its *'fair name'* alive, "Till *Rivers* leave to *run*, and *men* to *read'*.⁶² There is a quite different emphasis in Thomas's celebration of 'many a serious Hour' spent 'on the Banks of *Ysca'*. His verses, inserted near the end of *Anima Magica Abscondita*, describe the Usk valley at dawn with more closely observed detail than the highly literary exercise in which Henry declares his ambition to become its *genius loci*:

> 'Tis *Day*, my Chrystal *Usk*: now the sad *Night*
> Resignes her place, as *Tenant* to the *Light*.
> See, the *amazed mists* begin to *flye*,
> And the Victorious *Sun* hath got the *skie*.
> How shall I recompence thy *streams*, that keep
> Me and my Soul *awak'd* when others sleep?
> I *watch* my *stars*, I *move* on with the *skies*,
> And *weary* all the *Planets* with mine *Eyes*.

Locating himself firmly in the landscape as an intent observer of the river, the night sky, and the mists drawn up by the rising sun, he proceeds to interpret the details of the scene as emblems of simplicity, piety, and charity and to focus finally upon the lesson taught by the river about the true goal of the 'solid, *Christian*

---

60 'To Amoret gone from him', *HV Works*, pp. 17–18.
61 *HV Works*, p. 25.
62 *HV Works*, p. 173. See the discussion of this poem by Jonathan F.S. Post, *Henry Vaughan: The Unfolding Vision* (Princeton, NJ: Princeton University Press, 1982) pp. 30–33.

Philosopher': 'I see thy *course* anticipates my *Plea*, / I'le haste to *God*, as Thou dost to the *Sea*'.[63]

V

Thomas remembered being a pupil of Nature from his first youth and felt an early impulse to investigate the secrets of natural phenomena. By the time he began to write seriously in the late 1640s, the relationship of the physical realm to the spiritual and the role of God in creating and maintaining the natural world had become central to both his philosophy and his conception of scientific experiment. In *Anthroposophia Theomagica*, completed before he left Oxford in 1648, he pinned his colours to the mast in defiance of the ancient authority of Aristotle and his followers, known as the 'Peripatetics'. In an address to the reader, Thomas justifies his alternative vision of the universe with evidence of ongoing chemical and organic processes:

> The *Peripatetickes* look on *God*, as they do on *Carpenters*, who build with *stone* and *Timber*, without any *infusion* of *life*. But the *world*, which is *God's building*, is full of *Spirit*, *quick*, and *living*. This *Spirit* is the *cause* of *multiplication*, of several perpetuall *productions* of *minerals*, *vegetables*, and *creatures* ingendred by *putrefaction*: All which are *manifest*, *infallible Arguments* of *life*. Besides, the *Texture* of the *universe* clearly discovers its *animation*.[64]

In the discourse that follows, he explains that in his 'Perplexity' about the corrupt state of humankind in a world created by God, he 'quitted this *Book-businesse*, and thought it a better course to study *Nature* then *Opinion*'. Considering 'the World in generall' to be 'too large for *Inquisition*', he set himself to observe 'the Fruits of one Spring' and this convinced him that just as 'a great many *Vegetables* fresh, and beauteous in their *Time*' grew from seeds, so the entire natural world '*in the beginning was no such thing as it is*, but *some*

---

63 *TV Works*, pp. 135–36.
64 *TV Works*, p. 52.

other seed or *matter* out of which that *Fabricke* which I now behold, did arise'. Since 'God Almighty' is 'the only proper immediate *Agent* which actuates this *matter*', he opens his inquiry with this Creator, 'that we may know the *Cause* by his *Creatures*, and the *Creatures* by their *Cause*'. Then, using the Hermetic tradition to gloss the account of the Creation in Genesis, he develops a Trinitarian definition of the Godhead:

> God the *Father* is the *Metaphysicall, supercelestial Sun*, the *second Person* is the *light*, and the *Third* is *Amor Igneus*, or a *Divine heat* proceeding from *Both*. Now, without the *presence* of this *Heat* there is no *Reception* of the *Light*, and by Consequence no *Influx* from the Father of *Lights*. For this *Amor* is the *Medium* which *unites* the *Lover* to that which is *beloved*.

This identification of the distinct roles of the three Persons of God enables him to read the first verses of the Bible as a description of the process by which the physical universe was fashioned out of chaos or the First Matter:

> No sooner had the Divine *Light* pierced the *Bosom* of the Matter, but the *Idea*, or Pattern of the whole Material World appeared in those *primitive waters, like* an *Image* in a *Glasse*: by this Pattern it was that the Holy Ghost fram'd and modelled the Universal Structure.

He goes on to explain how this conception of the origin of the natural world is the basis for the '*Magical Analysis* of Bodies' undertaken by alchemists in their quest for the First Matter: 'For he that knows how to imitate the *Proto-Chymistrie* of the Spirit, by Separation of the Principles wherin the Life is Imprisoned, may see the Impresse of it Experimentally in the outward naturall vestments'.[65]

Further on in *Anthroposophia Theomagica*, Thomas extrapolates from the Trinity the three-fold nature of all created things: 'this *Triplicity* being the expresse Image of their *Author* and a Seal he hath laid upon his *Creature*'. Both the 'great World' and the human microcosm consist of three parts – 'the *Elemental*, the *Cœlestial* and the *Spiritual*' – and the celestial part, 'commonly called *Anima*

---

65 *TV Works*, pp. 54–55, 57–59.

media', is the means by which 'the Influences of the *Divine Nature*' are conveyed 'to the more material parts of the creature' and *'Man* is made subject to the Influence of the Stars'. This 'middle spirit', he insists, 'is in Man, in Beasts, in Vegetables, in Minerals; and in every thing it is the *mediate Cause* of Composition and Multiplication'.[66] It seems to be identical with the Universal Spirit of Nature whose operations are guided by 'a Seed or Glance of *Light*' from 'the *first Father of Lights*' in a passage from *Anima Magica Abscondita*, in which he describes how, 'seated *above all his Creatures*', the Father uses this channel 'to *hatch* as it were, and cherish them with *living Eternall Influences* which daily and hourely proceed from him'.[67] This cherishing of the natural world is also expressed in *Anthroposophia Theomagica* in one of Thomas's most explicit enunciations of a vitalist philosophy, which also implies the immanence of God in His creation:

> Now this Spirit was the Spirit of Life, the same with that Breath of Life which was breathed into the *First Man*, and he became a *Living Soule*: but without doubt the Breath or Spirit of Life is the *Spirit of God*. Neither is this Spirit in Man alone, but in all the *Great World* though after an other manner: For God *breathes continually*, and passeth through all things like an *Aire* that refresheth: wherefore also he is called of Pythagoras Ψυχωση τῶν ὅλων, *Animatio universorum* [the quickening of all].[68]

In *Anima Magia Abscondita*, registered with *Anthroposophia Theomagica* on 24 December 1649 and therefore written either in Oxford or during his first year in London, Thomas seems to identify Nature if not with God then with the life-giving force emanating from Him: 'For *Nature* is the Φωνή του θεού [Voice of God], not a meer sound or Command, but a substantiall active Breath, proceeding from the Creatour, and penetrating all things.'[69] In pronouncements of this kind, he comes very close to the pantheism that Hilary Llewellyn-Williams has found to be inextricable from the 'animist philosophy' of Hermetism, with its 'myriad gods, powers and spirits

---

66 *TV Works*, pp. 66, 76–77.
67 *TV Works*, p. 111.
68 *TV Works*, p. 88.
69 *TV Works*, p. 114.

in a constantly changing and limitless universe' however much it is 'disguised by Christian imagery'.[70]

In the poems that Henry Vaughan published or made ready for publication before 1648, nature was refracted through literary tradition and there is no indication – beyond fanciful images of an Elysium of lovers and poets, where trees are forever green – that there was any significant spiritual dimension to his engagement with the natural world in which he lived. Whatever the causes and processes of his transformation into the religious poet of *Silex Scintillans*, the beginnings of that spiritual and literary journey can be detected in verse translations of Boethius and Casimir that were added to *Olor Iscanus* from December 1647, when the dedicatory epistle was written, to 1651, when the volume was eventually published.[71] God figures for the first time in Henry's work as the 'great builder of this starrie frame', who gave 'a law to ev'ry starre' and controls the cycle of the seasons. This pagan creator in Boethius's *Consolation of Philosophy* does not extend his concern from the natural to the human realm, which is left 'to the flow / And Ebbe of Fortune'. And although this 'wise God' sealed from the beginning the 'proper time' for 'all things', the same 'divine decree' ordained that 'nothing mortall shall eternall be'.[72]

The first of the translations from the neo-Latin odes of the Polish Jesuit, Casimir Sarbiewski, is also addressed to an 'Allmighty *Spirit*', who rules everything 'here below' according to 'Set *turns* and *changes*'. In the closing lines, however, a more Christian note is struck for the first time in Henry Vaughan's work:

> But ô good God!
> While these for *dust* fight, and a *Clod*,
> Grant that poore I may *smile*, and be
> At rest, and *perfect peace* with thee.

70 Hilary Llewellyn-Williams, '"As Above, So Below": Reflections of the Hermetic Philosophy', *Scintilla*, 1 (1997), 72, 74.

71 Walley makes a strong case for dating these translations to the years 1648–51 and argues that the odes of Casimir led Vaughan on from the Stoic virtue of Boethius to 'find abiding peace within the recognition of that universal order which is the love of God' ('The Strange Case of *Olor Iscanus*', 32).

72 *Translations of Boethius*, Consolation of Philosophy Lib. 1. Metrum 5, Lib. 1. Metrum 6, Lib. 2. Metrum 3, *HV Works*, pp. 214–15, 216, 219.

Two more of Casimir's poems provided vehicles for some of the fundamental beliefs about God and Nature that he was to develop in *Silex Scintillans*. In one, the happy man of the Horatian tradition is recast as a Christian recluse, 'whose *longing Eyes* / Are ever *Pilgrims* in the *skyes*', where he 'views his *bright home*, and desires / To *shine* amongst those *glorious fires*'. The other, a formal reply to Horace's *Beatus ille* epode, expresses the yearning for both salvation and transcendence that echoes through many of the later devotional lyrics:

> He in the *Evening*, when on high
> The *Stars* shine in the *silent skye*
> Beholds th' *eternall flames* with mirth,
> And *globes* of *light* more large then E*arth*,
> Then weeps for *Joy*, and through his tears
> Looks on the *fire-enamel'd S*pheres,
> Where with his *Saviour* he would be
> Lifted above mortalitie.

Later in the poem, Henry's early literary confections about poetic paradises in the Priory Grove and River Isca poems have evolved into a Christian perception of the natural scene:

> In the Calme *Spring*, when the Earth *bears*,
> And feeds on *April's breath*, and *tears*,
> His Eyes accustom'd to the *skyes*
> Find here *fresh objects*, and like *spyes*
> Or busie *Bees* search the soft *flowres*
> Contemplate the *green fields*, and *Bowres*,
> Where he in *Veyles*, and *shades* doth see
> The *back Parts* of the *Deitye*.

This new attentiveness to the texture of life in an April landscape – giving birth, feeding, breathing, and searching – is rewarded with an intimation of the divine presence; and this in turn prompts a reflection on man's fallen state and an intuition about the sentience of plants that goes far beyond the rhetorical device of the pathetic fallacy:

> Then sadly sighing sayes, O *how*
> *These flowres With hasty, stretch'd heads grow*

> *And strive for heav'n, but rooted here*
> *Lament the distance with a teare!* [...]
> *And the Lillies hollow and bleak*
> *Look, as if they would something speak,*
> *They sigh at night to each soft gale,*
> *And at the day-spring weep it all.*
> *Shall I then only (wretched I!)*
> *Opprest with Earth, on Earth still lye?*[73]

Although Henry would later attribute his 'conversion' to the 'holy *life* and *verse*' of George Herbert, it is evident that the experience of translating the odes of Casimir had set him on the path not only towards writing devotional poetry but also towards some of his characteristic responses to the natural world.[74] The rest of this chapter will consider a number of specific areas in which his ideas about God and Nature as expressed in *Silex Scintillans* and his original and translated prose works coincided with or diverged from the system of belief developed by his brother.

VI

Much of the commentary on the relationship between the Vaughan twins as writers has been devoted to establishing the nature and extent of the poet's debt to the Hermetic philosophy and vocabulary of the alchemist.[75] In his quest for the origin of Henry's ideas about God in Nature, for example, A.C. Judson long ago affirmed that Thomas's influence on his poetic imagination was 'second only to that exerted by George Herbert', although he allowed the possibility that 'if he did not derive his ideas directly from his brother, he

---

73 *Translations of Casimir*, Lib. 4. Ode 28, Lib. 3. Ode 22, and 'The Praise of a Religious life', *HV* Works, pp. 222–23, 224, 227–28.

74 For the reference to George Herbert, see the 'Author's Preface' to *Silex Scintillans* (1655), *HV* Works, p. 558.

75 This is the burden of the Memorial Sermon preached by S.L. Bethell before members of the Brecknock Society in the parish church of Llansantffraed in 1952: 'The Theology of Henry and Thomas Vaughan', *Theology*, 56 (1953), 137–43.

probably made use of the same sources'.[76] For Robert Sencourt, it was 'impossible not to think that what guided the mind of Eugenius Philalethes would have affected his brother also, or that the clergyman would not have immediately committed to the physician his own conclusions as to Natural Science'; while Eluned Crawshaw found similar images and themes but different emphases in the work of the brothers, Henry being 'far more pessimistic than Thomas', who 'looks to renewal rather than mourning a paradise lost'.[77]

In her pioneering study, *Henry Vaughan and the Hermetic Philosophy*, Elizabeth Holmes argues that both twins had actively 'explored the natural world in search of hidden meanings' during the 1640s.[78] Indeed, a couplet in one of the poems printed in *Thalia Rediviva* implies that Henry had once taken more than a speculative interest in the secrets of nature: 'And my false *Magic*, which I did believe, / And mystic Lyes to *Saturn* I do give'.[79] Since Saturn 'presided over alchemical experiments', it seems likely that Vaughan is here 'repudiating an earlier interest in alchemy and occult studies fostered by his brother Thomas'.[80] 'Vanity of Spirit', from the first part of *Silex Scintillans*, recalls in more detail how his desire for knowledge of the Creator had led him to the kind of questions that exercised the natural philosophers:

> Quite spent with thoughts I left my Cell, and lay
> Where a shrill spring tun'd to the early day.
>   I beg'd here long, and gron'd to know
>   Who gave the Clouds so brave a bow,
>   Who bent the spheres, and circled in
>   Corruption with this glorious Ring,

---

76 A.C. Judson, 'The Source of Henry Vaughan's Ideas concerning God in Nature', *Studies in Philology*, 24 (1927), 605, 593.

77 Robert Sencourt, *Outflying Philosophy: A Literary Study of the Religious Element in the Poems and Letters of John Donne and in the Works of Sir Thomas Browne and of Henry Vaughan the Silurist* (London: Simpkin, Marshall, 1925), pp. 150–51; Eluned Crawshaw, 'The Relationship between the Works of Thomas and Henry Vaughan', *Poetry Wales*, 11 (1975), 80–81.

78 Elizabeth Holmes, *Henry Vaughan and the Hermetic Philosophy* (Oxford: Basil Blackwell, 1932), p. 15.

79 'The importunate Fortune, written to Doctor Powel of Cantre', *HV Works*, p. 742.

80 Quoted from the commentary on the poem in *HV Works*, p. 1345.

> What is his name, and how I might
> Descry some part of his great light.

His answer, it would seem from what follows, was to probe the secrets of the physical world by the experimental methods of the alchemists:

> I summon'd nature: peirced through all her store,
> Broke up some seales, which none had touch'd before,
>> Her wombe, her bosome, and her head
>> Where all her secrets lay a bed
>> I rifled quite, and having past
>> Through all the Creatures, came at last
>> To search my selfe, where I did find
>> Traces, and sounds of a strange kind.

This turn inwards, after the rifling of nature's womb, was rewarded with 'Ecchoes beaten from th' eternall hills'. Then, by 'weake beames' and flashes of fire, he caught sight of an ancient stone, covered in 'Hyeroglyphicks' and 'broken letters', but before he could piece them together to 'find out / The mystery' – 'That little light I had was gone'.[81] Thomas likewise personifies Nature and uses a similar image to describe his fear that he may have gone too far in unveiling some of her secrets in *Anima Magica Abscondita* – 'having allmost broken her Seale, and exposed her naked to the World'. But he goes on boldly to 'speake of greater matters' and explain the operations of the 'Seed or Glance of *Light*' that descends 'from the *first Father of Lights*'. He speaks as an alchemical adept who knows more than he is willing to tell of the mysteries of the natural world, 'For there is a necessity of reserving, as well as publishing some things'.[82] Henry closes 'Vanity of Spirit' more humbly with a move typical of the poetry he was writing at the end of the 1640s. Acknowledging his human limitations, he looks for a solution beyond this life:

> It griev'd me much.   At last, said I,
> *Since in these veyls my Ecclips'd Eye*
> *May not approach thee, (for at night*

---

[81] *HV Works*, pp. 80–81.
[82] *TV Works*, p. 111.

> *Who can have commerce with the light?)*
> *I'le disapparell, and to buy*
> *But one half glaunce, most gladly dye.*[83]

By the time he wrote the lyrics published in 1650, then, he was no longer engaged in his brother's alchemical quest for Nature's fundamental secret, the First Matter – identified in *Aula Lucis* as the Philosopher's Stone – which Thomas insisted was to be sought 'not only with the *Tong*, but with the *hand*', because the adept, as he affirms even more forcefully in *Magia Adamica*, 'must see it, handle it, and by *experimentall ocular Demonstrations* know the very *Central Invisible Essences*, and *Proprieties* of it'.[84]

Henry's religious temperament was nevertheless receptive to three ideas that were central to his brother's philosophy of Nature: the first is the vitalist conception of the world as *'God's building'* – 'full of *Spirit, quick*, and *living*' – in which the process of generation, even of minerals, is perpetual; the second is the certainty that all of Nature's creatures, again including minerals, will share in the resurrection; and the third is the possibility of ascent from the physical to the spiritual world.[85] His most powerful evocation of a natural scene imbued with life in every part is the first movement of 'The Morning-watch':

> O Joyes!   Infinite sweetnes! with what flowres,
> And shoots of glory, my soul breakes, and buds!
>   All the long houres
>   Of night, and Rest
>   Through the still shrouds
>   Of sleep, and Clouds,
>   This Dew fell on my Breast;
>   O how it *Blouds*,
> And *Spirits* all my Earth! heark!   In what Rings,
> And *Hymning Circulations* the quick world
>   Awakes, and sings;
>   The rising winds,
>   And falling springs,

---

83 *HV Works*, p. 81.
84 *TV Works*, pp. 459, 457, 198.
85 These aspects are addressed by Richard H. Walters, 'Henry Vaughan and the Alchemists', *Review of English Studies*, 23 (1947), 107–22.

> Birds, beasts, all things
> Adore him in their kinds.
> Thus all is hurl'd
> In sacred *Hymnes*, and *Order,* The great *Chime*
> And *Symphony* of nature.[86]

Comparison with the three passages quoted earlier, in which Thomas sets out his animist vision of Nature, will evince some significant differences of emphasis. The Hermetic philosopher – the proto-chemist – looks for evidence to support his proposition that the material world is infused with life, and finds it in the perpetual processes of putrefaction and generation that drive the *'multiplication'* of *'minerals, vegetables,* and *creatures'*. The devotional poet experiences himself as an integral part of a greater harmony to which all of Nature contributes – his soul 'breakes, and buds' into 'flowres, / And shoots of glory' like plants rooted in the earth and the blood courses through his body with the same life-sustaining energy as the *'Hymning Circulations'* of the quick and waking world of birds and beasts. In contrast to the virtual elision of God with Nature as the 'active Breath' that continually 'passeth through all things' in Thomas's other formulations of the animist principle, the God of Henry's morning worship remains in touch with but apart from his Creation – transcendent rather than immanent – as 'all things / Adore him in their kinds'. A celebrated stanza from 'Rules and Lessons' also implies a distinction between the world of creatures and the Creator who is known to them by natural instinct and can be known through them by an attentive human observer:

> Walk with thy fellow-creatures: note the *hush*
> And *whispers* amongst them.   There's not a *Spring,*
> Or *Leafe* but hath his *Morning-hymn*; Each *Bush*
> And *Oak* doth know *I AM.*[87]

The theme of an animate world waking to praise the God who cares for it is taken up again in 'The Bird'. The poet focuses first on the tiny creature of the poem's title that has been tossed by sullen storms all night:

86 *HV Works*, p. 87.
87 *HV Works*, p. 99.

> And now as fresh and chearful as the light
> Thy little heart in early hymns doth sing
> Unto that *Providence*, whose unseen arm
> Curb'd them, and cloath'd thee well and warm.

But then he turns to features of the natural scene that are usually regarded as inanimate:

> So hills and valleys into singing break,
> And though poor stones have neither speech nor tongue,
> While active winds and streams both run and speak,
> Yet stones are deep in admiration.[88]

There is an obvious precedent in the Psalms for attributing song to hills and valleys and speech to streams, but to find the very stones 'deep in admiration' of the Creator is the hallmark of a poet whose acute awareness of what Alan Rudrum has called 'a sphere beyond matter within the material world itself' rendered him 'intuitively a hermetist'.[89]

There was, in fact, authority for ascribing some degree of sentience to the entire created world in the Epistle to the Romans, which supplies one of Henry's poems with an epigraph (in Beza's Latin version): '*Etenim res Creatae exerto Capite observantes expectant revelationem Filiorum Dei*' [For the creatures, watching with lifted head, wait for the revelation of the sons of God].[90] He is delighted to find his intuition vindicated by Scripture:

---

88 *HV Works*, p. 582.
89 Alan Rudrum, 'The Influence of Alchemy in the Poems of Henry Vaughan', *Philological Quarterly*, 49 (1970), 480.
90 Alan Rudrum discusses the significance of the epigraph in the context of divergent views among Church fathers and early modern theologians about the meaning of the Greek word behind 'the creatures' and about the inclusion of the rest of the natural world in the resurrection ('Henry Vaughan, the Liberation of the Creatures, and Seventeenth-Century English Calvinism', *The Seventeenth Century*, 4 (1989), 33–54). In another article, he argues that Vaughan's use of the Latin wording (which Beza altered in later editions) was deliberately aimed at Calvinist commentators, who judged the creatures 'senselesse, and their state / Wholly Inanimate' ('For then the Earth shall be all Paradise: Milton, Vaughan and the neo-Calvinists on the Ecology of the Hereafter', *Scintilla*, 4 (2000), 50–52).

> And do they so? have they a Sense
> > Of ought but Influence?
> Can they their heads lift, and expect,
> > And grone too? why th' Elect
> Can do no more: my volumes said
> > They were all dull, and dead,
> They judg'd them senselesse, and their state
> > Wholly Inanimate.

In the second stanza, he takes '*res Creatae*' to include stones, trees, and flowers; and in the third, he contrasts his own inconstant attendance upon God with the steadfastness of plants, which 'peep from their beds' with erect heads, and of minerals buried in the earth, which 'cannot quit the womb' and yet 'Sigh there, and grone for thee, / Their liberty'.[91] These later stanzas draw upon the continuation of the Pauline passage:

> For wee know that the whole creation groaneth, and trauaileth in paine together until now. And not only *they*, but our selues also, which haue the first fruites of the spirit, euen we our selues groane within our selues, waiting for the adoption, *to wit*, the redemption of our body. (Romans 8:22–23)

Thomas quotes these same verses in *Magia Adamica* as part of his Hermetic commentary on the curse that followed the transgression of Adam and Eve and arrives at the conclusion that 'the *Creatures in General*' will participate in the resurrection: 'for as they were *cursed* in the *Fall* of *Man*, for *Man's* sake, so it seems in his *Restitution* they shall be also *blessed* for *his sake*'.[92] Thomas quotes Scripture to support his contention that the created world was implicated in the Fall of Man, whereas Henry is immersed in an experience of wonder at the constancy of unfallen Nature, which, as so often in his devotional poetry, shows up his own spiritual inadequacies.

91 'And do they so?', *HV Works*, p. 95.
92 *TV Works*, p. 159. Wardle considers the use made of the verses from Romans by the Vaughan brothers and concludes that 'we must content ourselves with the idea that the two men had discussed and settled this matter to their own satisfaction before Thomas left Wales' ('Thomas Vaughan's Influence upon the Poetry of Henry Vaughan', *Publications of the Modern Language Association*, 51 (1936), 951–52).

The idea that the whole of the natural world is yearning towards God and waiting for the return of Christ occurs frequently in the poems of *Silex Scintillans* – in 'The Tempest', for example, 'all things' show man the way to heaven, 'trees, herbs, flowres, all / Strive upwards stil, and point him the way home'; and in 'The day of Judgement', the poet cries with 'earnest groans for freedom', while 'My fellow-creatures too say, *Come*! / And stones, though speechless, are not dumb'.[93] He turns to Hermetic philosophy – and his brother's belief about the agency of the 'middle spirit' – to explain the origins of the instinct that draws the cockerel towards its Maker and Saviour:

> Father of lights! what Sunnie seed,
> What glance of day hast thou confin'd
> Into this bird? To all the breed
> This busie Ray thou hast assign'd;
>   Their magnetisme works all night,
>   And dreams of Paradise and light.
>
> Their eyes watch for the morning-hue,
> Their little grain expelling night
> So shines and sings, as if it knew
> The path unto the house of light.
>   It seems their candle, howe'r done,
>   Was tinn'd and lighted at the sunne.[94]

Thomas's passing reference in *Magia Adamica* to the involvement of the natural world in the ultimate restitution of humankind is elaborated in *Euphrates* as part of his argument that '*Scripture*, all the way, makes use of *Nature* and hath indeed discovered such *natural mysteries* as are not to be found in any of the philosophers'. He adds:

---

93 *HV Works*, pp. 126, 619–20.
94 'Cock-crowing', *HV Works*, p. 572. For detailed readings of this poem, see Don Cameron Allen, 'Vaughan's "Cock-Crowing" and the Tradition', *English Literary History*, 21 (1954), 94–106; June Sturrock, '"Cock-Crowing"', *Scintilla*, 5 (2001), 152–58; and Jonathan Nauman, '"The truth and light of things": Henry Vaughan and Nature', in *Henry Vaughan and the Usk Valley*, ed. Elizabeth Siberry and Robert Wilcher (Little Logaston Woonton Almeley: Logaston Press, 2016), pp. 67–69.

> For my own part, I fear not to say that *Nature* is so much the busines of *Scripture*, that to me, the *Spirit of God*, in those sacred Oracles, seems not onely to mind the *Restitution of Man in particular*, but even the *Redemption of Nature in generall*. We must not therefore *confine* this *Restitution* to our own *Species*, unless we can confine corruption to it withall, which doubtless we can not do [...] If it be true then that *Man* hath a Saviour, it is also true, that the whole Creation hath the same; God having reconciled all things to himself in Christ Jesus.[95]

Basing his certainty on intuition rather than deduction, Henry looks forward in 'The Jews' to a time when 'living waters' will flow to 'make drie dust, and dead trees grow' and prays in particular that he might see the 'proper [i.e. its own] branches' – now lying scattered and decayed – restored to the olive.[96] Elsewhere, he urges 'the new worlds new, quickning Sun' to 'fold up these skies, / This long worn veyl' and 'pierce and pass' through the creatures so that they may be fixed 'without blemish or decay' in 'a state / For evermore immaculate'. In such a 'state', they will be 'fit for the sight' of their Maker's 'pure and unveil'd eye'. And it is this state for which all God's creatures 'Travel and groan, and look and call'.[97] Most explicitly, in the closing lines of 'The Book', the poet who counselled an approach to the God of Nature by listening to the morning hymns of spring and leaf and oak begs to be included in the resurrection that will embrace every species of created thing:

> O knowing, glorious spirit! when
> Thou shalt restore trees, beasts and men,
> When thou shalt make all new again,
> Destroying onely death and pain,
> Give him amongst thy works a place,
> Who in them lov'd and sought thy face![98]

---

95 *TV Works*, pp. 517–18.
96 *HV Works*, p. 585.
97 'L'Envoy', *HV Works*, p. 631.
98 *HV Works*, p. 630. For a discussion of this poem, see A.W. Rudrum, 'Henry Vaughan's "The Book": A Hermetic Poem', *AUMLA: Journal of the Australasian Universities Language and Literature Association*, 16 (1961), 161–66.

In 'The Dawning', the poet who longed for the blissful 'state' of standing in the sight of God's 'pure and unveil'd eye' and gazing upon His 'face' joins the rest of the creatures in expecting 'some sudden matter' and watching for 'the Break' of the 'great day' when Christ Himself 'wil be the Sun' and free them from their material bonds.[99] In 'Disorder and frailty', he identifies with the upward striving of plants, feeling himself enlivened by the breath of the Spirit and the blood of Christ as they are by sunlight and dew:

> I threaten heaven, and from my Cell
> Of Clay, and frailty break, and bud
> Touch'd by thy fire, and breath; Thy bloud
> Too, is my Dew, and springing wel.

Later in the poem, the example of a 'sleeping Exhalation' that 'soars, and shines', drawn up by 'the heat, and beams' of 'that Comforter, the Sun', makes him too yearn for his soul to be hatched and given 'wings', so that it can 'fly / Up where thou art, amongst thy tire / Of Stars, above Infirmity'.[100] His hour's meditation on the winter sleep of a once 'gallant flowre', waiting to come forth 'most fair and young' in due season, culminates in a prayer that he might travel along that 'path unto the house of light' about which the rooster dreams and sings:

> O thou! whose spirit did at first inflame
>   And warm the dead,
> And by a sacred Incubation fed
>   With life this frame
> Which once had neither being, forme, nor name,
>   Grant I may so
>   Thy steps track here below,
>
> That in these Masques and shadows I may see
>   Thy sacred way,
> And by those hid ascents climb to that day
>   Which breaks from thee
> Who art in all things, though invisibly;

---

99 *HV Works*, pp. 116–17.
100 *HV Works*, pp. 109–10.

> Shew me thy peace,
> Thy mercy, love, and ease.[101]

As in 'Cock-crowing', which derives its 'house of light' from the Latin *aula lucis* (the title of one of Thomas's treatises), Hermetic philosophy has provided Henry with 'a coherent system of thought' and 'a terminology' for poetic expression.[102] Catching glimpses of the 'sacred way' by tracing the steps of the 'Father of lights' in the 'Masques and shadows' of the created world is one thing, but taking the 'path' to the 'house of light' where He dwells is another. The poet prays to 'soar and rise / Up to the skies' in celebrating Christ's ascension in the first of the new poems added to the 1655 *Silex Scintillans*. He acknowledges in the companion 'Ascension-Hymn', however, that he is clogged by 'Dust and clay / Man's antient wear' and that 'Who will ascend, must be undrest'. There are 'some / That know to die / Before death come' and 'Walk to the skie / Even in this life', but he accepts that such flights are not for the many, who must wait for the redemption and restoration promised through the sacrifice of Christ:

> Hee alone
> And none else can
> Bring bone to bone
> And rebuild man,
> And by his all subduing might
> Make clay ascend more quick then light.[103]

Thomas was more confident than his brother that an ascent from the elemental by way of the celestial into the spiritual realm of the three-fold universe – the ultimate goal of the Hermetist – was achievable before death. His desire for his own soul to make this journey is given expression in some verses near the beginning of *Anthroposophia Theomagica*:

> *She* would – though *here imprison'd*, see,
> Through all her *Dirt* thy *Throne* and *Thee*.

---

101 'I Walkt the other day', *HV Works*, pp. 144–45.
102 Rudrum, 'The Influence of Alchemy in the Poems of Henry Vaughan', 480.
103 *HV Works*, pp. 565, 566–67.

> *Lord* guide her out of this *sad Night*
> And say once more, *Let there be Light*.[104]

According to the Hermetic interpretation of Genesis that he elaborates in the rest of the discourse, the ascent must be initiated by a descent from the 'Father of Lights':

> You see now, if you be not *Durissimæ Cervicis Homines* [men of a most dense head], how man fell, and by Consequence you may guesse by what meanes he is to rise. He must be united to the *Divine Light* from whence by disobedience he was separated. A *Flash*, or *Tincture* of this must come, or he can no more discerne things spiritually, then he can distinguish Colours naturally without the light of the Sun. This light descends, and is united to him by the same meanes as his Soule was at first.[105]

In this early work, Thomas is less concerned with alchemical experiments than with the mystical principles of Cornelius Agrippa – 'He is indeed my Author, and next to God I owe all that I have unto Him'.[106] In its companion piece, *Anima Magica Abscondita*, he quotes with approval Agrippa's repudiation of maleficent necromancers and alchemists who persecute nature, and expounds 'the true *Essential mystery* of *Regeneration*, or the *Spiritual Death*' from the work of a magus known as 'Sapiens' to the Rosicrucian Brotherhood. Calling upon his soul and body to rise up and follow their higher soul, Sapiens conducts them to a high mountain, where there is a shining and impregnable tower. Refreshed from a fountain of living waters, the adept proceeds upwards to the abode of Wisdom, beyond which is a realm reached by very few:

> It is such a place which mortals may scarcely reach unless they are raised by the Divine Will to the state of immortality; and then, or ever they enter, they must put off the world, the hindering vesture of fallen life […]. Whosoever advances beyond these three regions passes from the sight of men.[107]

104 *TV Works*, p. 56.
105 *TV Works*, p. 81.
106 *TV Works*, p. 84.
107 *TV Works*, pp. 132, 127–28. The words of Sapiens, quoted in Latin in Rudrum's

Thomas adds his own comment on the destination of the mystical journey described by Sapiens: 'This is the *pitch* and *place*, to which if any man *ascends*, he enters into *Chariots* of *Fire* with *Horses* of *fire*, and is *translated* from the *earth*, *soul* and *Body*. Such was *Enoch*, such was *Elijah*, such was *Esdras*.' And he emphasizes that 'the *Period* and *Perfection*' of this magical art 'is no way *Physicall*', although he may have been led to it in the first place by an interest in natural secrets: 'In a word, it ascends *per lumen Naturæ in lumen Gratiæ* [by the light of Nature to the light of Grace], and the *last end* of it is *truely Theologicall*.'[108]

VII

Henry and Thomas Vaughan coincide most closely in their belief that the realm of Nature is quick and living, which means that it is always changing in that process of putrefaction and production that Thomas offered as proof of its animation against the materialists who denied any infusion of life.[109] As a corollary to this belief – confirmed for the Hermetic philosopher by chemical evidence and for the devotional poet by biblical authority – they also shared a conviction that all things would participate in the restitution prophesied in the Book of Revelation. They had different conceptions, however, of what that restitution would involve. Henry accepted the orthodox doctrines that Christ will rebuild man by reuniting scattered bones and dust and that preparation of the resurrected body for the final ascent to heaven is dependent on its being cleansed from sin – made possible only by the sacrifice of the Cross – when the Christ of 'Ascension-Hymn' returns on the Last Day: 'The Fuller, whose pure blood did flow / To make stain'd man more white then snow.'[110]

---

edition, are cited here from *Works of Thomas Vaughan*, ed. Arthur Edward Waite [1919] (Kessinger Publishing's Rare Mystical Reprints, n.d), p. 106.
108 *TV Works*, pp. 128, 129.
109 Bethell commented in 1952 that developments in contemporary science and theology mean that we are now in a better position to 'appreciate the rearguard action fought by the brothers Vaughan against a crudely materialistic science and the beginnings of deistical theology' ('The Theology of Henry and Thomas Vaughan', 139).
110 *HV Works*, p. 567.

Thomas conceives of the transformation described by St Paul – 'wee shall all be changed, in a moment, in the twinckling of an eye, at the last trumpe' (I Corinthians 15:51–52) – as a chemical process like the production of minerals in the earth, in which there is no emphasis on redemption from sin: 'In a word, *Salvation* it self is nothing else but *transmutation* [...]. God of his great Mercy *prepare* us for it, That from hard stubborn *Flints* of this *world*, we may prove *Chrysoliths* and *Jaspers* in the new, eternall *foundation*.'[111]

Thomas insisted near the end of his very first work that he was orthodox in religion – 'I am neither Papist, nor Sectary, but a true, resolute Protestant in the best sense of the Church of England' – and he closed it with some verses addressed to 'My sweetest *Jesus*!'[112] He never refers to his status as an ordained minister of that church, however, and unlike other ejected clergymen, he made no attempt to reclaim his living at Llansantffraed in 1660. Furthermore, allusions to the Church or to Christ and the need for redemption from sin are rarely found in his published writings.[113] His core beliefs are embodied in their most imaginatively convincing form in the vision of Thalia, who tells him, '*Hoc quicquid est, quo Condita manent, atque gubernantur, usitato cunctis Vocabulo Deum nomino*' [Whatsoever it is, by which the world is preserved and governed, I call by that usual name God]. The high point towards which the encounter with Thalia moves, which is narrated with a sense of religious awe, comes when he dips his hand into the river cascading from '*the* Mountains *of the* Moone' and feels 'a *certaine* kind of *Oile* of a *Waterie Complexion*', which has a '*viscous, fat, mineral nature*' and is '*bright* like *Pearls*, and *transparent* like *Chrystall*' – 'Hereupon *Thalia* told me it was the *first Matter*, and the very Naturall, true *Sperm* of the *great World*'.[114] He claimed in his notebook that he had discovered 'the Secret of extracting the oyle

---

111 *Lumen de Lumine*, *TV Works*, p. 357.
112 *Athroposophia Theomagica*, *TV Works*, pp. 92–93.
113 Thomas's manuscript notebook, *Aqua Vitae: Non Vitis*, however, is punctuated with exclamations and prayers invoking the name of Christ as Saviour in the hope of a reunion in heaven with Rebecca, e.g., 'T. R. V. 1658. Whom God has joined, Who will separate? O Christ Jesus! Light and Life of the World: Son of God: Son and Redeemer of Mankind: Draw me after Thee, We shall run' (p. 191).
114 *Lumen de Lumine*, pp. 306–08.

of Halcali [i.e. the First Matter] [...] in the Dayes of my most deare Wife', but that he had since 'made a hundred Attempts in vaine' to reproduce the experiment. On the day before Rebecca died, God had 'brought it againe into my mind' and on the day of her death he had 'extracted it by the former practice'.[115]

The equivalents of these supreme personal and spiritual moments in the poems of his twin brother are the climactic celebrations of the Eucharist in the two parts of *Silex Scintillans*.[116] For Henry, the church and its liturgy rather than the laboratory provide the context for an experience that looks forward to that final ascent into the eternal presence of God. In 1650, he invokes the language of the Book of Common Prayer to prepare himself for Easter Day: 'Thou holy, harmless, undefil'd high-priest! / The perfect, ful oblation for all sin, [...] Give to thy wretched one / Thy mysticall *Communion*.'[117] And, in 1655, he approaches the sacred feast as a foretaste, mediated by the church to those who 'sit lingring here', of that 'world of light'[118] towards which his soul yearned:

> Come then true bread,
> Quickning the dead,
>   Whose eater shall not, cannot dye,
> Come, antedate
> On me that state
>   Which brings poor dust the victory.[119]

---

115 *Aqua Vitae*, p. 31.
116 Thomas Calhoun sees the sequence of Easter poems leading up to Holy Communion in the 1650 collection as 'a carefully staged event' that results in a 'transcendent vision' and a 'moment of transformation', which is no sooner achieved than an inevitable descent is made into the everyday world in 'Affliction (I)' (*Henry Vaughan: The Achievement of Silex Scintillans* (Newark, DE: University of Delaware Press, 1981), pp. 177–82.
117 'Dressing', *HV Works*, p. 120.
118 'They are all gone into the world of light', *HV Works*, p. 567.
119 'The Feast', *HV Works*, p. 623. A contrary view is taken by Sophie Read in her recent study of how Eucharistic ideas are expressed by six early modern poets, in which she argues that because Vaughan was deprived of the rites of the Anglican Church, his experience of the 'mysticall *Communion*' of the Eucharist 'is not something that he lives through his verse in the same way that Herbert does', but is dominated by a 'sense of absence' rather than presence and is 'mediated through borrowed language'. See *Eucharist and the Poetic*

While there is some validity, therefore, in Hilary Llewellyn-Williams's judgement that Henry and Thomas were both 'devout Anglican Christians', who 'yet seem to have experienced no conflict between Christian doctrine and the Hermetic viewpoint', Michael Srigley gets closer to defining their distinctive positions in his remark that they are 'two sides of one coin' – 'Where Thomas assimilates Christianity to alchemy, Henry, it seems to me, subordinates alchemy to Christianity.'[120] That coin was part of the intellectual currency of the so-called 'Vitalist Moment' of the mid-century, which 'derived ultimately from the sixteenth-century alchemist Paracelsus' and 'linked man and the universe in a self-contained cosmic economy of interflux and exchange'.[121] The broader context for understanding the fervour with which the Vaughan twins embraced their animistic vision was the upsurge of mechanistic materialism associated with the philosophy of Descartes and the new 'atomism' of Pierre Gassendi, which had reached Oxford by the 1640s and was being widely disseminated throughout the country in the 1650s.[122] During the brief period of their most intense activity as authors, from 1648 to 1655, Henry and Thomas Vaughan played their different parts in mounting a rear-guard action against an intellectual movement that

Imagination in Early Modern England (Cambridge: Cambridge University Press, 2013), pp. 170–74.

120 Llewellyn-Williams, '"As Above, So Below"', 71; Michael Srigley, 'Ritual Entries: Some Approaches to Henry Vaughan's *Silex Scintillans*', *Scintilla*, 3 (1999), 53.

121 John Rogers, *The Matter of Revolution: Science, Poetry, and Politics in the Age of Milton* (Ithaca and London: Cornell University Press, 1996), p. 10. Henry Vaughan's participation in this moment is explored by Diane Kelsey McColley, 'Water, Wood, and Stone: The Living Earth in Poems of Vaughan and Milton', in *Of Paradise and Light: Essays on Henry Vaughan and John Milton in Honor of Alan Rudrum*, ed. Donald R. Dickson and Holly Faith Nelson (Newark, DE: University of Delaware Press, 2004), pp. 269–91. It is also discussed in Section VII of Chapter 9.

122 See Feingold for 'the early and widespread influence of Cartesian and Gassendist ideas at Oxford' ('Mathematical Sciences and New Philosophies', p. 411); and for a familiarity with the new ideas emanating from Paris at Owthorpe, the home of Colonel John Hutchinson in Nottinghamshire, in the 1650s, see Robert Wilcher, 'Lucy Hutchinson', in *The Oxford Handbook of Early Modern English Literature and Religion*, ed. Andrew Hiscock and Helen Wilcox (Oxford: Oxford University Press, 2017), pp. 363–65.

was calling in question the validity of an ancient way of conceiving and experiencing the relationship between the natural world and the God who created it.

CHAPTER THREE

Henry Vaughan and the Civil Wars

I

When Charles I raised his standard at Nottingham in August 1642, there were 'few overt supporters of the Parliamentary cause in Wales' and through the early years of the Civil War the Principality – apart from Pembrokeshire – was 'a bastion for the King, a prolific source of money and manpower'. This is why he set up his military headquarters at Shrewsbury a month later, made haste to occupy Chester, and sent the Prince of Wales to Raglan to drum up support in the south. In the first major battle, at Edgehill on 23 October, a sizeable proportion of his army had been recruited from across the border in North and South Wales. There are various reasons for this, and for the continued raising of troops to fight on the king's behalf right through to the autumn of 1645, when 'the royal position in Wales was crumbling rapidly, and whole counties were defecting to Parliament'.[1] For one thing, the majority of the Welsh people were loyal to Charles because the factors that led to rebellion in England and Scotland 'either did not exist or existed only on a very small scale in the greater part of Wales'.[2] In 1640, Puritanism had made few inroads beyond the Marches; most of the Welsh counties were economically backward, with hardly any large towns and little commercial development; and geographical remoteness

---

1 Philip Jenkins, *A History of Modern Wales 1536–1990* (London and New York: Longman, 1992), pp. 124–25, 131.
2 Hugh Thomas, *A History of Wales 1485–1660* (Cardiff: University of Wales Press, 1972), p. 197.

from court and parliament was compounded by the insulation of a predominantly Welsh-speaking population from the print war that preceded armed hostilities. Christopher Hill points out that not a single pamphlet 'sought to explain the Parliamentary standpoint in Welsh'.³ One Puritan preacher sneered that 'the common people addicted to the Kings service' – enlisted from among their tenants and dependants by such wealthy pro-Stuart landowners as the Earl of Worcester, whose main seat was Raglan Castle – 'have come out of blinde *Wales* and other dark corners of the Land'.⁴ Many of the more educated members of the community, who had 'undergone a period of legal training' and 'been responsible for the administration of the law at local level' were more concerned with the maintenance of legality 'as the framework of the social order' than with the religious and political issues that had ignited resistance to the rule of Charles I in other parts of his realm; and many of the same men were equally determined to defend the established church and its royal head as another bulwark against instability.⁵ Hill's claim that the 'gentry and clergy of Wales were royalist almost to a man', however, needs to be tempered by the observation of a more recent historian that 'reluctance to fight against the king did not imply an enthusiasm to fight for him' and that many in Wales 'were genuine in their indifference and sincere in their neutrality'.⁶

Hugh Thomas's explanation of the 'confused and complicated' reactions in Wales to the contest between king and parliament is that allegiance (whether active or passive) often depended upon 'such local issues as family alliances and feuds, and the patronage and persuasions of powerful individuals'.⁷ The Breconshire Vaughans had a history of military service to the English crown going back to the early fifteenth century, when Dafydd Gam supported Henry IV against Owen Glendower. Legend had it that he was subsequently knighted by Henry V on the field of battle and it is certain that he met

3 Christopher Hill, *Change and Continuity in Seventeenth-Century England* (London: Weidenfeld and Nicolson, 1974), pp. 23–24.
4 John Corbet, *An Historicall Relation of the Military Government of Gloucester* (London, 1645), p. 10.
5 Thomas, *A History of Wales*, pp. 199–200.
6 Hill, *Change and Continuity*, p. 23; John Davies, *A History of Wales* (Harmondsworth: Penguin Books, 1994), p. 278.
7 Thomas, *A History of Wales*, p. 197.

his death at Agincourt. Gam came from Penpont, a few miles west of Brecon, and his daughter, Gwladys, married Sir Roger Fychan of Bredwardine, who was also knighted and killed at Agincourt and whose descendants were the Vaughans of Tretower.[8] As head of the cadet branch of the family and a minor landowner, the father of the Vaughan twins, Thomas Vaughan of Newton, was a local magistrate and served as under-sheriff of his county in 1646. It appears that he was not content to be one of those Breconshire gentlemen who, in the diplomatic words of Roland Mathias, 'seem to have set the wish for a quiet life above a conspicuous loyalty'.[9] Hutchinson describes him as 'a most uncompromising royalist' and cites a letter dated 8 February 1653/54 in which he joined local opponents of the Puritan authorities in a campaign to discredit Jenkin Jones, one of the government's leading agents in the district.[10]

In his quest for the origins of the undoubted royalism displayed in Henry's later poetry, Mathias pointed out that the growing unrest in England and Scotland would have made little direct impact on his early life: 'An adolescence spent in the Usk valley before 1638 would hardly have been interrupted by sounds of dissidence from the other side of the Black Mountains.' Even the notorious Ship Money tax, which had been widely resisted and subject to a test case brought against John Hampden in 1637, was paid in Breconshire 'without undue demur'. And the disruptive activities of Puritan preachers like William Erbury, Walter Cradock, and Vavasor Powell had not yet penetrated beyond Cardiff and Newport in the south and Wrexham and Shrewsbury in the north.[11] Given the absence of any strong provocation to take sides before 1642, Mathias lights upon the religious and political attitudes of Matthew Herbert, tutor to the twins during their impressionable teenage years, as more significant for their ideological formation than either their mother's 'residual Catholicism' or the family's heroic past. The royalist and Laudian credentials of this formidable rector and schoolmaster are beyond dispute. He was sequestered and deprived of his livings at

---

8 See *Life*, pp. 4–6.
9 Roland Mathias, 'Reasons, Reasons', *Scintilla*, 4 (2000), 114.
10 See *Life*, pp. 116–18.
11 Mathias, 'Reasons, Reasons', 114, 112–13. For the dispute over Ship Money, see Kevin Sharpe, *The Personal Rule of Charles I* (New Haven, CT and London: Yale University Press, 1992), pp. 717–29.

Llangattock and Cefnyllis in Radnorshire as early as the winter of 1643/44, long before the widespread ejections of clergy loyal to the monarchy and the Church of England in 1649 and 1650; but he continued to preach to his former parishioners until the authorities compelled him to stop in 1655 and he was imprisoned more than once as a malignant, spending seventeen weeks in Brecon gaol during 1656.[12] Furthermore, while there is no record of the Vaughans of Tretower providing supplies or taking up arms for the king, there was 'a considerable focus of loyalty in and around Crickhowell', which was just across the river from the church and rectory at Llangattock. Mathias lists an impressive array of officers from this one locality, who served in various royalist regiments and who may well have enlisted due to the influence of Herbert – 'some of them perhaps his former pupils'. This is in striking contrast to the rest of Breconshire, where few of those who supported the king with money or horses were prepared to leave home and fight for his cause.[13]

Henry Vaughan left few records of his experiences at Oxford, but it can be assumed that whatever religious and political views he had begun to formulate under the tutelage of Matthew Herbert were strengthened among the undergraduates at Jesus College, who maintained what Mathias describes as 'a callow, unthinking loyalty to the King'.[14] If he had moved to London during the winter of 1639–40, he would have found himself in the middle of the crisis caused by the Pacification of Berwick, which had brought to an end the fiasco of the First Bishops' War against the Scottish Covenanters and triggered Charles I's decision to call a parliament in England for the first time in eleven years.[15] He would probably have been

12 Mathias, 'Reasons, Reasons', 112, 116; *Life*, pp. 109–10. Mathias points out that Hutchinson's later date of 1646 for Herbert's ejection was in fact the year in which a successor was presented to his livings (p. 116, note 23).
13 Mathias, 'Reasons, Reasons', 115–18. In a list of 'informations laid against the Breconshire gentry' on 5 February 1649, it is stated that various local men 'levied taxes in their parishes to maintain the war, bore arms in several rendezvous, encouraged others to take arms and led them as officers, and in Crickhowell and Llangroyne they took a fearful oath of association against Parliament' (*Old Wales*, Vol. I, ed. W.R. Williams ("Old Wales" Office, Talybont, Breconshire, 1905), pp. 68, 70).
14 Mathias, 'The Making of a Royalist', *Scintilla*, 3 (1999), 112.
15 For the war that took place in the summer of 1639 and ended without any serious engagement between the opposing armies, see Mark Charles Fissel, *The*

aware that Sir Herbert Price from the Priory was representing Brecon in the House of Commons and would have followed day by day the stubborn refusal of the Parliamentary leadership to grant resources for a resumption of the war until their long list of grievances had been attended to. After the king finally lost patience and dissolved the so-called Short Parliament within less than three weeks, Vaughan would have witnessed the preparations for the Second Bishops' War and the mixed reactions to the news that a Scottish army had crossed the Tweed on 20 August, overcome an English force at Newburn on the Tyne, and proceeded to occupy the northern counties of England.[16] If he had not taken up residence in the capital until the autumn of 1640, he would still have been there in time to experience the power of the London mob that broke into a session of the Court of High Commission in St Paul's Cathedral in October with shouts of 'No Bishop' and of the Puritan faction in the Long Parliament that assembled on 3 November and immediately set in train the 'constitutional revolution of the next eighteen months'.[17] The king's chief counsellor, the Earl of Strafford, was impeached on 11 November in a 'general atmosphere of plot and panic' and a fortnight later was 'taken in a closed coach through derisive crowds to the Tower of London'. Archbishop Laud was impeached on 18 December and sequestered from the Upper House. He, in his turn, was eventually driven 'through angry crowds to the Tower' on 1 March 1641.[18] Strafford was charged with High Treason on 22 March and his trial dragged on inconclusively until 21 April, when John Pym and his allies got a Bill of Attainder through its third reading in the Commons by two hundred and four votes to fifty-nine. This was an ancient device for condemning a man to death by Act of Parliament notwithstanding the lack of conclusive evidence against him. Among those who voted against it were George Digby, who was outraged by this circumvention of the due

Bishops' Wars: Charles I's Campaigns against Scotland, 1638–1640 (Cambridge: Cambridge University Press, 1994), pp. 22–39. For a discussion of the date of Henry's move from Oxford to London, see Chapter One, Note 17.

16 Fissel, *Bishops' Wars*, pp. 39–44.
17 C.V. Wedgwood, *The King's Peace 1637–1641* [1955] (London: Collins Fontana Library, 1966), pp. 327–29.
18 C.V. Wedgwood, *Thomas Wentworth First Earl of Strafford 1593–1641: A Revaluation* [1961] (London: Phoenix Press, 2000), pp. 316, 321, 323, 332–33.

process of law, and Sir Herbert Price, who rose more than once to support Digby's interventions on the floor of the House – facts that would not have escaped the attention of Henry Vaughan, especially when the names of the 'Straffordians' were posted up in public places. On 3 May, while the Bill was still awaiting endorsement by the House of Lords, Pym revealed details of an Army Plot to rescue Strafford from the Tower. This raised a storm of popular protest: Westminster was besieged by violent crowds baying for 'Justice, justice!' and the house of Digby's father, the Earl of Bristol, was attacked by a mob calling for vengeance on his 'false son'. The Bill authorizing Strafford's execution was passed in the Lords by twenty-six votes to nineteen on 8 May, but it still had to receive the royal assent. Throughout the next day and evening, a tide of angry Londoners 'surged shouting in the gates and alleys of Whitehall', around the palace where the king and his family were sheltering. At nine o'clock, Charles gave in – breaking a solemn promise to protect Strafford's life – and agreed to sign the Bill. On 12 May, Strafford was led to the block on Tower Hill before a multitude of spectators, who raised a 'deafening shout' of triumph 'as the executioner lifted the bleeding head'.[19]

These events made a lasting impression on Vaughan and informed his translation of Juvenal's tenth satire, but the earliest expression of his political stance during his time in London was in one of the original poems collected in his 1646 volume. Written 'occasionally' upon 'a meeting with some of his friends at the Globe Taverne', 'A Rhapsodie' celebrates the effects of 'royall, witty Sacke' imbibed by the poet and his companions.[20] The first thirty lines elaborate the association of 'Pot, and Poet' common in Cavalier verse and the moon depicted over the door of the tavern prompts the first of several poetic toasts, a verse convention that indicates that Vaughan belonged to a social group that rallied to the king and the Court party at a time when many who later became 'royalists' were in favour of the Long Parliament's early reforms.[21] The first part of the drinking bout provokes an imagined ramble through London, from

---

19 See Wedgwood, *Thomas Wentworth*, pp. 337–89. John Davies points out that Price was the only Welsh MP who 'wholly supported the king' during the first months of the Long Parliament (*A History of Wales*, p. 277).
20 *HV Works*, pp. 19–21.
21 Even Digby was initially among the reformers.

Tower Wharf in the east to Ludgate in the west, taking in 'Fleet street, & the Strand' where the Globe Tavern was situated:

> Should we goe now a wandring, we should meet
> With Catchpoles, whores, & Carts in ev'ry street:
> Now when each narrow lane, each nooke & Cave,
> Signe-posts, & shop-doors, pimp for ev'ry knave.

This is the crowded labyrinth of commerce and vice that harboured the rampant Puritanism from which Vaughan and his companions sought refuge in drunken conviviality.

The contemptuous description of London as it struck a young Welshman, who had found a congenial niche for himself in the poetic fraternity of those soon to be nominated Cavaliers, introduces a series of further toasts that use classical allusions to disguise contemporary politics.[22] The first, drunk to the Roman emperor Caligula, obliquely pours scorn on the Long Parliament, implicating it 'in the moral chaos and degeneracy which the previous paragraph has presented as the predominant qualities of London life'.[23]

> Come, take the other dish; it is to him
> That made his horse a Senatour: Each brim
> Looke big as mine; The gallant, jolly Beast
> Of all the Herd (you'le say) was not the least.

The next forges a parallel between Julius Caesar's bold flouting of Roman tradition when he marched towards Rome with an army after crossing the river that marked the boundary of the city and Charles I's intrusion into the House of Commons, backed by armed men, in an attempt to arrest Pym and four of his colleagues on charges of treason:

---

22 Louise Guiney and Gwenllian Morgan identified the topical relevance of these allusions in the notes inherited by F.E. Hutchinson and have been followed by most commentators. G.C. Moore Smith, in a review of Martin's 1914 edition of Vaughan's works, noted that the reference to Caligula's horse was 'clearly anti-Parliamentarian' and wondered if the later toasts to Caesar and Sylla concealed allusions to Charles I and Strafford (*Modern Language Review*, 11 (1916), 245).

23 James D. Simmonds, *Masques of God: Form and Theme in the Poetry of Henry Vaughan* (Pittsburgh, PA: University of Pittsburgh Press, 1972), p. 128.

> Now crown the second bowle, rich as his worth,
> I'le drinke it to; he! that like fire broke forth
> Into the Senates face, crost Rubicon,
> And the States pillars, with their Lawes thereon:
> And made the dull gray beards, & furr'd gowns fly
> Into *Brundusium* to consult, and lye.

The five members – the 'dull gray beards', some of them lawyers in 'furr'd gowns' – were forewarned and escaped into the City, where they were protected by the Common Council that had set up a Committee of Safety and taken control of London's trained bands. Vaughan drinks to Charles's defiance of Parliament but ignores the fact that the king was humiliated by the flight of his quarry and forced within a few days to leave his capital for the safety of Hampton Court. These events took place from 3 to 10 January 1642.[24] The last of his political toasts is to another Roman statesman whose position as a pillar of patrician rule and consequent bloody fate bring to mind the Earl of Strafford:

> This to brave *Sylla*! why should it be sed,
> We drinke more to the living, then the dead?
> Flatt'rers, and fooles doe use it: Let us laugh
> At our owne honest mirth; for they that quaffe
> To honour others, doe like those that sent
> Their gold and plate to strangers to be spent.

If the final couplet glances at Parliament's appeal in June 1642 'for loans of plate and money at eight per cent interest' to fund the war effort – which apparently 'met with an enthusiastic response'[25] – then it is likely that Vaughan had remained in London throughout the first half of that year, perhaps until war was formally declared in August and he was recalled to Breconshire by his father.

---

24 For an account of these turbulent few days, see Austin Woolrych, *Britain in Revolution 1625–1660* (Oxford: Oxford University Press, 2002), pp. 211–14.

25 C.V. Wedgwood, *The King's War 1641–1647* [1958] (London: Collins Fontana Library, 1966), p. 95.

II

Vaughan probably worked on the translation of Juvenal's tenth satire, which was printed in the second half of his 1646 volume of poems, during the first months of his rustication, before he entered the employment of Judge Marmaduke Lloyd and while the stirring events he had witnessed in the capital were still fresh in his mind. Simmonds comments that the ironic phrasing with which he introduced the translation in his preface is deliberately designed 'to establish a parallel between the state of England and the state of Rome as presented by Juvenal':[26]

> It is one of his, whose Roman Pen had as much true Passion, for the infirmities of that state, as we should have Pitty, to the distractions of our owne: Honest (I am sure) it is, and offensive cannot be, except it meet with such Spirits that will quarrell with Antiquitie, or purposely Arraigne themselves: These indeed may thinke, that they have slept out so many Centuries in this Satyre, and are now awaked; which, had it been still Latine, perhaps their Nap had been Everlasting.[27]

Simmonds recognizes the topical significance of the poet's contempt for those unlearned 'Spirits' – the 'mechanick preachers' of royalist propaganda – who 'quarrell with Antiquitie' in their rants against the ancient traditions of church and monarchy and who have up to now been protected from the force of Juvenal's satire by their ignorance of Latin. But in his analysis of the text itself, he merely notes that the story of Sejanus ends with reflections that 'seem to point it toward the rebel leaders of the Parliament and the army as a grim warning against what Vaughan saw as their ambitious aspiration to usurp the kingdom in the people's name'.[28] A closer scrutiny of Vaughan's translation, however, paying attention to additions and changes of emphasis, reveals more about the translator's attitude to the turbulent events he had witnessed in London. The insertion of 'Kingdomes' and the expansion of 'militia' into 'strife, and warre' in the opening paragraph turn Juvenal's general statement about the self-destructive

---

26 Simmonds, *Masques of God*, p. 86.
27 *HV Works*, p. 11.
28 Simmonds, *Masques of God*, pp. 89–91.

urges of mankind into an evocation of the horrors of civil war, which divides kin from kin:

> The easie gods mov'd by no other Fate,
> Then our owne pray'rs whole Kingdomes ruinate,
> And undoe Families, thus strife, and warre
> Are the swords prize, and a litigious barre
> The Gownes prime wish. (ll. 9–13)[29]

> [Whole households have been destroyed by the compliant Gods in answer to the masters' prayers; in camp (*militia*) and city (*toga*) alike we ask for things that will be our ruin.][30]

Much more specific are the topical allusions in a later passage that Vaughan developed from Juvenal's reference to Democritus, the philosopher who could not restrain his laughter at human folly:

> He knew their idle and superfluous vowes,
> And sacrifice, which such wrong zeale bestowes,
> Were meere Incendiaries; and that the gods
> Not pleas'd therewith, would ever be at ods. (ll. 83–6)

The inflammatory 'zeale' is that of the Puritans in the Long Parliament, who had drawn up a Protestation, which included an oath to 'maintain and defend [...] the true reformed religion [...] as also the power and privilege of Parliament, the lawful rights and liberties of the subjects'.[31] This oath – 'idle and superfluous' in Vaughan's eyes – was administered to members of both Houses in early May 1641, when the trial of Strafford was nearing its climax, and then distributed throughout the kingdom. Like the Scottish Covenant of 1638, it bound those who subscribed to it primarily to a cause rather

---

29 *HV Works*, p. 27. Line numbers of further quotations from the translation on pages 27–41 are given in the text.
30 Passages for comparison are from G.G. Ramsay's translation in *Juvenal and Persius*, Loeb Classical Library, rev. edn. (Cambridge, MA: Harvard University Press, 1940), p. 193. Line numbers of further quotations are given in the text.
31 *The Stuart Constitution 1603–1688: Documents and Commentary*, ed. J.P. Kenyon (Cambridge: Cambridge University Press, 1966), p. 223.

than a person (in contrast to the traditional oath of allegiance to the monarch), and it was later interpreted as authorizing armed resistance to a king who challenged its principles. Both the Covenant and the Protestation were for Vaughan 'meere Incendiaries', deliberately designed to provoke rebellion.

Another glance at the Protestation oath occurs at the beginning of a passage that contains his most detailed commentary on the fate of the Earl of Strafford and gives an insight into his personal reaction to the fall of Charles I's most controversial counsellor. Juvenal is directing his scorn at those responsible for the death of the emperor's favourite:

> Goe now fetch home fresh Bayes, and pay new vowes
> To thy dumbe Capitoll gods! thy life, thy house,
> And state are now secur'd; *Sejanus* lyes
> I'th' Lictors hands; ye gods! what hearts, & eyes
> Can one dayes fortune change? the solemne crye
> Of all the world is, Let *Sejanus* dye:
> They never lov'd the man they sweare, they know
> Nothing of all the matter; when, or how,
> By what accuser, for what cause, or why,
> By whose command, or sentence he must dye.
> But what needs this? the least pretence will hit,
> When Princes feare, or hate a Favourite.
> A large Epistle stuff'd with idle feare,
> Vaine dreames, and jealousies, directed here
> From *Caprea* does it; And thus ever dye
> Subjects, when once they grow prodigious high.
> (ll. 107–22)

[Up with the laurel-wreaths over your doors! Lead forth a grand chalked bull to the Capitol! Sejanus is being dragged along by a hook, as a show and joy to all! 'What a lip the fellow had! What a face!' – 'Believe me, I never liked the man!' – 'But on what charge was he condemned? Who informed against him? What was the evidence, who the witnesses, who made good the case?' – 'Nothing of the sort; a great and wordy letter came from Capri.' (ll. 65–72)]

It is Vaughan who adds the astute comment that the life, the house (perhaps contemporary readers would have picked up a covert reference to the House of Commons), and the state of those who formulate 'new vowes' are 'secur'd' now that Sejanus has been condemned to death. In this and in much of what follows, he is reflecting the political reality that made John Pym and his supporters in Parliament determined to destroy the strong man of Charles's government for fear of their own lives if he escaped their clutches ('th' Lictors hands'). The questions of Juvenal's Roman mob about the nature of the evidence that was brought against Sejanus culminate in Vaughan's pointed rendering of their final comment, when they hear that it was a letter from the emperor's island hideaway that sealed his fate: 'But what needs this? the least pretence will hit, / When Princes feare, or hate a Favourite.' In Vaughan's subtext, the 'large Epistle stuff'd with idle feare' sent from Capri has its counterpart in a Remonstrance dispatched in November 1640 from the Dublin parliament, accusing Strafford of oppression as Lord Lieutenant of Ireland and giving the managers of the Long Parliament sufficient 'pretence' for proclaiming (if not proving) him a traitor.[32] Further topical significance is imported into the passage in the words 'feare' and 'jealousies', which have no equivalent in Juvenal's text but that had echoed like a refrain in the paper war between the king and his opponents in the months before the raising of the royal standard at Nottingham.[33]

Vaughan's loathing for the parliamentary leadership and the London mob is clear enough, but his attitude to Strafford and the reluctant compliance of the king in his execution is more ambivalent. An interpolated passage expatiates on the abandonment of Sejanus by his friends:

> but tell me how
> This tooke his friends [Juvenal's 'mob of Remus']? no private murmurs now?
> No teares? no solemne mourner seene? [...]
> [...] they follow fortune still,
> And hate, or love discreetly, as their will
> And the time leades them; This tumultuous fate
> Puts all their painted favours out of date. (ll. 123–32)

---

32 See Wedgwood, *Thomas Wentworth*, pp. 320–21.
33 See Edward Hyde, Earl of Clarendon, *The History of the Rebellion and Civil Wars in England*, ed. W. Dunn Macray, 6 vols. (Oxford: Clarendon Press, 1888), Vol. I, p. 493.

The author's contempt for the pusillanimity of Strafford's former allies combines with admiration for the noble disdain with which the great man embraced disaster: 'Scorning a base, low ruine, as if he / Would of misfortune, make a Prodigie' (ll. 181–82); and ambiguity pervades another couplet he added to his Juvenalian source, in which it remains uncertain whether the greater 'shame' attaches to those who pursued or those who deserted the fallen statesman: 'But O what State can be so great, or good, / As to be bought with so much shame, and bloud!' (ll. 173–74).[34] In one further addition, Vaughan makes the murder of Pompey the occasion for a less oblique but still bitterly ironical allusion to Charles I's role in the tragedy of Strafford: 'Our publick vowes / Made *Caesar* guiltles' (ll. 440–41).[35]

Vaughan's rendering of Juvenal's satire, then, is laced with topical references; and if it is indeed the earliest of his extant verse translations, executed soon after his return to Breconshire, it may be read as evidence that, for all his hatred of the mob and horror at the effects of Civil War, he had not yet developed the unquestioning loyalty that would lead him to take up arms in 1645 and serve the cause of the outlawed church and beleaguered monarchy with his pen during the 1650s.

III

Even before war had been declared, both parties began to assemble armies – Parliament by means of the Militia Ordinance passed in March 1642, which gave it authority to summon the county trained bands, and the king by reviving Commissions of Array, which had been the traditional method of raising troops for the crown before the reign of Queen Elizabeth.[36] Anthony Fletcher shows that 'the region which responded most positively' to Charles's call 'was a long strip of western England, from Cornwall through Monmouthshire and the Marches of Wales to Cheshire and Lancashire, also the king's

---

34 See the note on 31:175–82 in *HV Works*, p. 867.
35 For a fuller account of the literary responses to Strafford's death, see Robert Wilcher, *The Writing of Royalism 1628–1660* (Cambridge: Cambridge University Press, 2001), pp. 61–66.
36 See Anthony Fletcher, *The Outbreak of the English Civil War* (London: Edward Arnold, 1981, corr. 1985), pp. 244–46, 322–24.

happiest recruiting ground for his field army'.[37] Across the border in Breconshire, the Members of Parliament for the county and the borough, William Morgan and Sir Herbert Price, held commissions of array, along with several other members of the local gentry, including John Jeffreys of Abercynrig and Vaughan's cousin, Charles Walbeoffe of Llanhamlach.[38] Colonel Price of the Priory was acting governor of Hereford when it surrendered to Sir William Waller in April 1643. A year later, he was back in Brecon raising troops to help royalists further west.[39]

Wales was important to the king not only as a source of new recruits and a base for military operations, but also because his long-term strategy was to bring reinforcements and munitions from Ireland through ports along the coasts of Wales, especially after an armistice was agreed with the Irish rebels in November 1643.[40] It was therefore crucial to both sides to keep control of the border counties and the early years of the Civil War saw the balance of power shifting back and forth along the Marches.[41] Elsewhere, however, the tide was beginning to turn in favour of Parliament. A crushing defeat of the main royalist army at Marston Moor on 2 July 1644 was followed by the surrender of York and the loss of the north; and the creation of the New Model Army under Sir Thomas Fairfax and Oliver Cromwell led to the decisive Battle of Naseby on 14 June 1645, in which the Welsh infantry was decimated. Charles withdrew to South Wales to try to repair his losses and made his headquarters at Raglan Castle, the seat of the Marquis of Worcester.[42]

In July, the king met the Commissioners of Array for South Wales at Abergavenny and stayed for two weeks at Raglan, waiting

---

37 Fletcher, *Outbreak of the Civil War*, p. 356. See Maps 7 and 9 for the distribution of territory between troops mustered by each side (pp. 347, 357).
38 See Sir Frederick Rees, 'Breconshire during the Civil War', *Brycheiniog*, 8 (1962), 1.
39 See *Life*, pp. 67–68.
40 For details of this strategy and its ultimate failure, see A.H. Dodd, *Studies in Stuart Wales*, 2nd edn. (Cardiff: University of Wales Press, 1971), pp. 87–100.
41 For details of the various campaigns and engagements, see Peter Gaunt, *A Nation Under Siege: The Civil War in Wales 1642–48*, Cadw Welsh Historic Monuments (London: HMSO, 1991), pp. 24–72.
42 The foregoing account is indebted to the section on 'Wales and the Civil War' in Thomas's *A History of Wales*, pp. 205–11.

in vain 'for the fulfilment' of their 'large promises'.⁴³ He was back in Breconshire early in August, after suffering another disappointment in Cardiff, where the 'Peaceable Army' of local gentry and their tenants refused to give further support to either side in the conflict. After trekking back across the Beacons, he spent the night of 5 August with Price at the Priory before heading north in the hope of joining the Earl of Montrose, who was at the height of his victorious campaign against the Covenanters in Scotland. Leaving Brecon by way of the King's Steps, the royal party made its way north through Radnorshire and got as far as Doncaster, before turning back and driving away a Scottish force that was besieging Hereford. On 7 September, Charles was again at Raglan, where he received the devastating news that Prince Rupert had surrendered Bristol to Fairfax; and his hopes of help from Scotland were dashed by the defeat of Montrose at Philiphaugh on 13 September. Any last chance of reinforcements from Ireland depended upon keeping control of Chester, so a week later he began a march through mid-Wales that took him by way of Newtown, Chirk, and Wrexham to reach the last port in royalist hands on 23 September. The next day he watched from the city walls as the royalist cavalry, including a troop commanded by Colonel Price, was routed at the Battle of Rowton Heath.⁴⁴

While the fortunes of war were ebbing and flowing to the east and west of the Usk Valley from 1642 to 1645 and the royalists were losing the most significant battles of the Civil War at Marston Moor and Naseby, Henry Vaughan was translating Juvenal, adding to his collection of original poetry, and working for the Chief Justice of the Brecon circuit. Since Judge Marmaduke Lloyd, an active royalist, was among those taken prisoner when Hereford fell once more into the hands of Parliament in December 1645, it is legitimate to wonder what kind of pressure there was on his clerk to express his loyalty to the king as a soldier before the summer of that year, when Charles I came to Breconshire in person. The belief that he took no part at all in the fighting, based largely on a misreading of the Latin poem *Ad Posteros* prefixed to *Olor Iscanus*, was effectively disposed of by Marilla many years ago, but there is no evidence that he enlisted

---

43 See Rees, 'Breconshire during the Civil War', 2–3.
44 Much of the information about Charles I's travels in the aftermath of Naseby is derived from Edward Parry's article, 'Charles I in South Wales, July to September 1645', *Brycheiniog*, 29 (1996–97), 39–46.

before 1645.⁴⁵ Mathias speculates that a combination of 'exemplary caution' by Thomas Vaughan senior over the safety of the heir to his estate and 'the lack of a horse and arms and the means to support himself as an officer in the Royal army' may have held him back 'until a noisy conscience' and the futility of his present employment 'brought him to the point of revolt'. He admits, however, that 'we know too little to do more than conjecture'.⁴⁶ What we do know from external evidence is that he served as a lieutenant and his twin brother as a captain under Sir Herbert Price.⁴⁷ That they took part in the campaign to defend Chester in the autumn of 1645 can be inferred from an entry in the diary of Richard Symonds, a Royal Life Guard, which records that Price's troop of horse was part of the army that reached Chester with the king on 23 September and engaged in the battle 'not farr from Beeston Castle'.⁴⁸

Two of his own poems supply more graphic witness to Vaughan's personal involvement in the battle and in the subsequent surrender of the castle, where the defeated royalists had taken refuge. 'An Elegie on the death of Mr. R.W. slain in the late unfortunate differences at Routon Heath, neer Chester, 1645', published in *Olor Iscanus* (1651), dates its composition internally. The poet has struggled with a 'full years griefe' since his last sight of his young friend – 'His years [...] could not be summ'd (alas!) / To a full *score*' – amid 'the *Fire* and *Cloud*' of the battlefield: 'like *shott* his active hand / Drew bloud, e'r well the foe could understand. / But here I lost him.' Now, one year on, he abandons the 'sandy hopes' that his companion in arms might have survived and yields to the tears he has denied for so long: 'But thou art gone! And the untimely losse / Like that one day, hath made all others Crosse [burdensome].'⁴⁹ A more light-hearted poem in the same volume thanks another friend – an unidentified Mr. J. Ridsley

---

45 See E.L. Marilla, 'Henry Vaughan and the Civil War', *Journal of English and Germanic Philology*, 41 (1942), 514–26. It is possible that he enlisted in 1644, when Price had also been recruiting for the royal service.

46 Mathias, 'Reasons, Reasons', 120–21.

47 Their names and ranks are listed among officers claiming financial relief for war service in February 1663 (*CSPD*, Vol. 68 (1663), No. 19), cited in *Life*, pp. 64–65).

48 *Richard Symonds's Diary of the Marches of the Royal Army*, ed. C.E. Long, Camden Classic Reprints 3 (Cambridge: Cambridge University Press, 1997), pp. 242–43.

49 *HV Works*, pp. 184–86.

– for the loan of a voluminous cloak that had afforded him protection from the elements 'on that day, when wee / Left craggie *Biston*, and the fatall *Dee*'.⁵⁰ A third poem in *Olor Iscanus*, which appears to have been written during the winter following these military experiences, reflects Vaughan's contempt for the inhabitants of his local town. They had not only written cravenly to Rowland Laugharne, who was advancing across South Wales from the parliamentary stronghold of Pembroke, but (as Richard Symonds recorded in his diary on 12 November) had 'pulld downe the castle of Brecknock, and the walls of the towne' to render it indefensible.⁵¹ The victorious major-general was welcomed by the townspeople on 23 November and a declaration was signed by the sheriff of Brecon and thirty-three members of the neighbouring gentry in which they disowned their previous acts of opposition to the Parliament.⁵² 'To his retired friend, an Invitation to Brecknock' sarcastically informs an erstwhile comrade of the shame that has been brought upon Brecon during his absence:

> The Town believes thee lost, and didst thou see
> But half her suffrings, now distrest for thee,
> Thou'ldst swear (like *Rome*) her foule, polluted walls
> Were sackt by *Brennus*, and his salvage *Gaules*.⁵³

Mocking the 'new fine *Worships*' who strut about the streets in the 'high Monumentall Hats' favoured by puritans, Vaughan reserves particular venom for 'an old *Saxon Fox*', who was probably the English replacement for his former employer, Judge Marmaduke Lloyd.⁵⁴ The depth of his cynical resignation at this time can be gauged in the remark that the tapsters at the inn 'have forgot thee, and exclaim / They have not seen thee here since *Charles* his reign', implying that the king's enemies are effectively governing the country, even though the capitulation of all the remaining royalist

---

50 'Upon a Cloke lent him by Mr. J. Ridsley', *HV Works*, pp. 187–89.
51 Symonds, *Diary*, p. 263.
52 See Rees, 'Breconshire during the Civil War', 4; Parry, 'Charles I in South Wales', 45. The names of John Jeffreys and Herbert Price were conspicuously absent from the document of surrender.
53 'To his retired friend, an Invitation to Brecknock', *HV Works*, pp. 180–82.
54 See *Life*, p. 83. Hutchinson wrongly dates the poem to March 1649, after the death of the king.

garrisons has not yet put an end to 'noise and War'. The 'mirth' that can insulate defeated Cavaliers from 'the times ridiculous miserie' is the best he can offer his friend, because there is nothing more they can do to help their king in an age 'that thus hath fool'd it selfe, and will / (Spite of thy teeth and mine) persist so still'.

During the spring of 1646, parliamentary armies were closing in on Oxford, where Charles was vacillating between attempts to negotiate with the English parliament and to agree terms with the Scottish commissioners. He was still nursing a forlorn hope that the armed struggle might be prolonged, but this evaporated when a royalist force under Sir Jacob Astley surrendered on 21 March, having been overtaken at Stow-on-the-Wold as it made its way towards Oxford. Before dawn on 27 April, the king rode out of his wartime capital disguised as a servant in attendance upon Michael Hudson, one of his chaplains dressed as a minister, and John Ashburnham, a groom of the bedchamber. With no clear plan of action, he passed through Dorchester, Henley-on-Thames, and St Albans, undecided whether to head for London, where he might rally support against the increasingly unpopular Army, or King's Lynn, where he might take boat for Ireland or Holland. At last, he opted to entrust his fortunes to the Scots, who were besieging Newark, and on 5 May gave himself up to the Earl of Lothian. As a mark of good will, he ordered the royalist soldiers defending Newark to lay down their arms and the garrison surrendered on the following day. The Scots soon moved him to Newcastle, however, and kept him under guard while they tried to persuade him to abandon the Church of England for their system of Presbyterianism. Eventually, on 30 January 1647, they handed him over to the English parliament on payment of £400,000 and withdrew their forces to Scotland.[55]

Meanwhile, after the retreat from Beeston Castle on 15 November 1645, news would have reached Vaughan of the fall of Chester on 3 February 1646 and Raglan Castle on 19 August. It was against this background of the failure of the royalist cause in Wales that he composed 'Upon a Cloke lent him by Mr. J. Ridsley' and 'An Invitation to Brecknock'. He also occupied himself with preparing a selection of his earlier verses for the press and *Poems, with the tenth Satyre of Iuvenal Englished* was duly registered for publication on

---

55 For details of this episode, see Charles Carlton, *Charles I: The Personal Monarch* (London: Ark Paperbacks, Routledge & Kegan Paul, 1984), pp. 302–13.

15 September 1646. The very act of publishing such a volume at this juncture may have been politically motivated. Until the 1630s, lyric poetry had usually been disseminated in manuscripts or in miscellanies of poems by various hands, but following the posthumous publication of Donne's *Poems* and George Herbert's *The Temple* in 1633, the printing of collections of shorter poems by a single author had become more common.[56] The edition of Thomas Carew's *Poems* in 1640 was certainly a monument to the leading court wit of the Caroline years, but there may have been a political as well as a commercial purpose in describing the author on the title-page as 'One of the Gentlemen of the Privie-Chamber, and Sewer in Ordinary of his Majesty'. By the time it appeared, the values of artistic refinement and disengagement from foreign wars that Carew had helped to propagate with his pen were being challenged by the revolt of the Scottish Covenanters; and when an enlarged second edition was published in 1642, the culture fostered by Charles I during a decade of peace was collapsing as the dispute between king and parliament headed towards armed conflict. The publication of Edmund Waller's *Poems* in 1645 by Humphrey Moseley was a more overt contribution to the propaganda war. Waller had been expelled from the House of Commons and imprisoned for plotting on behalf of the king. These royalist credentials, as well as the fact that his lyric poems had been set to music by Henry Lawes, 'Gentleman of the King's Chapell, and one of his Majesties Private Musick', featured on the title-page; and Moseley's preface emphasized the social pedigree of the contents (these 'exquisite poems' had been circulated in manuscript 'amongst persons of the best quality'), the fate the poet (who was now in exile, 'expos'd to the wide world' like his poems), and the taste of potential readers (to whom 'the choycest sort of invention' was sure to appeal).[57] Over the next eleven years, Moseley was responsible for editions of Crashaw, Shirley, Davenant, Carew (the third edition of 1651), Cartwright, Stanley, and Cowley – and Vaughan's *Olor Iscanus* – and earned himself the reputation of 'a guerrilla fighter on the front

---

56 See Arthur Marotti, *Manuscript, Print, and the English Renaissance Lyric* (Ithaca, NY: Cornell University Press, 1995). Among poets whose work was printed during the 1630s were Drayton, Randolph, Habington, Cowley, and Davenant.

57 The preface is reprinted by John Curtis Reed in 'Humphrey Moseley, Publisher', *Oxford Bibliographical Society Proceedings and Papers*, II (1927–30), 76.

line of high culture during the war and interregnum'.[58] The context for this determined effort to keep the royalist literary flame alive was the dispersal of the king's propaganda team after the fall of Oxford in the summer of 1646. Moseley took up the baton in earnest with the publication of *Fragmenta Aurea*, a collection of poems and plays by Sir John Suckling, which was entered in the Stationers' Register on 24 July and printed soon afterwards. He introduced the work of this 'Ornament of our Age' (who had fled to France after the failed plot to free Strafford in 1641 and died in Paris) to 'knowing Gentlemen' and 'the Ingenuous Reader';[59] and the very title of the volume – 'Golden Fragments' – presented its contents as 'the broken remains of a writer and a culture both now perceived to have been destroyed by the political turmoil occasioned by the Puritan and Parliamentary opposition to the king'.[60] Vaughan's prefatory epistle to 'Ingenious Lovers of Poesie', with its appeal to the *'more refined* Spirits' of readers who *'soare above the drudgerie of durty* Intelligence' – propaganda disseminated by parliamentary newsbooks – makes a contribution to the royalist self-image of cultural superiority being established by Moseley.[61]

In the poem for Ridsley and the invitation to Brecknock, both written in the aftermath of his personal experience of military action and defeat but excluded from *Poems*, Vaughan had veered between bitter cynicism and the consolations of friendship and mirth. The flight and submission of the king himself required a different kind of poetic response. Among those in Newark when it surrendered in May 1646 was John Cleveland, who was serving as Judge Advocate to the garrison. This royalist poet, who had been directing witty and often savage satires against the Puritans and the Scots throughout the conflict, began a poem entitled 'The Kings Disguise' by questioning an action that seemed to play into the hands of those who were intent on separating Charles from the divine authority that sanctions the

---

58 Ann Baynes Coiro, 'Milton and Class Identity: The Publication of *Areopagitica* and the 1645 *Poems*', *Journal of Medieval and Renaissance Studies*, 22 (1992), 277.

59 See Moseley's preface, in 'Humphrey Moseley, Publisher', pp. 76–77.

60 Thomas N. Corns, 'Thomas Carew, Sir John Suckling, and Richard Lovelace', in *The Cambridge Companion to English Poetry: Donne to Marvell*, ed. Thomas N. Corns (Cambridge: Cambridge University Press, 1993), p. 201.

61 *HV Works*, p. 11.

exercise of royal power: 'And why so coffin'd in this vile disguise, / Which who but sees blasphemes thee with his eyes?'[62] James Loxley sets it in the context of royalist ripostes to the propaganda coup achieved by Parliament in a pamphlet entitled *The King's Cabinet Opened* (1645), which printed compromising private papers belonging to the king that had been seized after the Battle of Naseby.[63] Through the first ninety lines, a sense of unease troubles the wit with which Cleveland scrutinizes Charles's deliberate occlusion of his royal self: 'Is't not enough thy Dignity's in thrall, / But thou'lt transcribe it in thy shape and all?'; 'the Sacriledge of thine Attire, / By which th'art halfe depos'd'; 'The Princely Eagle shrunke into a Bat'. The poet is too deeply committed to monarchy, however, to follow through the implications of his own disturbing conceits. Daniel Jaeckle describes how he puts 'a royalist spin on the disguise' in the latter part of the poem, in order to 'vindicate the king's strategy' and avoid portraying him as 'the cowardly deceiver that his enemies believe him to be' – which he does by appealing to the secret policy behind the 'dark mysterious dresse' and asserting that 'the divine nature of kingship puts it above human understanding'.[64] Just as the Gospel was 'couch in Parables', so Charles's 'vile disguise' must not be mistaken for the reality of his royal nature; and King Solomon, 'in Proverbs all array'd', provides another biblical example of a 'Text Royall' hidden from common view by 'so obscure a shade'. In this way, Cleveland salvaged his royalist faith, but he could not quite suppress what turned out to be prophetic misgivings about the course Charles was pursuing: 'May thy strange journey contradictions twist, / And force faire weather from a Scottish mist'.

Henry Vaughan invited comparison with Cleveland when his poem on the same subject was belatedly published in *Thalia Rediviva* (1678). The opening of 'The King Disguis'd. Written about the same

---

62 *Poems of John Cleveland*, pp. 6–9. Among Cleveland's earlier satires are 'Smectymnuus, or the Club-Divines', 'The Mixt Assembly', and 'The Rebell Scot'.

63 James Loxley, *Royalism and Poetry in the English Civil Wars: The Drawn Sword* (Houndmills, Basingstoke: Macmillan, 1997), p. 138.

64 Daniel Jaeckle, 'From Witty History to Typology: John Cleveland's "The Kings Disguise"', in *The English Civil Wars in the Literary Imagination*, ed. Claude J. Summers and Ted-Larry Pebworth (Columbia, MO and London: University of Missouri Press, 1999), pp. 75, 77.

time that Mr. John Cleveland wrote his' seems to replicate the older poet's anxiety that the royal mystique has been diminished by the ignominious flight from Oxford: 'A King and no King! Is he gone from us, / And stoln alive into his Coffin thus?'[65] But rather than dwelling at length on the damaging consequences of the disguise, Vaughan interprets this metaphorical death as an act of mercy that will save the 'Rebells' from a sin that would damn them: 'and therefore he / Himself deposed his own Majesty'. The conceits of the king 'coffin'd' in his disguise and deposing himself are not the only details in which the two poems overlap, which suggests that Vaughan's was not only contemporary with Cleveland's, but dependent upon it.[66] For instance, the perplexing 'Riddles' that Cleveland sought to resolve by likening them to 'Parables' and 'Proverbs' become for Vaughan the 'Royal Riddle'. He brings his poem to a close by transforming another of Cleveland's conceits – Charles as a temple fronted appropriately with 'Sphynxes' and 'puzling Pourtraitures'; and he echoes the warning about those to whom he has chosen to commit his person:

> Be sure to look no Sanctuary there,
> Nor hope for safety in a temple, where
> Buyers and Sellers trade: O strengthen not
> With too much trust the Treason of a Scot!

Cleveland's hope that Charles may be able to 'force faire weather from a Scottish mist' belongs to the historical moment of his reception at the headquarters of the army besieging Newark; Vaughan's reference to 'Buyers and Sellers' smacks more of hindsight and suggests that his poem, although originating in the same period, may have been completed later or retouched before it was published in 1678.

The sale of the king to Parliament may lie behind the contemptuous reference to '*Scotish zeale*' in some lines occasioned by the publication of *Comedies and Tragedies written by Francis Beaumont and John*

---

65 *HV Works*, pp. 731–32.
66 The coffin conceit did not appear in printed texts of Cleveland's poem until 1677, which might imply borrowing in the other direction; but since Vaughan's poem was not published until 1678 and is unlikely to have circulated in manuscript, it is more probable that he saw a version in which the earliest printed form of the first line – 'And why a Tenant to this vile disguise' (1647, 1653) – had already been emended.

Fletcher Gentlemen in 1647 and addressed to Fletcher.[67] In his view, the Jacobean dramatist had the good fortune to write before the country was 'into *Schismes* split' and before literary invention was subject to suspicious scrutiny by 'the *Kirk*' and 'the *Eares*' (i.e., Roundheads). Because he died before the '*stormes*' of Civil War shattered 'our *peace*', it is appropriate that the 'last fair *Issue*' of his genius should now make its appearance during '[t]his *breathing time*'. Marilla takes this allusion to the cessation of fighting as evidence that Vaughan's poem was composed before the various uprisings that constituted the Second Civil War broke out.[68]

Much of the unrest of 1648 was generated by resentment at malpractices by the county committees, which Parliament had set up to replace the traditional apparatus of government at local level. There had been disturbances in Glamorgan as early as June 1647 and subsequently 'both north and south Wales, especially the latter, were to be important centres of royalist insurgency in the Second Civil War'.[69] Vaughan had occasion to mourn another loss, not in Wales but in the north of England, where Pontefract Castle was seized by royalists in June. The garrison under Captain John Morrice made a number of daring assaults on the besieging army and managed to hold out until March 1649.[70] Several weeks before it fell, a royalist newsbook carried a report of the heroism of the defenders: 'From Pontefract I heare the valiant Cavalliers act their Parts to the Rebells admiration: they take constant sallies and beate up their Guards daily.'[71] It must have been during one of these raids that the man commemorated in 'An Elegie on the death of Mr. R. Hall, slain at Pontefract, 1648' was killed, if the following passage accurately indicates the occasion and manner of his death:

> Thy bloud hath hallow'd *Pomfret*, and this blow
> (Prophan'd before) hath Church'd the Castle now.

---

67 'Upon Mr. Fletchers Playes, published, 1647', *HV Works*, pp. 189–91.
68 Marilla, *Secular Poems*, p. 216.
69 See Robert Ashton, *Counter-Revolution: The Second Civil War and its Origins, 1646–8* (New Haven, CT and London: Yale University Press, 1994), pp. 97, 341.
70 Ashton, *Counter-Revolution*, pp. 405–06.
71 *Mercurius Pragmaticus*, No. 44, 17 February to 5 March 1648/49, quoted by Hutchinson, *Life*, p. 61.

> Nor is't a Common valour we deplore,
> But such as with *fifteen* a *hundred* bore,
> And lightning like (not coopt within a wall)
> In stormes of *fire* and *steele* fell on them all.
> Thou wert no *Wool-sack* souldier, nor of those
> Whose Courage lies in *winking* at their foes,
> That live at *loop-holes*, and consume their breath
> On *Match* or *Pipes*, and sometimes *peepe* at death.[72]

The idea that his blood has 'hallow'd' and 'Church'd' Pontefract and the odds in this particular sally beyond the walls of the Castle – while others were content to peer at their enemies through loop-holes rather than engaging with them in open fight – strongly suggest that he was the Dr. Hall, 'a Clergyman, and a valiant active man in arms for that garrison', who was one of a party of sixteen horse that 'charged and routed 140 of the Enemies horse' and whose death in action was 'very much lamented' in a letter dated 8 October 1648.[73] Earlier in the poem, as Loxley notes, Vaughan 'contrasts some royalists' lapse into inaction' after the first Civil War 'with his learned subject's continued armed service':[74]

> Thus when some quitted action, to their shame,
> And only got a *discreet Cowards* name,
> Thou with thy bloud mad'st purchase of renown,
> And diedst the glory of the *Sword* and *Gown*.

Mathias wonders, since the poet did not himself take part in the Second Civil War, whether 'in lauding Hall the cowardice he speaks of (however exaggerated the attribution may appear) is intendedly his own'.[75] This is not implausible, in the light of his other and greater loss in 1648 of his younger brother, William, in July. Hutchinson's surmise that William died 'as a result of wounds or sickness incurred in the Civil War', possibly at the Battle of St Fagan's, is strengthened by Henry's comment in *The Mount of Olives* that his 'furious and

---

72 *HV Works*, pp. 193–95.
73 Quoted in *Life*, note 4 on p. 61.
74 Loxley, *The Drawn Sword*, p. 209.
75 Roland Mathias, 'The Silurist Re-examined', *Scintilla*, 2 (1998), 75.

Implacable' enemies have 'washed their hands in the blood of my friends, my dearest and nearest relatives'.[76]

Vaughan's decision to print his *Poems* in 1646 was probably intended as a public declaration of his loyalty to the culture that had flourished under Charles I's personal rule and to the political cause that had just been defeated on the battlefield. His subsequent decision to withhold the volume he had prepared for the press in 1647 – containing the two elegies, the comic tribute to a former companion for the loan of a cloak, and the invitation to another – must have been partly the result of the closest and most painful of the losses lamented in *The Mount of Olives*. When he had recovered sufficiently to contemplate publishing again, he had undergone the conversion that he would later attribute to the influence of George Herbert's life and poetry.[77]

---

76 *Life*, p. 97; *HV Works*, p. 312.
77 For a discussion of the reasons for delaying the publication of *Olor Iscanus*, see the headnote to the volume in *HV Works*, pp. 149–53.

CHAPTER FOUR

Henry Vaughan and the Interregnum

I

The volumes of poetry and prose that Henry Vaughan published in the first half of the 1650s engaged directly with the religious and political situation in which defeated adherents of monarchy and the Church of England found themselves – particularly in his corner of Wales. Furthermore, the poems in *Silex Scintillans* (1650) and the material he added to *Olor Iscanus* between December 1647, when he wrote the dedicatory epistle for his projected second collection, and April 1651, the date of its eventual entry in the Stationers' Register, were composed during the years of personal crisis that would later cause him to desire the suppression of the products of his youthful pen.[1] One critic has described these years as 'the nadir of Royalist hopes'; and a contemporary observer remarked in 1652, 'The gentry and all the considerable persons in Wales [are] dejected and oppressed.'[2] Christopher Hill once expressed the opinion that Vaughan 'never showed anything like as much devotion to monarchy as to the church'.[3] It is certainly true, as the next chapter will demonstrate, that the present desolation and future

---

1 See the 'Authors Preface' to the 1655 *Silex Scintillans*, *HV Works*, p. 557.
2 M.M. Mahood, 'Vaughan: The Symphony of Nature', in *Poetry and Humanism* (London: Jonathan Cape, 1950), p. 290; *Mercurius Cambro-Britannicus* (1652), p. 8.
3 Christopher Hill, *The Collected Essays of Christopher Hill, Volume One: Writing and Revolution in 17th-Century England* (Brighton: Harvester Press, 1985), p. 218.

survival of the British Church – in its reformed Church of England manifestation – were significant concerns of *Silex Scintillans* and *The Mount of Olives*. As James Simmonds was one of the first to recognize, however, 'metaphysical idealism' and 'fanatical Royalism' often co-exist in Vaughan's devotional verse and some of the major poems in *Silex Scintillans* express a struggle to transcend 'hatred, or bitterness, or despair', which is political as well as religious in origin.[4]

Leaving aside the elegies and other poems that relate to Vaughan's experiences in the Civil War and its immediate aftermath, the first place to look for expressions of royalism and political resistance in the volumes published during the 1650s is the body of translations from Boethius's prison book, *The Consolation of Philosophy*, which Vaughan seems to have been working on in the period of distress leading up to the composition of *Silex Scintillans*. One of the earliest advises Stoic calm in the face of oppression:

> Dull Cowards then! why should we start
> To see these tyrants act their part?
> Nor hope, nor fear what may befall
> And you disarm their malice all.

Another became a vehicle for his poetic response to the fate of Charles I, contrasting the order of the natural world with a human society in which 'the wicked', clearly identified as the victorious Puritans, have taken control:

> No perjuries, nor damn'd pretence
> Colour'd with holy, lying sense
> Can them annoy, but when they mind
> To try their force, which most men find,

---

4 James D. Simmonds, *Masques of God: Form and Theme in the Poetry of Henry Vaughan* (Pittsburgh: University of Pittsburgh Press, 1972), p. 20. Other pioneering studies of the political dimension of Vaughan's religious poetry include Claude J. Summers and Ted-Larry Pebworth, 'Herbert, Vaughan, and Public Concerns in Private Modes', *George Herbert Journal*, 3 (1979–80), 1–21; Jonathan F.S. Post, 'Spitting out the Phlegm: The Conflict of Voices in Vaughan's *Silex Scintillans*', *Philological Quarterly*, 59 (1980), 165–86; Robert Wilcher, '"Then keep the ancient way!" A Study of Henry Vaughan's *Silex Scintillans*', *Durham University Journal*, new series, 45 (1983), 11–24.

> They from the highest sway of things
> Can pull down great, and pious Kings.

Yet another describes Fortune's power to throw the 'state of things' into turmoil, beating down with 'headlong force the highest Monarchs crown' and placing on the throne the 'despis'd looks of some mechanick wretch'.[5] These are representative examples of Vaughan's practice of mediating 'political commentary' through 'departures from the original' in his translations.[6]

A political reading of *Silex Scintillans* is best undertaken by dealing with the two parts separately. The 1650 volume was registered on 28 March 1650 and the poems collected in it had been written over the previous two years, the earliest probably dating from some months before the death of William. The poems added in 1655 were presumably written between early 1650 and 30 September 1654, the date of the preface to the augmented volume, or at the latest 20 March 1655, when it was registered. A chronological reading of the poems across the two parts will be shown to make both historical and psychological sense and may reflect roughly the order in which they were composed.[7] A difference in emphasis and attitude is marked by the decline in the number of first-person singular poems devoted to the speaker's own spiritual condition as one passes from Part One to Part Two; but there is no consistent pattern of progression from subjective to objective preoccupations, and expressions of personal helplessness and spiritual failure break through from time to time to the end of the 1655 volume. Nevertheless, an analysis that focusses attention on the political implications of Vaughan's poetry reveals the changing reactions of a steadfast royalist to his temporal situation with a clear turning-point about two-thirds of the way through Part One.

---

5 'Lib. 1, *Metrum* 4', 'Lib. 1, *Metrum* 5', 'Lib. 2, *Metrum* 1', *HV Works*, pp. 214, 215–16, 217.

6 Alan Rudrum, 'Paradoxical Persona: Henry Vaughan's Self-Fashioning', *Huntington Library Quarterly*, 62 (1999), 362.

7 See James Simmonds, 'The Date of Henry Vaughan's "Silex Scintillans"', *Notes and Queries*, 205 (1960), 64–65. He argues from evidence in two of the elegies for William Vaughan and from the arrangement of the elegies within the 1650 volume that 'the order of their printing may correspond to the order of their composition' and that March 1648 was 'the most likely date of his beginning to compose the first part of *Silex Scintillans*'.

II

Biblical epigraphs capture the mood and stance of many of the poems that follow the experience of awakening to sin and setting out on a spiritual pilgrimage in 'Regeneration'. A dialogue on 'Death' cites Job – '*A Land of darknesse, as darkness it selfe, and of the shadow of death, without any order, and where the light is as darknesse*' (Job 10: 22); and 'Resurrection and Immortality' cites Daniel – '*But goe thou thy way untill the end be, for thou shalt rest, and stand up in thy lot, at the end of the dayes*' (Daniel 12:13). The poems themselves express this contrast between life in a time-bound world – 'a gloomie sphere, / Where shadowes thicken, and the Cloud / Sits on the Suns brow all the yeare' – and the better life of eternity: 'One everlasting *Saboth* there shall runne / Without *Succession*, and without a *Sunne*'.[8] 'Day of Judgement' then contemplates the moment of transition between the two states of being:

> When like a scrowle the heavens shal passe
> And vanish cleane away,
> And nought must stand of that vast space
> Which held up night, and day.[9]

The ideas and images thus established are repeated in many of the subsequent poems. 'The Lampe' begins ''Tis dead night round about: Horrour doth creepe / And move on with the shades'; in 'Mans fall, and Recovery', the poet speaks for all his kind, oppressed by original sin – 'I'm Cast / Here under Clouds'; in 'The Call', he addresses his own heart and mind: 'How ill have we our selves bestow'd / Whose suns are all set in a Cloud?'[10] In the first two of the untitled elegies for William, this private despair is bound up with guilt – 'But 'twas my sinne that forc'd thy hand / To cull this *Prim-rose* out' – and looks for relief beyond the slow-moving hours of mourning in a world where 'Each day is grown a dozen year':

> Come, come!
> Such thoughts benum;

---

8 *HV Works*, pp. 59–62.
9 *HV Works*, p. 63.
10 *HV Works*, pp. 72, 73, 78.

> But I would be
> With him I weep
> A bed, and sleep
> To wake in thee.[11]

Another of the elegies extends this benumbing grief beyond a brother's sorrow to the wider community: '"tis now / Since thou art gone, / Twelve hundred houres, and not a brow / But Clouds hang on.'[12]

Some poems early in Part One look back to a better time rather than forward to an escape from time through death, often merging personal nostalgia with the universal experience of the descendants of Adam. 'The Search' longs for the 'those calme, golden Evenings' and 'white dayes' of the Old Testament patriarchs; in 'Man's fall, and Recovery', a human voice laments the loss of a 'traine of lights, which in those Sun-shine dayes / Were my sure guides'; 'The Retreate' remembers 'those early dayes! when I / Shin'd in my Angell-infancy'.[13] Another resource is to anticipate an end to grief and despair not merely in individual death but in the cessation of human history: 'Day of Judgemnt' describes *the end of all things*, which is said to be *at hand* in the epigraph from the First Letter of St Peter (4:7); and 'Buriall' complains that 'Tyme now / Is old, and slow, / His wings are dull, and sickly' and implores an end to the wearisome accumulation of days: 'Cutt then the summe, / Lord haste, Lord come, / O come Lord *Jesus* quickly!'[14] This solution is given a political dimension for the first time in 'The Brittish Church', which Wynn Thomas sees as a response to the claim by Welsh Puritans like Morgan Llwyd to be the true heirs of the earliest Christians in Britain 'by virtue of their resumption of the pure practices of the primitive Christian church'.[15] The first three lines add a royalist gloss to Vaughan's imagery for the psychological and spiritual predicament of the Church of England in particular and of sinful humanity in general:

---

11 'Thou that know'st for whom I mourne' and 'Come, come, what doe I here?', *HV Works*, pp. 79, 82–83.
12 'Silence, and stealth of dayes!', *HV Works*, p. 88.
13 *HV Works*, pp. 66, 73, 81.
14 *HV Works*, pp. 64, 91.
15 M. Wynn Thomas, '"No Englishman": Wales's Henry Vaughan', *The Swansea Review*, 15 (1995), 11.

> Ah! he is fled!
> And while these here their *mists*, and *shadowes* hatch,
> My glorious head
> Doth on those hills of Myrrhe, and Incense watch.
> Hast, hast my dear,
> The Souldiers here
> Cast in their lotts againe,
> That seamless coat
> The Iewes touch'd not,
> These dare divide, and staine.[16]

John Kerrigan teases out some of the political subtext of this passionate utterance, put into the mouth of the Church – the spouse of Christ, according to the traditional reading of the Song of Solomon (4:6) alluded to in the fourth line:

> 'Ah! he is fled!' is urgently unclear, like a cry heard in turmoil (the royalists routed in battle?); Christ emerges as the primary referent, yet the rhyme with 'head' adds an allusion to Charles I (head of the British church) that is sharpened by the contrast with the Welsh puritans who 'here' (in this corner of Brecknockshire, as well as in this mortal world) brood over spiritual bad weather and obscurity.[17]

The soldiers of the New Model Army, who 'divide, and staine' what George Herbert called the 'fit aray' of the established church in the poem that gave Vaughan his title, outdo their predecessors in the biblical account of the crucifixion by rending the 'coat [...] without a seam' (John, 19:23–24) instead of casting lots for it.[18] The second stanza invokes the Song of Solomon again, in words that plead for

---

16 *HV Works*, pp. 71–72.

17 John Kerrigan, *Archipelagic English: Literature, History, and Politics 1603–1707* (Oxford: Oxford University Press, 2008), p. 209.

18 See 'The British Church' (l. 7), in *The English Poems of George Herbert*, ed. Helen Wilcox (Cambridge: Cambridge University Press, 2007), p. 390. Vaughan is also alluding to Herbert's 'Church-rents and schismes' (pp. 488–89), in which 'debates and fretting jealousies' have left only 'shreds' of the once universal church.

an apocalyptic solution to the plight of the Church and its (largely royalist) adherents:

> O get thee wings!
> Or if as yet (untill these clouds depart,
> And the day springs,)
> Thou think'st it good to tarry where thou art,
> Write in thy bookes
> My ravish'd looks
> Slain flock, and pillag'd fleeces,
> And haste thee so
> As a young Roe
> Upon the mounts of spices.[19]

The embedded allusion to the books from which the dead are judged in Revelation (20:12) offers some consolation for the suffering inflicted upon their opponents by the victorious Parliamentarians. Christ is obviously the primary target of this urgent appeal, but a royalist reader might detect a covert glance not only at the martyred Charles I but also at his son and heir, biding his time abroad and keeping watch from afar on the desecration of his church and plunder of his kingdom.

The recourse to eschatology as an answer to the problems posed by sin and mortality lightens the endings of several meditations. A sense of urgency pervades 'The Dawning', from the initial questions – 'Ah! what time wilt thou come? when shall that crie / The *Bridegroom's Comming*! fil the sky?' – to the final affirmation of personal readiness:

> So when that day, and hour shal come
> In which thy self wil be the Sun,

---

19 See Song of Solomon: 'Vntill the day breake, and the shadowes flee away: turne, my beloued, and be thou like a Roe, or a yong Hart, vpon the mountaines of Bether' (2:17). Summers and Pebworth point out that the Hebrew word 'Bether' means 'separation' or 'division', which 'has a particularly poignant application to Vaughan's poem', considering the 'religious and political circumstances' of its composition ('Herbert, Vaughan, and Public Concerns in Private Modes', 16).

> Thou'lt find me drest and on my way,
> Watching the Break of thy great day.[20]

And 'Corruption' distils into four lines the desperate belief that there is only one way out of the political *cul-de-sac* into which royalists have been driven:

> All's in deep sleep, and night; Thick darknes lyes
>   And hatcheth o'r thy people;
> But hark! what trumpet's that? what Angel cries
>   *Arise! Thrust in thy sickle.*[21]

An important step in the psychological rehabilitation of the poet as an active member of his society is taken in 'The Match', when he accepts the challenge to 'thrust' his 'stubborn heart' into the *'Deed'* of inheritance drawn up by Herbert in 'Obedience'. The despair that led him to pray for death is put aside – 'Afford me life, / And save me from all inward strife!' – and at the close of this poem of self-dedication, he begins to contemplate a fruitful future in this world:

> And let this *grain* which here in tears I sow
>   Though *dead*, and *sick*,
> Through thy *Increase* grow *new*, and *quick*.[22]

The long poem that immediately follows, 'Rules and Lessons', is the first in the collection addressed to the reader and one of the few thus far not couched in the first-person singular. Along with instructions on how to conduct one's religious life throughout the day – 'never sleep the Sun up' (l. 7); 'When night comes, list thy deeds' (l. 115)) – the preaching poet finds room for political and social as well as spiritual duties: 'To God, thy Countrie, and thy friend be true, / If *Priest*, and *People* change, keep thou thy ground' (ll. 43–44).[23]

Although he continues to listen for the trumpet that will herald 'the Break of thy great day' and to lament that 'Winter is all my

---

20 *HV Works*, pp. 116–17.
21 *HV Works*, p. 104.
22 *HV Works*, pp. 98–99.
23 *HV Works*, pp. 99–103.

year', there are now stirrings of resistance to a government that had forbidden the celebration of Christmas – 'Thy birth now here / Must not be numbred in the year' – and kneeling to receive the Eucharist.[24] The title of 'Dressing' brings to mind Herbert's systematic clothing of himself with the attributes of Christ in order to perform his duties as a priest, culminating in the announcement, 'Come people; Aaron's drest'.[25] It begins by acknowledging that the call to service Vaughan had answered in 'The Match' will require psychological healing as well as spiritual cleansing from original and individual sin:

> touch with one Coal
> My frozen heart; and with thy secret key
>
> Open my desolate rooms; my gloomie Brest
> With thy cleer fire refine, burning to dust
> These dark Confusions, that within me nest,
> And soil thy Temple with a sinful rust.

The importance of the process taking place in 'Dressing' is indicated by Vaughan's allusion to the prophet whose lips were touched by a coal from the altar to prepare him for his mission of taking God's word to his people (Isaiah 6:1–10). The desolation and confusion expressed in so many of the earlier poems in *Silex Scintillans* must be overcome if Vaughan is to fulfil his public role as Herbert's successor in a world darkened by religious and political oppression. His personal victory is sealed by the defiant act of receiving the 'mysticall *Communion*' according to the rite in the banned Book of Common Prayer – invoked explicitly in 'The perfect, ful oblation for all sin' – and with a decency that deplored the beast-like irreverence of those who 'sit to thee, and eat / Thy body as their Common meat'.[26]

The three Easter poems for which 'Dressing' is a preparation mark the turning-point of the 1650 *Silex Scintillans*. The first, 'Easter-day', goes beyond the sermon-like didacticism of 'Rules and Lessons' in its impassioned appeal to others among the royalist faithful who have been languishing like the poet in the depths of depression:

---

24 'Idle Verse', 'Unprofitablenes', 'Christ's Nativity', *HV Works*, pp. 111, 105, 107.
25 'Aaron', *English Poems of Herbert*, p. 601.
26 *HV Works*, pp. 120–21.

> Thou, whose sad heart, and weeping head lyes low,
>   Whose Cloudy brest cold damps invade,
> Who never feel'st the Sun, nor smooth'st thy brow,
>   But sitt'st oppressed in the shade,
>   Awake, awake [...]
>   [...] and, like the Sun, disperse
>   All mists that would usurp this day.

The military and political connotations of the words 'invade', 'oppressed', and 'usurp' must be brought into play for the hidden message of this poem to be revealed. If not exactly a call to arms, it is a call to despondent royalists to resist oppression by celebrating Easter and so take a step towards dispersing the mists of Puritanism that '*would* usurp this day' – the mood of the verb itself denying the authority of those whose policy was to eradicate feast days from the nation's worship. Vaughan goes on to combine the Easter gospel of resurrection with the story of Christ healing a blind man with clay made from spittle:

>   Arise, arise,
> And with his healing bloud anoint thine Eys,
>   Thy inward Eys; his bloud will cure thy mind,
> Whose spittle only could restore the blind.[27]

He adapts them both, however, to serve the main burden of his poem by transferring the emphasis to the 'inward' eyes and the process of psychological healing: 'his bloud will cure thy *mind*' (italics added).

The other two poems embrace the renewed hope made possible by the sacrifice and resurrection of Christ: 'Easter Hymn' and 'The Holy Communion' open with complementary exclamations – 'Death, and darkness get you packing'; 'Welcome sweet, and sacred feast; welcome life!' – and celebrate a New Testament vision of a world of true faith, in which 'grace, and blessings' have 'quicken'd' one who was 'dead' and 'deep in trouble'.[28] From this point on, the political inflection of Vaughan's poetic voice is heard more frequently, punctuating or emerging from within poems that record his continuing spiritual pilgrimage. His version of 'Psalm 121'

---

27 *HV Works*, p. 121.
28 *HV Works*, pp. 121–22.

rejoices that 'He keeps me from the spite of foes, / Doth all their plots controul'; and 'Affliction' pauses in its demonstration that 'Sickness is wholsome' to observe that 'Kingdomes too have their Physick, and for steel, / Exchange their peace, and furrs'.[29] 'The Pilgrimage', in contrast to 'Regeneration' with its inward allegory of the individual's search for redemption, focuses on the 'accidents' that befall the traveller on his daily journey and the threat of dispossession or exile. Life regarded as an exile is, of course, a commonplace in Christian literature of all ages, but this ancient metaphor had a particular poignancy for royalists of Vaughan's generation. Landowners whose estates had been sequestered and priests deprived of their livings were like 'Birds rob'd of their native wood'; they pined 'with the thought of home' in a quite literal sense. Himself subject to 'tossings too and fro' as long as his lot is to 'linger here', Vaughan still nurses a desire for death, so that 'I may get me up, and go'; but he is now more resolute in journeying on, with God's help, until that release comes:

> O feed me then! and since I may
> Have yet more days, more nights to Count,
> So strengthen me, Lord, all the way,
> That I may travel to thy Mount.[30]

Towards the end of the volume, the frequency and directness of political material increases. When Vaughan contemplates the activities of the 'darksome States-man hung with weights and woe / Like a thick midnight-fog' in 'The World', his imagery suggests that he has contemporary politicians in mind. The secret mole-like work 'under ground', the feeding upon 'Churches and altars', the 'Perjuries', and the 'bloud and tears' that 'rain'd about him' create a composite impression of Charles I's political opponents – from John Pym's manipulation of Parliament and the London mob at the beginning of the 1640s through the bloodshed of the civil wars to Cromwell's obscure role in bringing the king to trial at the end – that would have been instantly recognized by a royalist reader in 1650.[31] In the next two poems, the problems created by contemporary

29 HV Works, pp. 124, 124–25.
30 HV Works, pp. 129–30.
31 HV Works, p. 132.

politics are addressed much more explicitly, first from a private and then from a public perspective.

The speaker in 'The Mutinie' likens himself to an ancient Israelite in bondage to Egyptian or Babylonian masters. When he wearily casts in his heart the 'after-burthens, and griefs yet to come', he is so shaken and dismayed by the 'heavy sum' that his thoughts storm at 'those bounds' placed upon them by his Creator. While accepting 'these barren grounds' to which he has been consigned by 'Destinie', he urges God to let him take a more active part in overthrowing their common adversaries:

> Let me so strive and struggle with thy foes
> (Not thine alone but mine too,) that when all
> Their Arts and force are built unto the height
>   That Babel-weight
> May prove thy glory, and their shame.

He prays that his eyes and ears may be sealed against the 'frothie noise' of enemy propaganda and is still tempted by the option of a 'shorter Cut' to an eternal 'home', but he is also ready to face the prospect of a longer journey 'through a wildernes'. Knowing that 'ful obedience' is required of the pilgrim, 'whatsoever path' has been 'decreed' by the divine will, he prays for strength to keep his mutinous thoughts in check:

>   that so seiz'd
> Of all I have, I may nor move thy wrath
>   Nor grieve thy *Dove*, but soft and mild
>   Both live and die thy Child.[32]

The first nine stanzas of 'The Constellation' develop the image of the 'Fair, order'd lights' of the night sky as an example of the '*Obedience, Order, Light*' of the created universe, which moves in harmonious accord with the Creator's will, unlike the rebellious protagonist of the preceding poem. The next three stanzas present a contrasting image of the experience of human beings:

---

32 *HV Works*, pp. 133-34.

> But here Commission'd by a black self-wil
>   The sons the father kil,
> The Children Chase the mother, and would heal
>   The wounds they give, by crying, zeale.
>
> Then Cast her bloud, and tears upon thy book
>   Where they for fashion look,
> And like that Lamb which had the Dragons voice
>   Seem mild, but are known by their noise.
>
> Thus by our lusts disorder'd into wars
>   Our guides prove wandring stars,
> Which for these mists, and black days were reserv'd,
>   What time we from our first love swerv'd.[33]

It is just possible to read the poem in an exclusively spiritual way as a version of the individual soul's 'dark journey, the pilgrimage from the City of Destruction to the Heavenly Jerusalem'.[34] This would mean taking 'here' to mean 'on earth' (rather than 'in Britain' or indeed 'in Wales') and 'our lusts' as a general reference to sinful mankind; but there are enough words and images heavy with contemporary significance to encourage us to read this poem as Vaughan's most explicit commentary on the horrors of civil war into which the country has been led by politicians who have proved 'wandring stars'. 'Commission'd' invokes the raising of troops; there is an allusion to fanatical Puritans in the poet's contempt for those who would 'heal / The wounds they give, by crying, zeale'; and the same hypocrisy taints those who 'for fashion look' upon the bible they have stained with blood. The images of sons slaughtering their father and children violating their mother, which are standard tropes for civil war, can be read more specifically as allusions to the execution of the king and the persecution of the Church of England; and the 'mists, and black days' have been firmly established in previous poems as symbols of the condition of the country under the joint rule of Army and Parliament. When Vaughan prays in the next stanza that God will 'guide us through this Darknes' for the sake of one 'who sits now

---

33 *HV Works*, pp. 134–36.
34 R.A. Durr, *On the Mystical Poetry of Henry Vaughan* (Cambridge, MA: Harvard University Press, 1962), p. 74.

by thee / All crown'd with victory', the word 'now' like the earlier 'here' invokes the immediate historical context in which Charles I, translated into glory, sits alongside the figure of Christ. Parallels between the sufferings and sacrifice of Christ and the martyred king were commonly invoked in royalist writing of the period; and the image of Charles, holding a crown of thorns in his hand and gazing upwards at a crown of immortality, was familiar from the engraved frontispiece of the *Eikon Basilike*, a collection of meditations and prayers (supposedly composed by the king during his years of captivity) that was on sale within a few days of his death.[35] In the closing stanzas, Vaughan prays that his fellow countrymen will be taught the lesson of obedience he has tried to learn in 'The Mutinie' and so become 'an humble, holy nation'; and that the English Church – the 'spouse' of Christ who bewailed her fate in an earlier poem – will regain 'her perfect, and pure dress'. Only then will men be able to say of the currently divided kingdom, '*Where God is, all agree*'.

The next poem, 'The Shepheards', offers an idealized example of 'harmles livers', whose humble cottages 'never harbour'd plots', in one of Vaughan's backward glances to a better world, guided by biblical '*Patriarchs, Saints, and Kings*'.[36] A life of 'holy leisure', however, is a distant ideal for the defeated royalist stirring restlessly under the new Commonwealth in his own secluded country retreat. 'Misery', a few poems from the end of the 1650 *Silex Scintillans*, records a spilling of rebellious thoughts more violent and various than those in 'The Mutinie'.[37] This breaking of 'the fence my own hands made' involves moral excesses, neglect of the Bible, and the wilful exclusion of 'my dear God from my mind'. But it also has a political dimension, which causes him to 'swel and fome and fret within' and issues in discontented utterance:

> "*The Age, the present times are not*
> "*To snudge in, and embrace a Cot,*
> "*Action and bloud now get the game,*

---

35 See Robert Wilcher, '*Eikon Basilike*: The Printing, Composition, Strategy, and Impact of "The King's Book"', in *The Oxford Handbook of Literature and the English Revolution*, ed. Laura Lunger Knoppers (Oxford: Oxford University Press, 2012), pp. 289–308.
36 *HV Works*, pp. 136–37.
37 *HV Works*, pp. 138–41.

> "Disdein treads on the peaceful name,
> "Who sits at home too bears a loade
> "Greater than those that gad abroad.

These emotions may have been bottled up since he had taken no part in the uprising in which William forfeited his young life.[38] Certainly the speech reflects the pressures upon a former royalist soldier who has chosen to *'snudge'* in quiet at a time when *'the peaceful name'* is held in contempt by committed diehards, even though those who endure oppression *'at home'* may feel that exile is an easier option. This outburst has a cathartic effect – 'So my fierce soul bustles about / And never rests til all be out' – and the poem moves forward to a plea similar to that at the end of 'The Mutinie':

> Open my rockie heart, and fil
> It with obedience to thy wil,
> Then seal it up, that as none see,
> So none may enter there but thee.

But before the poem comes to rest in the hope that God will 'both mend and make me thine', the poet gives voice to the anguish that must have been felt by many of the king's supporters, torn between a frustrated impulse to action and baffled submission not only to a triumphant enemy but also to the apparent will of the God of history:

> O let my Crie come to thy throne!
> My crie not pour'd with tears alone,
> (For tears alone are often foul)
> But with the bloud of all my soul.

Once the rebellious thoughts of 'The Mutinie' have been quelled, the public horrors of civil war confronted in 'The Constellation' and contrasted with the harmless lives of a simpler age in 'The Shepheards', and the poet's private demons of anger, guilt, and frustration exorcised in 'Misery', the collection moves quietly towards its conclusion. Looking back over the troubled course of the

---

38 Chris Fitter comments that this outburst 'is the restless self-accusation of Vaughan the non-combatant in the late 1640s' ('Henry Vaughan's Landscapes of Military Occupation', *Essays in Criticism*, 42 (1992), 134).

poet's life as individual and representative, 'The Sap' recommends the wine of the Eucharist as 'balm for souls that ake'; 'Mount of Olives' describes how his soul attained 'calm without all noise' after he had 'wander'd under tempests [...] bleak and bare in body as in mind'; 'Man' contemplates more objectively the contrast between the 'stedfastness' of the natural world and the 'ever restless and Irregular' state of humankind; and 'I Walkt the other day' brings the series of elegies to a tranquil close with the expectation of being reunited with the beloved dead in a realm 'without all pain'.[39] The volume ends with 'Begging', a simple prayer that the One who alone has the 'Art / To reduce a stubborn heart' will take complete control of the poet's: 'O my God, let it be thine!'[40]

III

Many of the poems in the 1650 *Silex Scintillans* embody spiritual, psychological, and political experiences of such intensity that it is easy to forget that the routines of everyday life were carrying on around Vaughan. Beyond the growing brood of small children in the family home at Newton, which must have often distracted him from his inner turmoil, there was a wider social world that had to be negotiated in the conditions imposed by the authorities at Westminster. Once the New Model Army had secured victory in 1647, the system of county committees set up by Parliament during the war to organize the defence of local communities in England had been extended to Wales, where it became a principal channel of communication between central and local government. One of the functions of these assessment committees was to sequester estates and impose fines on those who had openly supported the king. At the start of 1650, however, both regional and county bodies were replaced by a central committee in London, which nominated three subsidiary committees for North Wales, South Wales, and Monmouthshire. Local committees were renewed from time to time and Vaughan's close friends, Thomas Lewes, rector of Llanfigan, and Thomas Powell, rector of Cantref, were early victims of the Brecon sequestration committee, while among active royalists in

---

39 *HV Works*, pp. 141–46.
40 *HV Works*, p. 146.

his locality who chose to compound for their delinquency, John Jeffreys of Abercynrig retained his estate at a cost of £340 10 shillings. Another local man who compounded was Edmund Jones, 'a notorious trimmer', who was appointed Recorder of Brecon in 1650 and represented the town in the parliament of 1654.[41] The most significant of the ordinances relating to the government of the Welsh counties was An Act for the Better Propagation and Preaching of the Gospel in Wales, which was passed on 22 February 1650. Seventy-one commissioners were empowered to eject incumbents found guilty of 'delinquency, malignancy, and non-residence' and among the earliest to lose their livings were the rectors of Cantref and Llanfigan. Twenty-five approvers, including Walter Cradock and Vavasor Powell, were given the task of recommending candidates to fill the empty places.[42]

One consequence of the various arrangements for Wales put in place by the new regime from 1649 onwards was that 'committee members were drawn more exclusively from the staunch parliamentary supporters and the lower, newer sections of county landed gentry'; another was that the responsibilities of local officials were broadened to take in the enforcement of Puritan laws regulating marriage, the suppression of sports and revels, the observance of public fast days, and the detection and punishment of 'all conspiracies and secret meetings of disaffected persons who held opinions contrary to those of the Commonwealth authorities'.[43] One commentator has argued that this act 'remained the real government of Wales' until it was allowed to lapse in 1653 and another that the act 'invested immense power in a small cadre of ministers and laymen the best of whom were almost manically industrious and peripatetic in the prosecution of their duties'.[44] One of the most zealous approvers was Jenkin Jones

41 See Sir Frederick Rees, 'Breconshire during the Civil War', *Brycheiniog*, 8 (1962), 6.
42 A.M. Johnson, 'Wales during the Commonwealth and Protectorate', in *Puritans and Revolutionaries: Essays in Seventeenth-Century History Presented to Christopher Hill*, ed. Donald Pennington and Keith Thomas (Oxford: Clarendon Press, 1978), pp. 235–36.
43 Hugh Thomas, *A History of Wales 1485–1660* (Cardiff: University of Wales Press, 1972), pp. 232–33.
44 A.H. Dodd, *Studies in Stuart Wales*, 2nd edn. (Cardiff: University of Wales Press, 1971), p. 148; M. Wynn Thomas, '"In Occidentem & tenebras": Putting Henry Vaughan on the Map of Wales', *Scintilla*, 2 (1998), 11.

of Llandetty, formerly an officer in the parliamentary army, who sent a letter to Thomas Lewes in January 1654 warning that he would intervene with an armed troop at an intended 'cock-fight' (suspected of being a cover for illegal royalist activity) if the ejected minister and his companions did not 'forbear'. The threat was not carried out, but Henry Vaughan's father became involved in correspondence over the incident in what seems to have been a concerted local effort to discredit Jones with the recently instituted Protector, Oliver Cromwell. During February and March, both Lewes and Thomas Powell were engaged in another exchange of letters with Jones about whether ejected ministers might be permitted to preach the Gospel in the absence of replacement clergy.[45]

There is no evidence that Vaughan took any part in such direct challenges to political authority, although it seems likely that his help would have been enlisted in drafting his father's letter, which asked mischievously whether 'his Highness' had lately granted Jones 'a Commission' to keep up an armed troop 'privately'.[46] He did, however, insert subversive passages in the secular poems he continued to write alongside the devotional verses that were added in the two-part *Silex Scintillans*. Since the Latin poem '*Ad Posteros*' comes before the title-page of *Olor Iscanus*, it was probably written while the volume was in the press, which would date it to the early summer of 1651. By then, as Marilla puts it, 'the author had had time to feel the full impact of the new regime and to realize what the Parliamentarian triumph really signified'.[47] The same scholar had already scotched the earlier reading of the poem as a declaration of pacifist aloofness and went on to argue that, through Vaughan's 'peculiar gift at using words in a double sense', the poem 'refers subtly to the King's execution as well as to the overthrow of the monarchical government'.[48] Encoded in cryptic images, with Latin as a further precaution against the danger of being deciphered by his enemies, '*Ad Posteros*' was born of

---

45 The two sets of correspondence are discussed and reproduced in *Life*, pp. 116–20.
46 See the transcript of the letter in *Life*, p. 117.
47 *The Secular Poems of Henry Vaughan*, ed. E.L. Marilla (Uppsala: A.-B. Lundequistska Bokhandeln, 1958), p. 165. See also the headnote to '*Ad Posteros*' in *HV Works*, p. 978.
48 E.L. Marilla, 'Henry Vaughan and the Civil War', *Journal of English and Germanic Philology*, 41 (1942), 522, 525.

a need to be understood not only by posterity but also by those of his own party in the 'harsh' realities of the present:

> I lived at a time when religious schism had divided and fragmented the English people, amongst the furies of priest and populace. When these afflictions first raged through our pleasant land, a vile weed cast down the sacred rose, and the fountains were muddied; peace was drowned in the troubled waters, and a gloomy shadow overcast the days of splendour.[49]

Rudrum glosses 'the sacred rose' as 'Charles I'; the 'vile weed' clearly represents the Puritan parliamentarians who were despised by royalists as socially and culturally inferior; and the 'days of splendour' were the heyday of Caroline culture in the 1630s.[50] Having dissociated himself from the party that destroyed the ancient way of monarchy, Vaughan expresses his grief also for the church and denies any personal involvement in its overthrow:

> Thus I have taught myself to endure, like a chaste and faithful mother, and to ease the burden of my destiny with tears. I have never desecrated what is holy with hideous violence, neither was my mind or my hand stained.

For the 'righteous' and 'wise' readers to whom he addresses himself, the tears with which he has eased the pain of loss and defeat are the elegies and other poems that have already given 'innocent blood […] a voice' in the 1650 *Silex Scintillans*. Those responsible for the violence and desecration of the past decade, who are too ignorant to understand what he has written, are dismissed in the final words of the poem as 'the foolish'.

Several of the poems added to *Olor Iscanus* after 1647 celebrated the achievements of other writers as a means of criticizing the new regime. 'Upon the Poems and Playes of the ever memorable Mr. William Cartwright', also printed in the 1651 collection of the famous royalist's literary works, glances back at Vaughan's time in pre-war

---

49 '*Ad Posteros*' is quoted throughout this paragraph from Rudrum's translation in *HV Works*, p. 164.
50 Rudrum, *Complete Poems*, p. 466; Marilla, *Secular Poems*, p. 165. See also the note on 163:16 in *HV Works*, pp. 978–79.

Oxford in a punning and sarcastic evocation of the contrasting world of the 1650s:

> I did but *see* thee! And how *vain* it is
> To *vex* thee for it with *Remonstrances*,
> Though *things* in fashion, let those *Judge*, who sit
> Their *twelve-pence* out, to *clap* their *hands* at *wit*;
> I fear to *Sinne* thus *neer* thee; for (*great Saint!*)
> 'Tis known, *true beauty* hath no need of *paint*.[51]

For a reader who had lived through the 1640s, the word 'Remonstrances', with Vaughan's prompting about '*things* in fashion', could not fail to be recognized as a sneer at the Grand Remonstrance of 1641, in which Parliament had indicted the king, and to subsequent examples of this popular vehicle for setting out political demands and parading ideology. And the later lines would have reminded contemporaries of those other Saints who now had oversight of the country's morals, condemning cosmetics and closing the theatres lest they lead people into sin (hence Vaughan's mock fear of coming too close to a playwright). Every phrase is double-edged, being straight-forward praise of Cartwright and ironical rejection of the puritan ethics that made the continued performance of his plays impossible.[52]

A covert allusion to the regicide occurs in 'An Epitaph upon the Lady Elizabeth, Second Daughter to his late Majestie', Vaughan's elegy for the young princess who had died at Carisbrooke Castle on 8 September 1650 after years of custody in the households of various guardians appointed by the authorities:

> Thy portion here was *griefe*, thy years
> Distilld no other rain, but tears,
> Tears without noise, but (understood)
> As lowd, and shrill as any bloud.[53]

Marilla argued that the poem is 'as much an expression of political despair as of personal grief' and saw these lines as containing 'a

---

51 *HV Works*, p. 191.
52 See also the tributes to the Jacobean playwright, John Fletcher, and Sir William Davenant's *Gondibert* in *HV Works*, pp. 189–91, 199–201.
53 *HV Works*, p. 199.

specific, though obscure, reference to the execution of the King'.[54] Such a reading is strengthened by the lines that follow:

> Thou seem'st a *Rose-bud* born in *Snow*,
> A flowre of purpose sprung to bow
> To headless tempests, and the rage
> Of an Incensed, stormie Age.
> Others, e're their afflictions grow,
> Are tim'd, and season'd for the blow,
> But thine, as *Rhumes* the tend'rest part,
> Fell on a *young* and *harmless* heart.

Marilla glosses 'headless' as 'senseless; stupid' in his edition, but if he is right about the earlier passage then the word is a clue for the reader who has 'understood' the allusion to tears and blood, especially when the next couplet refers to others – older and more mature, like the young woman's own father – who are 'season'd for the blow' that literally renders them 'headless'.[55] Once the clues have been picked up, the entire passage can be seen as developing a comparison of two royal victims of the parliamentarians' rage: the tears of the daughter speak as loudly as the blood of the father; the princess has been compelled to bow to political tempests just as the king was forced to bow his head to the block; the blow has fallen on the young and harmless girl just as brutally as the axe fell upon the more seasoned enemy of the rebels. Not only do the parliamentarians murder their opponents; they are guilty, also, of the death of an innocent child.

Less overtly political, but very much part of a common strategy for keeping the royalist flame alive, are the familiar poems addressed to named individuals, who belonged to what Jonathan Post calls 'another circle of friends to replace the one whose demise the young author had recorded in *Poems 1646*'.[56] For example, 'To my worthy friend Master T. Lewes' describes a world in which trees

---

54 E.L. Marilla, '"The Publisher to the Reader" of *Olor Iscanus*', *Review of English Studies*, 24 (1948), 41.

55 Marilla, *Secular Poems*, p. 242. Hutchinson offers the same gloss, but also suggests that it may be a variant spelling of 'heedless' (*Life*, p. 80, note 3); Rudrum opts for 'brainless' (*Complete Poems*, p. 501).

56 Jonathan Post, *Henry Vaughan: The Unfolding Vision* (Princeton, NJ: Princeton University Press, 1982), p. 46.

are 'Opprest with snow' and rivers 'bound up in an *Icie Coat*', in a version of Earl Miner's 'Cavalier winter', with its hints of oppression and captivity.⁵⁷ The only remedy offered for the 'wild *Excentricks*' of the public sphere is the solace of friendship and continuity in the private sphere: 'Let us meet then! [...] / Keep wee, like nature, the same *Key*, / And walk in our forefathers way.' Nursing '*feare*, or *hope*' about 'what *may come*' or giving way to 'Sorrowes and sighes' will only concede victory to their 'foes'. Their best course of resistance is to partake of those 'discreet Joyes' of social intercourse, with an emphasis on necessary caution, 'Without which life were a disease'.⁵⁸

IV

Like the translations of Boethius and the occasional verses added to the original poems surviving from the project of 1647, the four translated items in prose that filled out *Olor Iscanus* are littered with partisan commentary on the political realities of life in South Wales after the victory of the New Model Army. Particularly pertinent for a community under the malevolent surveillance of Jenkin Jones were the warning that 'An Enemy is alwaies watchfull, lying *perdue* (as it were) to all thy actions, and (seeking an occasion to mischiefe thee) runs over all thy life with a most curious eye' and the consequent advice 'that thou have a care to live circumspectly, to be attentive to thy selfe, neither speak, nor act any thing negligently or unadvisedly, but keep thy tongue and thy hands within the *Lists*, and let thy maners be (as in a strict prescription of diet) uncorrupt, that thy very enemy may find no place for a just Reprehension'.⁵⁹ The account of an assembly in Asia, in which various 'Contestations' are 'canvased, decided, and grow up into mortall dissentions, betwixt the *undoer* and the *undone*' reads like a jaundiced view of the activities of the Long Parliament:

---

57 Earl Miner, *The Cavalier Mode: From Jonson to Cotton* (Princeton, NJ: Princeton University Press, 1971), pp. 179–80.
58 *HV Works*, pp. 196–97. For poems addressed to his closest friend, Thomas Powell, see *HV Works*, pp. 195–96, 740–43, 730.
59 'Of the benefit we may get by our Enemies', *HV Works*, p. 236.

What Feavers, what Agues, Malignant heats, or Superfluous humours ever so troubled mankind? If aswell as the men, you examine the grounds of their sutes and contentions in Law, you shall find some of them to proceed from a slight word spoken, some from malice, some from anger, others from a mad desire to be contentious, and all of them from *Covetousnesse*.[60]

The voice of a committed and defeated champion of monarchy can be heard in the rhetorical peroration of a lesson about the dangers of democratic politics as they had been played out in Vaughan's own experience:

O blessed Statesmen! this was your Reformation! Ruine, Confusion, prodigious Changes, nationall Miseries, and civill Inflammations were the religion, and liberty they had from you! so woefully pernicious is the Maladie of the Soul, if compared with the disease of the Body.[61]

The original prose work that gives its title to Vaughan's 1652 volume, *The Mount of Olives*, was designed to provide an alternative to The Book of Common Prayer for private use by faithful members of the Church of England so that the 'seed' that falls daily upon the heart 'may never be choak'd with the Cares of this world [...] nor wither away in these times of persecution and triall'.[62] In the prose meditation that follows, Vaughan observes that 'We have seen Princes brought to their graves by a new way, and the highest order of humane honours trampled upon by the lowest' and that 'A day, an hour, a minute [...] is sufficient to over-turn and extirpate the most settled Governments'.[63]

---

60 'Of the Diseases of the Mind and the Body', *HV Works*, pp. 248–49. A note on the word 'covetousness' in *HV Works*, 249:113 (p. 1056) quotes from Roger Edwin Wiehe's 1964 Ph.D. dissertation, 'The Prose Works of Henry Vaughan', p. 41: 'a key word encompassing the rise of the bourgeoisie, the tyranny of Parliament, and the loss of the old aristocracy'.
61 'Of the Diseases of the Mind, &c.', *HV Works*, p. 254; a note on 254:124–27 (p. 1058) quotes from Wiehe's dissertation, p. 47: 'Forgetting that "reformation" and "national" are not applicable to Athens, Vaughan anathematizes his contemporaries.'
62 *HV Works*, p. 295.
63 *Man in Darkness*, *HV Works*, p. 316.

Flores Solitudinis, the volume of prose translations published in 1654, was registered with the Stationers on 15 September 1653, eighteen months before the registration of the augmented edition of *Silex Scintillans* on 20 March 1655. The four works it contains were presumably written after those printed in *Olor Iscanus* and were therefore contemporary with some of Vaughan's later 'Sacred Poems and Private Ejaculations'.[64] The ills of interregnum Wales are addressed less frequently and explicitly in this volume than in *Olor Iscanus* and *The Mount of Olives*. Only once in these works does the Welsh translator directly invoke the political situation of his fellow royalists in demonstrating that death is 'a divine remedy' for all kinds of evils: 'We are surrounded with calamities, torn by inordinate wishes, hated by the world, persecuted, prest, and trodden upon by our enemies, disquieted with threatnings, which also torture and dishearten some.'[65] The translation of the life of Paulinus, a fourth-century convert to Christianity who gave away his wealth to live in seclusion and eventually became Bishop of Nola supplies a universal model for the kind of holy life that the volume was designed to advocate, but his experiences also provided several opportunities for Vaughan to emphasize their more particular relevance to his own time. Indeed, Susannah Monta claims that it was deliberately controversial and 'combative':

> Vaughan targets both complacent royalists tempted to make peace with Cromwell's regime and the saint discourse of the Cromwellian godly as he shapes for Anglicans a hagiographic model worthy of the traditional *imitatio sanctorum* and capable of revitalizing and sustaining that community through the bleak years of the Interregnum.[66]

---

64 Jonathan Nauman argues that the subject of the final text, to which Vaughan gave the title *Primitive Holiness, Set forth in the Life of blessed Paulinus*, 'was central and even pivotal to his stance as a sacred poet' and that his 'devotional reading in the poems and letters' of this fourth century bishop went back at least to the time of his younger brother's death in 1648 ('Classicism and Conversion: The Role of the Poems and Letters of St. Paulinus of Nola in Henry Vaughan's *Silex Scintillans*', *Scintilla*, 18 (2015), 14, 16).

65 *Of Life and Death, HV Works*, pp. 433–34.

66 Susannah Monta, 'Vaughan's Life of Paulinus: Recharting the Royalist Journey', in *Renaissance Tropologies: The Cultural Imagination of Early*

Taken together, the four works that make up Vaughan's 'Flowers of Solitude' continue further into the 1650s both the pursuit of his calling to personal holiness that began with 'Regeneration' and the commitment to a public mission of resistance to tyranny and persecution made in 'The Match' and carried forward in *The Mount of Olives*.

V

The interregnum prose, along with much of the secular poetry published in *Olor Iscanus* or held back until *Thalia Rediviva*, made an essential contribution to the literary, spiritual, and political enterprise that occupied Vaughan in the aftermath of the civil wars. It provides sufficient evidence of his awareness of social context and public responsibility to refute both the charge that the poet withdrew into 'self-isolation' after 'the debacle of 1648–9' and the allegation that *Silex Scintillans* 'conveys no effective sense of community with living men at all'.[67] Alan Rudrum replies that Vaughan deliberately excluded the contemporaneous 'social poems' from his editions of devotional verse 'because they were at odds with the literary persona he wished to project in his major contribution to the religio-political conflict'.[68] Noting that the two parts of the 1655 volume 'are clearly distinct in tone', E.C. Pettet had concentrated on 'Vaughan's spiritual development' from 'a struggle for assured faith and salvation … and often deep anguish' to 'a serener, more balanced attitude', in which 'spiritual distress' is now caused by 'the pangs of separation' from 'the Divine Light' and 'the intermittency of the vision'; and Jonathan Post places this personal development within a broader framework, suggesting that in the poems added to the edition of 1655 there is a 'decided increase in

---

Modern England, ed. Jeanne Shami (Pittsburgh, PA: Duquesne University Press, 2008), p. 126.
67 See A.J. Smith, 'Appraising The World', *Poetry Wales*, 11:2 (1975), 71.
68 Alan Rudrum, 'Resistance, Collaboration, and Silence: Henry Vaughan and Breconshire Royalism', in *The English Civil Wars in the Literary Imagination*, ed. Claude J. Summers and Ted-Larry Pebworth (Columbia, MO: University of Missouri Press, 1999), p. 103.

the tempo of history', which accompanies the poet's 'recognition of worldly time as winding down with startling speed'.[69]

The political implications of the interpretation of history in Part Two are explored in more detail by Madeleine Forey, who identifies two kinds of apocalyptic claim made by the prominent puritans Vavasor Powell and William Erbury, who were active in South Wales at the time Vaughan was composing his second collection of devotional lyrics.[70] Welcoming the Propagation Act in a Fast Sermon before Parliament on 28 February 1650, Powell had prophesied the return of Christ to reign over the earth: 'yea this yeare, 1650. that is coming [...] is to be the Saints yeare of Jubilee'; and Erbury, preaching in Brecon during August 1652, believed that the imminent millennium would not be the establishment of a kingdom but 'the full revelation of God in the hearts of puritan believers'.[71] It was against the backdrop of these ideas that Vaughan pursued 'both national (apocalyptic) renewal and personal transformation' in the new poems that were added to *Silex Scintillans* in 1655. In the 1650 edition, the recurring image of 'the author's heart of stone or flint', which also appeared as a visual emblem on the title-page, emphasizes the 'heart's passivity' as it awaits the moment of its transformation by God and thus distances the Anglican poet from the 'self-aggrandisement' of puritan prophets who 'laid claim to present revelation'. The enlarged edition 'performed a substantially different function', moving beyond the personal, spiritual apocalypse of the writer to 'the national responsibilities of the transformed poet, now prophet, within the context of the imminent general apocalypse'. One of Forey's most important insights is that the earlier poems were retained in order to serve as 'a testimony of personal conversion which becomes a vehicle for the calling of others', so that the complete volume takes over the formal qualities of contemporary puritan publications in 'combining the testimony of private experience with the didactic role of exemplar in the last

---

69 E.C. Pettet, *Of Paradise and Light: A Study of Vaughan's* Silex Scintillans (Cambridge: Cambridge University Press, 1960), pp. 200–03; Post, *The Unfolding Vision*, pp. 190–91, 198.
70 See Madeleine Forey, 'Poetry as Apocalypse: Henry Vaughan's *Silex Scintillans*', *The Seventeenth Century*, 11 (1996), 161–86.
71 Both quoted by Forey in 'Poetry as Apocalypse', 162.

days'.⁷² Michael Rothberg sees this as part of a process that 'creates a new kind of royalist subject' by thrusting the 'privacy' of the writer 'into the public sphere' and using the power of 'authorly authority' to 'defuse the Puritan individual, and to replace it with the desiring and dispossessed Anglican subject'.⁷³ Placing Vaughan's light and darkness imagery in the context of sectarians claiming divine illumination and of a county flooded by itinerant preachers as a result of the Propagation Act, Peter Thomas argues that '*Silex* as a whole constitutes a sustained, deliberate, even calculated engagement with current concerns and contentions' and that Vaughan's devotional verse of the 1650s 'is designed, not least, to challenge possession' of 'the vocabulary of spiritual and moral power' that had been 'hi-jacked' by puritans.⁷⁴

Vaughan makes his own political allegiance clear by referring to 'this Kingdom' in the very first sentence of the preface, a denial of the legitimacy of the new republic repeated in his 'complaint against *vitious verse*', which is said to be 'of some antiquity in this Kingdom'. Offering his 'poor *Talent* to the *Church*', Vaughan hopes that it will be 'as useful now in the *publick*, as it hath been to me in *private*' – flagging up the relation between 'testimony' and didactic purpose and the 'pragmatic intervention' into the political arena described by Forey and Rothberg – and places the volume 'under the *protection* and *conduct* of her *glorious Head*'. The political implications of the latter move are unavoidable in a statement dated just ten days after Oliver Cromwell assumed the title of Protector and in the light of its author's earlier play with the ambivalence of the phrase 'glorious head' in a poem put into the mouth of the British Church.⁷⁵

The first of the continuing series of meditations on the death of dear ones carries over into the new collection the shift of tone effected in later poems of Part One:

72 Forey, 'Poetry as Apocalypse', 175.
73 Michael Rothberg, 'An Emblematic Ideology: Images and Additions in Two Editions of Henry Vaughan's *Silex Scintillans*', *English Literary Renaissance*, 22 (1992), 88, 93.
74 Peter W. Thomas, 'The Language of Light: Henry Vaughan and the Puritans', *Scintilla*, 3 (1999), 21–22.
75 *HV Works*, pp. 555–56, 558–59.

> They are all gone into the world of light!
>   And I alone sit lingring here;
> Their very memory is fair and bright,
>   And my sad thoughts doth clear.

Although the two buoyant Ascension Day pieces that precede the elegy are dominated by 'fair thoughts' of Christ returning '[u]pon the Clouds again to judge this world!' and 'the Refiners fire' breaking forth on the Last Day to cleanse humankind, Vaughan is also prepared to look forward to an improvement in the earthly, time-bound realm of history. The closing stanza of the elegy captures this new optimism in alternative visions of what the future might have in store:

> Either disperse these mists, which blot and fill
>   My perspective (still) as they pass,
> Or else remove me hence unto that hill,
>   Where I shall need no glass.[76]

He can contemplate with equanimity either a general solution in time – the dispersal of the mists, with all their universal and more specifically political connotations – or an individual solution beyond time, when he will join those whom he imagines 'walking in an Air of glory'. The next poem, 'White Sunday', continues the liturgical sequence begun with the Ascension. The Spirit that descended upon the apostles in tongues of fire exposes the false claims to inspiration made by Vaughan's puritan opponents; and the final stanza longs for transformation by those same flames:

> O come! refine us with thy fire!
> Refine us! we are at a loss.
> Let not thy stars for *Balaams* hire
> Dissolve into the common dross![77]

The reference to Balaam, who refused offers by the king of the Moabites to promote him 'unto very great honour' (Numbers 22: 17) if he would curse his own people, implies that Vaughan had

---

76 See *HV Works*, pp. 565–69.
77 *HV Works*, pp. 569–70.

withstood pressure to follow other local members of the gentry in reaching an accommodation with the new authorities.

The use of plural first-person pronouns in the final stanza of 'White Sunday' calls attention to a body of faithful royalists who keep themselves aloof from 'the common dross' of collaborators. In the next poem, 'The Proffer', Vaughan takes up the same issue in more personal terms with 'an intensity and bitterness of mood' that Noel Thomas sees as reflecting both 'the depression in Breconshire following the Act of Propagation and his own feeling of desolation and loneliness'.[78] It opens with a stern rebuke – 'Be still black Parasites, / Flutter no more' – and in the third stanza develops the image of 'poys'nous, subtile fowls! / The flyes of hell / That buz in every ear'. The last four stanzas launch an outright attack on those who would seduce him from his loyalty to the royal cause:

>   Shall my short hour, my inch,
>   My one poor sand,
> And crum of life, now ready to disband
>   Revolt and flinch,
> And having born the burthen all the day,
>   Now cast at night my Crown away?
>
>   No, No; I am not he,
>   Go seek elsewhere.
> I skill not your fine tinsel, and false hair,
>   Your Sorcery
> And smooth seducements: I'le not stuff my story
>   With your Commonwealth and glory.
>
>   There are, that will sow tares
>   And scatter death
> Amongst the quick, selling their souls and breath
>   For any wares;
> But when thy Master comes, they'l finde and see
>   There's a reward for them and thee.

---

78 Noel Kennedy Thomas, *Henry Vaughan: Poet of Revelation* (Worthing: Churchman Publishing, 1986), p. 43.

> Then keep the antient way!
> Spit out their phlegm
> And fill thy brest with home; think on thy dream:
> A calm, bright day!
> A Land of flowers and spices! the word given,
> *If these be fair, O what is Heaven!*[79]

R.A. Durr ignores the topical signposts planted in such words as 'revolt', 'my Crown', 'your Commonwealth', 'the antient way' in favour of a reading that recognizes only the inner, spiritual pilgrimage. The 'black Parasites' are, for him, not sombrely dressed puritans, but 'the World's partisans, flocking about the flowers of heavenly gifts and virtues growing in the regenerate heart'. He sees the poem as prompted by a 'demonic proffer', which tempts the soul to cast away its crown of immortality, and he avoids the implication that the poet is being tempted to abandon 'the antient way' of monarchy and give up his allegiance to the crown of Charles II.[80] As Simmonds points out, however, the two readings are 'not in conflict': 'Both are valid, and therefore neither is adequate without the other, for in this poem, as is characteristic of his sacred verse, Vaughan perceives and interprets historical circumstances (which include his personal circumstances) in terms of the archetypal patterns of Christian myth.'[81] In many of his poems, Vaughan looks forward to a time when the contemporary darkness will give way to a 'calm, bright day' and the splendour of a newly risen sun will put the 'black Parasites' to flight. This will occur 'when thy Master comes', which is usually taken simply as a reference to the Second Coming of Christ. But in the kind of typology that Simmonds sees as characteristic of Vaughan's sacred verse, the 'Master' is not only Christ in the eternal dimension but also Charles II at this juncture in national history. The royalist waits for the restoration of an earthly king as well as the return of the King of Heaven; either event will scatter his enemies and 'reward' both sides appropriately for their faith and treachery. This means that the 'dream' that those who 'keep the antient way' are urged to 'think on' is one that can be fulfilled in historical time as well as at the end of history, and the

---

79 *HV Works*, pp. 571–72.
80 Durr, *On the Mystical Poetry of Henry Vaughan*, pp. 101, 103.
81 Simmonds, *Masques of God*, pp. 106–07.

'Land of flowers and spices' becomes a vision of a country under a restored monarchy as well as the paradise of justified souls. Read in this way, the poem is not the outcry of a defeated quietist waiting for a divinely imposed solution to the nightmare of the times but a defiant statement of political steadfastness. Vaughan may have shared the widespread hope that the world was speeding towards its end, but he also faced the possibility expressed in 'The Pilgrimage' that there may be 'yet more days, more nights to Count'.[82]

Once the strategy of a double focus on eternal verities and temporal realities has been recognized, political elements can be discerned in other poems. The 'home' to which 'Celestial natures' aspire in 'The Palm-tree', for example, is also the dwelling prepared for those who have given their lives in the royal cause or remain true to it in defeat:

> Here Spirits that have run their race and fought
> And won the fight, and have not fear'd the frowns
> Nor lov'd the smiles of greatness, but have wrought
> Their masters will, meet to receive their Crowns.[83]

Having served their divine and royal masters, like the speaker in 'The Proffer', they will receive the fitting 'reward' for their loyalty promised in the penultimate stanza of that poem. Again, a single stanza in 'Providence' arms the royalist who maintains his trust in God against giving up in the face of sequestration and other forms of persecution:

> I will not fear what man
> With all his plots and power can;
> Bags that wax old may plundered be,
> But none can sequester or let
> A state that with the Sun doth set
> And comes next morning fresh as he.[84]

And the single line that closes the celebration of a true saint's 'Art of love' in 'St. Mary Magdalen' glances disdainfully at the pretensions

---

[82] *HV Works*, p. 130.
[83] *HV Works*, p. 575.
[84] *HV Works*, p. 593.

of men like Erbury and Llwyd: 'Who Saint themselves, they are no *Saints*'.[85]

Other poems are more consistently engaged with the contemporary situation and the political hopes that keep the faith of the defeated party alive. 'The Bird' begins by evoking the innocent world of nature, in which the little songster joins its 'early hymns' to the general chorus of dawn praise sent up by 'hills and valleys', 'winds and streams' to the Providence that made and protects them. In the second half of the poem, the 'Birds of light' defy the authorities by chirping their 'solemn Matins' from the outlawed Book of Common Prayer. In opposition to this joyful traditional worship are the 'dark fowls', whose sombre version of religion makes 'all that hear them, sad' and under the shadow of whose power the once 'pleasant Land' turns to brimstone and the clear streams of faith are muddied. 'Brightness and mirth' are driven out by 'Owls and Satyrs', but only temporarily until – in words that echo the Benedictus recited each morning at Matins – 'the Day-spring breaks forth again from high'.[86] This looked-for dawn is not necessarily eschatological, since the word 'again' implies the continuing cycle of nature. The hidden message is that those who await the political equivalent of this daily event must continue to worship secretly in the 'ancient way'. The impact of this imagery, which places the rule of the 'dark fowls' as a mere episode, is quite different from those earlier desperate appeals in 1650 for the end of history: 'O come, Lord *Jesus* quickly!' and 'Ah! what time wilt thou come?'

Two poems further on, Vaughan offers another vision of historical restoration in 'The Jews', which invokes the ancient Jewish tradition that a Messiah will be sent by God to liberate his people. When this event occurs, the 'long frost' that benumbs their hearts will thaw and men and angels will once more 'familiarly confer / Beneath the Oke and Juniper', as they did in the Old Testament.[87] This vision of peace and revival on Earth contrasts with the poet's hopeless longing for the 'white days' of the Patriarchs and desire for personal death in Part One. Nabil Matar has shown that its context was the national debate about granting Jews permission to settle again in England and the belief among radical preachers that the conversion of the Jews

---

85 *HV Works*, p. 597.
86 *HV Works*, pp. 582–83.
87 *HV Works*, pp. 585–86.

was a necessary prelude to the establishment of Christ's kingdom on Earth.[88] For Vaughan, the idea of a Jewish Messiah merges with the Christian belief in the Second Coming to provide a vehicle for the hope that his own compatriots will find a political 'deliverer' in the person of Charles II, whose return will thaw the long frost of the Cavalier winter.

The policy of waiting for dark and wintry times to pass, while nurturing the values associated with 'the antient way' in the company of friends, finds its most powerful metaphorical expression in 'The Seed growing secretly'. A life of retirement, which felt like 'Lethargy, and meer disease' in 'Misery', only needs to be watered by the 'souls bright food' from above in order to 'blow / And spred and open' to the 'will' of its maker. Until the time is ripe for a more public display of allegiance, comfort can be derived from accepting that apparent quietism is part of a natural process: 'Dear, secret *Greenness*! nurst below / Tempests and windes, and winter-nights'. The political message of the poem for other 'secret' royalists is less covertly expressed in later stanzas:

> Let glory be their bait, whose mindes
> Are all too high for a low Cell:
> Though Hawks can prey through storms and winds,
> The poor Bee in her hive must dwel.
>
> Glory, the Crouds cheap tinsel still
> To what most takes them, is a drudge;
> And they too oft take good for ill,
> And thriving vice for vertue judge.

And a final stanza, with the apocalyptic imagery of its conclusion, invites a re-reading of the whole poem against the background of a neighbourhood (or even a nation) in which loyal supporters of the king are biding their time and refusing to be tempted by the 'noise' of their opponents in the expectation that their patience will one day be rewarded:

---

88 See Nabil I. Matar, 'George Herbert, Henry Vaughan, and the Conversion of the Jews', *Studies in English Literature*, 30 (1990), 79–92. Matar (84) cites sermons in Breconshire by Vavasor Powell and William Erbury during the early 1650s.

> Then bless thy secret growth, nor catch
> At noise, but thrive unseen and dumb;
> Keep clean, bear fruit, earn life and watch
> Till the white winged Reapers come!⁸⁹

Vaughan did not find it easy to maintain this ideal of quiet watchfulness, and poems towards the end of the volume reveal the continuing tensions of life under Cromwell's Protectorate. A weary longing to lie in the 'calm and sacred bed' of the grave and to be 'winged and free' returns in the elegies 'As time one day by me did pass' and 'Fair and yong light!'; the escapist attractions of the 'Dear, harmless age!' are felt again in 'Childe-hood'; and the last words of a 'troubled soul' in 'Anguish' are 'Or let me dye!'⁹⁰ And interspersed among such regressive pieces, the conflict between the impulse to action and the need for self-restraint and Christian fortitude is resumed. Above all, the instinct for revenge has to be quelled. 'The Men of War' cites as its epigraph a verse from St Luke's Gospel (23: 11), in which Herod and 'his men of war' mock Christ before sending him back to Pilate. The poem itself begins with a paraphrase of St John's words in Revelation (13:10):

> *He that into Captivity*
> *Leads others, shall a Captive be.*
> *Who with the sword doth others kill,*
> *A sword shall his blood likewise spill.*
> *Here is the patience of the Saints,*
> *And the true faith, which never faints.*

Vaughan goes on to distinguish between true saints and those who once tried to lure him 'for a temporal self-end' to join them in 'Successful wickedness'. Only the Word of God saved him from running 'to endless night' and enacting 'for *Saints* my self and mine', presumably by collaborating with his enemies. Now he must learn '*the patience of the Saints*', which leaves punishment to God and meets injustice and humiliation with Christ-like fortitude:

---

89 *HV Works*, pp. 598–99.
90 *HV Works*, pp. 600–02, 610, 615.

> For in this bright, instructing verse
> Thy Saints are not the Conquerers;
> But patient, meek, and overcome
> Like thee, when set at naught and dumb.

The conclusion prays for 'Contented thoughts, innoxious ease, / A sweet, revengeless, quiet minde' and looks forward to a restoration, when the poet's patience will be rewarded with a 'Crown', a *'Throne'* will be re-established, and the worldly *'Conquerors'* will fall before it. When that time comes, he hopes to be found among the 'chosen company' – both the saved and the faithful remnant of royalists – 'Who by no blood (here) overcame / But the blood of the *blessed Lamb'*.[91] Vaughan has here rehearsed in a quieter mood the political and spiritual difficulties that were expressed with greater vehemence in 'The Proffer'.

The conflict breaks out again in 'Abels blood', which demands retribution against the parliamentary soldiers in more strident tones:

> What thunders shall those men arraign
> Who cannot count those they have slain,
> Who bath not in a shallow flood,
> But in a deep, wide sea of blood?

This voice tells of a tide of complaint beating against the 'everlasting doors above', where the souls of the dead 'with one strong, incessant cry / Inquire *How long?* of the most high'. Another voice, at odds with it, takes over in the closing section of the poem, urging that the 'proudly spilt and despis'd blood' may be allowed to sleep or 'if it watch, forgive and weep / For those that spilt it'; and in the final couplet, the poet invokes 'his milde blood in voice and will, / *Who* pray'd for those that did him kill!'[92] The primary allusion is obviously to St Luke's Gospel: 'Then said Iesus, Father, forgiue them, for they know not what they doe' (23:34). But there was another victim of judicial violence, associated more directly with those whose blood was spilt in the civil wars, who echoed these words more than once and also prayed in *Eikon Basilike* that the cup of God's wrath 'may pass from all those, whose hands […]

---

91 *HV Works*, pp. 604–06.
92 *HV Works*, pp. 612–13.

are embrued with My blood'.[93] The poem embodies the troubled emotions of a devout Christian and steadfast royalist who cannot suppress the desire for vengeance, when he thinks of those who, in the words of his prose work, *The Mount of Olives*, 'have also washed their hands in the blood of my friends, my dearest and nearest relatives'.[94]

'L'Envoy', the parting shot of the volume, illustrates in its formal structure the double perspective that so often characterizes Vaughan's eschatological allusions. The first section looks forward to the moment when God will 'like old cloaths fold up these skies' and make all things 'Transparent as the purest day'. But for all his eager anticipation of a 'state' fit for God to look upon with 'pure and unveil'd eye', the poet is content to wait upon the divine will: 'we shall gladly sit / Till all be ready'. Then, as Rudrum observes, there is a passage of topical commentary that demonstrates that there has been no 'compromise in Vaughan's positioning on the political spectrum':[95]

> Onely, let not our haters brag,
> Thy seamless coat is grown a rag,
> Or that thy truth was not here known,
> Because we forc'd thy judgements down.
> Dry up their arms, who vex thy spouse,
> And take the glory of thy house
> To deck their own; then give thy saints
> That faithful zeal, which neither faints
> Nor wildly burns, but meekly still
> Dares own the truth, and shew the ill.
> Frustrate those cancerous, close arts
> Which cause solution in all parts,
> And strike them dumb, who for meer words
> Wound thy beloved, more then swords.

This passage gathers up the charges made against the Puritans in previous poems into a final indictment as a prelude to the closing

---

93 *Eikon Basilike with Selections from Eikonoklastes*, ed. Jim Daems and Holly Fairh Nelson (Peterborough, Ontario and New York: Broadview Press, 2006), p. 199. See also pp. 88 and 123.
94 *HV Works*, p. 312.
95 Rudrum, 'Resistance, Collaboration, and Silence', 115.

section, in which Vaughan turns again to a vision of a world transformed by the operation of grace. This is not, however, the radiant world 'without blemish or decay' that he imagined earlier, but an earthly society where 'sin (like water) hourly glides / By each mans door'. What he prays for is an end to dissension in religion and politics – 'That like true sheep, all in one fold / We may be fed, and one minde hold' – and a government in church and state that has learnt the lessons of the recent past and the present:

> Give watchful spirits to our guides! […]
> […] write in their hearts thy law,
> And let these long, sharp judgements aw
> Their very thoughts, that by their clear
> And holy lives, mercy may here
> Sit regent yet, and blessings flow
> As fast, as persecutions now.

The word 'regent' implies that that government will be monarchical and the last four lines of the poem commit the nation 'in war and peace' to the 'service' of the God who at some future point in its unfolding history – unless the Apocalypse intervenes – will have 'turn'd our sad captivity!'[96]

The experience of reading *Silex Scintillans* in the context of contemporary politics in Britain, and more particularly in South Wales, during the first half of the 1650s led Peter Thomas to the conclusion that, whatever part 'intuition' and 'a power inherent in the language itself' played in the process that resulted in this astonishing body of poetry, its author was 'also (as he must be if the language is to speak through him) calculatedly argumentative, a tough, combative controversialist, a sophisticated polemicist, an accomplished rhetorician, and a consummate craftsman with designs on his readers'.[97] It has been the purpose of this chapter to demonstrate the validity of this judgement and to extend it across the entire body of work in verse and prose that Vaughan devoted his time and talents to during the first five years of the Interregnum.

---

96 *HV Works*, pp. 631–32.
97 Thomas, 'The Language of Light', 28.

CHAPTER FIVE

Henry Vaughan and the Church

I

In a study of three generations of poets, whose religious experience centred upon the church that had emerged during the 1530s and 1540s and been established by the Elizabethan Settlement, John N. Wall argues that the English reformation was primarily liturgical not theological. Under the guiding hand of Archbishop Cranmer, the Edwardine church had grounded its Protestant assurance not in specific doctrines but in 'its life of worship made possible by the Book of Common Prayer, the Bible in English, and preaching as represented by the Book of Homilies'; and it had placed at the centre of its 'theological and social agenda' the project of transformation (of the community as well as the individual) by 'seeking to build up the Christian commonwealth through corporate worship'. Wall sees the poetry of Spenser, Herbert, and Vaughan not as 'imagining doctrines poetically' or 'reproducing understandings already arrived at in other words', but as actively contributing to both the agenda of transformation and the processes by which a sense of corporate distinctiveness was confirmed. Henry Vaughan was brought up during the 1630s to participate – like his poetic predecessors – 'in the tradition of liturgical enactment enabled by the Book of Common Prayer'.[1]

When he moved to Jesus College, Oxford, he would have encountered a particular brand of Anglicanism that had been

---

[1] John N. Wall, *Transformations of the Word: Spenser, Herbert, Vaughan* (Athens, GA: University of Georgia Press, 1988), pp. 5, 6, 275.

inspired by the devout practices of Lancelot Andrewes, Bishop of Winchester in the reign of James I, and elaborated during the 1620s and 1630s by Richard Neile, Bishop of Durham and later Archbishop of York, Matthew Wren, successively Bishop of Norwich and Ely, John Cosin, a leading figure at the University of Cambridge, and pre-eminently William Laud, who had begun his episcopal career at St David's in Wales and risen rapidly under the patronage of the Duke of Buckingham and Charles I to become Archbishop of Canterbury in 1633. The movement pioneered by Andrewes and later imposed by Laud 'sought to restore the order and beauty of pre-Reformation services as far as was compatible with the patterns of worship enjoined by the Book of Common Prayer'. Indeed, Graham Parry describes this phase in the development of the English church as 'a brief Anglican Counter-Reformation, driven by a surprising fervour for a richer devotional life, accompanied by a desire to see the Church of England ennobled by handsome ecclesiastical settings and decorous services'.[2]

At the time the Vaughan twins went up to Oxford, Laud was Chancellor of the university and Francis Mansell, the Master of Jesus College, was committed to carrying through his programme of reform. In 1636, the college chapel had been enlarged and fitted out with wood panelling and a marble floor, and the services attended by students in these newly beautified surroundings 'would have been formal and highly ceremonial'; and it is Parry's view that the 'lingering effects' of exposure to this fully developed Laudian dispensation at such a formative age would have stayed with Vaughan 'during the long years when the Church of England was dismantled and replaced by a Presbyterian-style National Church in the time of the Commonwealth'.[3] It should be pointed out, however, that there is no trace of devotion to the Church – whether Laudian in temper or not – in Vaughan's writing before the poems published in *Silex Scintillans*. In fact, the earliest mention of a church is in 'The Charnel-house', which was not printed until 1651 in *Olor Iscanus* but was presumably among the poems that Vaughan had prepared for the press in December 1647. This would place its composition in the period before the experiences that changed him

2 Graham Parry, *Glory, Laud and Honour: The Arts of the Anglican Counter-Reformation* (Woodbridge: The Boydell Press, 2006), pp. 23, 24.
3 Graham Parry, 'Vaughan and Laudianism', *Scintilla*, 13 (2009), 187.

from a secular poet into a predominantly religious one. The poem is a witty meditation on the vanity of all things mortal prompted by a vault where the bones of the dead are stored. The opening line suggests that this may have been occasioned by a visit to an actual ossuary, perhaps attached to St Bridget's at Llansantffraed or the Priory Church in Brecon: 'Blesse me! what damps are here? how stiffe an air?' In this gloomy adjunct to the building where God is worshipped, the 'Eloquent silence' of these 'Fragments of men, Rags of Anatomie' might cause an atheist to think again: 'Were I a *Lucian*, Nature in this dresse / Would make me wish a Saviour, and Confesse.' Vaughan's own affiliation at this time is hinted at when he begins to moralize the scene:

> *Chameleons* of state, Aire-monging band,
> Whose breath (like Gun-powder) blowes up a land,
> Come see your dissolution, and weigh
> What a loath'd nothing you shall be one day.[4]

If this is a contemptuous allusion to the victorious Puritans (since the chameleon was a metaphor for untrustworthiness and an 'air-monger' was a misguided visionary), then to associate them with Guy Fawkes's notorious Roman Catholic plot to blow up Parliament is an oblique means of endorsing the Church of England's middle way between dangerous extremes.[5] If there is any sense of personal commitment here, however, it has a political rather than a spiritual focus. The same anti-Puritan orientation is found in 'To his retired friend, an Invitation to Brecknock', which was probably written in the winter of 1645–46. The sneering reference to 'the brotherly Ruffs and Bands' and 'high Monumentall Hats' paraded in Brecon Shire-hall is part of the 'sweeping attack on the Anglo-puritan regime that came to dominate the town' described by John Kerrigan.[6]

Among the first moves by the Long Parliament towards a puritan reformation had been a Bill to deprive bishops of their seats in the

---

4 *HV Works*, pp. 175–77.
5 See the notes on 175:21 and 176:22 in *HV Works*, p. 990.
6 John Kerrigan, *Archipelagic English: Literature, History, and Politics 1603–1707* (Oxford: Oxford University Press, 2008), pp. 197–98. For the poem, see *HV Works*, pp. 180–82 and the notes on 181:23 and 181:24, p. 996.

House of Lords in May 1641 and a subsequent Root and Branch Bill to abolish episcopacy altogether, both of which failed to pass into law at the time because of opposition in the Lords. Nevertheless, as John Morrill has demonstrated, the failure of these early attempts at legislation did not prevent Parliament from toppling the Church of England as an effective *institution* by the time civil war was formally declared:

> Few bishops by the summer of 1642 retained any authority in their dioceses; most church courts had ceased to function; there was no mechanism to enforce, and parliamentary encouragement to modify, the liturgy and formal worship of the church; the outward and visible sign of Laudian innovation – the altar rail – had vanished in most parishes far more speedily than it had gone up. A vacuum had been created which the Houses were proceeding to fill.[7]

The instrument they created to deliberate on the future form and practices of the national church was the Westminster Assembly of Divines, which drew up a Directory of Public Worship. This legally replaced the Book of Common Prayer by order of Parliament on 4 January 1645. Six days later, Archbishop Laud was executed for treason, having been impeached and imprisoned as early as December 1640 and brought to trial in 1644. During the course of the 1640s, successive parliamentary ordinances transformed the church he had presided over, banning the observance of the feasts of Christmas, Easter, and Whitsun, ordering the destruction or removal from churches of crucifixes, images of saints, fonts, organs, and vestments, and forbidding the use of candles and basins on the communion tables that had replaced altars. The last consecration of a bishop took place in 1644 and in October 1646 the Lords finally accepted an ordinance that abolished the episcopal office.[8]

---

7 John Morrill, 'The Attack on the Church of England in the Long Parliament', in *The Nature of the English Revolution: Essays by John Morrill* (London: Longman, 1993), p. 86.

8 Jacqueline Eales points out that the Puritans objected not only to 'set forms of prayer' but also to 'the hierarchy of bishops, deans, chapters, and other ecclesiastical officers'; and that fourteen bishops were sequestered in 1643 and 'many of them later sought refuge in royalist regions in the West Country

It is no wonder that Vaughan's response to George Herbert's celebration of 'The British Church' – the 'deare Mother', whose 'perfect lineaments, and hue' presented a 'fine aspect in fit aray' to the world – took the form of a lament, in which the Church mourns over her 'ravish'd looks / Slain flock, and pillag'd fleeces'; and that 'The Constellation' ends with a prayer for the qualities that had characterized the Church of England in Herbert's day to be restored:

> Give to thy spouse her perfect, and pure dress,
>   *Beauty* and *holiness*,
> And so repair these Rents, that men may see
> And say, *Where God is, all agree*.⁹

By bringing together instances in his work where the idea of 'the church' is foregrounded – whether as a physical edifice, an institution, or a worshipping community – this chapter will demonstrate that Vaughan remained a faithful son of the 'British Church', in which George Herbert had served as a priest, and that he dedicated his talent to defending its beliefs and practices during his most productive years as a writer.¹⁰

---

and Wales'. See 'Religion in Times of War and Republic, 1642–60', in *The Oxford Handbook of Early Modern English Literature and Religion*, ed. Andrew Hiscock and Helen Wilcox (Oxford: Oxford University Press, 2017), pp. 85–86.

9 *HV Works*, pp. 72, 136. 'The Brittish Church' was placed near the beginning of the 1650 *Silex Scintillans*. For Herbert's poem, see *The English Poems of George Herbert*, ed. Helen Wilcox (Cambridge: Cambridge University Press, 2007), pp. 390–91.

10 Herbert's Oxford editor noted that he refers to the 'British' rather than the 'English' Church because 'full episcopacy had been reintroduced into Scotland in 1610' once the thrones of the two kingdoms had been united under James I and VI (*The Works of George Herbert*, ed. F.E. Hutchinson (Oxford: Clarendon Press, 1941), note on p. 515). His Cambridge editor adds that the term 'also suggests historical continuity with the church of ancient Britain' (*English Poems of George Herbert*, note on p. 391). Vaughan is obviously following Herbert in his choice of title and probably for the reason proposed by Wilcox. It was shorthand for the 'ancient way' that was under attack from Puritanism. John Kerrigan sees the 'hills and mists, fleeces and flocks' of Vaughan's poem as 'drenched in scripture and British history' (*Archipelagic English*, p. 208).

II

Various commentators have been busy uncovering the extent to which the religious lyrics and prose works that Vaughan published in the 1650s had engaged with Puritan efforts to extirpate what he more than once referred to as 'the ancient way'.[11] What he meant by that phrase can be illuminated by Judith Maltby's study of the degree of conformity among the English people to the national institution established in 1559. Evidence derived from the petitions, nearly thirty in number, provoked by demands for Root and Branch reform, points to widespread popular support from 1640 to 1642 for 'the lawful liturgy of the English church', which was based on the 'Prayer Book's harmony with antiquity which gave it authority', and the desire to maintain 'continuity with the worship of the early Christians'.[12] Another scholar confirms that Parliament's eventual ban on the Elizabethan liturgy served to reveal 'the strength of Prayer Book Protestantism'.[13] Even Anthony Milton, who argues that there was no clear and stable 'Anglican' identity before the restoration of the Church in 1660, admits that 'some contemporary royalists' saw themselves as 'united by their continued allegiance to a usurped Church and monarch, and sustained by private Prayer Book services'.[14]

11 See Claude J. Summers and Ted-Larry Pebworth, 'Herbert, Vaughan, and Public Concerns in Private Modes', *George Herbert Journal*, 3 (1979–80), 1–21; Jonathan F.S. Post, *Henry Vaughan: The Unfolding Vision* (Princeton, NJ: Princeton University Press, 1982); Robert Wilcher, '"Then keep the ancient way!": A Study of Henry Vaughan's *Silex Scintillans*', *Durham University Journal*, new series, 45 (1983), 11–24; Janet E. Halley, 'Versions of the Self and the Politics of Privacy in *Silex Scintillans*', *George Herbert Journal*, 7 (1983–84), 51–71; Noel Kennedy Thomas, *Henry Vaughan: Poet of Revelation* (Worthing: Churchman Publishing, 1986), Chapter 1; Graeme J. Watson, 'The Temple in "The Night": Henry Vaughan and the Collapse of the Established Church', *Modern Philology*, 84 (1986), 144–61.

12 Judith Maltby, *Prayer Book and People in Elizabethan and Early Stuart England*, Cambridge Studies in Early Modern British History (Cambridge: Cambridge University Press, 1998), pp. 114–15.

13 John Coffey, 'Religion', in *The Oxford Handbook of Literature and the English Revolution*, ed. Laura Lunger Knoppers (Oxford: Oxford University Press, 2012), p. 112.

14 'Introduction', in *The Oxford History of Anglicanism, Volume 1: Reformation*

John Wall explains how Vaughan, living now in a community prohibited from conducting its worship in the traditional way, transformed himself into 'the chronicler of the experience of that community when its source of Christian identity was no longer available'.[15] But he did more than simply chronicle its plight. In fact, the collection of devotional lyrics he published in 1650 and 1655 was described by Claude Summers as 'the masterwork of the poetry of Anglican survivalism', invoking a term that had been given currency by Morrill in his argument that the Long Parliament's attempt 'to eradicate Anglican worship and observance' came up against 'stubborn liturgical conservatism' and active resistance.[16] In a more extensive study of this resistance, John Spurr demonstrated that the experience of 'dispossession and persecution' among those who adhered to an ideal of decorous public worship during the 1650s was offset by 'renewed piety and ecclesiological confidence', so that the Church of England that re-emerged after 1660 had 'a distinct doctrinal, ecclesiological and spiritual identity'.[17] This was due in large measure to a survivalist movement inspired by Henry Hammond, former chaplain to Charles I, and spearheaded by a group of younger controversialists, who were to hold high ecclesiastical offices after the Restoration. While many of the orthodox clergy managed to retain their livings throughout the years of civil war and interregnum by varying degrees of conformity and collaboration, these more active opponents of the Puritan reforms encouraged each other in correspondence and used the printing press to mount a 'wide-ranging and resolute defence of the pre-1640 Church of England'.[18] For example, the principles behind the Elizabethan

and Identity c. 1520–1662, ed. Anthony Milton (Oxford: Oxford University Press, 2017), pp. 18–19.

15 Wall, *Transformations of the Word*, p. 275.

16 Claude J. Summers, 'Herrick, Vaughan, and the Poetry of Anglican Survivalism', in *New Perspectives on the Seventeenth-Century English Religious Lyric*, ed. John R. Roberts (Columbia, MO and London: University of Missouri Press, 1994), p. 64; John Morrill, 'The Church in England, 1642–9', in *Reactions to the English Civil War 1642–1649*, ed. John Morrill (Houndmills, Basingstoke: Macmillan, 1982), pp. 89–90, 107.

17 John Spurr, *The Restoration Church of England, 1646–1689* (New Haven, CT and London: Yale University Press, 1991), p. xiv.

18 Spurr, *The Restoration Church of England*, p. 11.

prayer book were upheld by Hammond himself in *A View of the New Directorie, and a Vindication of the Ancient Liturgie of the Church of England* (1645), Jeremy Taylor in *An Apology for Authorized and Set Forms of Liturgie: Against the Pretence of the Spirit* (1649), Robert Sanderson in *A Case of the Liturgy* (1652), and Lionel Gatford in *A Petition for the Vindication of the Publique Use of the Book of Common-Prayer* (1655).[19] These works were less concerned with defending the recent Laudian innovations than with preserving the 'ancient' forms of public worship embodied in the Prayer Book of 1559.

Hammond was well aware that the survival of the Elizabethan Church of England would depend upon something much more fundamental than the continuity of its clergy and the vigour of its apologists, as he made clear in a letter to Gilbert Sheldon dated 5 June 1654: 'The truth is, unless some care be taken otherwise to maintain the Communion of our Church, it is to little purpose what any write in defence of it. It will soon be destroyed.'[20] In the same year, Bishop Joseph Hall urged that 'Orthodox and genuine Sonnes of the Church of *England*' should 'firmly resolve' to countermine the 'Engineers of Hell', who were conspiring to destroy the church's traditional structures and practices, by entering into 'a safe, warrantable, *Holy Fraternity of Mourners in Sion*; Whose Profession, and worke shall be a peculiarity of Devotion'; and the first of his rules for this brotherhood was that 'wee shall hold up our private Devotions'.[21] It was precisely on this issue – how to succour the faithful remnant of a community rooted in the traditions of the Book of Common Prayer and to maintain its spiritual identity in a time of persecution – that many of Vaughan's activities as a writer in the first half of the 1650s were concentrated.[22]

19 These were part of an ongoing debate about composed and extempore prayer, in which a typical contribution from the other side was Thomas Cobbet's *A Practical Discourse of Prayer* (1654).
20 Quoted by John W. Packer, *The Transformation of Anglicanism 1643–1660* (Manchester: Manchester University Press, 1969), p. 46.
21 Joseph Hall, *The Holy Order: Or, Fraternity of Mourners in Sion* (London, 1654), pp. 3–5.
22 This public mission was an extension of the personal drama graphically expressed in the 'flashing flint' emblem on the title-page of the 1650 *Silex Scintillans*, which Peter Thomas has described as an 'icon of the trauma of loss and defeat and the struggle for survival and renewal that overtook Vaughan

The local circumstances in which Vaughan found himself at this time made the 'worke' of preserving the 'Communion' of Hall's 'Orthodox and genuine' members of the Church particularly pressing. Unlike some parts of the country, where 'prelatist clerics encountered little opposition in conducting their services in private',[23] South Wales came under strict Parliamentary control in the wake of the Act for the Better Propagation and Preaching of the Gospel in Wales of February 1650.[24] During the three years that it was in force, 196 ministers from South Wales and Monmouthshire were ejected, a substantial majority of them within the first twelve months. Only 127 were left in post across the region, and since replacements were hard to find, many churches remained closed.[25] This contrasts with the calculation that 'a national average of approximately 28 per cent' of clergy livings were under sequestration in England as a result of ejections for either 'scandal' or 'malignancy', although 'the geographical pattern of persecution varied considerably'.[26] In Breconshire, even Parliament's own officials (the county sequestrators John Gunter of Tredomen and William Thomas of Brecon) saw fit to inform the Committee of Compounding in London on 25 October 1651, 'All the ministers of this county were ousted two years past by the Commissioners named in the Act for the

---

mid-century'. See 'The "Desert Sanctified": Henry Vaughan's Church in the Wilderness', in *Sacred Text–Sacred Space: Architectural, Spiritual and Literary Convergences in England and Wales*, ed. Joseph Sterrett and Peter Thomas (Leiden and Boston, MA: Brill, 2011), p. 164.

23 Claire Cross, 'The Church in England 1646–1660', in *The Interregnum: The Quest for Settlement 1646–1660*, ed. G.E. Aylmer (London and Basingstoke: Macmillan, 1974), p. 114. Spurr suggests that in England 'perhaps 70 per cent or even 75 per cent of all parish ministers were left in possession of their benefices until their death or the Restoration' (*The Restoration Church of England*, pp. 6–7).

24 For a commentary on the strictness with which the act was implemented in South Wales and the consequences for orthodox members of the Church of England, see Peter Thomas, 'The "Desert Sanctified"', pp. 164–67.

25 See A.M. Johnson, 'Wales during the Commonwealth and Protectorate', in *Puritans and Revolutionaries: Essays in Seventeenth-Century History Presented to Christopher Hill*, ed. Donald Pennington and Keith Thomas (Oxford: Clarendon Press, 1978), pp. 237–38.

26 I.M. Green, 'The Persecution of "Scandalous" and "Malignant" Parish Clergy during the English Civil War', *English Historical Review*, 94 (1979), 522.

Propagation of the Gospel in Wales, since which none of these churches have been supplied.'²⁷ A general concern about the plight of the church in Wales was voiced by William Nicholson in *An Exposition of the Catechism of the Church of England* (1655):

> [The churches] are become like the prophet's lodge in a garden of cucumbers, deserted, ruined; no cottage on a hill more desolate, more defaced, the people having no encouragement to resort to that place where they have neither minister to pray with, or for them, or to sing praises to God with them, nor any at all in many places.²⁸

The parish of Llansantffraed was itself at the heart of an area in which the parliamentary Commissioners were extremely diligent. Noel Thomas notes that in the published list of twenty-five ejected clergy on which the name of Thomas Vaughan appears, 'no fewer than thirteen had their churches within six miles of Vaughan's home'; and he illustrates this situation by quoting from the parish register of Llanafan Fawr in Breconshire:

> After this time (sc. 1650) there was a general cessation of officiating in church either for Baptisme Marriadge or Buriall [...] All that while the Church & Chapells belonging to Lanavanfawr, were without prayer or preaching or officiating unless in some of them some itinerants came once in a month or quarter or year in some not at all during that time or as yet in 1659.²⁹

The situation in the neighbourhood of Newton needs to be set in the wider context of the struggle for conformist survival in South Wales during the Interregnum. The counties of Glamorgan, Carmarthen, and Brecon in particular had become the centre of 'a clandestine church movement' and a haven for members of the outlawed Church, including Francis Mansell, former Master

---

27 Quoted by R. Tudor Jones, 'Religion in Post-Restoration Brecknockshire 1660–1688', *Brycheiniog*, 8 (1962), 16. Jones adds that the sequestrators were removed from office on 16 December, after repeating their criticism of the Commissioners on 2 December 1651.

28 Quoted in Spurr, *The Restoration Church of England*, p. 23.

29 Thomas, *Henry Vaughan: Poet of Revelation*, p. 35.

of Jesus College, and Gilbert Sheldon, under whose wardenship the college of All Souls had become another nursery of Laudian reforms in Oxford during the 1630s.[30] Both Sheldon and Accepted Frewin, Bishop of Lichfield, joined Mansell at his brother's house in Carmarthenshire and later found refuge at the Aubrey house of Llantrithyd.[31] Significant among this group, and providing a link with Hammond's, was Jeremy Taylor, a former fellow of All Souls, who spent 'his most creative years', from 1646 to 1657, in Carmarthenshire.[32] After serving as a chaplain in the King's army, he set up a school in Newton Hall at Llanfihangel-Aberbythych and acted as chaplain to Richard Vaughan, the second earl of Carbery, at nearby Golden Grove, while keeping up a correspondence with Hammond 'and other Anglican luminaries' scattered across the country – 'sharing ideas and knowledge, swopping titbits of academic and royalist gossip, and encouraging each other in the service of "our distressed mother the church"'.[33] He fell foul of the authorities and was imprisoned in Chepstow Castle from May to October 1655, after which new government regulations against the employment of clergymen as chaplains and tutors in royalist households forced him to leave Golden Grove and take up residence about twelve miles away on the estate of his second wife at Mandiham.[34] It was during his years in Wales that he composed the works by which he is best remembered: *The Liberty of Prophesying* (1647), *The Rule and Exercises of Holy Living* (1650), *The Rule and Exercises of Holy Dying* (1651), and *The Golden Grove* (1655).

30 Thomas, *Poet of Revelation*, pp. 117, 130.
31 See Philip Jenkins, 'Welsh Anglicans and the Interregnum', *Journal of the Historical Society of the Church in Wales*, 27 (1990), 51–59.
32 See Harry Boone Porter, *Jeremy Taylor Liturgist (1613–1667)* (London: Alcuin Club/S.P.C.K., 1979), pp. 11–15.
33 Spurr, *The Restoration Church of England*, p. 10.
34 See the General Introduction to *Jeremy Taylor: Holy Living and Holy Dying*, ed. P.G. Stanwood, 2 vols. (Oxford: Clarendon Press, 1989), Vol. I, pp. xix–xx, xxiv–xxvi.

III

During the period when he was coming to terms with the defeat of the royalists and more personal losses in the Second Civil War of 1648, Henry Vaughan produced his most graphic and idyllic evocation of the Church in all its manifestations as place of worship, human institution, and community of worshippers, as it was preserved in his own memory and celebrated in the writings of George Herbert. It occurs in *The Praise and Happinesse of the Countrie-Life*, one of the prose translations appended to the poems in *Olor Iscanus* when it was eventually published in 1651:

> O what a pious and beautifull work it is, when *holy* and *solemne days* are observ'd in the Country, according to the *sacred rules* and *Ordinances* of *Religion*! The *doore-keepers* of the *house* of *God* set wide open their *beautifull gates*, The *Church-bels* Ring, and every pious Soule is ravish'd with the *Musick*, and is sick of *love* untill he come into the *Courts* of the *Lord*. The *Temples* and *Communion tables* are drest, and the *beauty of holinesse* shines every where. The poorest *Country-labourer* honours that day with his best *habit*; their *families*, their *beasts*, and their *catell* rest on that day, and every one in a decent and Christian *dresse* walks Religiously towards his *Parish Church*, where they hear Divine *Service*, performe all *holy duties*, and after Dinner release from all their labours *rest* in the *practice* of true *piety*.[35]

In this nostalgic vision derived from a Spanish original, Vaughan was lamenting what had already been lost and was now under further threat from Puritan reformers in the rural parishes of England and Wales. The dominant notes here are social and aesthetic rather than spiritual, and Philip West thinks that he may have chosen to translate this text and add it to the poems of *Olor Iscanus* primarily because it offered 'retreat as an honourable option for the defeated and frustrated'. As he approached the psychological and religious crisis embodied in the poems published in the 1650 *Silex Scintillans*, he passed through 'a transitional phase in which he increasingly sanctified the philosophy of retirement' through allusions to Old Testament prophets. One of the fruits of this process was a poem

---

35 *HV Works*, pp. 264–65.

entitled 'Retirement (II)', in which echoes of the prose translation from Guevara's Spanish support a date of about 1648, although it was not published until 1678 in *Thalia Rediviva*.[36]

In the first paragraph of the poem, Vaughan praises the rural retreats sought out by the patriarch Abraham, where the beauties of the natural world displayed the bounty and wisdom of their Maker:

> Fresh *fields* and *woods*! the Earth's fair *face*,
> God's *foot-stool*, and mans *dwelling-place*.
> I ask not why the first *Believer*
> Did love to be a Country liver?
> Who to secure pious content
> Did pitch by *groves* and *wells* his tent;
> Where he might view the boundless *skie*,
> And all those glorious *lights* on high.

In the second paragraph, the 'pious content' secured by the 'Country liver' depends less on his positive enjoyment of the countryside than on his relief at escaping from the corruptions and dangers of the wider world:

> All various Lusts in *Cities* still
> Are found; they are the *Thrones* of Ill.
> The dismal *Sinks*, where blood is spill'd,
> *Cages* with much uncleanness fill'd.
> But *rural shades* are the sweet fense
> Of piety and innocence.[37]

At this stage of his pilgrimage, Vaughan seems to have been inclined to embrace a quiet rural existence, in which 'piety and innocence' were safely preserved from the evils of politics and civil war. But developments emanating from the '*Thrones* of Ill' in the most prominent city of neighbouring England were soon to invade his sanctuary in the Breconshire countryside.

---

36 Philip West, *Henry Vaughan's* Silex Scintillans: *Scripture Uses* (Oxford: Oxford University Press, 2001), pp. 110–11.
37 *HV Works*, pp. 770–71.

IV

In the fifth book of his defence of the established English church, *Of the Laws of Ecclesiastical Polity* (1597), Richard Hooker included a discussion of the 'places' where the 'solemn duties of public service' were to be 'done unto God' and concluded that 'for performance of this service by the people of God assembled, we think not any place *so good* as the church, neither any exhortation so fit as that of David, "O worship the Lord in the beauty of holiness"'.[38] Foulke Robarts would later derive from Hooker his views on the sanctity of church buildings in *Gods Holy House and Service* (1639), which is described by West as 'perhaps the fullest exposition of Laudian sacrality'.[39] Joseph Hall, who 'remained distanced from Laudian ecclesiology', based his respect for places of worship directly upon the Scriptural account of Jacob's response to an encounter with God in his dream of a ladder that reached from Earth to heaven:

> And Iacob awaked out of his sleepe, and he said, Surely the LORD is in this place, and I knew it not. And he was afraid, and said, How dreadful *is* this place? this is none other, but the house of God, and this is the gate of heauen. And Jacob rose vp earely in the morning, and tooke the stone that hee had put for his pillowes, and set it vp for a pillar, and powred oile vpon the top of it. And hee called the name of that place Beth-el. (Genesis 28:16–19)

The then bishop of Exeter used this first instance in the Bible of the ritual consecration of a special site to the glory of God in order to discourse upon the special nature of the church as a building set apart, paraphrasing the biblical account in what West calls 'the more ecclesial language' of Anglicanism:

> How full of awe and reverend respect is this place, which God hath thus sanctified by his presence, having so familiarly manifested himselfe to me here, as men doe in their dwelling houses to their friends; this is no other than a representation of Gods spirituall house, his Church, by which we enter the glory of heaven […] The

---

38 Richard Hooker, *Of the Laws of Ecclesiastical Polity*, 2 vols., Everyman's Library (London: Dent, 1907), Vol. II, pp. 37, 52.
39 West, *Scripture Uses*, p. 38.

place where I set up this stone shalbe dedicated to the worship and service of my God, where I will build an altar to his name.[40]

He evidently saw Bethel 'as the first church to be both sanctified and dedicated in the Reformed Anglican sense'.[41]

In 'Sion', the poem at the centre of his collection of poetry, George Herbert insisted (as, indeed, had Hooker) that the inner temple of the penitent heart is more dear to God than the 'pomp and state' of 'Solomons sea of brasse and world of stone' in the temple at Jerusalem.[42] Nevertheless, he included a number of meditations on specific features of the buildings in which the services and ceremonies of the Church of England were conducted: 'The Altar', 'Church-monuments', 'Church-lock and Key', 'The Church-floor', and 'The Windows'. Since Henry Vaughan and his family were deprived of such a place of public worship by the closure of many churches in the Usk Valley, several commentators have suggested that he not only sought refuge in the countryside from the troubled human world around him but that he also discovered Beth-el, the house of God revealed to Jacob, among the woods and fields around Newton. Summers and Pebworth were the first to claim that 'Regeneration', the poem with which *Silex Scintillans* opens, not only enacts in allegorical mode the beginning of the poet's journey towards new spiritual life but also records his discovery of 'the architecture of Anglicanism' in a grove.[43] In this substitute church – 'Some call'd it, *Jacobs Bed*' – 'a little Fountain' near the entrance is the baptismal font, the nave consists of trees '[o]f stately height, whose branches met / And mixt on every side', a 'banke of flowers' supplies a raised altar, the 'thousand peeces' of 'vitall gold' shot through the canopy of leaves imitate the effect of stained-glass windows, and the interior has been censed ('[t]he aire was all in spice') and decked with flowers ('every bush / A garland wore') as for a religious festival.[44] West

---

40 Joseph Hall, *A Plaine and Familiar Explication of All the Hard Texts of the Whole Divine Scripture of the Old and New Testament* (London, 1633), p. 32.
41 For West's commentary on Hall's work, see *Scripture Uses*, p. 39.
42 *English Poems of George Herbert*, p. 382.
43 Claude J. Summers and Ted-Larry Pebworth, 'Vaughan's Temple in Nature and the Context of "Regeneration"', *Journal of English and Germanic Philology*, 74 (1975), 355–57.
44 *HV Works*, pp. 57–59.

has pointed out, however, that 'Regeneration' belongs to the late 1640s, before the wholesale ejection of ministers and closure of churches prompted by the Propagation Act, so that the poet would still have been able to attend his local church when he wrote it. Therefore, although *Jacobs Bed* is allegorically a church, there is 'no substantial historical evidence that Vaughan meant it to be a temple in nature'.[45]

More recently, Allan and Helen Wilcox have argued that Vaughan's profound and distinctive sense of place is also a fundamental feature of his personal spirituality. In the untitled poem beginning 'I walkt the other day', he describes how he found in a field near his home 'a sacred place – a location which is not the church building beloved of Herbert but the landscape of the Usk Valley', where he goes to spend his 'hour' of solitary communion with God.[46] Although this indicates a habit of praying and meditating alone in the countryside around his home, however, he also retained a deep allegiance to the Prayer Book ideal of communal worship. In a poem entitled 'Retirement (I)', published in the first edition of *Silex Scintillans*, he commits himself to resisting the Puritan position, which was exemplified by the declaration in The Directory for the Public Worship of God issued by Parliament in 1645 that 'no place is capable of any holiness under pretence of whatsoever Dedication or Consecration'.[47] He begins by relating how God, who keeps 'close house / Above the morning-starre', 'Did shew me home, and put me in the way'; in the second stanza, God explains that He has delayed thus directing him homewards until 'this day'; and in the third, the One who 'fram'd' him advises the sinful poet that, if he would come to his Maker's 'seat', he must turn away from 'th'applause, and feat / Of dust, and clay'. But in the last two stanzas, God reminds him that the heavenly mansion is not the only place in which he can expect to see and hear the truth:

---

45 West, *Scripture Uses*, pp. 36–37.
46 Allan and Helen Wilcox, 'Matter and Spirit Conjoined: Sacred Places in the Poetry of George Herbert, Henry Vaughan, R.S. Thomas and Rowan Williams', *Scintilla*, 11 (2007), 138–39.
47 The Directory was intended to replace the Book of Common Prayer in England and Wales.

> Now here below where yet untam'd
> Thou doest thus rove
> I have a house as well
> As there above,
> In it my *Name*, and *honour* both do dwell
> And shall until
> I make all new.[48]

The word 'house' is used by Jacob to designate the holy place where God dwells on Earth and in other scriptures to underline the importance of holy places, consecrated to the worship of God: 'Lord, I haue loued the habitation of thy house, and the place where thine honour dwelleth' (Psalm 26:8); 'I had rather be a doore keeper in the house of my God, then to dwell in the tents of wickednesse' (Psalm 84:10). In 'Retirement (I)', then, Vaughan's God is insistent that earthly buildings consecrated to his name and honour will remain his dwelling place until the end of time – when all shall be made new – in spite of the activities of sacrilegious Puritans who have stripped them of 'perfumes' and 'Array', leaving only bare 'stones'; and the tone in which he enjoins the poet not to abandon his house in the closing lines is both urgent and peremptory: 'Up then, and keep / Within those doors, (my doors) dost hear? *I will*'. This poem seems to grow out of Vaughan's struggle at the end of the 1640s to resist an impulse to retire from the transforming mission of his church either into the mansion above the stars or into the quietism of a rural retreat. With the words '*I will*', which are used to affirm personal commitment in the Prayer Book services of Baptism, Confirmation, Matrimony, and Ordination, Vaughan broadens the scope of his poetic vocation from the private sphere of devotion to the public sphere of service in the community of true worshippers.

V

'Retirement (I)' comes quite late in the 1650 volume. The resolution pronounced in its final words of assent and dedication was to bear fruit over the next four years in a series of prose works and an augmented edition of *Silex Scintillans*. While the new devotional

---

48 *HV Works*, pp. 127–28.

poems were accumulating, Vaughan entered the public arena with his own challenge to the opponents of 'the ancient way' of Cranmer, Hooker, and Herbert in *The Mount of Olives*, which was printed in 1652. The work's subtitle – 'Solitary Devotions' – is an acknowledgement that communal worship can no longer take place in sacred buildings and that the Church must now subsist primarily in the hearts of those who remain faithful to the tradition embodied in the Book of Common Prayer. A dedicatory epistle reminds fellow pilgrims that there is good precedent for their exile from the comforts of a 'house' of their own. The incarnate Son of God 'had no place to put his head in', so 'his *Servants* must not think the *present measure* too hard, seeing their *Master* himself took up his *nights-lodging* in the cold *Mount of Olives*'.[49] Donald Dickson observes that Vaughan was attempting to create a mental image of 'a sacred place through his figurative use of the Mount of Olives', which 'has special meaning for the British church in this time of trial'.[50] Then, in a preparatory '*short Exhortation*', he calls into public service the insights gained in his earlier personal struggle with the temptation to give up on the visible church and withdraw into the 'home' prepared for him in God's heavenly 'mansion':

> *Think not that thou art alone upon this Hill, there is an innumerable company both before and behinde thee. Those with their Palms in their hands, and these expecting them. If therefore the dust of this world chance to prick thine eyes, suffer it not to blinde them; but* running thy race with patience, look to JESUS the Authour and finisher of thy faith, who when he was reviled, reviled not againe. Presse thou towards the mark, *and let the people and their Seducers rage*; be faithful unto the death, and he will give thee a Crowne of life.[51]

The sense of isolation that might weaken the reader's resolve is countered with a reminder that the Church at its most fundamental is

---

49 *HV Works*, p. 283.
50 Donald R. Dickson, '*The Mount of Olives*: Vaughan's Book of Private Prayer', in *Of Paradise and Light: Essays on Henry Vaughan and John Milton in Honor of Alan Rudrum*, ed. Donald R. Dickson and Holly Faith Nelson (Newark, DE: University of Delaware Press, 2004), p. 210.
51 *HV Works*, pp. 285–86.

neither a building nor an institution but the *'innumerable company'* (in this world and the next) that makes up the Body of Christ; and the solitary pilgrim is urged to remain steadfast in the face of an aggressive multitude misled by false teachers.

The work itself was a handbook of admonitions, prayers, and prose ejaculations designed to hold the adherents of the outlawed church together in spirit when it was no longer possible for them to congregate in the parish church. In placing it in the hands of the 'Peaceful, humble, and pious READER', Vaughan positions himself carefully in relation to the contemporary debate about formal and extempore prayer:

> *I envie not their frequent* Extasies, *and raptures to the third heaven; I onely wish them real, and that their actions did not tell the world, they are rapt into some other place. Nor should they, who assume to themselves the glorious stile of Saints, be uncharitably moved, if we that are yet in the body, and carry our treasure in earthen vessels, have need of these helps.*[52]

In deriding the extemporal practice of the puritan 'Saints', he was aligning himself with the campaign in defence of a church grounded in the 'ancient' liturgy of the Elizabethan Prayer Book being conducted in print by Jeremy Taylor and other opponents of the Directory of Public Worship. Taylor would explain to his 'Pious and Devout Reader' that the purpose of *The Golden Grove* was to maintain the continuity of true religion in the current adverse climate by taking care that 'the young men who were born in the Captivity' should be 'taught how to worship the God of *Israel* after the manner of their forefathers'.[53] His exposition of one particular phrase from the Apostle's Creed – 'The Communion of Saints' – goes to the heart of the strategy for survival promoted by Hammond and Hall: 'which Communion must be kept in *inward things* always, and by all persons, and testified by *outward acts* always, when it is possible, and may be done upon just and holy conditions'.[54] Such sentiments would have been endorsed by the

---

52 *HV Works*, p. 285.
53 Jeremy Taylor, *The Golden Grove, Or, A Manuall of Daily Prayers and Letanies, Fitted to the Dayes of the Week* (London, 1655), sigs. A3^r, A7^r.
54 Taylor, *Golden Grove*, p. 40.

author of *The Mount of Olives*, who included instructions on how to prepare devoutly for the Lord's Supper, while acknowledging that the circumstances no longer existed for many members of the outlawed church to participate in this act of outward communion. For him, as for Taylor, only the rite according to the Book of Common Prayer provided the 'holy conditions' for the administration of the Eucharist.

In compiling an alternative to the banned Prayer Book, Vaughan was indebted not only to the Elizabethan liturgy itself but also to earlier handbooks – John Day's *A Book of Christian Prayers* (1578) and Lewis Bayly's *The Practice of Piety* (first published in 1612) – which met a need for aids to private prayer similar to the medieval Primers.[55] And, although it did not rival Bayly's handbook or Cranmer's liturgy in its contribution to *The Mount of Olives*, John Cosin's *A Collection of Private Devotions* (1627) was another significant source for Vaughan. This officially promoted volume was a Laudian revival of the Primer, with prayers for each of the nine canonical hours. In a prefatory discourse, 'Touching Prayer, and the Formes of Prayer', Cosin gives four reasons for renewing the 'ancient Pietie' of these daily devotions, two of which chime closely with the purposes of *The Mount of Olives* and *The Golden Grove*. The first is 'to continue & preserve the authority of the ancient *Lawes*, and old godly *Canons* of the Church' that were instituted so that men 'might know what to say, & avoid, as neer as might be, all extemporal effusions of irksome & indigested Prayers'; and the third is so that those 'whom earnest lets & impediments do often hinder from being partakers of the *Publicke* might have here a Daily & Devoute order of *Private Prayer*'. The preface ends with the hope that 'wee shall enjoy a perpetuall *Communion* with the *Saints*

---

[55] See Graeme J. Watson, 'Two New Sources for Henry Vaughan's *The Mount of Olives*', *Notes and Queries*, 230 (1985), 168–70 and Hilary M. Day, 'Bayly's *The Practice of Piety*: A New Source for Henry Vaughan's *The Mount of Olives*', *Notes and Queries*, 233 (1988), 163–65. John Wall gives enough examples to 'suggest the copiousness of Vaughan's allusions to the Prayer Book in *The Mount of Olives*' (*Transformations of the Word*, p. 285). For an account of the great variety of manuals of private prayer available during the sixteenth and seventeenth centuries, see Ian Green, *Print and Protestantism in Early Modern England* (Oxford: Oxford University Press, 2000), pp. 239–304.

triumphant, as well as militant', which is the very same thought elaborated in Vaughan's prefatory exhortation to his pious reader to think upon the *'innumerable company both before and behinde thee'*.⁵⁶

As he proceeds with his own contribution to the survivalist effort, Vaughan confirms his belief in the sanctity of the house of God:

> These reverend and sacred buildings (however now vilified and shut up) have ever been, and amongst true Christians still are the solemne and publike places of meeting for Divine Worship. There the *Flocks feed at noon-day*, there the great *Shepherd* and *Bishop* of their souls is *in the midst of them*, and where he is, that *Ground is holy*.

He also sends a message of encouragement to other followers of the ancient way, explaining how the church building can in itself inspire and support the true believer:

> Look seriously about thee, and Consider with thy self how many beauteous, wittie, and hopeful personages in their time lie now under thy feet; thou canst not tell but thy turn may be next. Humble thy self in this dust, and all vain Imaginations will flie from thee. Consider that thou art now in the *Cave of Macpelah*, in a sacred *Respositorie* where the Bodies of Saints are asleep, expecting that hour, *when those that are in the grave shall hear his voyce*.⁵⁷

The author of *The Mount of Olives* had travelled a long way on the road to sanctification since penning his witty conceits about human remains in his previous meditation on mortality in 'The Charnel-house'.

Elsewhere, a prayer to be used in time of persecution and heresy spells out the devastating effects of the activities of the local

---

56 *John Cosin: A Collection of Private Devotions*, ed. P.G. Stanwood (Oxford: Clarendon Press, 1967), pp. 9, 11, 14, 15. For more details of the place of *The Mount of Olives* in the context of manuals of private prayer, see Robert Wilcher, 'Henry Vaughan, Jeremy Taylor, Edward Sparke, and the Preservation of the Anglican Communion', *Scintilla*, 12 (2008), 144–51.

57 *HV Works*, pp. 293–94.

Approvers appointed by Parliament to carry out its religious policy in South Wales:

> The wayes of *Zion* do mourne, our beautiful gates are shut up, and the Comforter that should relieve our souls is gone far from us. Thy Service and thy Sabbaths, thy own sacred Institutions and the pledges of thy love are denied unto us; Thy Ministers are trodden down, and the basest of the people are set up in thy holy place.

And the sacrilegious practices now being imposed upon the people are contrasted with the proper way to make oneself ready for the celebration of Easter: 'Such was in our Church, that more strict and holy season, called *Lent*, and such still are the preparation-dayes before this glorious Sabbath in all true Churches.'[58] Vaughan had already made more covert reference to these 'preparation-dayes' in the sequence of Easter poems in the 1650 *Silex Scintilans*. As Wall has pointed out, the placing of a paraphrase of Psalm 121 immediately after 'Easter-day', 'Easter Hymn', and 'The Holy Communion' corresponds to the Prayer Book calendar for 1649, when that particular psalm was to be read in the week after Easter; and 'Dressing', which immediately precedes the Easter group, pleads for a share in 'Thy mysticall *Communion*' and 'echoes the appointed Psalm and lessons for Maundy Thursday, the Thursday of Holy Week, March 22, 1649'.[59] Vaughan clearly intended this section of his 1652 prose work to serve the same purpose – 'the creation of a community thinking about the Anglican Eucharist whether or not they could participate in it'[60] – and both make their contribution to Hammond's project of maintaining 'the Communion of our Church' at a time when the sharing of bread and wine according to the Elizabethan rite was denied to many of its members.[61]

---

58 *HV Works*, pp. 311, 302.
59 Wall, *Transfigurations of the Word*, p. 326.
60 Wall, *Transformations of the Word*, p. 327.
61 For a recent view of the role of the Eucharist in Vaughan's spiritual life, following the 'devastating rupture of continuity with the liturgical and literary past', see Sophie Read, *Eucharist and the Poetic Imagination in Early Modern England* (Cambridge: Cambridge University Press, 2013), pp. 154–78.

VI

As if to assert the continuing validity of the liturgical calendar that had governed the worshipping life of the Church of England, Vaughan opens the new collection of poems in the second part of *Silex Scintillans* with 'Ascension-day' and 'Ascension-Hymn', and follows these at intervals with 'White Sunday' and 'Trinity-Sunday'. The contemplation of the descent of the Holy Spirit at Pentecost reinforces his determination to defend the clarity of his vision of the true church against puritan claims to divine authority. Many of the radical preachers believed that they were illuminated by the same spiritual fire that had rested upon the Apostles and enabled them 'to speak with other tongues' (Acts 2:1–4). In 'White Sunday', Vaughan dismisses the vain boasts of such men:

> Can these new lights be like to those,
> These lights of Serpents like the Dove?
> Thou hadst no *gall*, ev'n for thy foes,
> And thy two wings were *Grief* and *Love*.
>
> Though then some boast that fire each day,
> And on Christs coat pin all their shreds;
> Not sparing openly to say,
> His candle shines upon their heads ...[62]

His mockery is directed at a particular dissenting group known as the 'New Lights' who had gathered around Morgan Llwyd in Wrexham during the late 1640s.[63] Originally converted by Walter Cradock, Llwyd later served with him and Vavasor Powell as one of the itinerant preachers entrusted by Parliament with the task of spreading the Gospel in Wales.

Of all the additional poems in the 1655 *Silex Scintillans*, 'The Palm-tree' embodies Vaughan's most confident delineation of what he meant by 'the church' when he came to communicate his 'poor *Talent*' to it in the preface.[64] Rosemary Freeman has pointed out

---

[62] *HV Works*, p. 569.
[63] See M. Wynn Thomas, *Morgan Llwyd*, Writers of Wales (Cardiff: University of Wales Press on behalf of the Welsh Arts Council, 1984), pp. 5–6.
[64] *HV Works*, p. 558.

that the image of 'the palm-tree borne down by a heavy weight yet still flourishing' was commonly used 'to signify perseverance and patience in life, or love, or religion'. She adds that Vaughan gave it 'a fuller and richer meaning' by drawing upon its associations with the 'Tree of Immortality' and the 'crown of victory' and so 'building up a complex idea of the nature of the religious life'.[65] What she does not remark is the relevance to Vaughan's poem of one particular instance of this emblem in the famous frontispiece of *Eikon Basilike* (1649). This book, attributed to Charles I, was hurried into print at the time of his execution to foster the myth of the Royal Martyr dying in defence of the Church of England.[66] William Marshall's engraving depicts the king kneeling before an altar with his eyes fixed on a crown of eternal life, a crown of thorns in his hand, and a crown of worldly vanity beneath his foot. On the left there is a rock beset by a stormy sea in the background and a palm tree loaded down with heavy weights in the foreground.

Editors have pointed out that the poem takes over words from Herbert's description of Solomon's temple in 'Sion' – 'flowers and carvings, mysticall and rare' – and that, through the Christian interpretation of the Song of Solomon, the palm tree had become a symbol for the Church. Vaughan begins by invoking the author of *The Temple*:

> Deare friend sit down, and bear awhile this shade
> As I have yours long since; This Plant, you see
> So prest and bow'd, before sin did degrade
> Both you and it, had equall liberty
>
> With other trees: but now shut from the breath
> And air of *Eden*, like a male-content
> It thrives no where. This makes these weights (like death
> And sin) hang on him; for the more he's bent

---

65 Rosemary Freeman, *English Emblem Books* (London: Chatto & Windus, 1948), pp. 150–51.
66 See Robert Wilcher, 'What was the King's Book for?: The Evolution of *Eikon Basilike*', *The Yearbook of English Studies*, 21 (1991), 218–28; and '*Eikon Basilike*: The Printing, Composition, Strategy, and Impact of "The King's Book"', in *The Oxford Handbook of Literature and the English Revolution*, ed. Laura Lunger Knoppers (Oxford: Oxford University Press, 2012), pp. 289–308.

> The more he grows. Celestial natures still
> Aspire for home; This *Solomon* of old
> By flowers and carvings and mysterious skill
> Of Wings, and Cherubims, and Palms foretold.[67]

The exact echo of Herbert's 'Love Unknown' in the first four words has been taken to imply that the older poet is either the speaker or the recipient.[68] The reference to the temple in Jerusalem and the allusion to Herbert's poem about it suggest that what we are overhearing is one side of a dialogue in which the Soul addresses the Body: the 'shade' cast by the physical over the spiritual part of the human creature is a burden that individual souls have carried since the Fall and now the palm tree, representing the material and institutional church, has also been degraded by sin and cast from Eden. But despite harassment by Puritans, the Church that currently seems to thrive 'no where' remains resilient: 'the more he's bent / The more he grows'. In the four stanzas that follow, Vaughan develops the idea of the Church as the body of true believers: it has a life 'hid above with Christ', which 'doth always (hidden) multiply', watered by the tears of those who suffer persecution for its sake and bestowing immortal crowns upon those who have 'won the fight' and withstood both the 'frowns' and the 'smiles' of the powerful. The Soul ends by promising its 'friend' that – provided it keeps the ancient way of faith – death will only effect a temporary parting and the Body will wake to receive 'a Garland' of immortality.

The poetic spokesman for a generation of dispossessed members of the Church of England in South Wales accepts in 'Jacobs Pillow, and Pillar' that for the time being, while 'Heathens rule / By God's permission', the 'dread place' and 'secret Ark, where the milde Dove doth dwell' must be the hearts of individual members of the true Church rather than 'the solemn temple'. This gloomy situation will only prevail, however, 'till he / With his strong arm turns our captivity'.[69] By the time Vaughan came to publish the augmented *Silex Scintillans*, the Propagation Act had lapsed (on Lady Day 1653) and there were

---

67 *HV Works*, p. 575.
68 See Thomas O. Calhoun, *Henry Vaughan: The Achievement of Silex Scintillans* (Newark, DE: University of Delaware Press, 1981), pp. 193–94; Post, *The Unfolding Vision*, p. 149.
69 *HV Works*, pp. 616–17. For 'Sion', see *English Poems of George Herbert*, p. 383.

hopes of a more tolerant church policy under the Protectorate of Oliver Cromwell. In the final poem of the volume, 'L'Envoy', the Welsh poet harks back to the imagery of 'The Brittish Church', which had been composed in the darkest days of the late 1640s:

> Onely, let not our haters brag,
> Thy seamless coat is grown a rag,
> Or that thy truth was not here known,
> Because we forc'd thy judgements down.
> Dry up their arms, who vex thy spouse,
> And take the glory of thy house
> To deck their own.

But now there is a more buoyant hope that the visible church may be guided by 'watchful spirits' and the rents in its fabric repaired, so that 'like true sheep, all in one fold / We may be fed, and one minde hold'. The Church to which Vaughan dedicated his completed body of divine poetry at the end of September 1654 was the faithful worshipping community that was being tested in the fire of war and persecution and would survive to be restored to its true place in the house of God in a future that is imagined as already accomplished in the prophetic tense of the poem's closing line:

> So shall we know in war and peace
> Thy service to be our sole ease,
> With prostrate souls adoring thee,
> Who turn'd our sad captivity!

While he was awaiting this delivery, Henry Vaughan moved on from poetry to medicine as another way of being 'useful' to his community; but for five years, he had laboured alongside, if not in direct collusion with, many others at the task of sustaining communion with those for whom he had prayed in the same valedictory poem:

> Then give thy saints
> That faithful zeal, which neither faints
> Nor wildly burns, but meekly still
> Dares own the truth, and shew the ill.[70]

70 *HV Works*, pp. 631–32.

As the poetic heir to George Herbert, he had bravely completed his own contribution in verse and prose to the survivalist project by standing up for the outlawed Church of England and exposing those who were abusing it.

PART TWO

Literary Practices

CHAPTER SIX

Henry Vaughan and the Art of Allusion

I

During the 1930s, when professional academic critics set about defining the characteristics and assessing the achievement of Henry Vaughan's poetry, their attention was drawn to a disconcerting feature of his poetic practice. George Williamson, in *The Donne Tradition* (1930), noted that the poems in his first volume 'were apparently for the most part inspired by Donne's love lyrics, to which they pay the homage of imitation', and went on to observe of the later religious poetry, 'Vaughan seems to have borrowed from the subject-matter of other poets; especially has he leaned upon Herbert in the titles and themes of his poems.'[1] In 1934, Joan Bennett opened the chapter on Vaughan in her *Four Metaphysical Poets* with the following summary of his development:

> Vaughan was fascinated by the phrases of other poets. This is not unusual in a young poet; but the habit of borrowing continued with Vaughan to the end. At first his borrowings strike no roots, they are picked blossoms that have caught his fancy, later they are young shoots that bloom anew in his poems.

She added that 'the most obvious debts' in the two secular volumes 'are to Donne and Habington' and that in *Silex Scintillans* he

---

1 George Williamson, *The Donne Tradition: A Study in English Poetry from Donne to the Death of Cowley* [1930] (New York: Noonday Press, 1958), pp. 125, 128.

'rehandles Herbert's themes, borrows his phrases, copies his metrical effects, repeats his titles and yet now the poem is his own'.[2] Two years later, Helen White registered her bemusement at the extent to which 'he borrowed figures, ideas, images, even phrases' from Herbert.[3]

It was not long before the inevitable accusation was made, in an article with the uncompromising subtitle 'A Study in Plagiarism'. Jean Robertson was mainly concerned with the pillaging of Owen Felltham's *Resolves* by a string of seventeenth-century essayists and pamphleteers, but the first culprit to be indicted was Vaughan, whose borrowings of words and ideas had been duly registered in the notes of L.C. Martin's edition. 'Only once,' she declares, 'does Vaughan announce that he is quoting, or pay any sort of tribute to Felltham (though not by name)',[4] and that is when he is preparing to lift an entire paragraph for use in his preface to *Silex Scintillans* and acknowledges that it was 'wisely considered, and piously said by one, *That he would read no idle books*'.[5] Robertson's own addition to the charge sheet is a passage from the translation of one of Ovid's *De Ponto* elegies in *Olor Iscanus*, which she traces to two different places in Felltham's work. Even longer passages were appropriated from Felltham in the translations of Juvenal's tenth satire (ll. 454–59) and two of the poems by Boethius from *The Consolation of Philosophy*.[6]

Such close and extensive borrowing as this is exceptional, but Vaughan's habit of taking over material from other texts has continued to attract unfavourable comment, even by those who recognize his unique gifts as a poet. Frank Kermode argues that when 'the necessary fusion of the alien matter and the personal meditative continuum' is effected, Vaughan produces one of those 'brilliant moments' that are the hallmark of his poetry, but when this fusion does not take place, 'there is left only the shabbiness of plagiarism';

---

2 Quoted from the later expanded version of Bennett's *Five Metaphysical Poets*, 3rd edn. (Cambridge: Cambridge University Press, 1964) p. 71.

3 Helen C. White, *The Metaphysical Poets: A Study in Religious Experience* [1936] quoted from Collier Books edition (London: Collier-Macmillan, 1962), p. 246.

4 Jean Robertson, 'The Use Made of Owen Felltham's "Resolves": A Study in Plagiarism', *Modern Language Review*, 39 (1944), 109.

5 *HV Works*, pp. 556–57.

6 *HV Works*, pp. 38–39, 221, 221–22. For the sources, see the notes on 221:1–6 and 221:1–15 in *HV Works*, p. 1043.

and Michael Bird regards many of Vaughan's 'simple magpie thefts' as an indication that 'he never outgrew the imitative need that binds Herbert's poetry (and before that Randolph's, Donne's and others) so closely to his own'.[7]

The charge of plagiarism is unavoidable in the case of the lengthy extracts lifted from Felltham's *Resolves* in the translations, but many of the instances of indebtedness recorded by Martin and other editors are in a different category. The range of terms used by critics to describe them hints at the nature of the critical problem: 'homage', 'borrowings', 'debts', 'echoes', 'imitation'. Vaughan's complex poetic relationship with George Herbert demands separate treatment and will be reserved for the next chapter, but, for the moment, a gathering of examples from the secular volumes, *Poems* (1646) and *Olor Iscanus* (1651), will provide a clearer picture of his early practice and help to establish some parameters for discussing this central feature of his work.

II

Vaughan's 'magpie' habit can be illustrated initially by his frequent borrowings from Thomas Randolph. The following are a representative sample: in 'To Amoret Weeping', the couplet 'I should perhaps eate Orphans, and sucke up / A dozen distrest widowes in one Cup' is adapted from 'Noe widdowe's curse caters a dish of mine, / I drinke no teares of Orphans in my wine'; a couplet in 'An Elegy' – 'I courted Angels from those upper joyes, / And made them leave their spheres to heare thy voice' – is elaborated from the single line, 'And call down Angels from their glorious Spheare'; and a tribute to Mr R. Hall contains an almost word-for-word theft from one of Randolph's elegies.[8] Furthermore, a simile in 'An Elegie on the death

---

7   Frank Kermode, 'The Private Imagery of Henry Vaughan', *Review of English Studies*, new series, 1 (1950), 208; Michael Bird, 'Nowhere but in the Dark: On the Poetry of Henry Vaughan', *English*, 33 (1984), 12, 3.
8   *HV Works*, pp. 23, 19, 195; and Randolph's 'On the Inestimable Content he Injoyes in the Muses', 'On the Death of a Nightingale', and 'An Elegy on the death of ... Sir Rowland Cotton', in *The Poems of Thomas Randolph*, ed. G. Thorn-Drury (London: Frederick Etchells and Hugh Macdonald, 1929), pp. 25, 93, 91.

of Mr. R.W.' – 'As some blind Dial, when the day is done, / Can tell us at mid-night, *There was a Sun*' – adopts both idea and details of expression from Robert Randolph's elegy 'To the Memory of his deare brother': 'And like Sun-dialls to a day that's gone, / Though poore in use, can tell there was a Sunne'; and lines from an encomium on Katherine Philips – 'These Raptures when I first did see / New miracles in Poetrie' – owe their rhythm and wording to the fusion of a commendatory poem in Randolph's *Poems* (1640) ('Blest Spirit, when I first did see / The Genius of thy Poetrie') and Randolph's own elegy on Sir Rowland Cotton ('A new strange miracle, wealth in Poetrie').[9]

William Habington was another important reservoir of material for Vaughan in his secular poems. For example, the closing lines of 'To my Ingenuous Friend, R.W.' – 'So they that did of these discusse, / Shall find their fables true in us' – were condensed from the final stanza of 'To Castara':

> So they whose wisdome did discusse
> Of these as fictions: shall in us
> Finde, they were more then fabulous.[10]

Other debts to *Castara*, which appeared in three editions from 1634 to 1640, include the phrases 'Eloquent silence' and 'loath'd nothing' in 'The Charnel-house', a single line in 'To the River Isca', and the reworking of 'that path / Which none but some sad Fairy beaten hath' into 'that sad path and seat / Which none but light-heeld *Nymphs* and *Fairies* beat' in 'Monsieur Gombauld'.[11]

Two of the 'Amoret' poems are related in more complex ways to the following stanzas from 'A Valediction: forbidding Mourning' by John Donne:

> Dull sublunary lovers' love
> (Whose soul is sense) cannot admit

---

9 *HV Works*, pp. 198, 186; *Poems of Thomas Randolph*, pp. 5, 89.
10 *HV Works*, p. 13; *The Poems of William Habington*, ed. Kenneth Allott (Liverpool: Liverpool University Press, 1969), p. 15.
11 *HV Works*, pp. 175–76, 173, 183; see 'To a Tombe', 'Elegie, 8', 'His Muse speakes to him', and 'To the Honourable my much honoured friend, R.B. Esquire' in *Poems of Habington*, pp. 71, 111, 73, 17.

> Absence, because it doth remove
>   Those things which elemented it.
>
> But we by a love, so much refined,
>   That our selves know not what it is,
> Inter-assured of the mind,
>   Care less, eyes, lips, and hands to miss.[12]

The first of these stanzas is mined in the final couplets of 'To Amoret gone from him':

> If Creatures then that have no sence,
> But the loose tye of influence,
> (Though fate, and time each day remove
> Those things that element their love)
> At such vast distance can agree,
>   Why, *Amoret*, why should not wee.[13]

Vaughan picks up both image and phrasing from 'Those things which elemented it' in his fourth line, copies the rhyming of 'love' and 'remove', turns the limitations of those whose 'soul is sense' into the even more limited creatures that 'have no sence' to suit his own argument in which 'distance' replaces the acoustically similar 'absence'. In the third and fourth stanzas of 'To Amoret, of the difference 'twixt him, and other Lovers, and what true Love is', he draws upon both of Donne's stanzas for images, words, rhymes, and ideas:

> Just so base, Sublunarie Lovers hearts
>   Fed on loose prophane desires,
>   May for an Eye,
>   Or face comply:
> But those removed, they will as soone depart,
>   And shew their Art,
>   And painted fires.

---

12 *John Donne: The Complete English Poems*, ed. A.J. Smith (Harmondsworth: Penguin Books, 1971), p. 84.
13 *HV Works*, pp. 17–18.

> Whil'st I by pow'rfull Love, so much refin'd,
> That my absent soule the same is,
> Carelesse to misse,
> A glaunce or kisse,
> Can with those Elements of lust and sence,
> Freely dispence,
> And court the mind.[14]

Although worked into a different stanza form, the rhymes of refined/mind and is/miss are adopted from Donne, as are the conceits of the 'absent soule', the 'Elements' feeding desires in the hearts of 'Sublunarie Lovers' that depart when they are 'removed', and the love 'so much refin'd' that courts 'the mind' and is 'Carelesse to misse' physical contact with the beloved.

The same two stanzas highlight a more perplexing aspect of Vaughan's intertextual methods. They obviously share a common source with the opening of Habington's 'To the World. The Perfection of Love':

> Yet are we so by love refin'd,
> From impure drosse we are all mind.
> Death could not more have conquer'd sence.
>
> How suddenly those flames expire
>   Which scorch our clay?
> *Prometheus*-like when we steale fire
> From heaven 'tis endlesse and intire
> It may know age, but not decay.[15]

Vaughan must have been aware that Habington had preceded him in copying the celebration of love's refining power from Donne; and the imagery of the first three lines, together with the image of expiring 'flames' in the next two, probably generated the extended conceit of the birth and death of a shooting star in the second stanza of his own poem, upon which his subsequent contrast between 'true Love' and the 'painted fires' of 'Sublunarie Lovers' is built:

14 *HV Works*, p. 22.
15 *Poems of Habington*, p. 49.

>They shoot their tinsill beames, and vanities,
>   Thredding with those false fires their way;
>   But as you stay,
>   And see them stray,
>You loose the flaming track, and subt'ly they
>   Languish away,
>   And cheate your Eyes.

Having described in stanza 1 how 'spurious flames suckt up from slime, and earth' – perhaps suggested by Habington's 'impure drosse' – soon return to 'their first, low birth', he charts their course across the evening sky until they fade from sight. The flames that 'expire', and the fire stolen from heaven that does 'not decay' in Habington's next conceit, may have prompted Vaughan's subsequent adaptation of Donne's contrast between merely sensual lovers and lovers united in mind and soul. And he may also have been recalling yet another echo of Donne's poem in Habington's volume: 'Tis no dull Sublunary flame / Burnes in her heart and mine'.[16] Something much more sophisticated than 'magpie' activity or simple plagiarism is going on in this interplay between Vaughan's text and the poetry of both Donne and Habington.

Although Felltham, Randolph, Habington, and Donne are the sources most often cited by the editors of Vaughan's secular poems, borrowings great or small – some more convincing than others – have been traced to the work of Michael Drayton, William Shakespeare, Ben Jonson, William Browne, Francis Beaumont, Thomas Carew, Sir John Suckling, John Cleveland, William Cartwright, Sir John Denham, and Sir William Davenant. Philip Macon Cheek has drawn up a similar catalogue of Vaughan's indebtedness to Latin authors – classical, medieval, and early modern – who 'influenced deeply his secular poetry and his prose, forming, indeed, the essential basis and fabric of much of it'. He demonstrates that Vaughan was 'very fond of inserting quotations into his works' and that 'in his own compositions he frequently echoed ideas, lines or phrases which had appealed to his fancy'. Even in *The Mount of Olives*, which is 'an elaborate tapestry of quotations', Catullus and Petronius 'stand side by side' with phrases from the Bible. Among the long train of classical authors that make an appearance in his

---

16 See 'The Harmony of Love', in *Poems of Habington*, p. 92.

work, including Persius, Juvenal, Lucan, Ovid, Plautus, Cicero, Livy, and Pliny, Cheek identifies Virgil and Horace as two of 'his favourites'. He concludes that Vaughan's 'extensive familiarity with Latin literature and thought from classical antiquity down to his own day' found literary expression both 'in his varied translations from Latin authors [...] and in the Latin influence on much of his secular poetry'.[17]

III

The foregoing sketch of the breadth and variety of Vaughan's use of other men's literary texts in his secular volumes poses a problem about the appropriate terminology for discussing his derivative practice and its reception. A more discriminating critical vocabulary is clearly needed to describe a poetic method that lies between direct 'quotation' (like many of the attributed extracts from Latin authors) at one end of a spectrum and 'plagiarism' (like the passages taken over without acknowledgement in some of the verse translations) at the other. 'Imitation' was the term most commonly used in the seventeenth century to describe the process of adoption and adaptation of ideas, images, and phrases exemplified by Vaughan's debts to Randolph, Donne, Habington, Horace, and the rest. Ben Jonson defined it as the poet's ability 'to convert the substance, or riches of another poet, to his own use [...] to draw forth out of the best, and choicest flowers, with the bee, and turn all into honey, work it into one relish, and savour'. Along with 'a goodness of natural wit' and 'exercise of those parts', he considered it to be one of the requisites of the successful poet.[18] During his time at Llangattock with Matthew Herbert and later at Oxford, Vaughan would have begun to master this art by undertaking the 'loose translation or textual glossing' of classical models, first in Latin and later in English, in the manner outlined by Thomas Calhoun: 'The writer was to retain select phrases and the overall structure of

17 Philip Macon Cheek, 'The Latin Element in Henry Vaughan', *Studies in Philology*, 44 (1947), 69, 77, 79, 88.
18 *Ben Jonson: The Complete Poems*, ed. George Parfitt (Harmondsworth: Penguin Books, 1975), pp. 446–48.

the original, while varying from the model in diction, subject and implication.'[19]

Some of the borrowings cited earlier provide a glimpse of Vaughan's method of composing by imitation of specific models. 'An Elegie on the death of Mr. R.W.' contains not only the adaptation of the sun-dial image from Robert Randolph's memorial to his brother, but also a longer passage (ll. 25–32) based upon ideas and images derived from the elegy 'upon The Honourable Henry Cambell' in *Castara*. Habington's poem begins with a conceit of the 'false Arithmaticke' by which Time can give 'but twenty yeares account' of Cambell's life whereas calculating his age by his 'vertues' would have him out-living Methuselah.[20] This is the basis for Vaughan's similar argument that although the years of R.W. 'could not be summ'd (alas!) / To a full *score*', he had 'purchas'd more of man' in 'so short a span' than those 'worthless livers' who have 'quite outgone their own *Arithmetick*'.[21] In the other elegy in *Olor Iscanus,* the statement that there is no need for tears to flow because Mr. R. Hall's honour 'must / Confin'd to those cold reliques sadly sit / In the same Cell an obscure Anchorite' is only slightly reworked from a passage in the poem by Robert Randolph that he had already drawn upon for his tribute to Mr. R.W.; and his other main debt is to 'An Elegy on the death of Sir Rowland Cotton' by Thomas Randolph himself.[22] Taken all together, these instances of imitation suggest that Vaughan consulted other memorials to the dead in volumes that he had to hand before embarking upon his own elegies. The lifting of phrases from Habington's 'To a Tomb' and from the eighth of his elegies to George Talbot (which is a meditation on the vault where his body lies) in 'The Charnel-house', and from a commendatory poem to Randolph for his own commendation of Katherine Philips, smacks of the same practice of trawling through suitable models for ideas and images. He may even have had his source volumes open beside him as he composed his verses.

A different perspective on some of the examples assembled from the secular poems may be opened up by invoking a critical

---

19 Thomas O. Calhoun, *Henry Vaughan: The Achievement of Silex Scintillans* (Newark, DE: University of Delaware Press, 1981), p. 68.
20 *Poems of Habington*, p. 87.
21 *HV Works*, p. 185.
22 *HV Works*, p. 193; and see *Poems of Randolph*, pp. 2, 90.

term that takes into account not only the phenomenon but also the literary purpose and effect of borrowing involved in imitation. The word 'allusion', meaning 'an implied, indirect, or passing reference to a person or thing', goes back at least to the early seventeenth century (*OED* 1. 1612). Its subsequent specialization as a term for a particular literary device can be traced in the development of the cognate verb 'allude'. The first recorded example of the meaning 'To make an oblique or indirect reference to' is dated 1531 (*OED* 2.a). An important new feature can be seen emerging in definitions of its use in the seventeenth century: 'to have fanciful or figurative reference to' (*OED* 3.b 1638, 1648, 1665) and 'to make a play on words' (*OED* 5.a 1607, 1634). Although often used interchangeably, there is a significant shade of difference between alluding and referring, which is only partly to do with the 'indirect' or 'passing' nature of an allusion. More important is its derivation from the Latin verb 'ludere' (to play), which comes to the fore in the seventeenth-century modification of its referential function — by play of words or fancy — and implies a literary rather than a discursive context. The entry in a twentieth-century glossary spells out the range of reference embraced by the term in critical discourse and seems to remove the restriction to that which is 'indirect or implied': 'Allusion in a literary text is a reference, explicit or indirect, to a well-known person, place, or event, or to another literary work or passage.'[23] What this formulation leaves out is the engagement of two participants in the game of allusion — the writer and the reader. According to modern semantic theory, a literary allusion is not a simple denotative reference because it 'directs our attention to one or more attributes of the source text' and 'these attributes or associated meanings are "recoverable" for the given audience — that is, they are part of the source text's connotation, which is public knowledge for a common cultural group'. For an allusion to contribute successfully to the meaning and effect of a literary text, therefore, 'the referent must be recognized and the relevant aspects of its connotation determined and applied' — that is, determined by the writer and applied by the reader.[24] This means that even the

---

23 M.H. Abrams, *A Glossary of Literary Terms*, 5th edn. (New York: Holt, Rinehart and Winston, 1985), p. 8.
24 Carmela Perri, 'On Alluding', *Poetics*, 7 (1978), 296, 292. An *OED* example from 1612 includes a qualifying phrase — 'as supposing a full knowing reader'

'explicit' reference apparently sanctioned by the glossary definition must activate *by implication* whatever connotations are 'relevant' to the context in which it is made. For instance, when Vaughan names 'Great *BEN*' and '*Randolph*' in 'To my Ingenuous Friend, R.W.', he has in mind a coterie of Caroline readers, whose response is 'determined' by a familiarity with Jonson's poem, 'An Epistle answering to One that Asked to be Sealed of the Tribe of Ben'.[25] A more personal case of the poet's expectation that an allusion will be 'applied' is the translation of Horace's description of an ice-bound countryside as the opening gambit in 'To my worthy friend Master T. Lewes'. A neighbour in the Usk valley, who was evicted from his rectory at Llanfigan in 1650, Thomas Lewes would have appreciated an invitation that began by alluding to a favourite poet and went on to offer the consolation of companionship and shared literary interests in difficult times:

> Let us meet then! And while this world
> In wild *Excentricks* now is hurld,
> Keep wee, like nature, the same *Key*,
> And walk in our forefathers way.[26]

The 'ancient way' Vaughan strove to preserve against the forces that were hurling his world off-course had strong cultural as well as religious connotations and his art of allusion was a means of activating them.

The condition that writer and reader belong to a community of mutual knowledge and interests is significant for the wider critical assessment of Vaughan's borrowings – especially in the light of a distinction made by Christopher Ricks: 'allusion is posited upon our calling the earlier work into play, whereas the one thing that plagiarism hopes is that the earlier work will not enter our heads'.[27] The line lifted word for word from Habington in 'To the River Isca' is a simple test case. It is part of Vaughan's list of rivers that have

---

 – in its use of the word 'allusion'. For a similar view, see William Irwin, 'What is an Allusion?', *The Journal of Aesthetics and Art Criticism*, 59 (2001), 287–97.
25 See *HV Works*, p. 12 and *Jonson: Complete Poems*, pp. 191–93.
26 *HV Works*, p. 197.
27 Christopher Ricks, *Allusion to the Poets* (Oxford: Oxford University Press, 2002), pp. 231–32.

been immortalized by poets whom he will emulate in 'redeeming' his native stream 'from *oblivious night*':

> Soft *Petrarch* (thaw'd by *Laura*'s flames) did weep
> On *Tybers* banks, when she (*proud fair!*) cou'd sleep;
> *Mosella* boasts *Ausonius*, and the *Thames*
> Doth murmure *SIDNEYS* Stella to her *streams*,
> While *Severn* swoln with *Joy* and *sorrow*, wears
> *Castara*'s smiles mixt with fair *Sabrin*'s tears.[28]

Habington's muse promises that Castara's name will be written in the 'Register of Fame' along with the poetic mistresses associated with a similar roll call of rivers famous in song:

> And though Imperiall *Tiber* boast alone
> *Ovids Corinna,* and to *Arn* is knowne
> But *Petrarchs Laura*; while our famous Thames
> Doth murmur *Sydneyes Stella* to her streames.
> Yet hast thou *Severne* left, and she can bring
> As many quires of Swans, as they to sing
> Thy glorious love: Which living shall by thee
> The onely Sov'raigne of those waters be.[29]

Castara's connection with the River Severn is mentioned in the couplet that immediately follows the 'stolen' line in Vaughan's poem, prompting recognition by members of the cultural group familiar with the source poem. More is at issue here than a simple homage to an admired poet, however, since Vaughan's allusion is also intended to bring to mind the relevance of Habington's 'many quires of Swans' to the poem that opens the volume in which he assumes the title of the Swan of Usk. Just as Habington has added himself to the list of celebrated poets by his association with a local river, so Vaughan stakes his claim to be admitted to their ranks.

Evidence that Vaughan is deliberately calling an earlier work 'into play' can be found in the epistle 'To all Ingenious Lovers of POESIE', which introduces his first collection of poetry and characterizes the love poetry that comprises most of the first half of the

---

28 *HV Works*, p. 173.
29 *Poems of Habington*, p. 73.

volume in terms that allude unmistakeably (for his chosen audience) to the author's preface in *Castara*: '*You have here a* Flame, *bright only in its owne* Innocence [...] *the fire at highest is but* Platonick.'[30] Habington had introduced his love poems with much the same disclaimer: 'In all those flames in which I burnt, I never felt a wanton heate; nor was my invention ever sinister from the straite way of chastity.'[31] Having positioned his readers as devotees of the coterie verse he has taken as his model, Vaughan can be confident that many of his allusions to the poems of Randolph (directly invoked in the first poem) and other Sons of Ben will be recognized and that his (belated) bid for a place in their company will be endorsed. Similarly, the explicit references to Sir Philip Sidney and *Castara*, the quotation of a line from Habington, and the adaptation of a passage from one of William Browne's pastoral songs in the first poem of the 1651 volume are all intended to alert readers to further allusions and to cement the author's place in a cultural tradition that stretches back to earlier generations of English poets and beyond. This clarifies the strategy of alluding to Donne's 'A Valediction: forbidding Mourning' by way of allusions to the same source in the work of Habington. The demonstration that, as a new poet, he stands at two removes from Donne's seminal love poem is a way of establishing himself as the next inheritor of a poetic culture that had flourished in the first half of the seventeenth century and was now under threat from the same forces that had dismantled the Church of England and challenged the political authority of the king.

The belief that Vaughan's occasional allusions to Donne's poetry are functional – not merely the random plucking of 'blossoms that have caught his fancy' or a misguided attempt to emulate his 'metaphysical' manner – finds support in James Simmonds's chapter-long demonstration that his initial conception and practice of the art of poetry was based on 'the traditional, classical principles propagated by Jonson in defiance of the new fashion for "strong-lined" verse of which Donne's is the most conspicuous example'.[32]

---

30 *HV Works*, p. 11.
31 *Poems of Habington*, p. 5.
32 James D. Simmonds, *Masques of God: Form and Theme in the Poetry of Henry Vaughan* (Pittsburgh, PA: University of Pittsburgh Press, 1972), p. 23. For Vaughan as a disciple of Jonson, see John T. Shawcross's argument that the thirteen original poems in the 1646 volume were inspired by Jonsonian

In 'To his Ingenuous Friend, R.W.', the poem that clears the ground for his courtship of Amoret, he sets up the Donne who wrote 'Hope not for mind in women', in 'Love's Alchemy', as a foil to the compatibility of mind between male friends: in the very first words – 'When we are dead' – he echoes the opening of 'The Damp', in which a contest between a mistress's disdain and his own male constancy ends with the carnal admission that 'Naked you have the odds of any man'; and the lover's 'device' in 'The Relic' that being buried with a bracelet of his beloved's hair will 'make their souls, at the last busy day, / Meet at this grave, and make a little stay' is appropriated to express the 'ancient love' that binds together R.W.'s 'genius' and the poet's 'mind':

> Wee'le beg the world would be so kinde,
> To give's one grave, as wee'de one minde;
> There (as the wiser few suspect,
> That spirits after death affect)
> Our soules shall meet …[33]

'A Song to Amoret' begins with an allusion to Donne's fantasy of haunting the mistress responsible for his death when she lies shivering in the 'worse arms' of a new lover:

> If I were dead, and in my place,
>   Some fresher youth design'd
> To warme thee with new fires, and grace
>   Those Armes I left behind …[34]

By invoking the angry sexual revenge poem, 'The Apparition', in which Donne threatens to return from beyond the grave, Vaughan establishes a contrast between the too earthly orientation of Amoret and 'the true resolved minde' of the less sexually preoccupied

---

principles and designed to subvert Donne's amatory verse ('Vaughan's "Amoret" Poems: A Jonsonian Sequence', in *Classic and Cavalier: Essays on Jonson and the Sons of Ben*, ed. Claude J. Summers and Ted-Larry Pebworth (Pittsburgh, PA: University of Pittsburgh Press, 1982), pp. 193–214).

33 *HV Poems*, p. 12. For the Donne poems cited, see *Donne: Complete English Poems*, pp. 65, 51, 75–76.

34 *HV Poems*, p. 18.

speaker.[35] And the extended analogy derived (via Habington) from Donne's exploration of the difference between 'sublunary' and 'refined' love in 'To Amoret, of the difference 'twixt him, and other Lovers' prepares the way for the celebration of chaste mutual love in 'To Amoret Weeping' (which contains verbal echoes of Habington's 'To Castara, Weeping') and the resolution of the courtship in betrothal or marriage in the concluding poem, 'Upon the Priorie Grove'.

IV

If Vaughan's many allusions to Donne have sometimes been misunderstood as an act of homage or evidence of poetic discipleship, the role of another major poet as an influence on his early poetry and an antagonist in his later work has been largely overlooked. A few more or less tentative attempts have been made to link the Welsh royalist poet and defender of Prayer Book worship with the Puritan poet and polemicist John Milton. Hutchinson compared the affectionate pastoral naming of Matthew Herbert as 'old *Amphion*' in 'Daphnis. An Elegiac Eclogue' with the reference to a Cambridge tutor as 'old *Damaetas*' in 'Lycidas'; Kenneth Friedenreich noted a similarity between the rhetorical stances adopted in the closing section of 'Il Penseroso' and the evocation of an idealized landscape that will inspire prophetic song in 'To the River Isca'; and Jonathan Post made a claim for Milton's presence in 'Upon the Priorie Grove, His usuall Retyrement' in a passage 'strongly reminiscent of the beginning of "L'Allegro"'.[36] As long ago as 1914, Louise Guiney had confidently affirmed that Vaughan had been 'from the first considerably preoccupied with his greatest contemporary'.[37] In support of this contention, she cited 'The Shepheards' (from the 1650 *Silex Scintillans*) and the earlier poems on the Priory Grove and the River Isca, and offered, by way of substantiating detail, Vaughan's

---

35 See *Donne; Complete English Poems*, pp. 42–43.
36 *Life*, p. 28; Kenneth Friedenreich, *Henry Vaughan*, Twayne's English Authors (Boston, MA: G.K. Hall, 1978), p. 88; Jonathan F.S. Post, *Henry Vaughan: The Unfolding Vision* (Princeton, NJ: Princeton University Press, 1982), p. 18.
37 See Louise Imogen Guiney, 'Milton and Vaughan', *The Quarterly Review*, 220 (1914), 355.

double compliment to Habington and the author of *Comus* in his description of the Severn wearing '*Castara's* smiles mixt with fair *Sabrin*'s tears'. He may, indeed, have expected informed readers to recognize Sabrina as the 'gentle nymph' who is conjured from the river by song in Milton's masque (ll. 823–900).[38]

This raises the question of when and in what texts Vaughan had come across the early poetry of Milton. He may have first become acquainted with *A Masque Presented in Ludlow Castle* [*Comus*] in the version seen into print by Henry Lawes in 1637 and 'Lycidas' was first published in 1638 in *Justa Eduardo King Naufrago*, the collection of Cambridge elegies on the death of Milton's fellow student, Edward King. He might have encountered these volumes during his time in Oxford, but it is more likely that they came to his attention in London at the beginning of the 1640s, when he was in touch with the royalist cultural circles in which Lawes was a prominent figure. Lawes supplied the music for Milton's Ludlow masque and, despite the subsequent divergence of their political paths, remained on good terms with the poet. Milton's sonnet in praise of the composer is dated 9 February 1646. For more than two decades, lyrics by most of the Court and Cavalier poets, including Carew, Waller, Suckling, Herrick, Cartwright, and Lovelace, were set to music by Lawes.[39] Other early poems by Milton to which allusions have been traced were not published until the 1645 volume, *Poems of Mr John Milton*. Vaughan may not have been aware that the author of 'L'Allegro' and 'Il Penseroso', *Comus*, and 'Lycidas' had already gone into print as a champion of radical church reform by the time he was imitating these pastoral poems in his own verse, although there are indications of his later familiarity with some of Milton's prose works.

Guiney's case can be strengthened by two more probable allusions to the Ludlow masque, which may have engaged the Welsh poet's imagination because it celebrated his own 'old, and haughty nation proud in arms' (l. 33). Verbal echoes, together with a striking similarity of subject matter, suggest that a couplet from 'To the River

---

38 For *Comus* and 'Lycidas' see *John Milton*, ed. Stephen Orgel and Jonathan Goldberg, The Oxford Authors (Oxford: Oxford University Press, 1990), pp. 39–71. Line numbers for quotations are given in the text.

39 See Ian Spink, *Henry Lawes: Cavalier Songwriter* (Oxford: Oxford University Press, 2000), pp. 23–62.

Isca' – 'Hence *th' Auncients* say, That, from this *sickly aire* / They passe to *Regions* more *refin'd* and *faire*' – was condensed from the Attendant Spirit's opening description of the 'regions mild of calm and serene air, / Above the smoke and stir of this dim spot, / Which men call earth' (ll. 4–6). It also seems likely that Comus's 'dazzling spells', which are 'Of power to cheat the eye with blear illusion, / And give it false presentments' (ll. 154–56), were in Vaughan's mind when he elaborated the image of the deceptive 'tinsill beames' and 'flaming track' of meteors that 'cheate your Eyes' in 'To Amoret, of the difference 'twixt him and other Lovers'.[40] The elevation of the drowned poet-priest to the position of 'genius of the shore' (l. 183) in 'Lycidas' may be glanced at in the conceit in 'To the River *Isca*' that *'Poets* (like *Angels*)' hallow the place in which they 'once appear' and so give rise to the 'aged faith, *That there their Genii live'*.[41] The idea of the dead poet becoming a local protective deity is part of the common classical inheritance of both writers, but the two poems are closely linked by their association with rivers and seas; and the conjunction of poets, angels, and genii in Vaughan's lines may owe something to the connection of Lycidas with the archangel of St Michael's Mount and the 'solemn troops' of 'saints above' (ll. 178–79).

More significant than Guiney's thinly supported case for Vaughan's indebtedness to Milton's early poetry is her contention that his initial admiration gave way to an antipathy towards a writer who came to symbolize for him the forces that had destroyed the church and executed the king. Indeed, as early as 1649 (if my belief that the pastoral dialogue, 'Daphnis', was originally drafted as an elegy for Charles I is correct), the author of *The Tenure of Kings and Magistrates* and *Eikonoklastes* was among those targeted in the epitaph that one of the mourning shepherds proposes for the murdered monarch: 'write o're his Hearse / For false, foul Prose-men this fair Truth in Verse' (ll. 95–96).[42] And an earlier exchange

---

40 See *HV Works*, pp. 173, 22.
41 *HV Works*, p. 173.
42 For the text of 'Daphnis', see *HV Works*, pp. 785–90; for my dating and interpretation of the poem, see '"Daphnis. An Elegiac Eclogue" by Henry Vaughan', *Durham University Journal*, new series, 36 (1974), 25–40. For a dissenting view, which sees the poem as an elegy for Thomas Vaughan written in 1666, see Graeme J. Watson, 'Political Change and Continuity of Vision in

between Damon and Menalcas can be seen as a comment on the man who was known to have been reaping the grimly appropriate harvest of blindness for his justification of the trial and execution of a king:

> *Men.* And is't not just to leave those to the night,
> That madly hate, and persecute the light?
> [............................]
> *Da.* The punishment still manifests the Sin,
> As outward signs shew the disease within. (ll. 35–40)

Milton had 'first noticed his sight growing weak and dull' as early as 1644 and by 1650 it was already a commonplace among royalist propagandists that this was a divine judgement on the man who had defended regicide with his pen.[43] Vaughan's potential readers would have had no difficulty in interpreting blindness as an outward sign of an inward disease.

For her part, Guiney was certain that there was an allusion to Milton in 'The Agreement', a poetic meditation on the Bible in the augmented edition of *Silex Scintillans*:

> Most modern books are blots on thee,
> Their doctrine chaff and windy fits:
> Darken'd along, as their scribes be,
> With those foul storms, when they were writ;
> While the man's zeal lays out and blends
> Onely self-worship and self-ends.[44]

A knowing reader in 1655 would have recognized how aptly this applied to the misguided zeal of a writer who had forfeited his eyesight in acting as scribe to those whose empty doctrines had brought darkness upon the land. Guiney also believed that she had uncovered an awareness of the prose pamphlets in the 'Authors Preface', in which Vaughan castigates the '*malady*' of '*vitious verse* and '*lascivious fictions*', just as Milton had once poured scorn upon

---

Henry Vaughan's "Daphnis. An Elegiac Eclogue"', *Studies in Philology*, 83 (1986), 158–81.

43 See William Riley Parker, *Milton: A Biography*, 2 vols. (Oxford: Clarendon Press, 1986), Vol. I, pp. 286, 389, 430.

44 *HV Works*, pp. 617–18. See Guiney, 'Milton and Vaughan', 363–64.

'the writings and interludes of libidinous and ignorant poetasters'.[45] While he was anxious to adopt the traditional moral stance of 'persons of eminent piety and learning', he was also concerned to dissociate himself from 'the seditious and *Schismatical*' – men like William Prynne and Milton, with whom he refused to 'meddle' – who might share his views on this particular issue. And when he went on to attack authors who had been 'so irreverendly bold, as to dash *Scriptures*, and the *sacred Relatives* of *God* with their impious conceits' and to lament that 'some of those desperate *adventurers* may (I think) be reckoned amongst the principal or most learned Writers of *English verse*', Guiney was sure that Vaughan 'knew very well, as we know, that there was but one "principal or most learned" writer living in England in 1654, who could be accused of founding his own novel views upon Bible texts'.[46] The implication of Vaughan's careful phrasing is that Milton was pre-eminent among those unspecified English poets whom he had once admired but who have since betrayed their calling by misusing the words of the Bible in a bad cause during the propaganda wars of the past decade.

Hutchinson was later to compare Milton's statement in 1642 'that he who would not be frustrate of his hope to write well hereafter in laudable things, ought himself to be a true poem' with Vaughan's similar declaration towards the end of the 1654 preface that in order to excel in 'holy writing' a man must 'strive (by all means) for *perfection* and true *holyness* [...] and then he will be able to write (with *Hierotheus* and holy *Herbert*) A *true Hymn*'.[47] What he failed to consider is the possibility that the allusion to Herbert might have had greater polemical impact if it were read as a conscious rebuke to another poet who, by pursuing 'impious conceits' and throwing in his lot with a rabble of 'desperate *adventurers*', had wilfully abandoned his own stated intention of being a 'true poem' and writing well.

The passage that Vaughan brings into play most effectively against its author is Milton's passionate argument for the living power of the printed word in *Areopgatica*:

45 *The Reason of Church Government* (1642), in *John Milton*, p. 171.
46 Guiney, 'Milton and Vaughan', 362. For the quotations from the 1654 preface, see *HV Works*, pp. 556–57.
47 See *Life*, pp. 100–01. For the parallel ideas in Milton and Vaughan, see *An Apology for Smectymnuus*, in *John Milton*, p. 180; and *HV Works*, p. 558.

> for books are not absolutely dead things, but do contain a potency of life in them to be as active as that soul was whose progeny they are; nay, they do preserve as in a vial the purest efficacy and extraction of that living intellect that bred them [...]. a good book is the precious life blood of a master-spirit, embalmed and treasured up on purpose to a life beyond life.⁴⁸

In his attack on the pernicious effects of bad books, Vaughan draws out the negative consequences of this belief:

> These *Vipers* survive their *Parents*, and for many ages after (like *Epidemic* diseases) infect whole Generations, corrupting always and unhallowing the best-gifted S*ouls*, and the most capable V*essels* [...] he that writes *idle books*, makes for himself another *body*, in which he always *lives*, and *sins* (after *death*) as *fast* and *foul*, as ever he did in his *life*.⁴⁹

The logic of Milton's own argument that the author of 'a good book' will enjoy 'a life beyond life' leads inevitably to the corollary that the writer whose words corrupt many will be consigned to '*the blackness of darkness for ever*' – a fate that has already overtaken the promoter and defender of regicide.

If the foregoing speculations carry any force, it is difficult to resist the conclusion that Vaughan's animosity was fuelled less by the simple fact that he and Milton had taken opposing sides in the great political and religious divisions of the age than by anger and dismay that the poet he had once honoured by imitation had betrayed his poetic calling and abused his undoubted gifts to become a 'foul prose-man' in the service of falsehood. The change in his perception of Milton was reflected not only in the shift from imitating to subverting the older writer's texts but also by the later allusions to Milton as a minatory example of a man who had allowed his God-given talent to be corrupted for political ends.

---

48 *John Milton*, pp. 239–40.
49 *HV Works*, pp. 555, 557.

V

Joan Bennett closes her account of Vaughan with the verdict that 'from first to last' he 'laid himself open to the influence of other poets' and Stevie Davies echoes Kermode's assertion that he was essentially 'a bookish poet':

> Vaughan's world was bookbound, its landscapes mountains of text through which fluent rivers of poetry streamed. His mind was compounded of many people's writings; the act of reading brought the ancient world to life and made Moses, Plato and Virgil his contemporaries.[50]

Leaving aside odd instances of near plagiarism, however, when he simply steals other men's words rather than bringing them into creative play, this chapter has sought to confirm the judgement of M.M. Mahood that he 'controls, and is not controlled by, his borrowings'.[51] His use of imitation and allusion tells us a good deal about the kind of reader he had in mind when he was composing his early secular poems; and the radical shift in subject-matter and purpose at the end of the 1640s can be charted in the changing nature of his relationship to the most famous of his literary contemporaries. That shift would take him into areas of experience and expression very different from those of the Jonsonian tradition in which he had begun to practice the art of poetry. The next two chapters will explore his dependence on two new sources of verbal, imaginative, and spiritual inspiration that resulted at times in an extraordinary level of creative intensity.

---

50 Bennett, *Five Metaphysical Poets*, p. 89; Kermode, 'The Private Imagery of Henry Vaughan', 206; Stevie Davies, *Henry Vaughan*, Border Lines Series (Bridgend: Seren, Poetry of Wales Press, 1995), p. 56.

51 Mahood, 'Vaughan: The Symphony of Nature', in *Poetry and Humanism* (London: Jonathan Cape, 1950), p. 270.

CHAPTER SEVEN

Henry Vaughan and George Herbert

I

Henry Lyte first remarked on the 'comfort and instruction' that Henry Vaughan drew from 'the writings of George Herbert' and on his consequent determination 'to make the life and compositions of that holy man his own future models'.[1] From the very beginning of Vaughan scholarship, therefore, there have been two lines of investigation into Herbert's influence on the author of *Silex Scintillans* – as man and as poet – which took their cue also from Vaughan's own statements that the 'holy *life* and *verse*' of the vicar of Bemerton had 'gained many pious *Converts*, (of whom I am the least)' and that his poetic ambition was to 'strive (by all means) for *perfection* and true *holyness*' in order to emulate Herbert and write 'A *true Hymn*'.[2] One line of argument, represented by H.C. Beeching, makes the literary impact of Herbert ancillary to the biographical: 'Vaughan owed to him his religious life, and so the practice of religious poetry'.[3] The other is represented by Frank Kermode, who accepts that 'the most important source of his poetry is the poetry of Herbert' but insists that this influence was entirely literary since Vaughan was always 'a poet with his roots in poetry rather than in

---

1 Silex Scintillans: *Sacred Poems and Private Ejaculations by Henry Vaughan*, ed. Rev. H.F. Lyte (London: Pickering, 1847), p. xxxii.
2 'The Authors Preface To the Following Hymns', *HV Works*, p. 558.
3 *Poems of Henry Vaughan Silurist*, ed. E.K. Chambers with an introduction by Canon Beeching, 2 vols., The Muses' Library (London: George Routledge & Sons, 1896), Vol. I, p. xli.

religious experience'.[4] The debate about the process and causes of Vaughan's 'conversion' has continued, but in this chapter it is the nature of the relationship between the poems in *The Temple* and the poems in *Silex Scintillans* that will be the focus of attention.

It was some time before the full extent of Vaughan's borrowing from Herbert came to light. Alexander Grosart, in the complete works of 1871, denied that the influence of *The Temple* went much beyond 'spiritual quickening, and the gift of gracious feeling'; and the editor of a facsimile reprint of the 1650 *Silex Scintillans* in 1885 rejected Lyte's claim that Herbert provided a significant model for Vaughan's poetry, finding only a few 'resemblances' between the two.[5] It was Louise Guiney who first demonstrated that 'numerous phrases and turns of thought descend from the master to the disciple'.[6] Beeching furthered the enquiry into 'the exact debt that the one poet owes to the other' by quoting several 'thoughts and metaphors simply "conveyed" from the elder poet by the younger' and other passages in which Vaughan employs a borrowed phrase 'with some change of sense, and so honestly makes it his own'.[7] In his 1905 edition of *Silex Scintillans*, Lewis Bettany traced the 'germinal idea[s]' of Vaughan's 'three leading themes' to Herbert and noted that he also took over twenty-eight titles and 'certain favourite expressions'. He considered, however, that 'the really significant features of resemblance between Herbert and Vaughan are to be discovered in that parallelism of phrase and of conceit which can be seen running right through *The Temple* and *Silex Scintillans*'. To supplement the discussion in his introduction, he printed fifty pages of parallel passages in an appendix.[8] Following

---

4 Frank Kermode, 'The Private Imagery of Henry Vaughan', *Review of English Studies*, new series, 1 (1950), 207, 217.
5 *The Works in Verse and Prose Complete of Henry Vaughan, Silurist*, ed. Alexander B. Grosart, 4 vols., The Fuller Worthies' Library (Blackburn, 1871), Vol. II, p. xc; *Silex Scintillans. Being a facsimile of the First Edition, published in 1650*, with an Introduction by the Rev. William Clare (London: Elliot Stock, 1885).
6 Louise Imogen Guiney, *A Little English Gallery* (New York: Harper & Brothers, 1894), pp. 97, 98–101. She noted a dozen instances, from single lines to entire stanzas.
7 *Poems of Henry Vaughan Silurist*, ed. Chambers, Vol. I, pp. xxxv–xxxix.
8 *Silex Scintillans by Henry Vaughan, Silurist*, intro. W.A. Lewis Bettany (London: Gresham Publishing, 1905), pp. xviii–xix, xxxiv–xxxv, 341–91.

the work of these pioneers, the identification of Herbertian sources has been a feature of the editions by L.C. Martin and Alan Rudrum, and the new *Works* of 2018; and surveys of the different kinds of borrowing from *The Temple* have subsequently been undertaken by E.C. Pettet and Mary Ellen Rickey.[9] Jonathan Post emphatically 'places Vaughan's relationship with Herbert at the center' of his study, because 'that relationship was at the center of the Welsh author's poetic life'.[10]

Once established, the fact of Vaughan's indebtedness to Herbert elicited a variety of critical responses, many of them negative or apologetic. Even Guiney was dismayed that 'a certain spirit of conformity and filial piety towards Herbert had betrayed Vaughan into frequent and flagrant imitations', which 'must have been voluntary' and could only be explained away as 'an intention to enforce the same truths in all but the same words'.[11] Bettany's diligence resulted in an uncompromising judgement on 'a parallelism so continuous and so close as to leave the reader no alternative save to regard the younger poet as his elder's deliberate plagiarist'.[12] Echoes of Guiney's uneasy ambivalence have continued to reverberate. For example, D.J. Enright sounded a note of reprehension in his mid-twentieth-century comment that Vaughan's 'borrowings are abundant and unashamed', but acknowledged that he was 'more suggestive, mysterious, than Herbert'.[13] At the start of the twenty-first century, David Reid remained in two minds about this unusual case 'of exclusive and uncritical absorption in another author', which at its best results in 'something entirely his own', but all too often

---

9 See E.C. Pettet, *Of Paradise and Light: A Study of Vaughan's* Silex Scintillans (Cambridge: Cambridge University Press, 1960), pp. 51–70; Mary Ellen Rickey, 'Vaughan, *The Temple*, and Poetic Form', *Studies in Philology*, 59 (1962), 162–70.

10 Jonathan F.S. Post, *Henry Vaughan: The Unfolding Vision* (Princeton, NJ: Princeton University Press, 1982), p. xvii. The book's index reflects a comprehensive approach to Vaughan's imitation of Herbert: pp. 70–77 (general), 77–97 (formalistic), 97–115 (thematic), 116–56 (figural), 156–62 (rhetorical), 186–88 (prophetic).

11 Guiney, *A Little English Gallery*, pp. 95–96.

12 Bettany, *Silex Scintillans*, p. xxxv.

13 D.J. Enright, 'George Herbert and the Devotional Poets', in *The Pelican Guide to English Literature, Volume 3: From Donne to Marvell*, ed. Boris Ford (Harmondsworth: Penguin Books, 1956), pp. 152, 153.

'flattens and conventionalizes' the original.[14] The two critics who have looked most closely at the scope and effects of Vaughan's debt to *The Temple* reach more positive verdicts. Having computed that sixty-odd poems 'contain some Herbert echo', Pettet points out that 'rather more than half carry a single parallel, often a mere phrase', so that simple lists of borrowings can create 'an entirely mistaken impression' of wholesale theft or slavish imitation. Indeed, he maintains that the finest of Vaughan's poems are 'on the whole the ones in which Herbert's presence is least felt'.[15] And for Jonathan Post, who declares that 'no one read Herbert with greater benefit or imagination', the most significant mark of the older poet's 'illuminating presence' in the work of the younger is not the abundance of verbal parallels but the skill of working 'in a smaller, tighter, and more volatile verbal space' – a skill that 'generated fifty-eight different verse forms' in the first part of *Silex Scintillans*. In addition to this crucial lesson in handling poetic structure, Vaughan also reaped 'significant thematic rewards' from 'a close reading of Herbert', not least among them 'the ministerial purpose' carried out in poetic commentaries on 'Scriptural passages and persons' and the art of exploring 'the inner configurations of the Christian life' that were 'simultaneously absorbed and commemorated in the younger writer's echoing songs'.[16]

This preliminary survey of critical attempts to come to terms with Vaughan's widespread borrowing from his great predecessor may be supplemented by a passage written from the perspective of a biographer, for whom life and art are woven inextricably into a single complex pattern:

> Everywhere in *Silex Scintillans* the debt to Herbert is felt; or rather, no debt but a gift received. To understand how Vaughan managed to convert his personal losses to spiritual and poetic gain, it is essential to reflect upon that relationship. Vaughan must have read or re-read George Herbert's *The Temple* in his most needy hours, perhaps while William was dying or in the shadow of his death [...]. He was empty and Herbert filled him; exhausted

---

14 David Reid, *The Metaphysical Poets* (Harlow: Longman/Pearson Education, 2000), pp. 177, 178.
15 Pettet, *Of Paradise and Light*, pp. 65, 67.
16 Post, *The Unfolding Vision*, pp. 111, 80–81, 97–98.

and Herbert refreshed him and relieved his spiritual poverty. Herbert put words in Vaughan's mouth, in a literal sense.[17]

Eloquent and persuasive as Stevie Davies's explanation of Herbert's gift to Vaughan is, however, it still leaves open important questions about a body of poetry that has been called 'derivative in a quite unprecedented way' and 'the most extreme example we have of one poet being influenced by another'.[18] Disagreements have arisen, for example, over the psychological dimension of Vaughan's literary relationship with Herbert. On one side, Post acknowledges Herbert's role as 'the catalyst in Vaughan's poetic career', but insists that he 'shaped rather than overwhelmed or displaced the Welsh poet's creative energies'.[19] On the other side, Gerald Hammond invokes Harold Bloom's theory of the 'anxiety of influence', arguing that Vaughan's 'admiration for Herbert was a troubled one' and that the two parts of *Silex Scintillans* embody the artistic conflict he underwent in 'freeing himself from the tyranny of Herbert's words'.[20] In a significant intervention in the debate, Sean McDowell has recently argued that 'the extremity and extensiveness of his borrowings' are the consequence of 'Vaughan's engagement with the bardic tradition of Welsh poetry', which 'placed a high emphasis on the rote memorization of the received traditions of natural and religious lore, poetic forms, extant works'. This leads him to the conclusion that 'Vaughan's treatment of Herbert as Welsh *bardd* accounts for the depth of his absorption of Herbert's language

---

17 Stevie Davies, *Henry Vaughan*, Border Lines Series (Bridgend: Seren, Poetry of Wales Press, 1995), p. 93.
18 A. Alvarez, *The School of Donne* [1961] (New York and Toronto: Mentor Books, New American Library, 1967), p. 68; Gerald Hammond, '"Poor dust should lie still low": George Herbert and Henry Vaughan', *English*, 35 (1986), 1.
19 Post, *The Unfolding Vision*, p. xx.
20 Hammond, '"Poor dust should lie still low"', 12, 20. Bloom's central theory, that the poetic influence of one strong poet on another always proceeds by a misreading – 'an act of creative correction', which involves psychological resistance to the power of the poetic 'father' – is distilled into the following summary: 'The history of fruitful poetic influence [...] is a history of anxiety and self-saving caricature, of distortion, of perverse, wilful revisionism' (Harold Bloom, *The Anxiety of Influence: A Theory of Poetry* (Oxford: Oxford University Press, 1975), p. 30).

within his own'.[21] His findings will need to be borne in mind during any examination of the multifarious nature of Vaughan's debt to *The Temple*.

II

The implications of Vaughan's borrowings from *The Temple* for the modern reception of many of his devotional lyrics are spelt out by Thomas Calhoun: 'Recognition of the old in the new, like recognition of distinct lines in polyphony, is an act of discovery (nowadays editorially preempted) that Vaughan must have anticipated from his readers.'[22] As Calhoun's parenthesis recognizes, few of today's readers will bring to *Silex Scintillans* the degree of familiarity with Herbert's poetry required for them to play their full part in deciphering its contribution to Vaughan's texts. Therefore, before embarking on a more detailed analysis of the various echoes, imitations, and allusions in the religious writings of Herbert's most devoted disciple, it is worth addressing the question of whether there were many in the 'linguistic and cultural community' that formed the readership for poetry in the mid-seventeenth century who would have been equipped to make the necessary 'act of discovery' to bring the Herbertian material into creative play.

In his first secular volume, the belated Son of Ben had been content to appeal to that elite band of 'Ingenious Lovers of Poesie' whom he identified as the '*more refined* Spirits' in '*these dull Times*'.[23] How confident could he have been in the 1650s that the kind of 'Peaceful, humble, and pious Reader' for whom he wrote *The Mount of Olives* in prose – the equivalent of Milton's 'fit audience, [...] though few'[24] – was well enough versed in the work of George Herbert to find the fruit of his own poetic talent 'as useful now in the *publick*, as it hath

---

21 Sean H. McDowell, 'Herbert as *Bardd* in the Imagination of Henry Vaughan', *George Herbert Journal*, 34 (2010–11), 103, 104, 106, 115.
22 Thomas O. Calhoun, *Henry Vaughan: The Achievement of Silex Scintillans* (Newark, DE: University of Delware Press, 1981), p. 72.
23 *HV Works*, p. 11.
24 *Paradise Lost*, Book VII, l. 31, *John Milton*, ed. Stephen Orgel and Jonathan Goldberg, The Oxford Authors (Oxford: Oxford University Press, 1990), p. 492.

been to me in *private*?'.²⁵ There is, in fact, plenty of evidence that there would have been a relatively large pool of suitably competent readers. No less than thirteen editions of *The Temple* were issued from 1633 to 1709 and, as Helen Wilcox has pointed out, Herbert's work was 'referred to, cited, imitated and reformulated by readers and writers from the complete spectrum of poetic, denominational and political allegiance'.²⁶ Robert Ray, in an essay that complements his catalogue of seventeenth-century allusions to Herbert, calculates that seventy per cent of them are by loyal Anglicans and Royalists; and a later critic adds that these included King Charles I, who was more than once reported as reading Herbert's divine poems.²⁷ Wilcox's demonstration that Vaughan was 'part of a generation of devotional writers', all of whom had 'a professed or implicit reliance' upon Herbert for inspiration and poetic models, not only offers 'a new context in which to read Vaughan's work' but also confirms that an audience well-versed in the poetry of George Herbert must have existed at the time.²⁸

III

Before identifying the different kinds and degrees of indebtedness to Herbert in particular examples of Vaughan's work, it is as well to bear in mind Christopher Ricks's formulation of the theoretical dilemma that is posed by any enquiry into the phenomenon of literary borrowing: '[A]lthough to speak of an allusion is always to predicate a source (and you cannot call into play something of which you have never heard), a source may not be an allusion, for it may

25 From the preface to the 1655 *Silex Scintillans*, *HV Works*, p. 558.
26 Helen Wilcox, '"Scribling under so faire a Coppy": The Presence of Herbert in the Poetry of Vaughan's Contemporaries', *Scintilla*, 7 (2003), 186.
27 Robert H. Ray, 'Herbert's Seventeenth-Century Reputation: A Summary and New Considerations', *George Herbert Journal*, 9:2 (1986), 1–15; Sidney Gottlieb, 'A Royalist Rewriting of George Herbert: *His Majesties Complaint to his Subjects* (1647)', *Modern Philology*, 89 (1991), 211, note 2. See also Robert H. Ray, 'The Herbert Allusion Book: Allusions to George Herbert in the Seventeenth Century', *Studies in Philology*, 83:4 (1986) and *George Herbert: The Critical Heritage*, ed. C.A. Patrides (London: Routledge and Kegan Paul, 1983).
28 Wilcox, '"Scribling under so faire a Coppy"', 185–86, 198.

not be called into play.'²⁹ Vaughan's practice, however, sometimes involves a different kind of allusiveness, in which the recognition of a phrase or image serves to impart a Herbertian resonance to a text without the need for its precise source to be identified or activated as an ingredient of meaning. It is nevertheless important to acknowledge that many of Vaughan's borrowings do deliberately extend an invitation to his readers to relate them to a particular poem. This practice is formally ratified in 'The Match', which stands at the centre of the 1650 *Silex Scintillans*. Addressed to the 'Dear friend! whose holy, ever-living lines / Have done much good / To many', it makes a solemn undertaking to 'joyn hands' with Herbert 'and thrust my stubborn heart / Into thy *Deed*, / There from no *Duties* to be freed'.³⁰ This is itself a direct invocation of Herbert's 'Obedience', in which the author of *The Temple* describes his poem as a 'speciall deed' conveying his heart 'and all it hath' to God and bequeathing his poetic discipleship to a worthy successor:

> He that will passe his land,
> As I have mine, may set his hand
> And heart unto this deed, when he hath read;
> And make the purchase spread
> To both our goods, if he to it will stand.³¹

Then follows the hope, alluded to directly by Vaughan, that 'some kinde man would thrust his heart / Into these lines'. Post interprets 'The Match' as defining 'the necessary ingredients for a successful transfer of power' and suggests that in his punning title 'the younger author traces the extent of his debts to Herbert and the terms of the overall "match" struck between himself and Christ'.³²

We must begin, however, by taking note of Hammond's insistence that material derived from *The Temple* can be disconcertingly limited in its allusive value according to Ricks's modernist criterion: 'Herbert's lines, images, and words often have no relevance to the

---

29 Christopher Ricks, *Allusion to the Poets* (Oxford: Oxford University Press, 2002), p. 3.
30 *HV Works*, pp. 97–98.
31 *The English Poems of George Herbert*, ed. Helen Wilcox (Cambridge: Cambridge University Press, 2007), pp. 374–75.
32 Post, *The Unfolding Vision*, p. 119.

Vaughan poem they find themselves in.'[33] As an example of a poem containing two such inert quotations, Hammond cites 'The Resolve'. The opening line introduces an urgent exhortation to abandon the false pleasures and distractions of this world and take another 'path' that leads to the spiritual traveller's true 'Home': 'I have consider'd it; and find / A longer stay / Is but excus'd neglect.'[34] The first line is taken over word for word from 'The Reprisall', in which Herbert meditates on the sinner's unpayable debt to the crucified Christ: 'I have consider'd it, and finde / There is no dealing with thy mighty passion.'[35] Readers who recognize the Herbertian phrase and trace it to its source will find that nothing is added to the semantic substance of Vaughan's poem. Even more 'perverse', in Hammond's view, is Vaughan's appropriation later in the poem of part of this stanza from 'Affliction (I)':

> At first thou gav'st me milk and sweetnesses;
>   I had my wish and way:
> My dayes were straw'd with flow'rs and happinesse;
>   There was no moneth but May.
> But with my yeares sorrow did twist and grow,
> And made a partie unawares for wo.[36]

Herbert is describing the shallow and immature joys he experienced in the initial stage of his service to God, before sickness, bereavement, and disappointed ambition darkened his life. In 'The Resolve', the same imagery and some of the same words are adopted to describe the deep and lasting joy that accompanies a life of Christian commitment:

> Follow the *Cry* no more: there is
>   An ancient way
> All strewed with flowres, and happiness
>   And fresh as *May*;
> There turn, and turn no more.

---

33 Hammond, '"Poor dust should still lie low"', 1.
34 *HV Works*, p. 97.
35 *English Poems of Herbert*, p. 116.
36 *English Poems of Herbert*, p. 162.

Although the borrowed material is fully integrated into the texture and argument of Vaughan's poem, as with the line from 'The Reprisall' there is no imaginative interplay with its source.

There is a similar lack of the kind of allusive energy looked for by Ricks in the appropriation of a conceit from 'Aaron'. Herbert writes as a man contemplating his unworthiness to carry out the task of an ordained priest – 'Profanenesse in my head, / Defects and darknesse in my breast' – but by the final stanza he has been transformed by clothing himself metaphorically in the attributes of Christ, the great High Priest: 'Come people; Aaron's drest.'[37] Drawing upon this source, Vaughan brings a long reflection upon his personal sinfulness in 'Repentance' to its climax with a plea for the salvation made available through the 'merits' of Christ:

> Defects, and darknes in my brest,
> Pollutions all my body wed,
> And even my soul to thee is dead,
> Only in him, on whom I feast,
> Both soul, and body are well drest.[38]

Beyond the satisfaction of tracing the origin of this passage, there seems little to be gained from linking the two poems. Nor does the final phrase – 'well drest' – which also occurs in Herbert's 'Prayer (I)', where it is one among many definitions of prayer, appear to carry an allusive charge of meaning in its new context.[39] In both these examples, it is enough for the reader to be aware that *Silex Scintillans* shares an undercurrent of phrase and image and religious temper with *The Temple*.

Even more striking instances of this apparently random lifting of material occur in 'The World', in which 'The doting Lover in his queintest strain' derives from 'The wanton lover in a curious strain' in Herbert's 'Dulnesse' and the sinister activities of the 'darksome States-man' – 'Yet dig'd the Mole, and lest his ways be found / Workt under ground, / Where he did Clutch his prey' – is taken from a simile in 'Confession', which describes the 'afflictions' visited upon humankind by God:

---

37 *English Poems of Herbert*, p. 601.
38 *HV Works*, p. 114.
39 See *English Poems of Herbert*, p. 178.

> We are the earth; and they,
> Like moles within us, heave, and cast about:
> And till they foot and clutch their prey,
> They never cool, much lesse give out.

The arguments of the two Herbert poems have no bearing on Vaughan's survey of the 'train' of worldly characters that are 'hurl'd' round beneath the 'great *Ring*' of eternity.[40]

In one last example of this looser kind of allusion, Vaughan expands upon some words from a passage in 'Complaining': 'Let not thy wrathfull power / Afflict my houre, / My inch of life'. Transplanted into 'The Proffer', one of the most overtly political poems in *Silex Scintillans*, Herbert's plea for divine mercy becomes part of a defiant response to an attempt by the local Puritan authorities to enlist the Welsh royalist poet in the service of the new republican state:

> Shall my short hour, my inch,
> My one poor sand,
> And crum of life, now ready to disband
> Revolt and flinch,
> And having born the burthen all the day,
> Now cast at night my Crown away?[41]

Although such instances might justify the conclusion that 'Vaughan merely used Herbert's poetry as a store-house of ideas and images, paying little obvious attention to their original application', Hammond goes too far in claiming that this is Vaughan's practice 'in the great majority of his poems'.[42] In the first place, many of the religious poems contain no trace of Herbert's influence on the choice of words or metaphors; and in the second, many of the obvious 'allusion-markers' in his devotional poetry are intended to draw attention to a significant relationship with their source.

---

40 *HV Works*, pp. 131–32; *English Poems of Herbert*, pp. 410, 443.
41 *English Poems of Herbert*, p. 501; *HV Works*, p. 571.
42 Hammond, '"Poor dust should still lie low"', 2.

IV

The case for the defence against Hammond's strictures may be developed further by means of John Hollander's contrast between 'poetic echo' and 'modes of more overt allusion'. He observes that 'poems seem to echo prior ones for the personal aural benefit of the poet, and of whichever poetic followers can overhear the reverberations' and adds the important corollary that poets 'also seem to echo earlier voices with full or suppressed consciousness'.[43] It is quite plausible that Vaughan's immersion in Herbert's poetry was so profound that some words and images found their way unbidden into his texts by a process that Pettet describes as involuntary borrowing, which may extend beyond isolated phrases to 'subconscious associations' of clusters of words.[44] The collocation 'work, and wind', for example, which occurs twice in *Silex Scintillans*, may be classed as an involuntary echo that has no allusive intent. In 'Midnight', it is used to describe the 'busie Ray' of each star that shines with 'ardour' in contrast to the 'Cold Affections / And slow motions' of the poet; and in 'Misery', it is absorbed into a simile – 'As flames about their fuel run / And work, and wind til all be done' – that describes the poet's quarrel with the divine will.[45] In the second of these instances, the fact that the phrase has its origin in a simile from Herbert's 'Jordan (II)' – 'As flames do work and winde, when they ascend, / So did I weave my self into the sense'[46] – may have been the subconscious trigger, although in neither case is Herbert's exploration of the pitfalls of writing religious verse brought into play. Indeed, in Hollander's terms, it may have been the pleasing sound of the alliterating verbs rather than their semantic context that lodged itself in Vaughan's mind.

A slightly longer phrase embedded in Herbert's 'Providence' – '*Rain*, do not hurt my flowers; but *gently spend / Your hony drops*' (italics added)[47] – may also have caught Vaughan's attention

---

43 John Hollander, *The Figure of Echo: A Mode of Allusion in Milton and After* (Berkeley, CA, Los Angeles, CA, and London: University of California Press, 1981), p. ix.
44 Pettet, *Of Paradise and Light*, pp. 61–64.
45 *HV Works*, pp. 83, 140.
46 *English Poems of Herbert*, p. 367.
47 *English Poems of Herbert*, p. 420.

as much for its aural appeal as for its imagery. In 'The Rain-bow', the omission of the intervening imperative clause brings the first word into direct contact with the internally chiming adverb and verb, which creates a metrically effective double stress at the start of the line and reinforces the subtle modulation of vowel sounds and the undercurrent of 'n' alliteration: 'Rain gently spends his honey-drops'.[48] The result is more striking for its verbal music than for any allusive value.

By way of contrast, an example of a phrase that clearly functions as an allusion rather than a mere echo occurs in 'Cock-crowing'.[49] Having pondered upon the 'Sunnie seed' planted in the bird, Vaughan prays that the 'cloke / And cloud' of the flesh that separates him from the 'immortall light and heat' of his Maker may be broken, because 'This veyle *thy full-ey'd love* denies, / And onely gleams and fractions spies' (italics added). The three-word phrase adopted from the last stanza of 'The Glance' brings with it the burden of the entire poem, in which Herbert recalls the promise vouchsafed when the 'sweet and gracious eye' of God first looked upon him:

> If thy first glance so powerfull be,
> A mirth but open'd and seal'd up again;
> What wonders shall we feel, when we shall see
>   Thy full-ey'd love![50]

Once the direct quotation of these three climactic words has called Herbert's poem into play, the 'first glance' that gave it its title can be read back into the opening lines of 'Cock-crowing' – 'Father of lights! What Sunnie seed, / What glance of day hast thou confin'd / Into this bird?' – and continues to reverberate in the 'gleams and fractions' of divine light perceived by Vaughan.

The first line of 'The Passion' – 'O My chief good!' – is obviously designed to call to mind Herbert's treatment of the same subject in 'Good Friday', which begins with the same exclamation.[51] As Vaughan continues his devotions at the foot of the Cross, he develops ideas and images derived from Herbert's 'The Agonie', which is a meditation

---

48 *HV Works*, p. 597.
49 *HV Works*, pp. 572–73.
50 *English Poems of Herbert*, pp. 589–90.
51 *HV Works*, pp. 93–94; *English Poems of Herbert*, p. 126.

on the role of 'two vast, spacious things' – 'Sinne and Love' – in the drama that began in Gethsemane and ended on Calvary:

> Sinne is that presse and vice, which forceth pain
> To hunt his cruell food through ev'ry vein.
>   [. . . . . . .]
> Love is that liquour sweet and most divine,
> Which my God feels as bloud; but I, as wine.[52]

The conceit of the 'presse and vice' provides the hint from which Vaughan develops his own evocation of the way human sin contributed to the physical agony of Christ:

> How did the weight
> Of all our sinnes,
> And death unite
> To wrench, and Rack thy blessed limbes!

And Herbert's final identification of Love as the blood and wine of the Eucharist is less obliquely recalled in a complex allusion that combines a wine-press with the 'press' that tortures the 'blessed limbes' or 'faire branches' of the True Vine to produce the saving 'juice' or 'liquour':

> Most blessed Vine!
> Whose juice so good
> I feel as Wine,
> But thy faire branches felt as bloud,
> How wert thou prest
> To be my feast!

Another poem about the 'strange wonders' of the saving power of divine love – 'The Incarnation, and Passion' – invites the reader to look back to the 'strange storie' of how 'my Lord JESUS di'd' told by Herbert in 'The Bag':

> The God of power, as he did ride
> In his majestick robes of glorie,

---

52 *English Poems of Herbert*, p. 119.

> Resolv'd to light; and so one day
> He did descend, undressing all the way.

Vaughan adapts these lines in his first stanza, turning Herbert's narrative into a personal address to his Saviour:

> Lord! When thou didst thy selfe undresse
> Laying by thy robes of glory,
> To make us more, thou wouldst be lesse,
> And becam'st a wofull story.

Herbert's telling of this story, which contains specific references to the 'inne' Christ first repaired to and the 'blow upon his side' received from 'a spear', provides the historical context for Vaughan's ensuing reflections on the various sacrifices endured by his 'deare Lord' after his 'translation' into human form in order to demonstrate that '*Love* / Is only stronger far than death'.[53]

Even the slightest of verbal markers may be enough to effect a meaningful allusion for the reader who is familiar with Herbert's poetry and Vaughan's methods. The second stanza of 'The Showre (I)' applies the preceding description of moisture rising from the surface of a 'drowsie Lake' as mist and falling again as rain to the prayer life of the poet:

> Ah! it is so with me; oft have I prest
> Heaven with a lazie breath, but fruitles this
> *Peirc'd not*; Love only can with *quick accesse*
>   Unlock the way. (italics added)

The italicized words invoke two contrasting perspectives on prayer in *The Temple*. 'Prayer (II)' begins 'Of what an easie quick accesse, / My blessed Lord, art thou! how suddenly / May our requests thine eare invade!' and 'Deniall' contradicts this happy optimism from bitter experience: 'When my devotions could not pierce / Thy silent eares; / Then was my heart broken, as was my verse.'[54] Together, these two products of Herbert's devotional life provide a rich context for Vaughan's poem.

---

53 *English Poems of Herbert*, p. 520; *HV Works*, p. 77.
54 *HV Works*, p. 74; *English Poems of Herbert*, pp. 371, 288.

V

Alongside these relatively brief echoes and adaptations of sources in *The Temple* are the variations that Vaughan plays at more length upon specific models. Two such poems were identified by Pettet as being 'so close to Herbert originals that they must be described as imitations'. One of these proclaims its dependence in a shared title – 'The Storm' – but Pettet himself admits that Vaughan 'makes much more of the literal "storm" than Herbert does' and that, although it contains 'a good deal of verbal reminiscence', in content it plays a series of variations on ideas expressed only in the opening and closing lines of its model.[55] The other is perhaps the most striking example of Vaughan's thorough-going imitation of a poem from *The Temple* and merits detailed analysis. The two poems are compact enough to quote in their entirety.

'The Dawning' is a characteristic product of Herbert's metrical virtuosity, with its varying line lengths and the refrain-like repetition of imperatives in the shortest line of each stanza:

> Awake sad heart, whom sorrow ever drowns;
>   Take up thine eyes, which feed on earth;
> Unfold thy forehead gather'd into frowns:
>   Thy Saviour comes, and with him mirth:
>   Awake, awake;
> And with a thankfull heart his comforts take.
>   But thou dost still lament, and pine, and crie;
>   And feel his death, but not his victorie.
>
> Arise sad heart; if thou dost not withstand,
>   Christs resurrection thine may be:
> Do not by hanging down break from the hand,
>   Which as it riseth, raiseth thee:
>   Arise, arise;
> And with his burial-linen drie thine eyes:
>   Christ left his grave-clothes, that we might, when grief
> Draws tears, or bloud, not want an handkerchief.[56]

---

55 Pettet, *Of Paradise and Light*, pp. 52–53.
56 *English Poems of Herbert*, p. 399.

Vaughan copies the stanza form, echoes the imperatives, and follows the dynamic curve from despair to the dawning of new hope made possible by the event celebrated at Easter:

> Thou, whose sad heart, and weeping head lyes low,
>   Whose Cloudy brest cold damps invade,
> Who never feel'st the Sun, nor smooth'st thy brow,
>   But sitt'st oppressed in the shade,
>   Awake, awake,
> And in his Resurrection partake,
>   Who on this day (that thou might'st rise as he,)
>   Rose up, and cancell'd two deaths due to thee.
>
> Awake, awake; and, like the Sun, disperse
>   All mists that would usurp this day;
> Where are thy Palmes, thy branches, and thy verse?
>   *Hosannah*! heark; why doest thou stay?
>   Arise, arise,
> And with his healing bloud anoint thine Eys,
>   Thy inward Eys; his bloud will cure thy mind,
>   Whose spittle only could restore the blind.[57]

Herbert's imagery and phrasing are both adopted and adapted throughout – eyes drowned in sorrow and feeding on earth become a weeping head that lies low; unfolding the forehead becomes smoothing the brow; the Saviour who brings comforts becomes the Sun/Son who rises; the verbal play on 'riseth, raiseth' prompts the similar play on 'rise' and 'Rose up'; the burial-linen that supplies a handkerchief to wipe tearful eyes becomes the healing blood that will cure the mind as Christ's spittle restored sight to blind eyes. But this is more than almost line-by-line paraphrase of a model of excellence. In carrying through his imitation of the source poem, Vaughan transforms it from a call to the sinner to recognize and embrace as his own Christ's victory over death into a rallying cry to other royalists and Anglicans who sit 'oppressed in the shade' of a Puritan regime that 'would usurp this day' – by banning church festivals like Easter – and eclipse the sun of kingship as well as dishonouring the Son of God. Following the method of imitation recommended by

---

57 'Easter-day', *HV Works*, p. 121.

Jonson, Vaughan has converted the substance of another poet's work into the 'relish, and savour' of his own poetic 'honey'; or, in terms of McDowell's situating of Vaughan within the Welsh bardic tradition, he has treated his predecessor's work 'not only as a repository of poetic models but also as a word-hoard', which he has 'uploaded into the text of his composing self'.[58]

Pettet proposed Vaughan's 'Son-dayes' as a possible third instance of imitation and it has been frequently compared with 'Prayer (I)' because both poems exemplify the Welsh poetic technique of *dyfalu*, described by Herbert's modern editor as 'accumulated definitions of a single idea, often in a sequence without conjunctions'.[59] The poems differ in subject matter, but there is some verbal interplay: 'Prayer the Churches banquet', the first of Herbert's sequence of phrases in apposition, mutates into 'The Churches love-feasts'; the 'six-daies world' is echoed in 'six-days-showres'; and Herbert's 'milkie way' is expanded into 'The milky way Chalkt out with Suns'. Linking conjunctions and main verbs are meticulously avoided by both poets right through to Herbert's 'something understood' and Vaughan's 'the Out Courts of glory'.[60]

In addition to Pettet's three exhibits, 'Praise' announces its debt to 'Praise (II)' not only in its title but also in its stanza form and its opening apostrophe, which modifies Herbert's 'King of Glorie, King of Peace' to suit Vaughan's different emphasis:

> King of Comforts! King of life!
>   Thou hast cheer'd me,
> And when fears, and doubts were rife,
>   Thou hast cleer'd me!

Later stanzas follow the model more closely in content: Herbert's 'Wherefore with my utmost art / I will sing thee' is carried over into 'Wherefore with my utmost strength / I wil praise thee'; and 'Sev'n whole dayes, not one in seven, / I will praise thee' is slightly varied

---

58 'Timber: or Discoveries', in *Ben Jonson: The Complete Poems*, ed. George Parfitt (Harmondsworth: Penguin Books, 1975), p. 448; McDowell, 'Herbert as *Bardd* in the Imagination of Henry Vaughan', 109.
59 Headnote under 'Sources' of 'Prayer (I)' in *English Poems of Herbert*, p. 176.
60 *HV Works*, pp. 111–12; *English Poems of Herbert*, p. 178.

in 'Day, and night, not once a day / I will blesse thee'.⁶¹ After eight stanzas modelled formally on 'Praise (II)', Vaughan adopts a six-line unit for the last four stanzas, the third of which signals in its final word the origin of this manipulation of different verse forms:

> If then, dread Lord,
> When to thy board
> Thy wretch comes begging,
> He hath a flowre
> Or (to his pow'r,)
> Some such poor Off'ring.

This is the metre and rhyme scheme used in the second half of Herbert's 'An Offering', which switches from iambic pentameters to this more lyrical form for the 'hymne' presented in response to the poem's opening invitation, 'Come, bring thy gift'.⁶² The fact that 'An Offering' follows 'Praise (II)' immediately in *The Temple* suggests that Vaughan had the book open before him as he combined his imitation of the form and content of one poem with a formal device typical of Herbert's poetic art – together with the very stanza form in which it is effected – in the second.⁶³

VI

This survey of the variety of Vaughan's poetic debts to Herbert will conclude with an analysis of the complex tissue of verbal and conceptual connections linking one of his major poems with poems in *The Temple* and with other poems in *Silex Scintillans*. It will be undertaken in the light – or admonitory shadow – of Ricks's reminder about the other side of the hermeneutic equation:

---

61 *English Poems of Herbert*, pp. 506–07; *HV Works*, pp. 118–19.
62 *English Poems of Herbert*, pp. 509–10.
63 Rickey discusses the 'Herbertian trick' of changing the stanza form part way through a poem in 'Vaughan, *The Temple*, and Poetic Form', 166–67. If Vaughan regularly had a copy of *The Temple* to hand as he wrote, McDowell's case for bardic memorization of Herbert's oeuvre 'by rote' may need to be questioned.

Readers always have to decide – if they accept that such-and-such is indeed a *source* for certain lines – whether it is also more than a source, being part not only of the making of the poem but of its meaning.[64]

The poem chosen for this exercise – 'Misery' – is included by Post among those poems from *Silex Scintillans* that share with 'their prototypes in *The Temple*' the project of exploring 'the inner configurations of the Christian life'.[65] It is useful for the purposes of this chapter because its title relates it to a specific Herbert model and because Vaughan's editors have identified within its 114 lines an extraordinary array of reminiscences from elsewhere in Herbert's work – 'The Church-porch', 'Sighs and Groans', 'Church-monuments', 'The Glimpse', 'Mortification', 'Giddiness', 'Nature', 'Jordan (II)', 'The Collar', 'Sion', 'The Starre', 'The Glance', and 'Love (II)' – though not all of these will figure in what follows.

The central debt to Herbert's 'Miserie' is thematic rather than formal: the earlier poem is in six-line stanzas of varying line lengths, whereas Vaughan uses octosyllabic couplets; but both poets are concerned with exploring the human tendency to rebel against the service owed to God. From the start, however, there are important and characteristic differences of approach. In the very last line, Herbert applies everything he has said about Man to his own predicament: 'A sick toss'd vessel, dashing on each thing; / Nay, his own shelf: / My God, I mean my self.'[66] Up till then, he has conducted an apparently objective survey of the effects of 'Folly and Sinne' on the behaviour of human beings, who are only kept from the disaster of wilfully rejecting their Maker by His own unfailing love for them:

> They quarrell thee, and would give over
> The bargain made to serve thee: but thy love
>   Holds them unto it, and doth cover
> Their follies with the wing of thy milde Dove,
>   Not suff'ring those
>   Who would, to be thy foes. (ll. 25–30)

---

64 Ricks, *Allusion to the Poets*, pp. 3–4.
65 Post, *The Unfolding Vision*, p. 98.
66 All quotations from 'Miserie' are from *English Poems of Herbert*, pp. 359–61 and are supplied with line references in the text.

Vaughan picks up the words 'serve, 'hold', and 'quarrel' from this passage in his opening lines, but presents the situation in more explicitly personal terms:

> Lord, bind me up, and let me lye
> A Pris'ner to my libertie,
> If such a state at all can be
> As an Impris'ment *serving* thee;
> The wind, though gather'd in thy fist,
> Yet doth it blow stil where it list,
> And yet shouldst thou let go thy *hold*
> Those gusts might *quarrel* and grow bold. (italics added)[67]

In the ensuing description of the way in which his 'spilt thoughts [...] / Take the down-rode to vanitie', Vaughan's speaker enacts in his own person the follies that Herbert lays at the door of Man, who is 'a foolish thing, a foolish thing' (l. 2). Adopting the role of an advocate for God, Herbert is scornful of the human creature's stubborn obtuseness before an all-seeing Creator – 'No man shall beat into his head, / That thou within his curtains drawn canst see' (ll. 15–16) – and censures his commitment to his own pleasures: 'Why, he'l not lose a cup of drink for thee: / Bid him but temper his excesse; / Not he …' (ll. 8–10). Glancing obliquely at these lines, Vaughan incorporates this particular human vice into the account of his own more comprehensive self-indulgence:

> Some fig-leafs stil I do devise
> As if thou hadst nor ears, nor Eyes.
> Excesse of friends, of words, and wine
> Take up my day … (ll. 23–26)

Borrowings from elsewhere in *The Temple* follow a similar pattern, transforming the general into the personal, distilling the individual from the universal. For example, 'I break the fence my own hands made' (l. 21) derives from the phrase 'Man breaks the fence' in 'The Church-porch' and another observation from the same poem – 'The drunkard forfets Man, and doth devest / All worldly right, save what

---

67 All quotations from 'Misery' are from *HV Works* pp. 138–41, and are supplied with line references in the text.

he hath by beast'[68] – is expanded into Vaughan's climactic confession of slavery to appetite:

> But I go on, haste to Devest
> My self of reason, till opprest
> And buried in my surfeits I
> Prove my own shame and miserie. (ll. 41–44)

It may be that the meaningful allusions in this passage – the unusual word 'devest' and the idea of a bestial loss of human reason – prompted the aural echo of 'forfets' in 'surfeits'. Up to this point, the difference between 'Miserie' and 'Misery' has been one of approach to the common theme of obedience: Herbert examines the wretchedness of a race of creatures that betrays its own best interests in refusing to serve the God who made and sustains it; and Vaughan expresses the 'shame and miserie' of one who is only too aware of his own foolishness and ingratitude in excluding from his mind the God 'who of that Cel / Would make a Court, should he there dwel' (ll. 35–36) – an image that harks back to the idea of imprisonment in the opening lines and owes something to an image in Herbert's 'The Glimpse':

> Thou knowst how grief and sinne
> Disturb the work. O make me not their sport,
> Who by thy coming may be made a court.[69]

Vaughan's next series of borrowings, however, takes his poem into another dimension of experience.

An interlude, in which God responds to his cry and pours 'a showr / Of healing sweets' (ll. 49–50) into the speaker's self-inflicted wounds, culminates in an evocation of the limited peace that comes with self-discipline:

> I School my Eys, and strictly dwel
> Within the Circle of my Cel,
> That Calm and silence are my Joys
> Which to thy peace are but meer noise. (ll. 57–60)

---

68 *English Poems of Herbert*, pp. 50, 51.
69 *English Poems of Herbert*, p. 531.

By accepting confinement to the cell of service in which he can lie 'A Pris'ner to my libertie' (l. 2), he opens himself to the transforming power of that divine love that is able to 'make a Court' of the mind that admits it. But the passage from Herbert's 'Mortification' which lies behind Vaughan's lines prompts a more specific reading of the later poet's situation. It is the fourth stanza of six in a meditation on human mortality and the journey from infancy to old age:

> When man grows staid and wise,
> Getting a house and home, where he may move
> Within the circle of his breath,
> Schooling his eyes;
> That dumbe inclosure maketh love
> Unto the coffin, that attends his death.[70]

The man of mature years in Herbert's poem, after the 'frank and free' season of youth, reads the enclosure of his own 'house and home' as an emblem of the coffin that will be his final resting-place, and schools his eyes to accept the inevitability of death. Vaughan must school himself not to face the fact of mortality like Herbert's representative of human kind, but to accept his strict confinement in the cell or dwelling-place in which God has appointed him to live in peace as an individual. That this cell is the 'house and home' to which he retired to enjoy 'Calm and silence' (l. 59) after the more active service of the Civil War is strongly suggested by what follows. Impatience at being bound up and fenced in erupts once more, and he eventually delivers a speech ringing with echoes of Herbert:

> At length I feel my head to ake,
> My fingers Itch, and burn to take
> Some new Imployment, I begin
> To swel and fome and fret within.
>   *"The Age, the present times are not*
>   *"To snudge in, and embrace a Cot,*
>   *"Action and bloud now get the game,*
>   *"Disdein treads on the peaceful name,*
>   *"Who sits at home too bears a loade*
>   *"Greater than those that gad abroad.* (ll. 61–70)

---

[70] *English Poems of Herbert*, p. 354.

The unusual word 'snudge' is picked up from 'Giddinesse', another of Herbert's objective meditations on Man, in which the inconstancy and waywardness of the human creature are highlighted. But the word brings its immediate context with it into Vaughan's poem:

> Now he will fight it out, and to the warres;
>   Now eat his bread in peace,
> And snudge in quiet: now he scorns increase,
>   Now all day spares.[71]

In Herbert's 'Miserie', Man is 'a foolish thing' because he allows 'Folly and Sinne' to 'play all his game' (l. 3). Vaughan, in the Wales of the late 1640s, knows that *'Action and bloud now get the game'* and the pressure upon him not to 'snudge in quiet' is more specific than the mere fickleness of human nature. 'Wars' and 'peace' are metaphors for contradictory impulses in 'Giddinesse'; in Vaughan's poem, there is a contemporary and local context that gives social and political force to the line *'Disdein treads on the peaceful name'*. The final couplet of the rebellious speech transforms the spiritual mutiny of another Herbert poem into a royalist commentary on the political realities of *'the present times'*. In 'The Collar', Herbert had repudiated his apparently fruitless obedience to God with the reiterated cry, 'I will abroad.' Towards the end of the poem, this line had been paired in rhyme with the same word that Vaughan uses in 'Misery':

>   Away; take heed:
>   I will abroad.
> Call in thy deaths head there: tie up thy fears.
>   He that forbears
>   To suit and serve his need,
>   Deserves his load.[72]

Vaughan's complaint seems to be that those who curb their impulse to 'take / Some new Imployment' – who accept the Christian discipline of dwelling strictly within the circle of peace – are in danger of being reviled for cowardice or indifference, as if they were content

---

71 *English Poems of Herbert*, p. 446.
72 *English Poems of Herbert*, p. 526.

to *'embrace a Cot'* rather than endure the hardships of action or exile with their king. But the fretful speaker knows the weight of the burden he bears by staying *'at home'* and not (like Herbert's rebel in 'The Collar') choosing to 'suit and serve his need' for more positive engagement.

Another of Herbert's expressions of resistance to divine control of his life contributes phrases to the later stages of 'Misery' and as before they gain political edge from the context that Vaughan has established for them. 'Nature' begins by invoking four possible acts of defiance against God's sovereignty:

> Full of rebellion, I would die,
> Or fight, or travell, or denie
> That thou hast ought to do with me.[73]

Vaughan's comment on the mutinous speech that he sets apart in italics in 'Misery' picks up three of these options:

> Thus do I make thy gifts giv'n me
> The onely quarrellers with thee,
> I'd loose those knots thy hands did tie,
> Then would go travel, fight or die. (ll. 71–74)

Each of the verbs taken over from Herbert's poem has more than metaphorical or rhetorical value for the defeated supporter of the king and persecuted member of the Church of England, who feels that his Christian duty requires him to snudge in quiet. In the final stanza of 'Nature', Herbert prays that God will 'smooth my rugged heart, and there / Engrave thy rev'rend law and fear'. Vaughan brings the analysis of his particular brand of politically generated misery towards its conclusion with a similar prayer. In it, he pleads not merely that he may respect God's law in general but that his heart may be strong enough to do whatever God requires of it:

> O send me from thy holy hil
> So much of strength, as may fulfil
> All thy delights (what e'er they be)

---

73 *English Poems of Herbert*, p. 155.

>   And sacred Institutes in me;
>   Open my rockie heart, and fil
>   It with obedience to thy wil. (ll. 97–102)

The change from 'rugged' to 'rockie' glances back at the emblem of the heart-shaped flint on the title page of the first edition of *Silex Scintillans*, perhaps prompted by the verb 'engrave' in the Herbert source.

The precise nature of his duty of obedience, in relation to what he had earlier dubbed 'these mutinies' – times when, 'wilded by a peevish heart', he had stormed at God, 'calling my peace, / A Lethargy, and meer disease' (ll. 81–84) – comes more sharply into focus when 'Misery' is read in the context provided for it by the three poems that precede it in *Silex Scintillans* and by the allusions to Herbert's poetry that bind all four together as a group. The first of them, entitled 'The Mutinie', is a rendering of his religious and political plight in terms of the captivity of the Israelites in Egypt.[74] Pondering on the 'after-burthens, and griefs yet to come', the captive in this Old Testament analogue to the 'Impris'ment' to God's will explored in 'Misery' recounts how his thoughts 'quit their troubled Channel' and stormed at the 'banks' that confined them, like the 'spilt thoughts' of the later poem. Again, like the 'Pris'ner' who burns for some 'new Imployment' in 'Misery', this Israelite pleads with God to let him 'strive and struggle with thy foes / (Not thine alone, but mine too)'. He also begs that his eye and ear may be sealed up against 'all this fome / And frothie noise which up and down doth flie' – an image that connects with Vaughan's 'fome and fret within' in 'Misery' but needs the context supplied by another poem by Herbert for its full significance to be released. 'The Familie' begins with the question, 'What doth this noise of thoughts within my heart / As if they had a part?' Then, after a prayer that the Lord will 'Turn out these wranglers, which defile thy seat', it goes on to celebrate the 'Peace and Silence', 'Order', and 'Humble Obedience' that should characterize the 'house and familie' of God.[75] Summers and Pebworth have convincingly argued that the poem has 'a public dimension', which is anti-Puritan in emphasis, and have suggested that it 'may glance

---

74 *HV Works*, pp. 133–34.
75 *English Poems of Herbert*, pp. 477–78.

approvingly at the practice of ejecting non-conforming ministers from their livings'.[76]

That the 'fome / And frothie noise' in 'The Mutinie' are related to the noise of the Puritan wranglers who disturbed the peace of the Caroline church in 'The Familie' is confirmed by the next poem in *Silex Scintillans*. 'The Constellation' contemplates the 'exact obedience' with which the 'order'd lights' of the stars move 'without noise' in their 'vast progressions' across the night sky. In contrast, the British nation is 'disorder'd into wars'; and those who seek to justify the destruction of their father and mother (king and church), unable to conceal their true nature behind a show of piety, 'Seem mild, but are known by their noise'.[77] Two more of Herbert's poems, 'The British church' and 'Church-rents and schismes', which are among his most overt treatments of the state of the contemporary world, are then brought into play.[78] Vaughan's powerful metaphor for the effects of civil war in 'The Constellation' is an obvious allusion to Herbert's personification of the Church of England as 'deare Mother' and 'Mother deare and kinde' in these poems: 'The Children Chase the mother, and would heal / The wounds they give, by crying, zeale'. The alternative image of a restored church as the Bride of Christ in the last stanza draws upon details of Herbert's portrait of the 'perfect lineaments, and hue', 'Beautie', and 'fit aray' of his 'dearest Mother' in 'The British church' and glances at the damage to church unity caused by Puritan dissenters that Herbert laments in 'Church-rents and schismes':

> Give to thy spouse her perfect, and pure dress,
>   *Beauty* and *holiness*,
> And so repair these Rents, that men may see
>   And say, *Where God is, all agree.*

---

76 Claude J. Summers and Ted-Larry Pebworth, 'The Politics of *The Temple*: "The British Church" and "The Familie"', *George Herbert Journal*, 8 (1984), 7, 9–10.
77 *HV Works*, pp. 134–36.
78 *English Poems of Herbert*, pp. 390–91, 488–89. Summers and Pebworth discuss the political dimensions of these two poems and compare 'The British Church' with the poem to which Vaughan gave the same title, in 'Herbert, Vaughan, and Public Concerns in Private Modes', *George Herbert Journal*, 3 (1979–80), 1–21.

The setting for Vaughan's 'Misery' is completed by 'The Shepheards', a Nativity poem that begins by evoking a Biblical golden age when the national leaders were *'Patriarchs*, Saints, and Kings' – in bitter contrast to the guides who 'prove wandring stars' in 'The Constellation'. But by the time of the birth of Christ that age was long past, and the true faith was sustained in the 'humble Cotts' of Bethlehem rather than the 'stately Piles' of Jerusalem. Vaughan's description of the homes of the shepherds contains various details that reach backwards and forwards to neighbouring poems in *Silex Scintillans*:

> No costly pride, no soft-cloath'd luxurie
>   In those thin *Cels* could lie,
> Each stirring wind and storm blew through their *Cots*
>   Which never harbour'd plots,
> Only Content, and love, and humble joys
>   Lived there without all *noise*. (italics added)[79]

In the context of these three companion poems, which explore from a variety of perspectives the difficulty of maintaining a Christian stance of peace and humility in a period of disorder, persecution, and successful rebellion, Vaughan's 'Misery' emerges as a powerful and subtle statement of the political as well as the spiritual predicament of a 'fierce soul' that 'bustles about / And never rests til all be out' (ll. 79–80). And a great part of its subtlety lies in the complex tissue of allusions by means of which it draws both inspiration and authority from the work of a great poet whose name, by the end of the 1640s, had become associated among members of one substantial community of Herbert's readers with the cause of an outlawed church and the king who had died for it.[80]

---

79 *HV Works*, p. 137.
80 Helen Wilcox identifies, among 'different generations and groupings' of readers who 'learned to appreciate different Herberts', those who 'looked back from the 1650s and saw an emblem of pre-Civil War Anglicanism' ('In the *Temple* Precincts: George Herbert and Seventeenth-Century Community-Making', in *Studies in Community-Making and Cultural Memory 1558–1689*, ed. Roger D. Bell and Anthony W. Johnson (Farnham, Surrey: Ashgate, 2009), pp. 262, 264).

VII

A shift in the nature and purpose of allusion similar to that discussed in Chapter Six in relation to Milton can be discerned in the changing roles played by George Herbert in the course of Vaughan's career as a devotional writer. It has been observed by more than one scholar that the process of intertextual osmosis was at its most intense in the poems of the 1650 *Silex Scintillans*, when Herbert's work was functioning as both a spiritual inspiration and a literary model for a poet who was going through the trauma of remaking himself. Pettet, for example, notes that the borrowings from Herbert 'are four times as numerous in Part I as in Part II'.[81] For Stevie Davies, Vaughan's most powerful religious lyrics are the medium in which his conversion was not only recorded but to a large extent accomplished in the aftermath of his younger brother's death:

> He studied and mirrored Herbert; became for a span a latter-day twin of his relative. Herbert taught him not just a poetic manner, the power of virtuoso verse-forms, piety and a confessional art, but a new language of the heart and a means of communicating with his own innermost self.[82]

Post observes that this situation altered during the first half of the 1650s, when Vaughan was growing in boldness as 'a surrogate minister of Christ opposing Puritan attitudes', in which role he published *The Mount of Olives: Or, Solitary Devotions* in 1652.[83] Early in the first part of that collection of prayers and meditations for use by the faithful Anglican in place of the prohibited Book of Common Prayer, Vaughan prints a stanza from Herbert's 'The Church-porch' in support of his comment on the closure and vilification of 'reverend and sacred buildings'.[84] In the section devoted to preparation for receiving Holy Communion, he quotes two lines from Herbert's 'The Priesthood': 'O what pure things, most pure, must those hands be / which bring my God to me!'[85] A verse

---

81 Pettet, *Of Paradise and Light*, p. 64.
82 Davies, *Henry Vaughan*, pp. 93–94.
83 Post, *The Unfolding Vision*, p. 127.
84 *HV Works*, p. 293.
85 *HV Works*, p. 302.

introduction to the discourse on death, which makes up the second part of *The Mount of Olives*, owes a line to Herbert's 'Vanitie (II)'; and the doxology that closes the volume echoes that at the end of *The Temple*: '*Glory be to God on high, and on earth peace, good will towards men!*'[86] Several lines and phrases from poems by Herbert are woven into the fabric of Vaughan's prose meditation on dying and twice there are more extensive quotations from the work of 'the most obedient *Son* that ever his *Mother* had, and yet a most glorious true *Saint* and a *Seer*'.[87] In the same work, Vaughan singles him out as a representative of the 'many blessed Patterns of a holy life in the *Brittish Church*', names 'Mr. *George Herbert* of blessed memory' in a marginal gloss, and cites 'Church-musick', 'Church-rents and schisms', and 'The Church Militant' as examples of 'his incomparable prophetick Poems'.[88] These are not among the great devotional lyrics from which Vaughan had drawn spiritual and artistic sustenance when he was in the throes of the experience of regeneration that lies at the heart of the 1650 edition of *Silex Scintillans*. They seem to have been selected, like the earlier quotations from 'The Church-porch' and 'The Priesthood', to reinforce Herbert's status as a model of traditional piety and obedience to the practices of the church that he had once celebrated as his 'deare Mother'.

As Vaughan assumed a more public stance in the prose works of the early 1650s, then, Herbert's hold on his creative imagination evidently began to slacken and the foremost poetic talent of the Church of England was accorded a new kind of significance as an authority to be invoked and an ideologically powerful symbol to be exploited in the Silurist's literary offensive against triumphant Puritanism. It is in this changed role that the poet of *The Temple* figures in the collection of prose translations that Vaughan published as *Flores Solitudinis* in 1654. He quotes two stanzas from 'Content' in the epistle to the reader; and in *The Life of Paulinus*, he makes a passing reference to 'blessed Mr. *Herbert*' and glances at him again when he comes to consider the effects of advancing years on his subject: 'Holy *Paulinus* had now attained a good old age,

---

86 *HV Works*, pp. 313, 336.
87 *HV Works*, p. 332. The whole of 'Life' is quoted (p. 332) and a stanza from 'Death' (p. 334).
88 *HV Works*, p. 332.

the fore-runners (as Master *Herbert* saith) were come.'[89] This new status accorded to Herbert in *Flores Solitudinis* and the augmented edition of *Silex Scintilans* may well have been influenced not only by Vaughan's changed perception of his own role but also by the publication of *A Priest to the Temple, Or, The Country Parson* in a volume entitled *Herbert's Remains* in 1652. Sharon Achinstein sees this, with its 'Prefatory View' of Herbert's life by Barnabas Oley, as designed to promote the vicar of Bemerton as a pattern of service in the now outlawed Church of England and 'a rallying symbol for the excluded clergy'.[90] By the time Vaughan composed the 'Authors Preface' in 1654, 'the blessed man, Mr. *George Herbert*', as saint and poet of the true British church, had assumed a central place in his conception of his own vocation. Only by taking to heart his exemplary life and work would it be possible for a poet to become his successor in any meaningful sense; and it was to that position that Henry Vaughan aspired as he offered his 'poor *Talent* to the *Church*' in the hope that he too might serve the cause of religion by writing 'A *true Hymn*'.[91]

---

89 *HV Works*, pp. 373, 526, 529. The last reference is to Herbert's poem 'The Forerunners'.

90 Sharon Achinstein, 'Reading George Herbert in the Restoration', *English Literary Renaissance*, 36 (2006), 443.

91 *HV Works*, p. 558. For a discussion of Vaughan's dismissal of would-be imitators of George Herbert whose verse did not live up to his prescription for a 'true Hymn', see my essay 'The "true, practic piety" of "holy writing": Henry Vaughan, Richard Crashaw, Christopher Harvey, and *The Temple*', in *Of Paradise and Light*, ed. Dickson and Nelson, pp. 50–70.

CHAPTER EIGHT

Henry Vaughan and the Scriptures

I

In her chapter on the art of *Silex Scintillans*, M.M. Mahood recognized that '[b]y far the largest of Vaughan's English debts is to the Authorised Version'. She went on: 'Probably there is no poet of the period whose work reveals a more intimate knowledge of the Bible [...]. Others might expound the letter; Vaughan lived the text.'[1] The surprising thing is that the nature of this debt had not become a subject of scholarly attention much earlier. As another mid-century critic observed, it was very odd that the Bible had been 'all but ignored' in the 'search for sources'.[2] Among Vaughan's editors, Grosart had begun the process of identifying allusions to the Bible in footnotes to the text, but had not been followed by his immediate successors.[3]

---

1 M.M. Mahood, 'Vaughan: The Symphony of Nature', *Poetry and Humanism* (London: Jonathan Cape, 1950), p. 255. Stevie Davies would later develop the idea of living the text: 'For the Anglican after the eviction of the ministers, it could be the only resort. Henry Vaughan's Bible was therefore a kind of tabernacle into which he could withdraw from the world to look for Jesus [...]. His pilgrim eyes travelled the tracks of print through the sacred pages, and Christ the Word was counsellor to his own words' (Stevie Davies, *Henry Vaughan*, Border Lines Series (Bridgend: Seren, Poetry of Wales Press, 1995), pp. 113–14).
2 R.A. Durr, *On the Mystical Poetry of Henry Vaughan* (Cambridge, MA: Harvard University Press, 1962), p. 15.
3 *The Works in Verse and Prose Complete of Henry Vaughan, Silurist*, ed. Alexander B. Grosart, 4 vols., The Fuller Worthies' Library (Blackburn, 1871).

Chambers confined himself to a handful of explanatory notes and Martin confessed in his 1914 preface that his endeavour to record the sources for all quotations in Vaughan's original work did not extend to 'those from the Bible, which are so numerous, and sometimes so involved, that to annotate them would only obscure matter of more real interest'.[4] He relented somewhat in his second edition of 1957, but still felt that it 'seemed unnecessary to give chapter and verse for all Vaughan's citations and reminiscences of the Bible', adding that he had pointed out some of 'the less obvious ones', as well as 'some which might be missed through their close welding into the poet's own creative thought'.[5] The reluctance to annotate this aspect of Vaughan's text, therefore, was based on the assumption that readers would be familiar enough with the scriptures to pick up most biblical references without editorial assistance. Within four years of Martin's second edition, however, the result of a general decline in knowledge of the Bible in Western society was highlighted by Douglas Bush: 'The most pervasive and important element in Vaughan is biblical allusion and symbol, and these, in our day, are often not readily grasped'; and towards the end of the century, Christopher Hill confessed that 'we now miss' many of the biblical allusions that 'the literature of the age is crammed with'.[6] This situation had already been addressed by

Grosart identified some thirty biblical quotations or allusions in the 1650 *Silex Scintillans* and nearly three times as many in the preface and poems added in 1655.

4 *The Works of Henry Vaughan*, ed. Leonard Cyril Martin, 2 vols. (Oxford: Clarendon Press, 1914), Vol. I, p. iv. Chambers confined his notes to an explanation of 'Balaam's hire' (Numbers 22:18) in 'White Sunday'; an elucidation of the phrase 'Pistic nard' in 'St. Mary Magdalen', variously translated from the Greek in the gospels of Mark and John; and the sources of three other allusions to Judges in 'The Constellation', the gospels of John and Matthew in 'Ascension Day' and Luke in 'St. Mary Magdalen'. See *The Poems of Henry Vaughan Silurist*, ed. E.K. Chambers, 2 vols., The Muses' Library (London: George Routledge & Sons, 1896), Vol. I, pp. 309, 313, 307, 309, 313.

5 *The Works of Henry Vaughan*, ed. L.C. Martin, 2nd edn. (Oxford: Clarendon Press, 1957), p. iv.

6 Douglas Bush, *English Literature in the Earlier Seventeenth Century 1600–1660*, The Oxford History of English Literature, 2nd edn., revised (Oxford: Clarendon Press, 1962), p. 155; Christopher Hill, *The English Bible and the Seventeenth-Century Revolution* (London: Allen Lane, The Penguin Press, 1993), p. 31.

Christopher Dixon in the headnote to his commentary on a selection of Vaughan's poetry published in 1967:

> Wherever possible I have quoted Biblical passages relevant to Vaughan as fully as possible. If the sources are merely cited, readers may well not have a Bible to hand, and may not have the leisure or inclination to pursue the references.[7]

Philip West applauded the next major edition for doing Vaughan and his readers 'the great service of identifying many of the poems' hundreds of scripture borrowings'.[8] This achievement by Alan Rudrum has since been supplemented by the editors of the 'Oxford Authors' *George Herbert and Henry Vaughan* and the recently published *Works*.[9]

It is one thing to respond to the fact of Vaughan's immersion in the Scriptures by recording the mass of biblical material – quotations, characters, stories, language, and symbolism – in his poetry, but quite another to rise to the critical challenge issued in Rudrum's preface, 'that serious reading of Vaughan involves an awareness of *how he employed* his biblical sources' (italics added).[10] Early in the twentieth century, there had been a tentative account of Vaughan's adoption of the biblical symbolism of light and darkness and there was a mid-century examination of a 'cluster' of biblical images in 'The Night'.[11] It was not until 1960, however, that a whole chapter was devoted to illustrating the variety of ways in which Vaughan actually used the Scriptures. This pioneering venture by E.C. Pettet drew attention to various aspects of Vaughan's creative engagement

---

7 *A Selection from Henry Vaughan*, ed. Christopher Dixon (London: Longman, 1967), p. 108.
8 Philip West, *Henry Vaughan's* Silex Scintillans: *Scripture Uses* (Oxford: Oxford University Press, 2001), p. 1. The edition was Alan Rudrum's *Henry Vaughan: The Complete Poems* (Harmondsworth: Penguin Books, 1976, revised 1983).
9 See *George Herbert and Henry Vaughan*, ed. Louis L. Martz, The Oxford Authors (Oxford: Oxford University Press, 1986) and *The Works of Henry Vaughan*, ed. Donald R. Dickson, Alan Rudrum, and Robert Wilcher, 3 vols. (Oxford: Oxford University Press, 2018).
10 *Complete Poems*, ed. Rudrum, p. 18.
11 Helen Sard Hughes, 'Night in the Poetry of Henry Vaughan', *Modern Language Notes*, 28 (1913), 208–11; Fern Farnham, 'The Imagery of Henry Vaughan's "The Night"', *Philological Quarterly*, 38 (1959), 425–35.

with the Bible beyond simple meditations on characters and narrative episodes: the 'picture of Nature' that is 'intensely and continually coloured with Biblical reminiscences'; 'Scriptural allusions' both 'straightforward' and adapted; and above all 'the matter of language', from 'phrases taken straight from the Bible' and longer 'quotations or near-quotations' to 'Bible-inspired images'.[12] His critical verdict, however, was that the biblical 'echoes' in Vaughan's work 'are far less interesting than those from Herbert'.[13] Nevertheless, a spark had been ignited and studies of individual poems began to explore the complexities of Vaughan's poetic management of his biblical resources. Leland Chambers, for example, concluded that in composing 'The Night' Vaughan was 'scrupulous in the practice of his unique allusive technique', bringing the 'entire scriptural context' to bear 'on the development of the poem's meaning'; and Cleanth Brooks showed how close readings of 'The Retreat' and 'The Night' are enriched by an awareness of the scriptural origins of particular phrases in Revelation, Deuteronomy, the gospels of St Mark and St John, Malachi, and the Song of Solomon.[14] Others began to look more widely at the uses Vaughan made of biblical material. Robert Duvall claimed that biblical allusion is not merely 'ornament' or 'external inspiration' but 'an integral aspect of Vaughan's religious poetics' and argued the need for 'Biblical literacy' among Vaughan's readers; Eluned Brown showed that the 'hallowed places' of the Old Testament are as much part of the landscape of Vaughan's poetry as 'his own neighbourhood'; and Kenneth Friedenreich included a section on 'The Bible' in his chapter on important characteristics of Vaughan's style.[15] Eventually, a book-length study by

12 E.C. Pettet, *Of Paradise and Light: A Study of Vaughan's* Silex Scintillans (Cambridge: Cambridge University Press, 1960), pp. 32, 34–35, 36, 38, 42.
13 Pettet, *Of Paradise and Light*, p. 40.
14 Leland H. Chambers, 'Henry Vaughan's Allusive Technique: Biblical Allusions in "The Night"', *Modern Language Quarterly*, 27 (1966), 387; Cleanth Brooks, 'Henry Vaughan: Quietism and Mysticism', in *Essays in Honor of Esmond Linworth Marilla* , ed. Thomas Austin Kirby and William John Olive (Baton Rouge, LA: Louisiana State University Press, 1970), pp. 15–23. See also James Dale, 'Biblical Allusions in Vaughan's "The World"', *English Studies*, 51 (1970), 336–39; and Geoffrey Hill, 'A Pharisee to Pharisees: Reflections on Vaughan's "The Night"', *English*, 38 (1989), 97–113.
15 Robert Duvall, 'The Biblical Character of Henry Vaughan's *Silex Scintillans*', *Pacific Coast Philology*, 6 (1971), 13, 14; Eluned Brown, 'Henry Vaughan's

N.K. Thomas was devoted to explicating ways in which Vaughan 're-lives some of the major experiences of the Old Testament and the New' in his poetry and draws upon the Bible – especially 'the apocalyptic sections' – to process 'his own troubled experience in seventeenth century Puritan Britain'.[16] The culmination of this activity to date has been Philip West's demonstration that 'the most fruitful criticism of Vaughan begins and ends by consulting the bible' and his insistence that the critical focus should be shifted from the *presence* of biblical material in Vaughan's texts to the *uses* to which it is put in what was fundamentally a 'scripture-using culture'.[17] In this chapter, therefore, the emphasis will be on the *artistic* dimension of Vaughan's dependency on the Bible, since, for him, poetry 'is itself a *scripture-use*, a custom inspired by scripture, authorized by scriptural stories […] as well as consisting, in part, of scripture's words'.[18]

II

West notes that Vaughan was 'one of the first Welshmen to grow up able to read a Church of England bible in his native tongue', since the Welsh translation produced by William Morgan in 1588 was conformed to the Authorized Version in 1620. There is no trace of this in Vaughan's work, however, although there is evidence that he consulted the Catholic Vulgate, the Protestant Junius–Tremellius Latin bible, Beza's Latin New Testament, and the Geneva Bible, as well as taking 'the overwhelming majority' of his biblical citations from the Authorized Version.[19] Both the Genevan and the King James translations owed a great deal to the pioneering work of William Tyndale in the 1520s and 1530s, but it was the Bible produced in Geneva by Protestant exiles from the reign of the Catholic

---

Biblical Landscape', *Essays and Studies*, new series, 30 (1977), 57; Kenneth Friedenreich, *Henry Vaughan*, Twayne's English Authors (Boston, MA: G.K. Hall, 1978), pp. 34–38.
16 Noel Kennedy Thomas, *Henry Vaughan: Poet of Revelation* (Worthing: Churchman Publishing, 1986), pp. 13–14.
17 West, *Scripture Uses*, pp. 1, 18.
18 West, *Scripture Uses*, p. 20.
19 West, *Scripture Uses*, pp. 19–20.

Queen Mary that became the version favoured by Separatists and the Puritan faction in the Church of England. Reprinted frequently in handy quarto editions after its first publication in 1560, it was intended primarily for private study. Although its users included such senior conservative clerics as Lancelot Andrewes and William Laud, various features were designed to help less sophisticated readers navigate and understand the text: for the first time, chapters were divided into numbered verses for easy reference and descriptive chapter headings, concordances, and interpretative marginal notes were also supplied. For several decades after the 1611 translation authorized by King James had become the official Bible for reading in Church of England services, the Geneva Bible remained popular and new editions continued to appear until 1644 in spite of efforts to suppress it.[20]

An examination of all the passages from Scripture quoted as epigraphs to poems in *Silex Scintillans* reveals that one is taken from Beza's Latin, one combines phrases from the Latin versions of Junius–Tremellius and the Vulgate, four are from Geneva, and three have a composite wording from the Geneva and the Authorized versions.[21] The reason for this eclectic approach perhaps lies in the role allotted to the Bible by the Protestant reformers. As a lifelong member of the Church of England, Vaughan would have subscribed to the sixth of the Thirty-nine Articles set out in the Book of Common Prayer:

> Holy Scriptures containeth all things necessary to salvation: so that whatsoever is not read therein, nor may be proved thereby, is not to be required of any man, that it should be believed as an article of the faith, or be thought requisite or necessary to salvation.[22]

---

20 See Hill, *The English Bible and the Seventeenth-Century Revolution*, pp. 56–66.

21 In three further epigraphs, there are no differences between the wording in the Geneva and King James versions. These are postscripts to 'Resurrection and Immortality', 'The Pilgrimage', and 'The Law, and the Gospel'. See *HV Works*, pp. 62, 130, 131. For a fuller treatment of this topic, see my forthcoming article, 'Henry Vaughan's Use of Biblical Epigraphs in *Silex Scintuillans*', *Scintilla*, 24 (2021).

22 *The Book of Common Prayer: The Texts of 1549, 1559, and 1662*, ed. Brian Cummings (Oxford: Oxford University Press, 2011), p. 675.

The search for the truths contained in the Scriptures, however, was complicated by the fact that the versions read out in church or studied in private often differed from each other in wording. Vaughan had inherited the Protestant belief that contradictions and disagreements over the meaning of Scripture 'were the product of bad reading, not a problem with the Word itself'; and that the truth embodied in the Bible 'was explicable only in terms of itself'.[23] Donald Dickson explains that the standard methods for seeking the meaning of a given passage involved not only an etymological analysis of the original Hebrew and Greek of the Old and New Testaments, but also the 'diligent comparison of text with text', so that 'multiple levels of signification' – typological, Christological, personal, and historical – could be recovered 'by collating text with text, image with image'.[24] The ideal goal of this process is summed up by George Herbert in his second poem entitled 'The H. Scriptures':

> Oh that I knew how all thy lights combine,
>   And the configurations of their glorie!
>   Seeing not onely how each verse doth shine,
> But all the constellation of the storie.
>
> This verse marks that, and both do make a motion
>   Unto a third, that ten leaves off doth lie:
>   Then as dispersed herbs do watch a potion,
> These three make up some Christians destinie.[25]

Problems arose for Vaughan's generation, however, when rival factions arrived at mutually antagonistic interpretations in applying this system of 'collation'. In 'White Sunday', for example, an account of the 'Prophetic fire' that inspired the Apostles at Pentecost prompts a warning against being misled by contemporary pretenders to similar inspiration in interpreting the Word of God:

---

23 West, *Scripture Uses*, pp. 11, 12.
24 Donald R. Dickson, *The Fountain of Living Waters: The Typology of the Waters of Life in Herbert, Vaughan, and Traherne* (Columbia, MO: University of Missouri Press, 1987), pp. 33, 45.
25 *The English Poems of George Herbert*, ed. Helen Wilcox (Cambridge: Cambridge University Press, 2007), p. 210.

> Though some then boast that fire each day,
> And on Christs coat pin all their shreds;
> Not sparing openly to say,
> His candle shines upon their heads.[26]

West observes that Vaughan goes out of his way to identify passages frequently appropriated by his Puritan opponents to serve their religious and political ends and describes how he in turn 'ranges widely across the bible' – in both *Silex Scintillans* and *The Mount of Olives* – assembling around them 'other scriptures which mark each other from far off as correct guides to interpretation'. He cites as an example 'Ascension-day', which 'brings together prophecies from Malachi, Luke's gospel, Revelation and Acts to support its anti-radical visions', and concludes that Vaughan could be 'every bit as partisan in his readings' as his opponents and 'every bit as convinced by what he read'.[27]

In the context of this practice, then, his quotations from the Geneva Bible in the epigraphs attached to certain poems may have been intended as an act of re-appropriation – a way of affirming that the Geneva version was not in itself corrupt: its use by bad men and wilful *mis*use on occasion did not render it any more or less the authentic Word of God than the Authorized Version. Furthermore, the very fact that he consulted and quoted from a range of translations in Latin and English indicates his scholarly awareness that both caution and discernment were necessary in searching out the true meaning from a variety of human translations of a divinely inspired original.

His preference for Beza's Latin over any English version for the headnote to one of the untitled lyrics has been widely discussed. Rudrum, for example, explains that its wording of a verse from Romans 8:19 – '*Etenim res Creatæ exerto Capite observantes expectant revelationem Filiorum Dei*' [For the creatures, watching with lifted head, wait for the revelation of the sons of God] – plunges what follows into a theological debate about the status of animals in the divine scheme of things, which is highlighted by the excited questions of the opening lines:

---

26 *HV Works*, p. 569.
27 West, *Scripture Uses*, p 13.

> And do they so? Have they a Sense
>   Of ought but influence?
> Can they their heads lift, and expect,
>   And grone too? Why th'Elect
> Can do no more ...[28]

This is not the only poem for which he appears to have selected a particular version of the Scriptures to suit his poetic or doctrinal purpose. In 'Isaacs Marriage', he substitutes 'pray' from the Geneva Bible for 'meditate' in an epigraph otherwise taken word for word from the King James translation – 'Praying! And to be married? It was rare, / But now 'tis monstrous' – in order to provoke this incredulous exclamation and to justify his later conceit of the young patriarch's soul taking flight towards God in the 'incense' of prayer.[29] The theological significance of the story of Adam's fall into sin and subsequent redemption by the 'saving wound' of Christ, which is the subject of 'Man's fall, and Recovery', is distilled into a verse from one of St Paul's letters: *'As by the offence of one, the fault came on all men to condemnation; So by the Righteousness of one, the benefit abounded towards all men to the justification of life'* (Romans 5:18).[30] The moral contrast between Adam and Christ is sharpened by the adoption of 'the fault' from Geneva instead of the Authorized Version's 'iudgment' and the latter's 'righteousnes' instead of Geneva's 'iustifying'; and doctrinal considerations may lie behind the preference for Geneva's 'the benefit abounded towards all men' over 'the free gift came vpon all men' in the 1611 Bible. Whatever the reasons for the eclectic nature of the epigraph, it provides an authoritative summary of the central issue of Sin and Salvation in the universal history of the human race.

The epigraph chosen for 'Disorder and frailty' has a rather different function. The poem is a guilt-laden complaint by a wayward, weak, and perverse sinner who has repeatedly failed to maintain his initial responsiveness to the life-giving actions of his Saviour: he breaks 'the link' established with God; he sees hopeful buds turn into 'yielding

---

28 *HV Works*, p. 95. For Rudrum's reading of the poem, see 'Henry Vaughan, the Liberation of the Creatures, and Seventeenth-Century English Calvinism', *The Seventeenth Century*, 4 (1989), 33–54.
29 *HV Works*, pp. 68–71.
30 *HV Works*, pp. 73–74. Vaughan wrongly places the quotation in Romans 18:19.

leaves', poisoned by flies and beaten off by rain; he watches his 'weak fire' soar towards 'that Comforter, the Sun' only to descend to earth as soon as it is 'Cool'd by the damps of night'; and he begs in a final stanza for his soul to be granted 'wings' and to be watered by 'grace'. A verse from one of the minor Prophets then imposes a different perspective on the disorder and frailty of the speaker: '*O Ephraim what shall I do unto thee? O Judah how shall I intreat thee? for thy goodness is as a morning Cloud, and as the early Dew it goeth away?*' (Hosea 6:4).[31] The sense of divine disappointment is made more poignant by the substitution of a word from the Geneva translation in a text that is mainly quoted from the Authorized Version. In place of the rhetorical reiteration of the 1611 translators – 'O Iudah, what shall I do vnto thee?' – the poet inserts into this second question the verb with which the Protestant reformers expressed their sense of the Creator's yearning over his people's lack of steadfastness and perseverance: 'O Judah, how shall I *entreat* thee?'[32] This switching from the point of view of the self-absorbed poet to that of the deity whose loving approaches have so often come to nothing is one of Vaughan's most creative uses of an epigraph.

III

Fundamental to Vaughan's use of the Bible in his poetry is his conviction, expressed in the 1650 poem 'H. Scriptures', that the 'dear book' is not only his 'souls Joy, and food' and 'lifes Charter', but also the 'Key that opens to all Mysteries'.[33] Over the Christian centuries, a complex system of hermeneutics had evolved for explicating the 'Mysteries' encoded in the written (and later printed) text of the Bible – what Vaughan called the '*Word* in Characters' in another of the phrases in 'H. Scriptures'. A fourfold method, developed by Augustine and Aquinas, had been widely employed during the Middle Ages, which added typological, tropological (or moral), and anagogical (or eschatological) levels of meaning to the literal or historical signification of the words. Typology, a special kind of allegory in which

---

31 *HV Works*, pp. 108–10.
32 Ephraim and Judah were the two tribes of Israel occupying territory to the north and south of Jerusalem.
33 *HV Works*, p. 104.

persons and events in the Old Testament were read as prefiguring Christ and events in the New Testament, was authorized by Christ's own practice, when he 'expounded vnto them in all the Scriptures, the things concerning himselfe' (Luke 24:27), making direct links between the Old Testament and his own role and destiny: 'For as Ionas was a signe vnto the Nineuites, so shall also the Sonne of man be to this generation' (Luke 11:30); 'And as Moses lifted vp the serpent in the wildernesse: euen so must the Sonne of man be lifted vp' (John 3:14). St Paul frequently taught that the Old Testament was fulfilled in the New: 'For it is written, that Abraham had two sonnes, the one by a bond-maid, the other by a free woman [...] Which things are an Allegorie; for these are the two Couenants' (Galatians 4:22–24); the law was merely 'a shadow of good things to come' and has now been superseded by 'the very Image' of those things (Hebrews 10:1); Adam was 'the figure of him that was to come' (Romans 5:14).

Barbara Lewalski summarizes the traditional method of typological exegesis as 'a pattern of signification in which type and antitype, as historically real entities with independent meaning and validity, form patterns of prefiguration, recapitulation, and fulfillment by reason of God's providential control of history'. She goes on to describe how the reformers of the sixteenth century adapted this medieval system so that history came to be regarded 'as a continuum' rather than two distinct eras separated by the Incarnation of Christ and 'the contemporary Christian' replaced Christ as 'the primary antitype'. This shift of emphasis meant that Protestants could read 'the experiences recorded in the Old and also the New Testament' as types of 'their own spiritual experience' and the events of individual lives were assimilated 'to the pervasive typological patterns discerned in biblical and later Christian history'.[34] This method of applying Old Testament history and prophecy to the personal situation of a modern speaker is set out in the middle two stanzas of George Herbert's 'The bunch of grapes':

---

34 Barbara K. Lewalski, 'Typology and Poetry: A Consideration of Herbert, Vaughan, and Marvell', in *Illustrious Evidence: Approaches to English Literature of the Early Seventeenth Century*, ed. Earl Miner (Berkeley, CA and London: University of California Press, 1975), pp. 42–43. West notes that the new method of reading scriptural experiences 'as types of the spiritual lives of individual believers' was a development from 'the *tropological* or moral sense of scripture' (*Scripture Uses*, p. 42).

> For as the Jews of old by Gods command
>   Travell'd, and saw no town:
> So now each Christian hath his journeys spann'd:
>   Their storie pennes and sets us down.
>   A single deed is small renown.
> Gods works are wide, and let in future times;
> His ancient justice overflows our crimes.
>
> Then have we too our guardian fires and clouds;
>   Our Scripture-dew drops fast:
> We have our sands and serpents, tents and shrowds;
>   Alas! our murmurings come not last.
>   But where's the cluster? Where's the taste
> Of mine inheritance? Lord, if I must borrow,
> Let me as well take up their joy, as sorrow.[35]

In her later study of Protestant poetics, Lewalski describes this poem as 'the most explicit statement of Herbert's conception of typology as God's symbolism', since it not only depends upon 'the traditional typological relationships' between the 'cluster of grapes' brought back by the spies sent into Canaan by Moses (see Numbers 13:17–25) and Christ, 'the true vine pressed in the winepress of the Passion' (see Isaiah 63:3), but also locates 'the entire typological relationship in the heart of the speaker'.[36] For, although these central stanzas see the journey of 'each Christian' prefigured in the story of justice and grace dispensed to 'the Jews of old', the first and fourth stanzas express the poet's more personal sense that although he has drawn back from the brink of the promised land 'to the Red sea, the sea of shame', he can still claim his share in the joyful 'inheritance' of the redeeming wine 'pressed for my sake'.

Something similar happens in Vaughan's 'The Law, and the Gospel', in which the type of Mount Sinai, where God delivered the Ten Commandments to Moses, is answered by the antitype of Mount Sion – literally, one of the hills on which the historical Jerusalem was built – which is associated in the New Testament with the 'heauenly Ierusalem' and with 'Iesus the mediatour of

---

35 *English Poems of George Herbert*, p. 449.
36 Barbara Kiefer Lewalski, *Protestant Poetics and the Seventeenth-Century Religious Lyric* (Princeton, NJ: Princeton University Press, 1979), pp. 312–13.

the new Couenant' (Hebrews 12:18–24). There is a corresponding movement from the Israelites, who '[w]hisper'd obedience' and inclined *'their* heads' in the first stanza, to the followers of Christ – 'With filial Confidence *we* touch ev'n thee' – in the second (italics added); but these plural pronouns are superseded in the last two stanzas by the first-person singular of the poet, who pleads to have both Law and Gospel planted in his heart, so that the threat of 'a Just Curse' may be complemented in his own experience by the promise of 'mercies' obtained by the crucifixion of the one who 'bore my pain'.[37]

The three brief stanzas of 'Trinity-Sunday' move from the eternal reality of the Three Persons in One God (in heaven) by way of their general manifestation in human history (through the Incarnation) to their personal effects on the speaker, in whom the types are fulfilled:

> So let the *Anti-types* in me
> Elected, bought and seal'd for free,
> Be own'd, sav'd, *Sainted* by you three![38]

In 'Ascension-day', Vaughan finds fulfilment of a distant Scriptural event in his own spiritual elation:

> Thy glorious, bright Ascension (though remov'd
> So many Ages from me) is so prov'd
> And by thy Spirit seal'd to me, that I
> Feel me a sharer in thy victory.

Then, having recapitulated in his own imagination the 'secret commerce' between Christ and his disciples during the 'forty days' after his resurrection, Vaughan ends the poem by reading Christ's ascension as a type of his Second Coming: 'Come then thou faithful witness! come dear Lord / Upon the Clouds again to judge this world!'[39]

Vaughan's own approval of the typological method is expressed most directly in 'White Sunday', which owes something to the first of the stanzas from Herbert's 'The bunch of grapes' quoted above:

37 *HV Works*, pp. 130–31.
38 *HV Works*, p. 579.
39 *HV Works*, pp. 565–66.

> Besides, thy method with thy own,
> Thy own dear people pens our times,
> Our stories are in theirs set down
> And penalties spread to our Crimes.[40]

'The Mutinie' is an obvious case of Vaughan's use of typology to reveal, as Jonathan Post observes, 'both personal and political significance' in his own situation.[41] The opening lines – 'Weary of this same Clay, and straw, I laid / Me down to breath' – clearly evoke the plight of the Israelites in Egypt, in bondage under a new Pharaoh and forced to serve him 'with rigour' (Exodus 1:1–14). Spiritual exhaustion and rebellion take on a political dimension as the poet turns to address the God of history who has permitted the present state of affairs:

> If yet these barren grounds
> And thirstie brick must be (said I)
> My taske, and Destinie,
>
> Let me so strive and struggle with thy foes
> (Not thine alone but mine too,) that when all
> Their Arts and force are built unto the height
> That Babel-weight
> May prove thy glory, and their shame.

Mobilizing another Old Testament type – the Tower of Babel – Vaughan calls upon God to humble his oppressors as he once scattered 'the children of men' when they strove to make themselves 'a name' by raising up 'a city and a tower, whose top may *reach vnto heauen*' (Genesis 11:1–9). The fact that God's punishment involved the confounding of 'their language' may have appealed to the poet who elsewhere condemned the Puritans in his own day for corrupting the pure spring of Religion with 'False *Ecchoes*, and Confused sounds' and for stuffing their books with 'chaff and windy fits'.[42] In the final stanza, the mutinous poet enlists the story

---

40 *HV Works*, pp. 569–70.
41 Jonathan F.S. Post, *Henry Vaughan: The Unfolding Vision* (Princeton, NJ: Princeton University Press, 1982), p. 178. For 'The Mutinie', see *HV Works*, pp. 133–34.
42 See 'Religion' and 'The Agreement', *HV Works*, pp. 64–65, 617–19.

of the Israelites wandering in the desert, one of his favourite Old Testament types:

> Not but I know thou hast a shorter Cut
> To bring me home, than through a wildernes,
> A Sea, or Sands and Serpents ...

One detail is picked up not from Exodus but from Numbers 21:6: 'And the Lord sent fierie serpents among the people, and they bit the people, and much people of Israel died.' The contemporary antitype is the havoc wrought among the royalist and Anglican faithful by parliamentary zealots.

Vaughan's perception that the experiences of the recent Civil War had their biblical type in the Old Testament also informs his invocation of the feud between Jacob and Esau:

> But blessed *Jacob*, though thy sad distress
> Was just the same with ours, and nothing less,
> For thou a brother, and blood-thirsty too
> Didst flye, whose children wrought thy childrens wo.[43]

Jacob's prayer when he learns that Esau is coming to meet him with 'foure hundred men' is perhaps the specific source of Vaughan's couplets: 'Deliuer me, I pray thee, from the hand of my brother, from the hand of Esau: for I feare him, lest he will come, and smite me, and the mother with the children' (Genesis 32:6, 11).[44] The poem in question, 'Jacobs Pillow, and Pillar', is one of Vaughan's most sustained exercises in this particular way of using Scripture. Its main source is the story of how Jacob made a pillow of stones, dreamed of a ladder with 'the Angels of God ascending and descending on it', and next day set up one of the stones as a pillar, which he anointed with oil and dedicated as 'Gods house' (Genesis 28:10–22). Joseph Galdon explains that this pillar became 'a type of the temple, the House of God and the Gate of Heaven'. Elsewhere in the poem, Vaughan invokes the ark of Noah, which also became a symbol of God's dwelling-place, and both the ark and the pillar were read as

---

43 *HV Works*, pp. 616–17.
44 In a footnote, Vaughan himself cites passages about Esau's 'violence' against Jacob and his pursuit of his brother 'with the sword' from Obadiah and Amos.

types of 'the heart, the Temple of the individual soul, where God is worshipped even after the historical temple is destroyed'.[45] Christ's own prophecy that the time will come when the Father will be worshipped 'neither in this mountaine, nor yet at Hierusalem' but 'in spirit, and in trueth' (John 4:21–23) is also recalled in lines that resonate with the contemporary significance of this cluster of biblical types for those whose churches had been closed by their Puritan rulers:

>   he foretold the place,
> And form to serve him in, should be true grace
> And the meek heart, not in a Mount, nor at
> *Jerusalem*, with blood of beasts, and fat.
> A heart is that dread place, that awful Cell,
> That secret Ark, where the milde Dove doth dwell
> When the proud waters rage: when Heathens rule
> By Gods permission, and man turns a Mule.

Galdon sums up the complex typology of the Temple that lies at the heart of the poem: 'There is the historical temple of the Old Testament, but there is also the temple of the New Testament, the Church of God, and finally there is the temple of the individual soul.'[46] At the end of 'Jacobs Pillow, and Pillar', Vaughan forges further typological links – between Jacob and Christ and contemporary Christians – which stress the historical continuity implied by the method of exegesis he has been employing throughout the text:

> Thou from the Day-star a long way didst stand
> And all that distance was Law and command.
> But we a healing Sun by day and night,
> Have our sure Guardian, and our leading light;
> What thou didst hope for and believe, we finde
> And feel a friend most ready, sure and kinde.
> Thy pillow was but type and shade at best,
> But we the substance have, and on him rest.

---

45 Joseph A. Galdon S.J., *Typology and Seventeenth-Century Literature* (The Hague and Paris: Mouton, 1975), pp. 132–34.

46 Galdon, *Typology and Seventeenth-Century Literature*, p. 136.

What Jacob, living under the dispensation of Old Testament Law, could only 'hope for' has since been manifested in the 'healing Sun' of the 'Day-star', Christ; and Christ himself – according to Augustine – is an antitype of the anointed pillar, 'because Christ comes from the Greek *chrism*' and was 'the anointed of God'.[47]

The story of Jacob features in several of Vaughan's other works. In 'Rules and Lessons', for example, his night-long wrestling with a stranger (Genesis 32:24–30) is a type of the contemporary Christian's spiritual struggle with God:

> Serve God before the world: let him not go
> Until thou hast a blessing , then resigne
> The whole unto him; and remember who
> Prevail'd by *wrestling* ere the *Sun* did *shine*.[48]

And West points out – in a chapter on the typological significance of the patriarchs for Vaughan – that Jacob's flight from the murderous wrath of Esau figures more than once in *The Mount of Olives*, where it finds its antitype in 'the persecuted and afflicted Anglicans of the Interregnum', perhaps most strikingly in a prayer for use when departing from home: 'Thou that didst go out with *Jacob* from *Beer-she-ba* unto *Padan-aran*, guiding him in the *waste plaines*, and watching over him on his *Pillow of stones*, be not now farre from me.'[49] Another 'central conceit' in *Silex Scintillans*, explored in detail by Donald Dickson, is that 'the stony heart of the believer can flow with living waters'. It originates in God's command to Moses to strike water from 'the rocke in Horeb [...] that the people may drinke' (Exodus 17:6), which was interpreted by St Paul as a type of the 'spirituall drinke' flowing from the 'spirituall Rocke [...] and that Rocke was Christ' (1 Corinthians 10:4).[50] A straightforward example occurs in 'White Sunday':

> Yet thou the great eternal Rock
> Whose height above all ages shines,

---

47 West, *Scripture Uses*, p. 42.
48 *HV Works*, p. 99.
49 West, *Scripture Uses*, p. 45; *HV Works*, p. 292.
50 Dickson, *Fountain of Living Waters*, p. 142.

> Art still the same, and canst unlock
> Thy waters to a soul that pines.⁵¹

Extending right through Vaughan's devotional poetry, from the 1650 emblem of the 'flinty heart' (derived from Ezekiel 11:19) to the 'eschatological imagery' of 'thy eternal, living wells' in 'The Seed growing secretly', the 'living fountains' of 'Fair and yong light!' and the 'Fountains of life, where the Lamb goes' in 'The Water-fall' (derived from Revelation 7:17), the 'typology of the waters of life serves as a framing device' against which the speaker 'can understand, measure, and give form to his own life's story'.⁵²

IV

Pettet notes that, quite apart from the formal parallels of type and antitype, 'Vaughan's poems are filled with Scriptural allusions' and 'replete with phrases taken straight from the Bible'.⁵³ These observations might suggest that Vaughan was indebted to the Scriptures in much the same way that he was indebted to Randolph and Habington in his secular verse and to George Herbert in his religious poetry. But the critical consensus seems to be that the words and images and ideas of the Bible played an even more fundamental role in his practice of the art of poetry than either the system of typology or any other literary source. Gerald Hammond found the 'Biblical echoes' to be more 'precise and purposeful' than echoes of *The Temple*; Robert Duvall declared that 'Vaughan's method is more than borrowing', fusing public 'biblical detail' with 'private, immediate, mystical experience' into 'a rich idiom which is, finally, and manifestly, his own'; and John Wall argued that the '[w]eaving and reweaving' of biblical material into 'an allusive web' gives his poems 'a feeling of employing a private or privately understood or highly coded vocabulary'.⁵⁴ Duvall

---

51 *HV Works*, p. 570.
52 Dickson, *Fountain of Living Waters*, p. 139.
53 Pettet, *Of Paradise and Light*, pp. 34, 36.
54 Hammond, '"Poor dust should lie still low"', 1; Duvall, 'The Biblical Character of Vaughan's *Silex Scintillans*', 18; John N. Wall, *Transformations of the Word: Spenser, Herbert, Vaughan* (Athens, GA: University of Georgia Press, 1988), p. 332.

explains how this Scripture-based poetic art was developed to meet a particular set of cultural circumstances:

> Vaughan's unique, private vision returns again and again for a kind of *verification* to experiences recorded in the Bible – experiences Vaughan knew would be known by his audience. Drawing on a great common stock of allusions broadens the range of the poetry and by the technique of inter-related images and allusions intentionally appeals to the Biblically-minded seventeenth-century readers.[55]

Just as he expected the gentlemen to whom he addressed his earliest poems to recognize his allusions to the popular poets of the Caroline court, so he expected his later readers to bring an appropriate knowledge of the Bible to the task of decoding his religious poems.

'Regeneration' illustrates at the very beginning of Vaughan's 1650 volume the variety of his allusive practice, ranging from simple to complex and from commonplace to recondite.[56] At line 25, the pilgrim–poet is summoned East to a place that '[s]ome call'd [...] *Jacobs Bed*'. Duvall's biblically literate reader would have known from the familiar story of Jacob's dream that Jacob himself had 'called the name of that place Beth-el' (Genesis 28:19) and that his anointing of a stone pillar there was widely interpreted as 'a sort of church dedication' – a symbolic event of great significance for Vaughan's fellow Anglicans.[57] When a 'rushing wind' breaks in upon the speaker's 'musing' later in the poem, the two words would have been enough to identify it as the 'rushing mighty wind' of the Holy Spirit that inspired the Apostles at Pentecost (Acts 2:1–2); and this would have been confirmed when he hears the whispered words, '*Where I please*', which is a simple allusion to Christ's explanation to Nicodemus that the wind of the Spirit 'bloweth where it listeth' (John 3:8). Much greater demands are made upon the reader's biblical knowledge by the more abstruse reference to the 'Prophets, and friends of God', who alone are permitted to tread upon the consecrated soil of Bethel. The relevant verse – from one of the apocryphal books that were included in the 1611 edition of the Authorized Version – teaches that Wisdom

---

55 Duvall, 'The Biblical Character of Vaughan's *Silex Scintillans*', 18.
56 See *HV Works*, pp. 57–59.
57 West, *Scripture Uses*, p. 39.

'maketh al things new: and in all ages entring into the holy soules, she maketh them friends of God, & Prophets' (Wisdom of Solomon 7:27). The idea of renewal and growing intimacy with God has an obvious bearing on the subject of regeneration, but those who recognized a further allusion to the General Epistle of James – 'Abraham beleeued God, and it was imputed vnto him for righteousnes: and he was called the friend of God' (James 2:23) – would have recalled that James used the phrase in the course of demonstrating that Abraham was justified 'by workes […] and not by faith only' (2:24), a statement critical for the post-Reformation debate about the theology of salvation. Even more complex is the stanza devoted to 'a little Fountain' flowing into a 'Cisterne full / Of divers stones, some bright, and round / Others ill-shap'd, and dull'. Many readers would probably have understood the fountain as a symbol of Christ's grace – derived from references like that to the 'well of water springing vp into euerlasting life' (John 4:14); but to interpret the 'divers stones' and the 'Cisterne', they would have had to bring together verses from the Old and New Testaments: 'they haue forsaken me, the fountaine of liuing waters, *and* hewed them out cisternes, broken cisternes that can hold no water' (Jeremiah 2:13) and 'Ye also as liuely stones, are built vp a spirituall house, an holy Priesthood to offer vp spirituall sacrifice' (1 Peter 2:5).

Often the briefest of verbal signals will trigger an allusion that makes a significant contribution to the texture and meaning of a poem. For example, 'our Pillar-fires' in the third of the untitled elegies, 'the gourd of sin' in 'Repentance', the 'lost Son' in 'The Jews', and 'the *weeping Lad*' in 'Begging (II)' are enough to remind the reader well-versed in Bible stories of the Israelites' journey through the wilderness towards the promised land (Exodus 13:21), God's causing a gourd to grow and wither in a single day and night to teach Jonah a lesson (Jonah 4:6–11), Christ's parable of the prodigal son (Luke 15:11–32), and the plight of the outcast Ishmael (Genesis 21:19).[58] Similarly, the phrases the 'narrow way' in 'Son-dayes', 'hid in thee' in 'I walkt the other day', 'Bring bone to bone' in 'Ascension-Hymn', and 'Co-heirs' in 'Faith' are sufficient reminders of significant biblical teachings not to require spelling out in any more detail: that 'strait is the gate, and narrow is the way which leadeth vnto life, and few there be that finde it' (Matthew 7:14); that 'yee are dead, and your life is hid

---

58 See *HV Works*, pp. 86, 113, 586, 587.

with Christ in God. When Christ, who is our life, shall appeare, then shall yee also appeare with him in glorie' (Colossians 3:3–4); that there will be a resurrection of the body, 'and beholde a shaking, and the bones came together, bone to his bone' (Ezekiel 37:7), as prophesied in the Old Testament; and that 'we are the children of God. And if children, then heires, heires of God, and ioint heires with Christ: if so be that we suffer with *him*, that wee may be also glorified together' (Romans 8:16–17).[59] Sometimes it is merely a matter of incorporating descriptive or narrative phrases into the text of a poem: 'the heauen departed as a scrowle when it is rolled together' (Revelation 6:14) becomes 'like a scrowle the heavens shal passe' in 'Day of Judgement'; 'the starres in their courses fought' (Judges 5:20) figures in 'The Constellation'; the sky *'which is* strong, *and* as a molten looking glasse' (Job 37:18) reappears in 'Ascension-day', where the 'Heav'n above them shin'd like molten glass'.[60]

West demonstrates from a stanza in 'White Sunday' that 'even single words might change the sense of a whole poem by implying framing scriptural contexts'.[61] Having noted that 'some rays' of the light of the Spirit that shone so brightly at Pentecost still provide genuine illumination in the pages of 'thy Book', Vaughan discerns a present danger 'by these glances of the flock', that is, by glimpses of the true nature of some who claim to be followers of the Good Shepherd:

> For though thou doest that great light lock,
> And by this lesser [i.e. the rays] commerce keep:
> Yet by these glances of the flock
> I can discern Wolves from the Sheep.

Two words in the fourth line call up for 'a scripture-using readership' a verse that was popular 'in anti-clerical literature of the earlier seventeenth century': 'Beware of false prophets, which come to you in sheepes clothing, but inwardly they are rauening wolues' (Matthew 7:15). Once activated, this allusion alters the direction of a poem that began as a celebration of Whitsunday and sets in train 'a series of biblical allusions designed to identify Puritan *new lights* as these false

---

59 *HV Works*, pp. 111, 146, 567, 115.
60 *HV Works*, pp. 63, 135, 566.
61 West, *Scripture Uses*, p. 173. For 'White Sunday', see *HV Works*, pp. 569–70.

prophets'.[62] Something similar is effected not just for a single poem but for *Silex Scintillans* as a whole by the two words that bring the final poem to a close. In an adaptation of the prayer that God will 'Turne againe our captiuitie' (Psalm 126:4), the poet looks forward to a future time when his oppressed people will adore the God 'Who turn'd our sad captivity!' – an allusion that also brings into play the long history of the Israelites, who were twice exiled and twice restored to their own land from servitude in Egypt and Babylon.[63]

V

The implications of Vaughan's careful and varied management of biblical material for an understanding of his ideal conception and actual practice of the art of religious poetry are spelled out in the sestet of the sonnet entitled 'H. Scriptures'. The last of the descriptive phrases that make up the octave are 'The *Word* in Characters [i.e. letters of the alphabet], God in the *Voice*'. They specify the two ways in which the divine *Logos* is manifested in the realm of human culture as language in its written and spoken forms; and together they inform the sestet's prayer for a fruitful collaboration between the language of the Bible and the language of the poet:

> O that I had deep Cut in my hard heart
>   Each line in thee! Then would I plead in groans
>   Of my Lords penning, and by sweetest Art
> Return upon himself the *Law*, and *Stones*.
>   Read here, my faults are thine. This Book, and I
> Will tell thee so; *Sweet Saviour thou didst dye!*[64]

Lewalski sees in these lines Vaughan's desire to have the Bible as 'the standard for his art'.[65] For if the poet were to take the words of the Scriptures so fully to heart that they were metaphorically engraved upon it, then there would be no essential difference between his utterance (the 'groans' that are recorded in print) and the sacred

---

62 See West, *Scripture Uses*, p. 173.
63 See 'L'Envoy', *HV Works*, p. 632.
64 *HV Works*, p. 104.
65 Lewalski, *Protestant Poetics*, p. 228.

written text.⁶⁶ Furthermore, this integrating of human and divine language 'by sweetest Art' would be an effective means of laying claim to the salvation gained through Christ's sacrificial death on the Cross, which is promised in the text of the holy Book and expressed as a certain faith in the last words of the poem: '*Sweet Saviour thou didst dye*!' The italic font, by a convention that Vaughan employs more than once in *Silex Scintillans*, indicates words spoken aloud, which 'tell' Christ the truth that is also told in the 'Book' and printed in the poem for him to 'Read here'.⁶⁷

Voices speaking aloud from the pages of Scripture permeate a poem that seems designed to demonstrate the 'sweetest Art' by which New Testament mercy engraved upon the 'hard heart' of the poet counteracts the demand for Old Testament justice in an utterance that seamlessly weaves together the poet's language with biblical words and images. The first move of 'Abels Blood', as Post observes, is to establish 'the lines of continuity between past and present'.⁶⁸ In a six-line prologue to the three stanzas of varying length that follow, Vaughan recalls the story of Cain's crime against his brother and its abiding significance in human history:

> Sad, purple well! whose bubbling eye
> Did first against a Murth'rer cry;
> Whose streams still vocal, still complain
>   Of bloody *Cain*,
> And now at evening are as red
> As in the morning when first shed.⁶⁹

In the account of the first murder, God tells Cain that 'the voyce of thy brothers blood cryeth vnto me from the ground' (Genesis 4:10).

---

66 Madeleine Forey's gloss on these lines – 'the authority in the language is Christ's and not his own' – is useful, except that the tense in the poem is conditional, not indicative: 'Then would I plead.' See her article, 'Poetry and Apocalypse: Henry Vaughan's *Silex Scintillans*', *The Seventeenth Century*, 11 (1996), 169.

67 For other uses of the convention of italics to indicate utterance, see the last three lines of 'Regeneration', which record words spoken by God and by the poet; lines 20 and 40 of 'Corruption', spoken by Man and an Angel; and the extended speech by the poet in lines 65–70 of 'Misery' (*HV Works*, pp. 59, 104, 139–40).

68 Post, *The Unfolding Vision*, p. 169.

69 For 'Abels blood', see *HV Works*, pp. 612–13.

And for Vaughan, the streams that flow from Abel are 'still vocal' and 'still complain' across the ages as a symbol of the instinctive clamour for justice, even 'now', as human history draws to a close:

> If single thou
> (Though single voices are but low,)
> Coulds't such a shrill and long cry rear
> As speaks still in thy makers ear,
> What thunders shall those men arraign
> Who cannot count those they have slain,
> Who bath not in a shallow flood,
> But in a deep, wide sea of blood?

If that 'single' cry has carried into the present and 'speaks still' in the ear of the Creator, there must be 'thunders' of divine punishment due to those contemporary murderers who 'cannot count' the number of their victims and who wade 'in a deep wide sea of blood'. That climactic image sets in train a succession of biblical phrases and contexts that culminate in a New Testament echo of the 'shrill and long cry' for vengeance provoked by the first murder:

> A sea, whose lowd waves cannot sleep,
> But *Deep* still calleth upon *deep*:
> Whose urgent *sound* like unto that
> *Of many waters*, beateth at
> The everlasting doors above,
> Where souls behind the altar move,
> And with one strong, incessant cry
> Inquire *How long?* of the most high.

The 'lowd waves' of the 'sea of blood' call up a poetic voice from long ago: 'Deepe calleth vnto deepe at the noyse of thy water-spouts: all thy waues and thy billowes are gone ouer me' (Psalm 42:7). The Psalmist, overwhelmed by a sense of abandonment and injustice, goes on to give voice to his frustration in words that mirror the plight of the contemporary poet:

> I will say vnto God, My rocke, why hast thou forgotten me? why goe I mourning, because of the oppression of the enemy? *As* with

a sword in my bones, mine enemies reproch mee: while they say dayly vnto me, Where *is* thy God? (Psalm 42:9–10)

The urgency of the message of those waves is vividly expressed in imagery that runs together 'voices' from the Old and New Testaments: 'his voice as the sound of many waters' (Revelation 1:15); 'Lift vp your heads, O yee gates; and be ye lift vp, ye euerlasting doores; and the King of glory shall come in' (Psalm 24:7); 'And when hee had opened the fift seale, I saw vnder the altar, the soules of them that were slaine for the word of God, and for the testimony which they held. And they cried with a lowd voice, saying, How long, O Lord, holy and true, doest thou not iudge and auenge our blood on them that dwell on the earth?' (Revelation 6:9–10).

Psalm 42 does not end, however, with the bewildered complaint of a drowning man. An alternative internal voice brings this Old Testament poem to an end on a different note: 'Why art thou cast downe, O my soule? and why art thou disquieted within me? hope thou in God, for I shall yet praise him, *who is* the health of my countenance, and my God' (Psalm 42:11). Vaughan's modern complaint also turns back upon itself – exactly half way through the poem, as Post points out – with a direct address to the eternal author and dispenser of justice; and the speaker 'adopts a new tone, a new voice, a new message' that 'seems literally to transform [...] the turbulent wake of voices in the first half of the poem':[70]

> Almighty Judge!
> At whose just laws no just men grudge;
> Whose blessed, sweet commands do pour
> Comforts and joys, and hopes each hour
> On those that keep them; O accept
> Of his vow'd heart, whom thou hast kept
> From bloody men! and grant, I may
> That sworn memorial duly pay
> To thy bright arm, which was my light
> And leader through thick death and night!

The assurance of comfort and hope is filtered into the poem through the personal witness of the speaker, who has been preserved from

---

[70] Post, *The Unfolding Vision*, pp. 170–71.

the hands of 'bloody men' by a vow that he now promises to honour by duly paying the 'sworn memorial' to the God who led him safely 'through thick death and night' on the field of battle – perhaps a reminiscence of the 'day of darknesse and of gloominesse, a day of clouds and of thicke darknesse' foreseen by one of the minor prophets, when 'the LORD shall vtter his voyce before his armie' (Joel 2:2, 11). This experience prompts the acceptance of a different response to the spilling of blood in a final stanza that is intricately woven from New Testament texts into a prayer – another kind of utterance – based on a new dispensation:

> I, may that flood,
> That proudly spilt and despis'd blood,
> Speechless and calm, as Infants sleep!
> Or if it watch, forgive and weep
> For those that spilt it! May no cries
> From the low earth to high Heaven rise,
> But what (like his, whose blood peace brings)
> Shall (when they rise) *speak better things*,
> Then *Abels* doth! may *Abel* be
> Still single heard, while these agree
> With his milde blood in voice and will,
> *Who* pray'd for those that did him kill!

The injunction to 'forgive and weep' for the 'bloody men' who have repeated the crime of Cain in the present age is based on St Paul's teaching to the 'saints and faithfull brethren' of Colosse that the 'peace' available through the shedding of Christ's blood is attained not by revenge but by reconciliation: 'For it pleased *the Father* that in him should all fulness dwell, And (hauing made peace through the blood of his crosse) by him to reconcile all things vnto himself' (Colossians 1:19–20). Vaughan then quotes the explicit revocation of the Old Testament image of Abel's blood crying for justice in another of the New Testament epistles, in which the writer reminds his readers that they are summoned not to Mount Sinai, but 'vnto mount Sion' and 'to Iesus the mediatour of the new Couenant, and to the blood of sprinckling, that speaketh better things than that of Abel' (Hebrews 12:18, 22, 24). Finally, to drive home the point of speaking with the new voice of forgiveness and reconciliation, he invokes the supreme demonstration of those qualities: 'And when they were come to the place which is called Caluarie, there they crucified him [...] Then said Iesus , Father, forgiue them, for they know not what they doe' (Luke 23:33–34).

This extraordinary poem sets in motion a debate about the moral complexities of a symbolic event from the distant past that still reverberates in the here and now.[71] By merging his own voice with those of the Psalmist, St John the Divine, St Paul, and Christ himself, Vaughan creates a kaleidoscope of different perspectives – human and divine, universal and personal, historical and contemporary – upon the paradox of a God whose dealings with his creatures are both just and merciful. Through the exercise of the 'sweetest Art' described in 'H. Scriptures', he expresses poetically 'in groans / Of my Lords penning' the great mystery and challenge of a divine plan in which the 'milde blood' of a crucified Saviour provides a solution to the moral dilemma posed by the hot blood of murder and revenge.

In one of the earliest of the many detailed analyses of 'The Night', Fern Farnham speaks of 'the warp drawn from the Bible upon which the poem is woven'; and in a later article, Geoffrey Hill offers the alternative image of a mosaic, made 'out of Mosaic (and many other) echoes', which becomes a 'living work'.[72] There is no space here to tease out all the allusions, ranging from Genesis through Old Testament narrative and prophetic books and New Testament gospels and epistles to Revelation, that give such rich poetic life to one of Vaughan's finest achievements.[73] For the purposes of this chapter, a few of the most prominent or pervasive threads will be highlighted and followed through its intricately woven texture. The first two stanzas reflect upon the implications of the epigraph from the Gospel of St John, in which the evangelist records the visit of Nicodemus, 'a ruler of ye Iewes', to Jesus 'by night', drawn to him by the 'miracles' that he has performed:[74]

---

71 For a discussion of the debate about the significance of Cain, see the article by Joe Sterrett, 'The Dynamic of Despair: Evolving Toleration for Cain in Herbert and Vaughan', *Scintilla*, 16 (2012), 81–91.

72 Farnham, 'The Imagery of Henry Vaughan's "The Night"', 428; Geoffrey Hill, 'A Pharisee to Pharisees', 100.

73 A full list would include Exodus, Numbers, 1 Kings, 2 Chronicles, Psalms, Song of Solomon, Isaiah, Malachi, Mark, Luke, John, Colossians, 1 John, and Hebrews.

74 Vaughan wrongly cites John 2:3, whereas the record of the encounter begins in John 3:1–2. For the text of the poem, see *HV Works*, pp. 610–12.

> Through that pure *Virgin-shrine*,
> That sacred vail drawn o'r thy glorious noon
> That men might look and live as Glo-worms shine,
>   And face the Moon:
> Wise *Nicodemus* saw such light
> As made him know his God by night.
>
> Most blest believer he!
> Who in that of land darkness and blinde eyes
> Thy long expected healing wings could see,
>   When thou didst rise,
> And what can never more be done,
> Did at mid-night speak with the Sun!

The key phrase is obviously 'by night', which not only gives the poem its theme and title but is also associated with Nicodemus on the two other occasions when he makes an appearance in John's narrative: he is among the Pharisees who receive a report from the officers of the temple on their failure to apprehend Jesus and is carefully set apart from the rest as 'He that came to Iesus by night' (John 7:45–51); and he accompanies Joseph of Arimathæa in seeking permission from Pilate to bury the body of Jesus, when he is again distinguished as the man 'which at the first came to Iesus by night' (John 19:39). Very few biblical commentators agreed with the judgement that Nicodemus deserved the epithet 'wise', which Vaughan accorded him for recognizing the 'light' in a land where most eyes were 'blind' to the divinity of Christ.[75] This is because of the inconclusive nature of the conversation that follows the verse cited in the epigraph, in which Nicodemus finds it difficult to grasp what Christ means by being 'born again'. As Allan Wilcox has shown, it is only when the other passages containing the phrase 'by night' are brought into play that it becomes possible to regard him as a 'Most blest believer', who knew on this first occasion that he was speaking with the Sun/Son 'at mid-night'.[76]

The 'sacred vail' that shields human eyes from the 'glorious noon' of God's presence is most obviously the bodily form assumed by Christ at the Incarnation, which opened up 'a new and liuing way

---

75 See Hill, 'A Pharisee to Pharisees', 98.
76 See Allan Wilcox, 'Nicodemus and "The Night"', *Scintilla*, 15 (2011), 141–55.

which hee hath consecrated for vs, through the vaile, that is to say, His flesh' (Hebrews 10:20). Behind these lines, however, there are also Old Testament allusions to the unbearable brightness of the godhead – 'And he said, Thou canst not see my face: for there shall no man see mee, and liue' (Exodus 33:20) – and to both the veil that Moses wore before the children of Israel to hide the shining of his own face after his encounter with God on Mount Sinai (Exodus 34:29–35) and the veil made out of 'blew, and purple, and scarlet, and fine twined linnen' that covered the Ark of the Covenant (Exodus 26:31–33) and later hung before the Holy of Holies in the temple built by Solomon (2 Chronicles 3:14). The allusion may also be picked up in Stanza 7 in the reference to 'thy dark Tent, / Whose peace but by some *Angels* wing or voice / Is seldom rent' (ll. 38–40). The word 'rent' recalls the rending of the veil in the temple 'from the top to the bottome' at the moment of Christ's death on the Cross, recorded in three of the gospels (Matthew 27:51, Mark 15:38, Luke 23:45) – a connection all the more resonant, since the 'dark Tent' alludes to the curtained tent in which the Ark of the Covenant was kept during the wanderings of the Israelites in the wilderness: 'And on the day that the Tabernacle was reared vp the cloud couered the Tabernacle, *namely* the Tent of the Testimony' (Numbers 9:15). For the Psalmist, the original dark tent in which God dwelt was the night itself: 'He made the darkenes his secret place: his pauilion round about him, *were* darke waters, *and* thicke cloudes of the skies' (Psalm 18:11). In the context of the seventeenth century, it has become the tabernacle where Christ may be encountered and peace can still be found, insulated from the 'loud, evil days' inhabited by Vaughan, which are reminiscent of the 'clamour, and euill speaking' that caused St Paul to advise his converts to redeem the time 'because the dayes are euill' (Ephesians 4:31, 5:16). The 'dark Tent' may even be symbolic of Christ, who is 'the true Tabernacle, which the Lord pitched, and not man' (Hebrews 8:2). As a metaphor for the night, it also resolves the problem that Vaughan posed at the start of Stanza 3, 'O who will tell me, where / He found thee at that dead and silent hour!' The answer – in negative and positive terms – is given in Stanza 4:

> No mercy-seat of gold,
> No dead and dusty *Cherub*, nor carv'd stone,
> But his own living works did my Lord hold
>   And lodge alone.

Allusions to the decoration of the desert tabernacle and the temple in Jerusalem (Exodus 25:17–18; 2 Chronicles 3:8–13) give place to Christ's solitary refuge under the natural cover of the night sky – 'And it came to passe in those dayes, that hee went out into a mountaine to pray, and continued all night in prayer'; 'at night hee went out, and abode in the mount that is called the mount of Oliues' (Luke 6:12; 21:37) – and behind the whole passage, indeed the entire poem, hovers the New Testament summary of the shift from one dispensation to another:

> Then verily the first *Couenant* had also ordinances of diuine Seruice, and a worldly Sanctuary. For there was a Tabernacle made [...] which is called the Sanctuarie. And after the second vaile, the Tabernacle which is called ye Holiest of all [...] And ouer it the Cherubims of glory shadowing the Mercyseat [...] But Christ being come an high Priest of good things to come, by a greater and more perfect Tabernacle, not made with hands, that is to say, not of this building. (Hebrews 9:1–11)

The wisdom that set Nicodemus apart from his fellow Pharisees was his ability to see who the miracle worker from Galilee – rising on his 'long expected healing wings' – really was. Noel Thomas points out that the first of these epithets derives from the eagerly awaited fulfilment of Old Testament prophecies about the coming of a Messiah.[77] It also alludes to the Christian expectation of the Second Coming of Christ to judge the world, which is foretold in the last book of the Old Testament in the passage that supplies the rest of the phrase: 'But vnto you that feare my Name, shall the Sunne of righteousnesse arise with healing in his wings' (Malachi 4:2). In the rest of this short chapter, the prophet foretells the day when the wicked will be burnt like stubble and Elijah will be sent, 'before the comming of the great and dreadfull day of the LORD', to turn the hearts of fathers and children towards each other. The 'Sunne of righteousnesse' lies behind the sun references in the first two stanzas and the 'healing wings' look forward to the first line of Stanza 6, the second of two stanzas addressed to 'Dear night!':

---

77 See Thomas, *Poet of Revelation*, p. 162.

>   Gods silent, searching flight:
>   When my Lords head is fill'd with dew, and all
>   His locks are wet with the clear drops of night;
>   His still, soft call;
>   His knocking time; The souls dumb watch,
>   When Spirits their fair kinred catch.

Post calls this 'the devotional high point' of the poem, in which the Welsh *dyfalu* technique of 'building phrase upon phrase' fuses 'the temporal with the timeless', enabling Vaughan to 'join Nicodemus in the past' and enter the presence of Christ.[78] The wonderful development of the image of the 'healing wings' leads into an elaborated quotation from the Song of Solomon – 'for my head is filled with dewe, *and* my lockes with the drops of the night' (5:2) – and more allusions fall effortlessly into place in the *dyfalu* structure: the 'still small voice' heard by Elijah (1 Kings 19:12) and 'the voyce of my beloued that knocketh, *saying*, Open to me' (from the same verse in the Song), which is echoed in the well-known passage from Revelation: 'Behold, I stand at the doore, and knocke: if any man heare my voyce, and open the doore, I will come in to him, and will sup with him, and he with me' (3:20). Then, after two stanzas that dump the poet back into the harsh reality of a world where 'all mix and tyre / Themselves and others', Vaughan turns again to the 'deep, but dazling darkness' of God and the poem comes to rest in a prayer that draws upon St Paul's image of being 'hid with Christ in God' (Colossians 3:3): 'O for that night! where I in him / Might live invisible and dim.' 'The Night' is perhaps the supreme example in *Silex Scintillans* of an art that incorporates biblical phrases and allusions – including the contexts they bring with them – so organically into its poetic idiom that they become expressive of the poet's own most profound and intimate experiences.

VI

Given Vaughan's discriminating use of a variety of translations for his epigraphs from the Bible and the obvious familiarity with Puritan commentaries that stokes his animosity towards those who 'dash

---

78 Post, *The Unfolding Vision*, pp. 205–06.

the *Scriptures* [...] with their impious conceits', it can be assumed that his own practice was informed by traditions of biblical exegesis of a more congenial kind. West notes, however, that 'this side of his reading proves extremely difficult to reconstruct'.[79] As Barbara Lewalski explains and as this chapter has demonstrated, he exploited 'the familiar biblical metaphors and typological strategies' found in 'the English Protestant tradition in theology and poetics'.[80] West adds confirmation that he had absorbed the 'new emphasis within typology' that was 'widespread in seventeenth-century England'.[81] From an early age, he would have imbibed that tradition both from sermons, which were 'expositions of biblical terms, and rich in quotations from the Bible', and from the Book of Common Prayer, with, for example, its 'typological references to the Patriarchs and their wives in the Marriage ceremony'.[82] He must also have been acquainted with the work of some of the Fathers of the Church – Augustine, Tertullian, Origen, Jerome, Ambrose – who had established the methods of 'typological, figural interpretation' and have been described as 'almost as popular as the Bible itself in the seventeenth century'.[83] And there can be little doubt that Vaughan was widely read in such Protestant contributions as Calvin's commentaries on Genesis and Isaiah and Joseph Hall's *A Plaine and Familiar Explication of All the Hard Texts of the Whole Divine Scripture of the Old and New Testament* (1633) and *Contemplations upon the Principall Passages of the Holy Scriptures* (1642).[84] He almost certainly knew Hall's *The Holy Order: Or, Fraternity of Mourners in Zion* 1654), which takes a phrase – 'Songs in the night' – as the title for an appended collection of prose meditations from the same passage in Job that Vaughan used on the title-page of the 1655 *Silex Scintillans*.[85]

In the absence of direct quotation from or citation of patristic or reformed commentaries, however, scholars can only assemble examples of similar interpretations or typological strategies from

---

79 West, *Scripture Uses*, p. 12.
80 Lewalski, *Protestant Poetics*, p. 332.
81 West, *Scripture Uses*, p. 42.
82 Galdon, *Typology and Seventeenth-Century Literature*, pp. 13, 15.
83 Galdon, *Typology and Seventeenth-Century Literature*, p. 17.
84 Cited by West, *Scripture Uses*, p. 39 and Lewalski, 'Typology and Poetry', 46.
85 See the headnote to *Silex Scintillans* (1655), *HV Works*, p. 1199.

material that Vaughan might have encountered. For instance, Lewalski establishes that the basis for 'the imagery and development' of 'Regeneration' derives from 'conventional Protestant exegesis of the allegory of Canticles 2:10–12' by citing a sermon by George Gifford.[86] She also finds parallels to Vaughan's 'metaphor of the Christian pilgrimage' as 'an antitype of the wanderings of the Old Testament patriarchs' in the notes of the Geneva Bible and in commentaries by Calvin (translated 1605) and John Diodati (1648).[87] In his discussion of 'Midnight', with its epigraph from Matthew 3:11, Dickson invokes Augustin Marlarat's *A Catholike and Ecclesiasticall exposition of the holy Gospel after S. Mathewe* (translated by Thomas Tymme in 1570) and Richard Ward's *Theologicall Questions, Dogmaticall Observations, and Evangelicall Essays, upon Matthew* (1640).[88] West mentions sermons by Robert Bruce and Robert Harris, published in 1617 and 1626 respectively, and also Adam Littleton's *Hezekiah's Return of Praise for his Recovery* (1668), as an appropriate context for reading Vaughan's application of the story of Hezekiah to his own situation; and works by Egeon Askew (1605), Henry Ainsworth (1621) and John Diodati (1651) are cited to corroborate Vaughan's reading of Jacob as 'a type of the elect'.[89]

In the end, however, Vaughan's greatest debt was to the Scriptures themselves. It is not surprising that the final poem in the completed collection of religious verse in the 1655 *Silex Scintillans*, before the formal dismissal of 'L'Envoy', is addressed 'To the Holy Bible'. Hailed by the poet as his 'life's guide' – his 'first cheap Book', from the pages of which he 'learnt to read' – it is credited with actively wooing his eye away from 'vanity' – 'And oft left open would'st convey / A sudden and most searching ray / Into my soul' – and, through its 'milde art of love', with bringing him 'home' and showing him 'that pearl' he had so long 'sought elsewhere'. Vaughan seems to acknowledge here what Mahood was the first to recognize: that he had, indeed, 'lived the text' rather than merely expounding it. Writing his tribute during what he thought was a terminal illness, he looks beyond the benefits he has received from it in this life:

86 Lewalski, *Protestant Poetics*, p. 320.
87 Lewalski, 'Typology and Poetry', 55.
88 Dickson, *Fountain of Living Waters*, pp. 144–45.
89 West, *Scripture Uses*, pp. 81–87, 45–48.

> Living, thou wert my souls sure ease,
> And dying mak'st me go in peace:
> Thy next *Effects* no tongue can tell;
> Farewel O book of God! farewel![90]

What he modestly leaves out of this valedictory salute to the most potent of all the influences that shaped him as man and poet is the incalculable contribution it made to the flowering of the 'poor *Talent*' that he begged leave to communicate 'to the *Church*' in the preface to *Silex Scintillans*.[91]

---

90 *HV Works*, pp. 630–31.
91 *HV Works*, p. 558.

CHAPTER NINE

Henry Vaughan and the Book of Nature

I

In *Man and the Natural World*, Keith Thomas explored 'the profound shift in sensibilities [...] which occurred in England between the sixteenth and late eighteenth centuries'. During this protracted cultural revolution, 'some long-established dogmas about man's place in nature were discarded' and the 'relationship of man to other species was redefined', with particular emphasis on 'his right to exploit those species for his own advantage'.[1] Two snapshots of trees in poetry before and after this radical 'shift in sensibilities' will provide some points of reference. A passage from the first canto of Edmund Spenser's *The Faerie Queene* (first printed in 1590) exemplifies several of the traditional values of trees as poetic material. The Red Cross Knight and his Lady seek refuge from an impending storm in a 'shadie groue':

>   Much can they prayse the trees so straight and hy,
>   The sayling Pine, the Cedar proud and tall,
>   The vine-prop Elme, the Poplar neuer dry,
>   The builder Oake, sole king of forrests all,
>   The Aspine good for staues, the Cypresse funerall.
>
>   The Laurell, meed of mightie Conquerours
>   And Poets sage, the Firre that weepeth still,

---

1 Keith Thomas, *Man and the Natural World: Changing Attitudes in England 1500–1800* (London: Penguin Books, 1984), p. 15.

> The Willow worne of forlorne Paramours,
> The Eugh obedient to the benders will,
> The Birch for shaftes, the Sallow for the mill,
> The Mirrhe sweete bleeding in the bitter wound,
> The warlike Beech, the Ash for nothing ill,
> The fruitfull Oliue, and the Platane round,
> The caruer Holme, the Maple seeldom inward sound.
>   (I.i.8–9)[2]

Almost every epithet indicates the usefulness or meaning of the tree in the human world: on the one hand, the pine that supplied masts for sailing ships, the oak used in building, the aspen, birch, and yew from which staves, arrows, and bows were fashioned, the holm suitable for carving, and the versatile ash, 'for nothing ill'; and on the other hand, the cedar that was symbolic of pride, the oak that was emblematic of kingship, the laurel woven into wreaths of honour for victorious soldiers and wise poets, and the willow associated with forsaken lovers. Even those descriptive terms that might seem to focus on the 'thingness' of the tree rather than its absorption into the human realm turn out on further inspection to be as 'obedient to the benders will' as the yew: the poplar is not only 'neuer dry' because it grows by water but also because the Heliades, weeping for their brother Phaeton's death, were transformed into poplars and their tears into oozing amber; and the maple is 'seeldom inward sound' not only because it tends to rot inwardly but also because the treacherous Trojan horse was made of it.[3] Only the fir 'that weepeth still' seems to be mediated to the reader's mind without some freight of practical or moral or symbolic or mythic value, and even then it is perceived in anthropomorphic terms as 'weeping' rather than exuding resin as a natural process. The complete subordination of the natural phenomena of pine and oak and willow to the human perspective is reinforced by the fact that the sixteenth-century poet's catalogue of trees has a long poetic pedigree, stretching back through Chaucer to Ovid and Virgil.[4]

---

2 *Edmund Spenser: The Faerie Queene*, ed. A.C. Hamilton, Longman Annotated English Poets (London and New York: Longman, 1977, corr. 1980), pp. 31–32.

3 All the information about the significance of trees in this passage is taken from the notes to Hamilton's edition.

4 See Chaucer, *The Parliament of Fowls*, ll. 172–82; Ovid, *Metamorphoses*, X, 90–105; Virgil, *Aeneid*, VI, 179–82.

One strain in Christian thought, authoritatively formulated by Thomas Aquinas, held that the rest of the creation had been set under the 'dominion' of the newly created man and woman in Genesis 1: 28–30, and this strain was so prevalent in 1600 that Keith Thomas could assert that a reader coming to the moral and theological writings of Elizabethan and early Stuart England for the first time 'could be forgiven for inferring that their main purpose was to define the special status of man and to justify his rule over other creatures'.[5] Francis Bacon summed up the dominant attitude: 'Man, if we look to final causes, may be regarded as the centre of the world, insomuch that if man were taken away from the world, the rest would seem to be all astray, without aim or purpose.'[6]

Some of the significant changes in perception and attitude that had taken place by the end of the eighteenth century can be seen in a passage from *The Excursion* by William Wordsworth, published in 1814.[7] The Pastor's account of people buried in the churchyard of his mountain parish is interrupted by the sight of a 'giant oak' being transported by an old man on a 'massy timber wain'. The 'good Vicar' cannot help feeling 'a motion of despite' towards this member of his flock, who bears such a 'conspicuous part / In works of havoc':

> "Full oft his doings leave me to deplore
> Tall ash-tree, sown by winds, by vapours nursed,
> In the dry crannies of the pendent rocks;
> Light birch, aloft upon the horizon's edge,
> A veil of glory for the ascending moon;
> And oak whose roots by noontide dew were damped,
> And on whose forehead inaccessible
> The raven lodged in safety."

---

5 Thomas, *Man and the Natural World*, p. 25.

6 'Prometheus, or the State of Man', Chapter XXVI of *De Sapientia* [*The Wisdom of the Ancients*], in *The Works of Francis Bacon*, ed. James Spedding and Douglas Denon Heath, Vol. VI (London: Longman, Green, Longman, and Roberts, 1861), p. 747.

7 See *The Excursion*, Book VII, ll. 590–624, in *The Poetical Works of William Wordsworth*, Vol. V, ed. Ernest de Selincourt and Helen Darbishire (Oxford: Clarendon Press, 1949), pp. 248–51.

At the start of this 'digression on the fall of beautiful and interesting Trees', as it is called in the Argument to Book VII, each species is characterized on quite different principles from those underlying Spenser's catalogue. The ash-tree is described entirely in terms of its existence within the processes of nature – growing from a seed blown by the wind and nourished by moisture from the air in a crevice of the rocks; the oak, rooted in the dew-dampened earth and with ravens nesting in its topmost branches, is presented as part of a complex habitat that sustains many forms of life; and the birch, although filtered through human aesthetic values, has a unique contribution to make to the beauty of a scene that exists only when viewed from a particular spot at a particular moment in the earth's rotation – 'upon the horizon's edge' between an observer and 'the ascending moon'.

This conception of trees in their environment – in which man's role is to be conscious of the interconnectedness of the natural world and to appreciate its beauty – is set against the 'havoc' wrought by the ancient peasant:

> "— Many a ship
> Launched into Morecamb-bay, to *him* hath owed
> Her strong knee-timbers, and the mast that bears
> The loftiest of her pendants; He, from park
> Or forest, fetched the enormous axle-tree
> That whirls (how slow itself!) ten thousand spindles:
> And the vast engine labouring in the mine,
> Content with meaner prowess, must have lacked
> The trunk and body of its marvellous strength,
> If his undaunted enterprise had failed
> Among the mountain coves."

For him, the 'proudest ornaments' of the mountains and valleys are no more than raw material to be exploited in the construction of ships and industrial machinery, like Spenser's 'sayling Pine' and 'Sallow for the mill'.

The next section acknowledges ways in which trees can be absorbed into the human world without being destroyed or forfeiting their independent existence:

> "That sycamore, which annually holds
> Within its shade, as in a stately tent

> On all sides open to the fanning breeze,
> A grave assemblage, seated while they shear
> The fleece-encumbered flock – the JOYFUL ELM,
> Around whose trunk the maidens dance in May –
> And the LORD'S OAK – would plead their several rights
> In vain, if he were master of their fate;
> His sentence to the axe would doom them all."

The men involved in the annual sheep-shearing merely enjoy the amenities of 'shade' and 'fanning breeze' provided by '[t]hat sycamore' rather than exploiting the tree in any way that interferes with its own life; and the 'JOYFUL ELM' and 'LORD'S OAK' owe their capitalization to the special significance assigned to them within the human community that shares this particular environment with them and protects them from the axe of the old man. Such significance, specific to this place and this community in Wordsworth's Romantic catalogue of trees, is different in kind from the generalized symbolic values associated with cypress and laurel and willow in classical and Renaissance poetry.

II

The editors and critics who rediscovered Vaughan in the nineteenth century were particularly attracted by elements in his poetry that reminded them of the Romantic response to the natural world. One Victorian commentator accorded Vaughan a prominent place in 'any history of the development of the love of the present age for Nature'; another asserted that he was the earliest 'of all our poets' to perceive 'the innermost charm and magic of Nature' and to exhibit 'a deep imaginative sympathy with tree and blossom, animal and bird'; and a third wrote of Vaughan's 'passionate love of Nature' and claimed that he was ahead of his time in treating 'external nature subjectively rather than objectively'.[8] The presence of a vivid awareness of the natural world in Vaughan's poetry has continued to be part of his

---

8 George MacDonald, *England's Antiphon* (London: Macmillan & Co., 1874), p. 262; Francis T. Palgrave, *Landscape in Poetry from Homer to Tennyson* (London: Macmillan, 1897), pp. 161, 163; John Brown, *Horae Subsecivae*, new edition in 3 vols. (London: Adam and Charles Black, 1900), Vol. I, pp. 293, 294

appeal to later readers. Rachel Trickett, for example, pointed out that Vaughan's 'water imagery' is 'remarkably detailed', as in this simile from 'Misery':

> As waters here, headlong and loose
> The lower grounds stil chase, and choose,
> Where spreading all the way they seek
> And search out ev'ry hole and Creek.⁹

And a twenty-first century critic has insisted that there are 'moments in Vaughan's poems when he awakes our senses to particular natural phenomena – flowers and trees and wild creatures, and the effects of weather and seasons'.¹⁰

Often, such 'moments' are signalled by a direct appeal to the senses involved in perceiving them. In one of the Amoret poems, the poet foregrounds the visual experience of tracking the 'flames' of a meteor across the evening sky – 'Marke', 'you stay / And see them stray', 'they … cheate your Eyes' – and also calls attention to the breeze that cools the 'afflicted ayre' of a sultry afternoon. Being a man of his age, however, he picks up the ethical dimension of the word 'cheate' to condemn the 'false fires' that 'shoot their tinsill beames, and vanities'. A significant pointer to his future methods is the easy combination of physical and moral elements: the word 'tinsill' signifies both sparkling brightness and cheap gaudiness (*OED*, n. and adj. 1 and 5), so that the flames are simultaneously 'beames' and 'vanities'.¹¹

Sometimes, the poet 'awakes our senses' by the simple use of a demonstrative that grounds an observation in a familiar landscape. The move from an indefinite 'some' to the precision of 'those' and 'this' sharpens the visual impact from the general to the particular in a stanza from one of the elegies:

> (the quotations are from 'Henry Vaughan' in the first series of critical essays by Brown initially published in 1882).

9 *HV Works*, p. 138. See Rachel Trickett, 'Henry Vaughan and the Poetry of Vision', *Essays and Studies*, new series, 34 (1981), 89.
10 Jeremy Hooker, '"Pure and endless light": Henry Vaughan in his Landscape', in *Henry Vaughan and the Usk Valley*, ed. Elizabeth Siberry and Robert Wilcher (Little Logaston Woonton Almeley: Logaston Press, 2016), p. 4.
11 See 'To Amoret, of the difference 'twixt him, and other Lovers, and what true Love is', *HV Works*, p. 22.

> It glows and glitters in my cloudy brest
> > Like stars upon some gloomy grove,
> Or those faint beams in which this hill is drest,
> > After the Sun's remove.[12]

The last two lines prompted an influential mid-twentieth-century commentator to declare that he knew of no earlier passage in English poetry in which 'the details of a specific, privately-observed natural landscape' were presented in such a way that readers must 'imagine and respond to' a sight 'which only the speaker has seen' – 'as if the afterglow on *this* hill were different from that on any other'.[13] The hill in question is presumably the one that rose behind the farmhouse in which Vaughan lived.

Sometimes, it is the combining of different senses in the evocation of a natural scene that creates an impression of observed reality. In 'The Water-fall', the poet repeats an experience frequently savoured in the past – 'Dear stream! dear bank, where often I / Have sate, and pleas'd my pensive eye' – in an opening description that involves sound, sight, and touch, and kinesis in conveying the ceaseless motion and momentary stasis as the stream appears to hesitate before plunging over the brink:

> With what deep murmurs through times silent stealth
> Doth thy transparent, cool and watry wealth
> > Here flowing fall,
> > And chide, and call,
> As if his liquid, loose Retinue staid
> Lingring, and were of this steep place afraid ...[14]

A personal experience of nature takes over from the dominant mode of allegory in 'Regeneration', when the poet enters a grove of stately trees, where 'a new spring / Did all my senses greet': the sun 'shot vitall gold / A thousand peeces' through the leaves; the 'azure' sky was 'Checquer'd with snowie fleeces'; the air was 'all in spice'; 'every bush' wore a 'garland'; and 'all the Eare lay hush', save for 'a little

---

12 'They are all gone into the world of light!', *HV Works*, p. 568.
13 Joseph H. Summers, *The Heirs of Donne and Jonson* (London: Chatto & Windus, 1970), p. 128.
14 *HV Works*, p. 626.

Fountain' that 'lent / Some use for Eares'.[15] In another poem, he finds a metaphor for the 'boyling stremes' of his own blood in the 'curling force, and hisse' of his native river, which takes on a blood-like hue from the local soil when it is in spate – a detail corroborated in a letter that Gwenllian Morgan sent to Louise Guiney: 'There have been the reddest of red floods in the Usk: I never saw him redder.'[16]

III

The 'deep imaginative sympathy' with the non-human world and the 'subjective' treatment of 'external nature' that drew nineteenth-century readers to Vaughan have also continued to stimulate interest in his poetry. In 1927, Edmund Blunden was captivated by the way 'he speaks with nature familiarly and reverently' and by his humble 'consciousness that there is a sense in a bird or a bee which man has almost lost'.[17] Glyn Pursglove comments on the 'affectionate tenderness' with which Vaughan writes of a little creature's 'vulnerability and resilience' and the 'delightful and intimate touches' of its 'warm wing' and 'harmless head' in the opening stanza of 'The Bird'.[18] What Blunden described as 'this Franciscan companionship' meant that Vaughan had a quite different sensibility from an older contemporary like John Donne, who saw fit to sneer at those credulous enough to swallow the fanciful stories told about the medieval saint: 'They will needs make us believe,' he told his congregation, 'that St. *Francis* preached to Birds, and Beasts, and Stones; but they will not go about to make us believe that those Birds, and Beasts, and Stones joyned with St. *Francis* in prayer [...] of all onely Man can speak to God'.[19] The poet who had been brought up in the

---

15 *HV Works*, p. 58.
16 The poem in question is 'The Storm', *HV Works*, p. 86. For the letter, see the note on 86:4 in *HV Works*, p. 916.
17 Edmund Blunden, *On the Poems of Henry Vaughan: Characteristics and Intimations* (London: Richard Cobden-Sanderson, 1927), pp. 42–43.
18 Glyn Pursglove, '"Winged and free": Henry Vaughan's Birds', in *Of Paradise and Light: Essays on Henry Vaughan and John Milton in Honor of Alan Rudrum*, ed. Donald R. Dickson and Holly Faith Nelson (Newark, DE: University of Delaware Press, 2004), pp. 252–53. For 'The Bird', see *HV Works*, p. 582.
19 See Blunden, *On the Poems of Henry Vaughan*, p. 43; John Donne is quoted by

Usk Valley rather than the streets of London possessed a natural empathy that convinced him otherwise. The plants that waited upon Christ in 'Palm-Sunday' and continued, along with 'birds, beasts & stones', to 'expect' the return of 'the lamb', are imagined in 'The Night' as keeping faithful watch while he prayed in his last lonely vigil on the Mount of Olives: 'Where *trees* and *herbs* did watch and peep / And wonder, while the *Jews* did sleep'.[20]

Vaughan's 'intimate identification with every aspect of nature' was attributed by Leona Spitz to his 'spiritual search' for his own place in 'the renewal and regeneration of the world', which led him to see himself 'as part of natural process'.[21] On the one hand, this enabled him to imagine the marigold as a real flower growing in the soil and opening its petals to the warmth of the morning sun instead of merely exploiting the flower's 'unfolding' as a simile for the desired emergence of a friend from the 'quiet *Cell*' in which he has retired from the 'sad distractions' of the time:

> But as the *Mary-gold* in Feasts of Dew
> And early Sun-beams, though but thin and few,
> Unfolds its self, then from the Earths cold breast
> Heaves gently, and salutes the hopeful *East*.[22]

And in another simile, he claims intimate knowledge of the secret life of a flower in terms that are appropriate to the marriage-song it graces:

> Sweet as the flowres *first breath*, and Close
> As th'*unseen spreadings* of the Rose,
> When he unfolds his Curtain'd head,
> And makes his bosome the *Suns bed*.[23]

Elizabeth Holmes in *Henry Vaughan and the Hermetic Philosophy* (Oxford: Basil Blackwell, 1932), p. 46.
20 *HV Works*, pp. 588, 611.
21 Leona Spitz, 'Process and Stasis: Aspects of Nature in Vaughan and Marvell', *Huntington Library Quarterly*, 32 (1968–69), 137.
22 'To his Learned Friend and Loyal Fellow-Prisoner, Thomas Powel of Cant. Doctor of Divinity', *HV Works*, p. 730.
23 'To the best, and most accomplish'd Couple —', *HV Works*, p. 192.

On the other hand, as Alan Rudrum notes, his intuitive grasp of the inner life of plants provides him with a means of exploring 'the invisible processes of his own soul by reference to visible, but strictly analogous, processes in the world of nature'.[24] The second stanza of 'Disorder and frailty' describes one such invisible process in terms derived from the vicissitudes that befall the vegetable creation:

> I threaten heaven, and from my Cell
> Of Clay, and frailty break, and bud
> Touch'd by thy fire, and breath; Thy bloud
> Too, is my Dew, and springing wel.
>   But while I grow
> And stretch to thee, ayming at all
>   Thy stars, and spangled hall,
>   Each fly doth tast,
>   Poyson, and blast
> My yielding leaves; sometimes a showr
> Beats them quite off, and in an hour
>   Not one poor shoot
>   But the bare root
> Hid under ground survives the fall.[25]

The 'Cell / Of Clay' is the human body, in which the soul depends upon the 'fire' of the Holy Spirit and the blood of Christ for birth and growth; it is also the soil, in which the seed's germination depends upon the warmth of the sun and the moisture of dew and rain. The soul stretches towards heaven and the plant reaches towards the light; and both soul and plant are subject to corruption (flies) and the vagaries of external forces (weather), so that they withdraw from the active life for which they were beckoned from 'the womb of darknes' in the first stanza of the poem.[26]

---

24 Alan Rudrum, 'The Influence of Alchemy in the Poems of Henry Vaughan', *Philological Quarterly*, 49 (1970), 477.
25 *HV Works*, p. 109.
26 A similar merging of plant and human processes is sustained throughout 'Unprofitablenes' (*HV Works*, p. 105).

IV

Amidst the chorus of admiration for Vaughan's apparent modernity in the poetic treatment of Nature, sceptical voices have been raised. Placing him firmly in his own time, Pettet – in a chapter entitled 'The Book of Nature' – was adamant that the occasional 'fine descriptive passage' and 'touches of first-hand observation' were not enough to justify the poet's earlier reputation as a precursor of Wordsworth and the Romantics.[27] This is because, as Leona Spitz was to point out, '[f]or Vaughan [...] no physical aspect of nature had significance apart from its spiritual application'; or, in Jeremy Hooker's blunter formulation, 'Without the existence of God, nature would have meant nothing to Henry Vaughan.'[28] One of the instructions he issues in 'Rules and Lessons' brings together his Franciscan sense of companionship with the non-human creation and an affirmation of the teaching role of the Book of Nature: 'Walk with thy fellow-creatures: note the *hush* / And *whispers* amongst them [...] Each *Bush* / And *Oak* doth know *I AM*.'[29] In a recent paper, Jonathan Post describes such a walk as 'a peripatetic lesson' about 'the separate but shared essences of God's two creations', which depends upon the poet's 'recognition of a separate self-hood enjoyed by plants'.[30]

Vaughan's conception of the created universe as a second source of revelation to be read alongside the Book of the Scriptures lies behind the role played by many of the natural details in his poetry – a role that he often refers to quite explicitly. In one of the poems he translated from Boethius, he had found this advice for one who sought an 'unclouded' view of 'the Laws' set down by the 'eternal

---

27 E.C. Pettet, *Of Paradise and Light: A Study of Vaughan's* Silex Scintillans (Cambridge: Cambridge University Press, 1960), pp. 86, 90–91. R.A. Durr traces the motif of the Book of Nature back to Alcmaeon and cites scriptural authority for it: 'But ask now the beasts, and they shall teach thee; and the fowls of the air, and they shall tell thee: Or speak to the earth, and it shall teach thee: and the fishes of the sea shall declare unto thee' (Job 12:7–8). See Appendix B in *On the Mystical Poetry of Henry Vaughan* (Cambridge, MA: Harvard University Press, 1962), p. 133.

28 Leona Spitz, 'Process and Stasis', 137; Jeremy Hooker, 'Henry Vaughan: Image-Maker, Iconoclast', *The Swansea Review*, 15 (1995), 22.

29 *HV Works*, p. 99.

30 Jonathan F.S. Post, 'Walking with Vaughan in *Silex Scintillans*', *Scintilla*, 22 (2019), 21.

Cause': 'Let him with careful thoughts and eyes / Observe the high and spatious Skyes'; and in 'The Starre', he affirmed God's authorship of the Book of Nature, which functions as a primer for the human race:

> Yet, seeing all things that subsist and be,
> Have their Commissions from Divinitie,
>   And teach us duty; I will see
>   What man may learn from thee.[31]

What he learns from contemplating this star 'with careful thoughts and eyes' is that, where 'desire, cellestial, pure desire' takes root 'and grows', God brings about 'a Commerce' with his creatures and 'sheds / His Secret on their heads'. Taking stock of his more immediate surroundings, he begins 'The Tempest' with the thought that '[t]his late, long heat' may be a source of 'Instruction' and goes on to lament that 'man' is reluctant to 'hear / The world read to him', even though one purpose of 'the Creation' is to make up 'lectures [in the old sense of 'readings'] for his eie, and ear'. The lesson that earthbound man – astray in the 'darkness' – might read by paying proper attention to the natural environment is spelled out a couple of stanzas later:

> All things here shew him heaven; *Waters* that fall
>   Chide, and fly up; *Mists* of corruptest fome
>   Quit their first beds & mount; trees, herbs, flowres, all
> Strive upwards stil, and point him the way home.[32]

Looking beyond what can be taught by a single star, he discovers in 'The Constellation' that the 'vast progressions' of a whole formation of stars across the night sky, moving in an 'exact obedience' to the will of the Creator, put 'poor man' to shame as he 'grops beneath here, and with restless Care / First makes, then hugs a snare'. The lesson takes a political turn, when he contrasts the 'calm and wel-trained flight' of the heavenly bodies with the fate of his countrymen – 'by our lusts disorder'd into wars'.[33] This habit of reading the details of the natural world for 'instructions', which was one of the staples of

---

31 *HV Works*, pp. 758–59; 574.
32 *HV Works*, pp. 125–26.
33 *HV Works*, pp. 134–36.

Vaughan's poetic technique, has much in common with the emblem poetry that was popular in the sixteenth and seventeenth centuries.

In one of the poems to Etesia, he glances at the way items from the Book of Nature are enlisted to express something beyond themselves:

> The gallant *Tulip* and the *Rose*,
> Emblems which some use to disclose
> Bodyed *Idea's*.[34]

'The Water-fall', which is often cited as evidence of Vaughan's love of Nature and close observation of natural phenomena, is chosen by Rosemary Freeman as an example of a poem that 'follows the structure of an emblem exactly'. She notes that it is 'divided into three sharply distinguished sections, each marked by a change in form and rhythm': the first is the description of the waterfall; the second is the 'interpretation'; the third is the 'application', which sets out the deeper truths and themes 'embodied in the waterfall and its meaning'. She highlights the way in which the meaning elicited in the second section – that 'what God takes', he will 'restore' – is 'already implied in the vocabulary of the second half of the description'.[35] In fact, it is characteristic of Vaughan's mode of imagination and expression to charge the descriptive part of the emblem with a strong symbolic force drawn from Christian doctrine and imagery that goes far beyond the rational procedures of the emblem tradition:

> The common pass
> Where, clear as glass,
> All must descend
> Not to an end:
> But quicknd by this deep and rocky grave,
> Rise to a longer course more bright and brave.[36]

The stream flowing through the Breconshire landscape is perceived at the same time as a symbol of the transience of earthly existence as

---

34 See 'To Etesia (for Timander,) the first Sight', *HV Works*, p. 750.
35 Rosemary Freeman, *English Emblem Books* (London: Chatto & Windus, 1948), pp. 151–53.
36 *HV Works*, pp. 626–27.

it flows through 'times silent stealth'. Human terms are employed to describe its approach to the edge and its inevitable descent – it chides and calls and lingers fearfully – and then the symbolic significance of the 'common pass' through which 'All must descend' is clinched by the more explicit image of the 'deep and rocky grave'. The Christian hope hinted at in 'Not to an end' is confirmed by the verb 'quickned' and by the assurance of resurrection in a final couplet that describes simultaneously the re-establishment of the stream's onward course after the turmoil of the waterfall and the better life enjoyed after the turmoil of death. In this passage there is an instantaneous apprehension of the physical and the spiritual in one movement of mind, rather than the pedestrian deduction of one from the other familiar to readers of the emblem books.

Although the waterfall is nearer to symbol than emblem, however, the 'sublime truths, and wholesome themes' that Vaughan discovers lodged in its 'mystical, deep streams' in the third section of the poem belong to a pre-existing system of beliefs that are not dependent on the natural phenomenon of the waterfall for their revelation. The poetic procedure involved here can be seen more clearly in a comparison with Wordsworth's 'The Simplon Pass', which also arrives at sublime truths through the contemplation of river scenery. In the Romantic poem, the physical details of the landscape play a more active role in the generation of emotion and visionary insight. The mountain river is a self-sufficient expression of an eternal reality that is bound up with the temporal phenomena through which it is perceived. Wordsworth interprets the 'torrents' and the '[b]lack drizzling crags' as 'Characters of the great Apocalypse, / The types and symbols of Eternity, / Of first, and last, and midst, and without end'.[37] Whereas the Romantic poet's intuition of transcendent modes of being is generated by his experience of Alpine scenery, the sight of a Breconshire waterfall stimulates in Vaughan a more intense awareness of beliefs and attitudes already instilled in him by his Christian faith. The stream's water is a 'useful Element and clear', because it is the material symbol of baptism and because it helps him meditate on spiritual things, but it never becomes – like Wordsworth's 'stationary blasts of waterfalls' – a revelation of the 'workings of one mind' not accessible by other means.

37 *The Poetical Works of William Wordsworth*, Vol. II, ed. Ernest de Selincourt, 2nd edn. (Oxford: Clarendon Press, 1952), pp. 212–13.

The contemplation of a natural phenomenon has a slightly different emblematic function in 'The Showre (I)'. The first stanza promises a poetic treatment similar to that of the waterfall by fixing attention on a feature of the rural environment, which is described accurately but felt to have significance beyond itself. The lake is 'drowsie'; mist 'breath'd' from 'her faint bosome' is 'the disease / Of her sick waters'; in the evening, 'Too grosse for heaven', the water vapour condenses into a shower, weeping for its 'mistake'. As in other poems that focus upon the world of Nature, Vaughan insists upon his role as observer – ''Twas so, I saw thy birth.' But it is the physical processes that matter rather than the visual qualities of the scene. With the second stanza – equivalent to the 'interpretation' phase of an emblem – the poem begins to develop a different emphasis from 'The Water-fall'. 'Ah! it is so with me' introduces a personal perspective, in which the 'I' is not the medium for a meditation that ranges over universal Christian truths but for an expression of the experience of an individual sinner, who has often 'prest / Heaven with a lazie breath' to no avail and discovers that only 'Love' can 'Unlock the way' to God, while everything else is 'smoke, and Exhalations of the brest', like the sick vapours that rose from the lake. The speaker's problem is resolved in the third stanza by the hope of softening his 'hard heart' with tears as the shower had made soft the earth: then perhaps 'at last / (Some such showres past,) / My God would give a Sun-shine after raine'.[38] The poem demonstrates once again Vaughan's ability to express the physical and the spiritual in terms of each other without any sense of contrivance. The mist breathed from the lake and the lazy breath of the speaker are two manifestations of the same essential process: both result from sickness and both are eased by the shedding of tears. The 'Sun-shine' of the last line has complete realization in both realms.

Vaughan's habitual poetic method is foregrounded in the cry 'I see the use' that opens 'The Storm', as he prepares to engage both 'thoughts and eyes' in a comparison of the 'tempests in my bloud' with the waters of the River Usk, 'uncalmed' by 'storms, and wind' into a red flood. Like the spiritually and emblematically 'useful Element' of water in 'The Water-fall', the 'inraged air' and the billowing 'waters' provide both imagery and vocabulary for the 'quick blasts' of penitent sighs and the 'storme' that are needed to 'purge' the 'mind' of one 'made foul' by 'sinfull ease': 'And *wind* and

38 *HV Works*, pp. 74–75.

water to thy use / Both *wash*, and *wing* my soul'.³⁹ In the context of the current argument, the emendation of the initial phrase to 'I see the *Usk*' (italics added) in the new edition of Vaughan's *Works* is open to question, since the word 'use', in its now obsolete meaning of the 'practical application of doctrine' in a sermon (*OED*, use, n. 13d), makes perfectly good sense in the light of Vaughan's poetic way with details from the world of nature.⁴⁰

V

There have been various surveys of the poetic functions of particular features of the natural world in Vaughan's poetry. Helen Hughes, for instance, has explored manifestations of 'his love of night' in 'conventional figures and phrases of poetic diction drawn from both Biblical and classical sources' and in the 'more individual expression of personal observation and feeling'; and Belinda Humfrey has written about 'this poet's extraordinary admiration for plant-life', with emphasis on 'green plants or herbs', rather than his 'persistent imagery of flowers'.⁴¹ Glyn Pursglove has analysed more thoroughly the birds 'that occur with some frequency' in his poetry, from those that suggest 'personal observation' – such as the 'Birds rob'd of their native wood' that still pine 'with the thought of home' in their well-fed captivity and the 'fledged birds nest' from which the occupant has 'flown' – to those derived from 'the rich tradition of avian symbolism', like 'the surviving turtle' in Vaughan's elegy for his first wife and the eagle, with its fabled ability to stare directly at the sun and 'fly to enormous heights', which has a long secular poem all to itself.⁴² Hutchinson may have been exaggerating in his claim that there are 'many poems of Henry Vaughan that illustrate his love of trees and his watchful observance of their growth', but the role of

---

39 *HV Works*, pp. 86–87.
40 For a discussion of the emendation, see the note on 86:1 in *HV Works*, p. 916.
41 Helen Sard Hughes, 'Night in the Poetry of Henry Vaughan', *Modern Language Notes*, 28 (1913), 209; Belinda Humfrey, 'Vaughan and Vegetables', *Scintilla*, 3 (1999), 137.
42 Pursglove, '"Winged and free"', pp. 251, 252, 258, 260-64. See 'The Pilgrimage', 'They are all gone into the world of light!', 'Fair and yong light!', and 'The Eagle', in *HV Works*, pp. 129, 568, 601, 732–34.

the arboreal creation does figure significantly in his poetic oeuvre and has been largely neglected by the critical community.[43] The rest of this chapter, therefore, will focus on Vaughan's poetic use of trees – as topographical feature, metaphor, simile, emblem, symbol – to place his approaches to nature within the longer process of cultural change investigated by Keith Thomas.

The few references to trees in Vaughan's early secular verse tend to be drawn from traditional resources and mediated through conventional language. For example, in the 1646 volume, we encounter the ghost of Ben Jonson 'in the shade of his owne bayes' – the laurel reduced to its symbolic function as a wreath of honour – and enter the 'sacred shades' of the 'coole, leavie House', where the poet courted Catherine Wise in the grounds of Brecon Priory.[44] Also derivative, but to more purposeful effect, is a passage from one of the elegies in *Olor Iscanus* (1651), which commemorates a soldier friend in an epic manner by likening his death in battle to the fall of noble trees, rent 'from the ground' and 'overborn' by the 'full-mouth'd blast' of a 'fatall sullen whirle-wind'.[45] The classical provenance of such a simile is part of an appropriately elevated style, but not all its details are derived from the passages in Virgil and Catullus cited by Vaughan's modern editors: the description of the leafy tops caught by 'the Morning-ray', beckoning to the sun, and whispering 'to the day', supplements the classical analogues in ways that are typical of Vaughan's idiosyncratic responses to the natural scene.[46] Even more resonant of his individual voice and vision is a couplet inserted into one of his translations from Boethius in *Olor Iscanus*. In 'that first white age', when human beings lived in harmony with the earth, 'The shadie Pine in the Suns heat / Was their Coole and known Retreat'. Vaughan adds a rider to this familiar classical topos: 'For then 'twas not cut down, but stood / The youth and glory of the wood.'[47] The sense that the tree has a life and a value that are

43 *Life*, p. 22.
44 'To my Ingenuous Friend R.W.', *HV Works*, p. 12; 'Upon the Priorie Grove, His usuall Retyrement', *HV Works*, pp. 24–25.
45 'An Elegie on the death of Mr. R.W. slain in the late unfortunate differences at Routon Heath, neer Chester, 1645', *HV Works*, p. 184.
46 See Catullus, 64: 105–09; Virgil's *Aeneid* 9: 679–82 and 2: 626–31, cited in *HV Works*, note on 184: 9–18, p. 1003.
47 Lib. 2, Metrum 5, in *HV Works*, p. 220.

independent of human needs or symbolic meanings has more in common with Wordsworth than Spenser; and the note of indignant regret at its fate is an indication of the cultural change that had already begun to make itself felt by the middle of the seventeenth century.

The most extended and complex allusion to a tree among the secular poems occurs in 'Daphnis. An Elegiac Eclogue', which was printed in the late volume, *Thalia Rediviva* (1678).[48] The real existence of this tree is not in doubt, since it is clearly located in the Usk valley at the beginning of the passage in question:

> So where swift *Isca* from our lofty hills
> With lowd farewels descends, and foming fills
> A wider Channel, like some great port-vein,
> With large rich streams to feed the humble plain:
> I saw an Oak, whose stately height and shade
> Projected far, a goodly shelter made,
> And from the top with thick diffused Boughs
> In distant rounds grew, like a Wood-nymphs house.
> (ll. 43–50)

Hutchinson wonders if this was the same tree that featured in a dream about 'the great Oake, which growes before the Court yard of my fathers house' recorded by Thomas Vaughan in 1658; and Stevie Davies surmises that Henry's tree 'seems to have grown near Matthew Herbert's rectory at Llangattock and may have resembled the oak-tree at Newton'.[49] The connection with the tree at Llangattock is suggested by the continuation of the passage in 'Daphnis':

> And many times had old *Amphion* made
> His beauteous Flock acquainted with this shade;
> A Flock, whose fleeces were as smooth and white

---

48 *HV Works*, pp. 785–90. Line numbers for quotations from 'Daphnis' are given in the text.

49 *Life*, p. 20; Stevie Davies, *Henry Vaughan*, Border Lines Series (Bridgend: Seren, Poetry of Wales Press, 1995), p. 42. The letter is quoted from *Thomas and Rebecca Vaughan's* Aqua Vitae: Non Vitis, ed. and trans. Donald R. Dickson, Medieval and Renaissance Texts and Studies, Vol. 217 (Tempe, AZ: Arizona Center for Medieval and Renaissance Studies, 2001), p. 239.

> As those, the wellkin shews in Moonshine night.
> Here, when the careless world did sleep, have I
> In dark records and numbers noblie high
> The visions of our black, but brightest Bard
> From old *Amphion's* mouth full often heard;
> With all those plagues poor shepheards since have known.
> (ll. 55–63)

If 'old *Amphion*' is indeed Matthew Herbert, who tutored the Vaughan twins for six years, then his flock are the youngsters who gathered round to hear him recite bardic poetry beneath an imposing tree.

The oak-tree in 'Daphnis', which may derive from a composite memory of those at Newton and Llangattock, becomes the focus for an evocation of Vaughan's adolescence during the 1630s, which is refracted through the pastoral myth as another 'white age', when he was growing up under its 'goodly shelter'. With its 'thick diffused Boughs' that grew in 'distant rounds' towards the top, it has a more distinctive linguistic and physical presence than the trees in the Priory Grove, with their conventional 'greene curles'. The fact that the poet's idyllic early life flourished under the protection of an oak-tree, however, suggests a more allegorical reading based on the traditional emblem of the oak as – in Spenser's words – 'sole king of forrests all'. Such an interpretation goes beyond the generalized pastoral myth of innocent pleasure and invokes the peaceful years of Charles I's reign, before the onset of 'those plagues poor shepheards since have known' – the revolt of Parliament that led to civil war. This gives a political significance to the lines in which the fate of the tree is related:

> But the curs'd owner from the trembling top
> To the firm brink, did all those branches lop,
> And in one hour what many years had bred,
> The pride and beauty of the plain lay dead. (ll. 67–70)

If the traditional symbolism of the oak has a more specific connection with the 'happy days' of the Caroline peace, then this account of the savage pruning and felling of the king of trees becomes an allegory of the failed royalist cause and the execution of Charles I. In this reading, Damon's antipathy towards the 'curs'd owner' and the 'hated Hewer' has a more political charge than the Wordsworthian Pastor's 'motion of despite' against the tree-felling activities of the old man.[50]

The weaving together of the natural and the political in describing the recovery of the violated tree in the final lines of the passage is typical of Vaughan's method of fusing vehicle and tenor in poems like 'The Water-fall' and 'The Showre', so that the workings of nature and theology, morality or politics are apprehended in a single movement of mind and language:

> But Nature, which (like vertue) scorns to yield
> Brought new recruits and succours to the Field;
> For by next Spring the check'd Sap wak'd from sleep
> And upwards still to feel the Sun did creep,
> Till at those wounds, the hated Hewer made,
> There sprang a thicker and a fresher shade. (ll. 67–72)

Neither 'Nature' nor the 'vertue' of a just cause yields permanently to destructive force. Natural processes may be uppermost here – Davies points out that Vaughan gives an 'accurate description of the ability of oaks to "coppice" after felling' – but the pun on 'succours/suckers' and the military metaphors ('new recruits' and 'the Field') release the oak tree's significance as a symbol of embattled monarchy.[51]

The more literal dimension of Vaughan's oak as a focus for communal activities and personal reminiscence places it in a long line of trees commemorated in literature for their association with the human world, from the one known locally as 'My Lady's Oak' in Ben Jonson's 'To Penshurst' – so-called because a Lady Leicester went into labour beneath its branches – right through to 'the LORD'S OAK' in *The Excursion*.[52] These include Aemilia Lanyer's

---

50 Andrew Marvell made a similar allusion to the death of Charles I in the woodland sequence of *Upon Appleton House*: 'While the oak seems to fall content, / Viewing the treason's punishment' (ll. 559–60). See the commentary on the association of tree symbolism and the royalist cause in *The Poems of Andrew Marvell*, ed. Nigel Smith, Longman Annotated English Poets, rev. edn. (London and New York: Pearson Education, 2007), p. 233.

51 Davies, *Henry Vaughan*, pp. 42–43. For different political readings of this pastoral elegy, see the headnote and commentary in *HV Works*, pp. 1376–82.

52 *Ben Jonson: The Complete Poems*, ed. George Parfitt (Harmondsworth: Penguin Books, 1975), p. 96 and the note on l. 18, p. 508.

poignant farewell to an oak tree on the royal estate at Cookham, where she had spent an idyllic interlude of intellectual female companionship with the Countess of Cumberland and her daughter during the first decade of the seventeenth century; Anne Finch's memory of the 'delightful shade' bestowed upon her by an unidentified tree, in gratitude for which she hopes that it may escape 'the axe' till its 'large stock of sap is spent' and 'grace' attends its natural end; and a tribute by the Dorset dialect poet, William Barnes, who fondly recalls how one particular tree has been woven into the fabric of his life – as the site of his parents' relaxation 'At evenen down below the wide / Woak's head', his own boyhood games ('I there've a-climb'd, an' there've a-zwung'), and his courtship – and finds consolation in the thought of the continuity such a tree represents: 'An' let en grow, an' let en spread, / An' let en live when I be dead.'[53]

Vaughan may have shared some of the attitudes towards trees as living creatures and human companions that were being given poetic expression during the seventeenth and eighteenth centuries, but the *aesthetic* dimension of this emerging sensibility is signally missing from his poetry. The 'stately height' of the oak in the Usk valley, for instance, is noted for the 'goodly shelter' it provides rather than its beauty. There is nothing to compare with William Cowper's pleasure in the contribution made by trees – now sadly 'felled' – to the prospect in 'The Poplar Field': 'Twelve years have elapsed since I first took a view / Of my favourite field, and the bank where they grew.'[54] In his poetry, Vaughan does not celebrate views of this kind, composed of field and bank and poplars; nor is he one to deplore, like Gerard Manley Hopkins, the 'strokes of havoc' that have hewn down those more famous poplars at Binsey because they

---

53 See Aemilia Lanyer, 'The Description of Cooke-ham', in *Kissing the Rod: An Anthology of Seventeenth-Century Women's Poetry*, ed. Germaine Greer, Susan Hastings, Jeslyn Medoff, and Melinda Sansone (London: Virago Press, 1988), pp. 46–51; Anne Finch, Countess Winchilsea, 'The Tree', in *Minor Poets of the Eighteenth Century*, ed. Hugh I'A. Fausset (London: Dent, 1930), pp. 114–15; William Barnes, 'The Girt Woak Tree that's in the Dell', in *The Poems of William Barnes*, ed. Bernard Jones, 2 vols. (Carbondale, IL: Southern Illinois University Press, 1962), Vol. I, pp. 81–83.

54 *The Poetical Works of William Cowper*, ed. William Benham (London: Macmillan, 1879), p. 323.

unselved a 'Sweet especial rural scene'.[55] He is more responsive to the play of light than any other visual phenomenon, so that when trees do become part of a 'Scene of fine sights' (in a passage near the beginning of 'Daphnis'), it is only in association with sunset: 'The green wood glitter'd with the golden Sun / And all the West like Silver shin'd.'[56] For the most distinctive impact that trees made on his poetic imagination, however, we need to turn to the role they played in the expression of his *spiritual* vision of the natural world in *Silex Scintillans*.

VI

One of the primary sources of Vaughan's idiosyncratic response to nature is highlighted by Eluned Brown's observations that the 'hallowed places' of the early Patriarchs 'are as much part of his landscape as his own neighbourhood'.[57] In 'Religion', for example, the divine revelation that breathes through the 'leaves' of Old Testament scripture merges with the immanence of God in the arboreal creation; and the groves of Breconshire are transfigured by references to three angelic visitations to produce a highly individual version of the poetic catalogue of trees:

> My God, when I walke in those groves,
> And leaves thy spirit doth still fan,
> I see in each shade that there growes
> An Angell talking with a man.
>
> Under a *Juniper*, some house,
> Or the coole *Mirtles* canopie,
> Others beneath an *Oakes* greene boughs,
> Or at some *fountaines* bubling Eye.[58]

---

55 'Binsey Poplars', in *The Poems of Gerard Manley Hopkins*, ed. W.H. Gardner and N.H. MacKenzie, 4th edn. (London, Oxford, New York: Oxford University Press, 1970), pp. 78–79.
56 *HV Works*, p. 786.
57 Eluned Brown, 'Henry Vaughan's Biblical Landscape', *Essays and Studies*, new series (1977), 57.
58 *HV Works*, p. 64.

The poem goes on to specify the encounters with angels by Jacob, Elias, and Abraham. The restoration of such intimacy is looked forward to in 'The Jews', a meditation on the time of deliverance for the Jewish people prophesied by St Paul, when the inhabitants of Earth and heaven will once again 'familiarly confer / Beneath the Oke and Juniper'.[59]

Vaughan's conception of the special role of trees in the divine dispensation of the wider natural world is expressed in his version of 'Psalme 104':

> Thou giv'st the trees their greenness, ev'n to those
>   Cedars in *Lebanon*, in whose thick boughs
> The birds their nests build; though the Stork doth choose
>   The fir-trees for her house.[60]

But the trees are not only imbued with greenness so that they can contribute to the economy of nature; they have their own degree of sentience and join in the universal worship of the Creator. One of the stanzas in 'Rules and Lessons', for example, asserts that every leaf 'hath his *Morning-hymn*'; and another advises the pious reader to look upon the natural world not for exemplary lessons or aesthetic qualities but for what it reveals of its divine author: 'Thou canst not misse his Praise; Each *tree, herb, flowre* / Are shadows of his *wisedome*, and his Pow'r.'[61] In Vaughan's religious poetry, trees tend to figure frequently in this kind of generic list as participants in a universe that is both created and animated by God. 'Trees, flowers & herbs' share the anticipation of the rest of the natural and human world as they wait for Christ to make his triumphal entry into Jerusalem in 'Palm-Sunday'; and in 'The Night', '*trees* and *herbs* did watch and peep / And wonder', keeping wakeful vigil while he prays.[62]

It is because of his intuition that all created things have the ability to worship and watch and wonder – to join in the 'great *Chime* / And *Symphony* of nature', as he puts it in 'The Morning-watch' – that Vaughan longs for the steadfastness that is

---

59 *HV Works*, p. 585.
60 *HV Works*, p. 580.
61 *HV Works*, pp. 99, 102.
62 *HV Works*, pp. 588, 611.

lacking in humankind: 'I would I were a stone, or tree, / Or flowre by pedigree.'⁶³ In other poems, Vaughan insists that trees will be restored along with the rest of creation. When the Jews share in the general deliverance at the Second Coming of Christ, the 'bright *Dove*' will descend from heaven and 'living waters flow / To make drie dust, and dead trees grow'.⁶⁴ 'The Book' traces each of the components from which the volume in the poet's hand has been manufactured back to their origins as living parts of the universe created by God:

> Thou knew'st this *Tree*, when a green *shade*
> Cover'd it, since a *Cover* made,
> And where it flourish'd, grew and spread,
> As if it never should be dead.⁶⁵

In the final section of the poem, Vaughan prays that he will have 'a place' among the other works of the Creator, when 'trees, beasts and men' are restored and all is made 'new again'.

VII

Henry Vaughan's conviction that trees are spiritually alive with a God-given greenness and that they will share in the general resurrection placed him in the company not only of his hermeticist brother but also of other participants in what John Rogers has called 'the Vitalist Moment'. Rogers locates this moment between 1649 and 1652, the very time when Thomas was seeing his first hermetic books into print and Henry was composing the lyrics that were published in *Silex Scintillans*, and defines Vitalism as a philosophy that 'holds in its tamest manifestation the inseparability of body and soul and, in its boldest, the infusion of all material substance with the power of reason and self-motion'. He explains 'the unprecedented, and largely unrepeated, burst of interest in the specifically vitalist forms of Paracelsian speculation' as a reaction against the 'amoral ascendancy of spiritless physical force implicit in the materialist

---

63 See 'And do they so?', *HV Works*, p. 95.
64 'The Jews', *HV Works*, p. 585.
65 *HV Works*, p. 629.

philosophies of Hobbes and Descartes'.⁶⁶ In an earlier study of the animist materialism of Milton, Stephen Fallon had demonstrated that the poet of *Paradise Lost* celebrated 'the vitality of all matter' and rejected Cartesian dualism in favour of the belief that spirit and matter are 'two modes of the same substance'.⁶⁷ Donald Dickson has since argued that two works by Thomas Vaughan published in 1650 – *Anthroposophia Theomagica* and *Anima Magica Abscondita* – 'ought to be seen as a part of the firestorm sparked by the fear that Descartes had depicted an atheistic, mechanistic universe'.⁶⁸ Whatever these works imply for Thomas's theological position, however, one should be wary of consigning Henry to the 'boldest' end of the Vitalist spectrum, where the more extreme sectaries of the 1650s denied the transcendence of God and embraced a kind of pantheism.⁶⁹ As M.M. Mahood pointed out, the poet's 'vivid awareness of the physical world's intersection with the spiritual world' makes nonsense of the Cartesian dualism against which his twin brother waged polemical war in his hermetic treatises; but it is as well to remember her further observation, 'Thomas Vaughan speaks from speculation, Henry Vaughan from experience.'⁷⁰ When that experience was formulated into intellectual beliefs, the result is neither heretical animism nor pantheism because, as Ross Garner's close analysis of 'And do they so?' demonstrates, 'the order of nature' in Vaughan's work, 'is kept distinct from the order of grace throughout'.⁷¹

66 John Rogers, *The Matter of Revolution: Science, Poetry, and Politics in the Age of Milton* (Ithaca, NY and London: Cornell University Press, 1996), pp. 1, 9.
67 Stephen M. Fallon, *Milton among the Philosophers: Poetry and Materialism in Seventeenth-Century England* (Ithaca, NY and London: Cornell University Press, 1991), pp. 107, 80.
68 Donald R. Dickson, 'Thomas Vaughan and the Iatrochemical Revolution', *The Seventeenth Century*, 15 (2000), 18.
69 Stevie Davies quotes from Jacob Bauthumley's *The Light and Dark Sides of God* (1650): 'Nay, I see that God is in all Creatures, Man and Beast, Fish and Fowle, and every green thing, from the highest Cedar to the Ivey on the wall; and that God is the life and being of them all, and that God doth really dwell, and if you will personally [...] and hath his Being no where else but in the Creatures' (*Henry Vaughan*, p. 130).
70 M.M. Mahood, 'Vaughan: The Symphony of Nature', in *Poetry and Humanism* (London: Jonathan Cape, 1950), p. 289.
71 Ross Garner, *Henry Vaughan: Experience and the Tradition* (Chicago, IL and London: University of Chicago Press, 1959), p. 103.

The research of Fallon and Rogers has informed recent developments in a critical movement that has extended ecological readings from Romantic poetry and American wilderness literature back into the early modern period, initially in relation to *Paradise Lost*.[72] Diane McColley highlighted the reading of 'The Book' by Alan Rudrum as a pioneering piece of ecocritical analysis in its recognition that 'attitudes toward other-than-human beings were matters of theological and philosophical contention that vitally concerned the Vaughans and other early modern writers' and that Henry's poem perceives Earth 'as the shared habitat of various lives, each with its own *telos*, unfolding out of the great mystery of being in its own way'.[73] In a more recent study, she returns to 'The Book' for its awareness of the 'cost to the earth, to habitats, to species, to individuals of those species' of the artefacts familiar in our daily lives.[74] This observation can serve to introduce the only poems in *Silex Scintillans* devoted entirely to poetic lucubrations prompted by a tree: 'The Palm-tree' and 'The Timber'. Together, they confirm that Henry Vaughan was a man of his age – a seventeenth-century Christian for whom it was a matter of habit to subordinate the natural world to the preoccupations of fallen humankind, turning trees into emblems.

The meditation in 'The Palm-tree' owes much to the emblem tradition, weaving in references to that other tree 'ne'r to be pric'd, / A Tree, whose fruit is immortality' and interpreting the palm as a symbol of both the faith and the patience 'of the Saints', which is 'water'd by their tears, as flowers are fed / With dew by night'.[75]

---

72 See Diane McColley, *Milton's Eve* (Urbana, IL: University of Illinois Press, 1983); Diane Kelsey McColley, *A Gust for Paradise: Milton's Eden and the Visual Arts* (Urbana, IL: University of Illinois Press, 1993); Ken Hiltner, *Milton and Ecology* (Cambridge: Cambridge University Press, 2003); Robert N. Watson, *Back to Nature: The Green and the Real in the Late Renaissance* (Philadelphia, PA: University of Pennsylvania Press, 2006).

73 Diane Kelsey McColley, 'Water, Wood, and Stone: The Living Earth in Poems of Vaughan and Milton', in *Of Paradise and Light: Essays on Henry Vaughan and John Milton in Honor of Alan Rudrum*, ed. Donald R. Dickson and Holly Faith Nelson (Newark, DE: University of Delaware Press, 2004), p. 270.

74 Diane Kelsey McColley, *Poetry and Ecology in the Age of Milton and Marvell* (Aldershot: Ashgate, 2007), pp. 1, 113.

75 *HV Works*, p. 575.

Although richer in texture than the kind of verse that doggedly explicated the woodcuts in an emblem book, it remains resolutely inside the mode of thought that produced Spenser's catalogue of trees. In the opening movement of 'The Timber', however, we seem to enter a quite different kind of poetic experience – much closer to Wordsworth's evocation of the sycamore nursed by 'vapours' in its dry crevice of rock – as Vaughan feels his way into what it must have been like to be the tree that now lies fallen:

> Sure thou didst flourish once! and many Springs,
> Many bright mornings, much dew, many showers
> Past ore thy head: many light *Hearts* and *Wings*
> Which now are dead, lodg'd in thy living bowers.
>
> And still a new succession sings and flies;
> Fresh Groves grow up, and their green branches shoot
> Towards the old and still enduring skies,
> While the low V*iolet* thrives at their root.
>
> But thou beneath the sad and heavy *Line*
> Of death, dost waste all senseless, cold and dark;
> Where not so much as dreams of light may shine,
> Nor any thought of greenness, leaf or bark.
>
> And yet (as if some deep hate and dissent,
> Bred in thy growth betwixt high winds and thee,
> Were still alive) thou dost great storms resent
> Before they come, and know'st how near they be.
>
> Else all at rest thou lyest, and the fierce breath
> Of tempests can no more disturb thy ease;
> But this thy strange resentment after death
> Means onely those, who broke (in life) thy peace.[76]

Two critics from an earlier generation had picked out this 'fine descriptive passage' as 'one that was most likely prompted by the actual sight of some fallen tree' and 'the resentient cry of cut timber at an approaching storm' as an instance of Vaughan's finding proof 'of

---

76 *HV Works*, pp. 583–85.

the Creator's presence in His world'.⁷⁷ A more ecologically minded reader like Stevie Davies sees in it 'a green inspiration' that is 'full of love for rooted things', and that balances 'the loss of an ancient home and shelter for generations of winged creatures' in the first stanza against the demonstration of the biosphere's 'principle of recycling' in the second stanza. In the 'conditions for new growth' created by the natural phenomena of death and decay, 'saplings spring amongst the ruins of the old trees and compete for the light'.⁷⁸

McColley does not include 'The Timber' in her account of 'hylozoic poems', but these five stanzas might be taken as a prime example of the way poets in the seventeenth century 'increasingly went beyond emblematic uses of plants to heed the processes of their lives'.⁷⁹ Vaughan's empathy for what might be called the 'inner life' of the tree is particularly strong in the third, fourth, and fifth stanzas, after his initial observations on its place in the natural environment: the normal concerns of arboreal existence – 'dreams of light' and thoughts 'of greenness, leaf or bark' – are extinguished, and all that remains of former sentience is a 'strange resentment' (an uneasy stirring of former feelings) at the approach of a storm. But the poem does not end here: in nine further stanzas, Vaughan interprets each detail as if the foregoing passage were an emblematic woodcut. His meditation begins with the fallen tree's likeness to a murdered man whose 'dead blood' flows in the presence of his killer, and he goes on to raise issues of sin, repentance, and salvation:

> And is there any murth'rer worse then sin?
> Or any storms more foul then a lewd life?
> Or what *Resentient* can work more within,
> Then true remorse, when with past sins at strife.

He does not call upon arboreal imagery again until near the end, when he introduces the 'trees of life' that can only be watered by 'streams sent from above'; and the poem is printed with an epigraph from Romans 6:7 – '*He that is dead, is freed from sin*' – which suggests that Vaughan approached the dead tree from the start with

---

77 Pettet, *Of Paradise and Light*, p. 86; Mahood, 'Vaughan: The Symphony of Nature', in *Poetry and Humanism*, p. 289.
78 Davies, *Henry Vaughan*, pp. 143–44.
79 McColley, *Poetry and Ecology*, p. 111.

this text in mind. For all its sensitivity to the life in other parts of the created world, this is not a Romantic or an ecological poem before its time; but nor is Vaughan merely 'expressing, with extraordinary inwardness, his own sense of sin' in terms of a natural object, as one critic has described the strategy of 'The Timber'.[80] He fuses in a single imaginative act two vital elements of his personal experience and his poetic art: the intuitive (which was in tune with the 'profound shift in sensibilities' that Keith Thomas saw as leading eventually to both the Romantic and the ecological movements in Western culture) and the devotional (which grounded him firmly in established habits of Christian meditation).

80 A. Alvarez, *The School of Donne* [1961] (New York and Toronto: Mentor Books, The New American Library, 1967), p. 70.

CHAPTER TEN

Henry Vaughan and the Practice of Poetry

I

The very first appreciation of Vaughan's poetry – an anonymous article on *Olor Iscanus* published in 1821 – praised it in general terms for 'a considerable command of forcible language, and an occasional richness of imagery', but condemned many of the poems for 'obscurity' and the poet for spending 'his strength on frigid and bombastic conceits'.[1] The nineteenth-century prejudice against the 'metaphysical' style meant that even the 'most favourable specimen' that had been selected from the secular poems to reintroduce Vaughan to modern readers in 1801 was thought to be 'too much marked by quaintness and conceit'; and the editor who first reprinted a few items from *Silex Scintillans* in 1819 regarded their author as 'one of the harshest even of the inferior order of the school of conceit'.[2] The charges of 'obscurity' and 'quaintness' were repeated in Lyte's 1847 edition; even Louise Guiney admitted that his 'figures' are 'too bold and too many' and 'come from strange corners'; and an early twentieth-century namesake of Vaughan blamed 'some of the greatest conceits which disfigure his more distinctively religious verses' on the influence of George Herbert.[3]

---

1 *The Retrospective Review*, 3:2 (1821), 336.
2 George Ellis, *Specimens of the Early English Poets*, 3 vols. (London: G & W. Nicol and J. Wright, 1801), Vol. III, p. 304 (the poem chosen was abridged from 'To the best, and most accomplished Couple'); Thomas Campbell, *Specimens of the British Poets*, 7 vols. (London: John Murray, 1819), Vol. IV, p. 347.
3 Silex Scintillans: *Sacred Poems and Private Ejaculations by Henry Vaughan*,

In the 1930s, when Vaughan was being read more systematically as a Metaphysical Poet belonging to the Donne tradition, efforts were made to distinguish him from his peers by arguing that the conceit was 'a fashion he accepted rather than the outcome of his own habit of mind' and that his 'use of the conceit is simpler and less intellectual than Donne's'.[4]

Later critics moved beyond these early generalizations, but still concentrated largely on Vaughan's imagery. M.M. Mahood demonstrated that his images 'group themselves in a few well-defined clusters', notably those that gather round 'the idea of magnetism', 'light symbolism', 'clouds and mists', and 'the human soul as a plant'.[5] For E.C. Pettet, imagery was 'of quite exceptional importance in his poems, in their inspiration, structure, and general effect', and much of his labour was directed towards identifying 'key-images' that are 'prefigured in the earlier poems' and developed with greater 'symbolical richness and complexity' in the religious poetry. He also highlighted the phenomenon of 'recurrent image-clusters' and showed how variety is added to the religious poetry by figures drawn not only from 'esoteric sources' but also from 'everyday and domestic life' in the manner of George Herbert.[6] R.A. Durr found traditional 'symbols of the Christian life of prayer' – 'revivified with fresh nuances' – to be 'at once the center and circumference' of Vaughan's poetry; and more recently, Donald Dickson has explored the ways in which 'the metaphor of water out of the rock springing to life everlasting' was developed 'as a central conceit in *Silex*'.[7]

---

ed. Rev. H.F. Lyte (London: Pickering, 1847), p. xlvii; Louise Imogen Guiney, 'Henry Vaughan', in *A Little English Gallery* (New York: Harper & Brothers, 1894), pp. 80–81; J. Vaughan, 'Henry Vaughan, Silurist', *The Nineteenth Century and After*, 67 (1910), 497.

4 Joan Bennett, *Five Metaphysical Poets* [originally *Four Metaphysical Poets*, 1934], 3rd edn. (Cambridge: Cambridge University Press, 1964), p. 73; George Williamson, *The Donne Tradition: A Study in English Poetry from Donne to the Death of Cowley* [1930] (New York: The Noonday Press, 1958), p. 130.

5 M.M. Mahood, 'Vaughan: The Symphony of Nature', in *Poetry and Humanism* (London: Jonathan Cape, 1950), pp. 271–78.

6 E.C. Pettet, *Of Paradise and Light: A Study of Vaughan's* Silex Scintillans (Cambridge: Cambridge University Press, 1960), pp. 4–11, 24–31, 169–78.

7 R.A. Durr, *On the Mystical Poetry of Henry Vaughan* (Cambridge, MA: Harvard University Press, 1962), pp. 29–30; Donald R. Dickson, *The Fountain*

A few examples must suffice to illustrate Vaughan's choice and management of imagery in more detail. The opening stanzas of one of the love poems in his first volume illustrate the kind of extended conceit that his earliest critics would have condemned as 'quaint' or 'bombastic':

> If *Amoret*, that glorious Eye,
>   In the first birth of light,
>   And death of Night,
> Had with those elder fires you spye
>   Scatter'd so high
>   Received forme, and sight;
>
> We might suspect in the vast Ring,
>   Amidst these golden glories,
>   And fierie stories;
> Whether the Sunne had been the King,
>   And guide of Day,
>   Or your brighter eye should sway.[8]

Governed by 'If', a single twelve-line sentence pursues with apparent logic a hyperbolical comparison (not revealed as such until the final line) between the bright eye of the beloved and the sun, which was created in the beginning – when God 'divided the light from the darkness' (Genesis 1:4) – to rule the 'elder fires' (the stars) in the 'vast Ring' of the spherical heavens and to control the cycle of day and night here upon Earth. This is an early instance of Vaughan's ability to breathe new life into a hackneyed comparison, which gains narrative credibility from being set on a 'starry evening', when 'those elder fires you spye' are directly above the heads of the strolling couple.

In another of the love poems, Vaughan uses the analogy of magnetism to describe the force that draws the speaker towards his lady without the gross intermediaries of 'lust and sence' needed by 'Sublunarie Lovers':

---

of Living Waters: The Typology of the Waters of Life in Herbert, Vaughan, and Traherne (Columbia, MO: University of Missouri Press, 1987), p. 142.

8 From 'To Amoret, Walking in a Starry Evening', *HV Works*, p. 16.

> Thus to the North the Loadstones move,
> And thus to them th' enamour'd steel aspires:
> Thus *Amoret*,
> I doe affect.[9]

In affecting – that is, both aiming at and loving – Amoret, he is like loadstones attracted to the North and steel attracted to loadstones. Vaughan was here invoking the ancient conception of magnetism as a natural force exerted by a greater body on a lesser one.[10] But when he drew upon magnetic imagery again in a tribute to the friendship he enjoyed with Thomas Powell, he had evidently encountered the ideas of William Gilbert, who had established that 'in magnetism motion is not caused by attraction but by a coming together or agreeing together of both parts: the attractive power, as it were, not in one only but in both'.[11] As in the Amoret poem, he uses magnetism as an analogy for the effects of love, but he builds into it an assertion that his understanding of the phenomenon has kept pace with the newest revelations of science:

> 'Tis a kind Soul in *Magnets*, that attones
> Such two hard things as *Iron* and *Stones*,
> And in their dumb *compliance* we learn more
> Of Love, than ever Books could speak before.
> For though *attraction* hath got all the name,
> As if that *power* but from one side came,
> Which both unites; yet, where there is no *sence*,
> There is no *Passion*, nor *Intelligence*:
> And so by consequence we cannot state
> A Commerce, unless both we animate.[12]

---

9 'To Amoret, of the difference 'twixt him, and other Lovers, and what true Love is', *HV Works*, p. 22.

10 See A.U. Chapman, 'Henry Vaughan and Magnetic Philosophy', in *Essential Articles for the Study of Henry Vaughan*, ed. Alan Rudrum (Hamden, CT: Archon Books, 1987), p. 160.

11 Quoted (and translated) from Gilbert's *De Magnete* of 1612 by Chapman, 'Henry Vaughan and Magnetic Philosophy', note 25, p. 168.

12 'To his Learned Friend and Loyal Fellow-Prisoner, Thomas Powel of Cant. Doctor of Divinity', *HV Works*, pp. 729–30.

The conceit of learning about love from the 'dumb *compliance*' of objects in the natural world may have been dragged from 'strange corners', but the insight it offers into the nature of true friendship is based on a sophisticated knowledge of both new science and human psychology. One's critical response to such an intellectually worked-through analogy will depend upon a choice between Samuel Johnson's famous charge against Metaphysical conceits that 'the most heterogeneous ideas are yoked *by violence* together' and T.S. Eliot's counterclaim that all genuine poetry involves 'a degree of heterogeneity of material *compelled into unity* by the operation of the poet's mind' (italics added in each quotation).[13]

A stanza from a devotional poem, which contains one more reference to the theory of magnetism, will serve to illustrate another feature of the metaphysical style: the rapid movement from conceit to conceit in order to describe a state of mind or being from different perspectives. A meditation on the restless condition of humankind in 'Man' ends with this series of observations on the wanderer's search for 'home':

> He knocks at all doors, strays and roams,
> Nay hath not so much wit as some stones have
> Which in the darkest nights point to their homes,
>   By some hid sense their Maker gave;
> Man is the shuttle, to whose winding quest
>   And passage through these looms
> God order'd motion, but ordain'd no rest.[14]

The frequent Vaughan image of the homeless traveller, astray in a dark world, elides into a contrast with the 'wit' that enables 'some stones' (that is, loadstones) to locate their 'homes' in the north even in darkness, because their Maker has planted a natural force within them that is responsive to the force that draws them homewards. This conceit then abruptly gives way to an alternative image of man

---

13 Samuel Johnson, 'The Life of Cowley', in *Lives of the English Poets*, 2 vols., Everyman's Library [1925] (London: Dent, 1961), Vol. I, p. 11; T.S. Eliot, 'The Metaphysical Poets', in *Selected Essays*, 3rd edn. (London: Faber & Faber, 1951), p. 283.
14 *HV Works*, p. 144.

as a shuttle condemned to a perpetual 'winding quest' through the 'looms' of his restless existence.

Another Metaphysical device – the heaping together of brief conceits – is used to appropriately humorous effect in a passage from one of the occasional pieces in *Olor Iscanus*. The soldier-poet ruefully records the consequences of sleeping out all night after the surrender of Beeston Castle, clad only in a wire-stiffened cloak lent him by a friend:

> O that thou hadst been there next morn, that I
> Might teach thee new *Micro-cosmo-graphie*!
> Thou would'st have ta'ne me, as I naked stood,
> For one of th' *seven pillars* before the floud,
> Such *Characters* and *Hierogliphicks* were
> In one night worn, that thou mightst justly swear
> I'd slept in *Cere-cloth*, or at *Bedlam* where
> The mad men lodge in straw, I'le not forbear
> To tell thee all, his wild *Impress* and *tricks*
> Like *Speeds* old *Britans* made me look, or *Picts*.[15]

The initial comparison likens the microcosm of his body, lined with indentations, to a map of the macrocosm or greater world (perhaps with a glance at John Earle's famous *Microcosmographie* of 1628). In the second conceit, the cloak has imprinted upon his bare flesh hieroglyphic characters like those engraved upon two (not seven) pillars by Noah's son, Seth; in a third and fourth, his body bears marks that might have been left by wax-impregnated cloths used as winding-sheets or by the straw upon which inmates slept in the madhouse; in a fifth, he looks like the tattooed natives of ancient Britain depicted in John Speed's *History of Great Britaine* published in 1611. Such wittily conceived and far-fetched comparisons were designed to entertain the 'ingenious' readers Vaughan aimed at in his early secular poetry. This may have been the kind of thing that Melissa Wanamaker had in mind when she complained, 'Vaughan casually drops disconnected images helter-skelter into poems as if by accident, capriciously, or, worse, inattention to craft.'[16] Since she was mainly concerned with *Silex Scintillans*, however, she may

---

15 'Upon a Cloke lent him by Mr. J. Ridsley', *HV Works*, p. 188.
16 See Melissa Cynthia Wanamaker, *'Discordia Concors*: The Metaphysical Wit of

have been thinking of some such poem as 'Son-dayes', which, like Herbert's 'Prayer (I)', consists entirely of heterogeneous and syntactically isolated metaphors.[17]

II

The anonymous critic of 1821 had noted 'the facility of the rhyme, and the variety and ease of the rhythm' in one of the secular poems and these aspects of Vaughan's poetic art were often taken up by later critics.[18] Lyte observed that his rhymes were 'frequently defective' and commented at some length on his habit of 'making the sense of one line run over into the line following': this 'is doubtless a beauty in versification', which redeems it from monotony, but it can itself become monotonous if 'overdone'.[19] Guiney was at pains to rebut the accusation that Vaughan's verse was 'untunable', adducing in particular the positive rhythmic effects achieved by his habit of playing with pauses. Nevertheless, she classed the 'overflow' of run-on lines as a formal defect inherited from Jonson.[20] Although he regarded Vaughan's 'disjunctions of rhythm' as an imperfection, Edmund Blunden identified 'one vital gift' that invigorated the movement of his verse: he was 'a master' of iambic measures, particularly 'the eight-syllable couplet', in which he 'conveys the majority of his finest ideas'.[21] Simmonds observed that Vaughan employed couplets more extensively than any other verse form, especially in his earlier work, and that these, together with 'simple combinations of quatrains and couplets', are 'the basic measures of his poetry'; and Louis Martz calculated that *Silex Scintillans* contains

Henry Vaughan's *Silex Scintillans*', *Texas Studies in Literature and Language*, 16 (1974–75), 465.
17 *HV Works*, p. 111. Herbert's own poem, 'Sundays', begins with a similar list of images but does not sustain it beyond the first few lines. For other examples of this technique of traditional Welsh poetry, known as *dyfalu*, see Vaughan's 'The Charnel-house', 'H. Scriptures', 'Joy', 'The Night', 'To his Books', 'Retirement (II)', in *HV Works*, pp. 175, 104, 576, 611, 767, 770.
18 *The Retrospective Review* (1821), 343.
19 Lyte, *Sacred Poems*, pp. xlviii–lix.
20 Guiney, *A Little English Gallery*, pp. 81–82, 110.
21 Edmund Blunden, *On the Poems of Henry Vaughan: Characteristics and Intimations* (London: Richard Cobden-Sanderson, 1927), pp. 45–46.

'no less than thirty poems wholly or mainly in couplets – ten in the first part and twice that many in the second part'.[22]

Simmonds supplies a number of examples of self-contained couplets that achieve the kind of 'symmetry' and 'balance' associated with the later use of the form by Dryden and Pope. From an early secular poem, 'To his friend—', he quotes two lines that maintain a regular iambic beat – 'So wèe are mèerly thròwn upòn the stàge / The mìrth of fòoles, and Lègend òf the àge' (ll. 27–28) – and comments that 'the breaking of one line slows the rhythm' and also gives it 'internal balance and compact force, in contrast to the thrusting vigor of the unbroken line'. And he finds the same 'controlled and ordered energy' in a couplet from 'Vanity of Spirit' – 'Hère of this mìghty sprìng, I foùnd some drìlls, / With Ècchoes bèaten fròm th' etèrnall hìlls' (ll. 17–18).[23] But in this case, the impact of the steady rhythm of the second line is dependent not only on the caesura in the line before but also on the inversion of its initial foot, which is a common metrical variation in iambic pentameter verse. Such smoothly flowing couplets are not typical of Vaughan's handling of the form, however, as Lyte and Blunden recognized. The energy and variety created by disrupting the formal expectations set up by the enclosing rhymes and the underlying iambic rhythm are more characteristic of his verse than symmetry and balance. This was apparent in his first collection, in which the very first poem begins with a twenty-line movement that vividly evokes the bustle and camaraderie of student life and displays an easy mastery of the octosyllabic couplet:

> When we are dead, and now, no more
> Our harmles mirth, our wit, and score
> Distracts the Towne; when all is spent
> That the base niggard world hath lent
> Thy purse, or mine; when the loath'd noise

---

22 James D. Simmonds, *Masques of God: Form and Theme in the Poetry of Henry Vaughan* (Pittsburgh, PA: University of Pittsburgh Press, 1972), p. 44; Louis L. Martz, 'Vaughan and Rembrandt: The Protestant Baroque', in *From Renaissance to Baroque: Essays on Literature and Art* (Columbia, SC and London: University of Missouri Press, 1991), p. 235.

23 Simmonds, *Masques of God*, pp. 44–45. The two poems are in *HV Works*, pp. 179, 81.

> Of Drawers, Prentises, and boyes
> Hath left us, and the clam'rous barre
> Items no pints i'th' Moone, or Starre;
> [.........]
> When all these Mulcts are paid, and I
> From thee, deare wit, must part, and dye;
> Wee'le beg the world would be so kinde,
> To give's one grave, as wee'de one minde.[24]

A regular iambic beat on alternate syllables is established in the first three lines, but the spilling over of meaning and syntax from lines three and four disturbs the rhythm to force emphasis onto key words: 'When àll is spènt / That the bàse nìggard wòrld hath lènt / Thỳ purse, or mìne; when the loàth'd noìse / Of Dràwers ...' Throughout most of the twenty lines (eight of which are omitted above), the formal parameters of the couplet are disrupted in this way by strong pauses and runover lines. The result is a dynamic forward march that gradually subsides into a regular closed couplet at the end to bring to completion the syntactical movement orchestrated by the repeated 'when' clauses. In the penultimate couplet, the cessation of shared activity is heralded when the severance of the companions is mimicked rhythmically by the runover and the sequence of reluctant hesitations between the metrical feet: 'and Ì / From thèe, deare wìt, must pàrt, and dỳe'.

Equally vigorous, this time in decasyllabic rhyming couplets, is the contempt for Fortune – which the choice of vocabulary clearly identifies with the current political regime – conveyed by heavy caesuras and run-on lines at the start of a poem not published until 1678:

> For shame desist, why should'st thou seek my fall?
> It cannot make thee more Monarchical.
> Leave off; thy Empire is already built;
> To ruine me were to inlarge thy guilt,
> Not thy Prerogative. I am not he
> Must be the measure of thy victory.[25]

---

24 'To my Ingenuous Friend, *R.W.*', *HV Works*, p. 12.
25 'The importunate Fortune, written to Doctor Powel of Cantre', *HV Works*, pp. 740–41.

Each couplet uses the device of pairing a regularly moving iambic line and one interrupted by a caesura, with variety injected by positioning the pauses after the fourth, second, and sixth syllables. And the elision between the second and third couplets forces emphases onto the key word 'guilt' and the defining negative: 'thy guìlt / Nòt thy Preròogative'. Part of the satiric effect here is achieved by setting the moral stigma of the monosyllabic 'guilt' against the political crime implied by the polysyllabic 'Prerogative', the traditional authority that has been usurped from the king; part resides in the emphatic disturbance of metrical regularity in the last four syllables after the strong pause, which forces them to flow over into the final line: 'Ì am not hè', a metrical inversion (far more common in the first two feet of an iambic line) that blunts the triumph of the rhyme word 'victory'.

The rapid forward motion of the octosyllabic couplet is particularly suited to narrative. 'The Search' is typical of the way Vaughan exploits its resources for this purpose, playing off syntax against verse form by means of run-on lines and carefully placed pauses:

> 'Tis now cleare day: I see a Rose
> Bud in the bright East, and disclose
> The Pilgrim-Sunne; all night have I
> Spent in a roving Extasie
> To find my Saviour; I have been
> As far as *Bethlem*, and have seen
> His Inne, and Cradle; Being there
> I met the *Wise-men*, askt them where
> He might be found, or what starre can
> Now point him out, grown up a Man?[26]

Especially expressive are disruptions of the regular metrical beat not only to vary the rhythm but also to orchestrate meaning: 'I sèe a Ròse / Bùd in the brìght Eàst'; 'àll nìght have Ì / Spènt in a ròving …'; 'or whàt Stàrre càn / Nòw poìnt him oùt'. A quite different effect is achieved in 'The Retreate', where no caesuras break up the measured pace of the verse and each rhymed unit is self-contained:

> O how I long to travell back
> And tread again that ancient track!

---

26 *HV Works*, p. 66.

> That I might once more reach that plaine,
> Where first I left my glorious traine,
> From whence th' Inightened spirit sees
> That shady City of Palme trees;
> But (ah!) my soul with too much stay
> Is drunk, and staggers in the way.
> Some men a forward motion love,
> But I by backward steps would move,
> And when this dust falls to the urn
> In that state I came return.[27]

The rhythm is disturbed only twice, in order to imitate the action described: once, by means of enjambement and caesura – 'with too much stay / Is drunk, and staggers ...'; and once, when a slight pause, engineered by adjacent stresses, makes the rhythm teeter before a key verb – 'And whèn this dùst | fàlls to the ùrn'. The switch from iambic to trochaic metre in the last line then brings the poem to a close with a sense of finality created by the suppressed syllable at the end: 'Ìn that stàte I càme retùrn (˘).'

Simmonds, who has devoted more space to analysing Vaughan's handling of the couplet form than any other critic, concludes that 'his modifications of the basic rhythm' produce 'a marked increase in the internal activity of the verse', so that the 'normative line' in his early work and in the best of his couplet poems in *Silex Scintillans* 'becomes an organic form molded by the dynamic pressures of imagery and thought'. He also demonstrates that Vaughan frequently exploited the 'more spacious form' of the quatrain and observes that he 'usually respects the integrity of the unit', within which he can achieve both 'formal symmetry' and 'organic versification'.[28]

Two examples will illustrate the varied music available within the simple octosyllabic quatrain. At the end of 'The Incarnation, and Passion', the bewildered question articulated in the first two lines is answered by the word 'Love', which is not only repeated but given metrical prominence by the two pauses in the third line and the consequent runover into the final line, so that the negative force of the clinching rhyme word, 'death', is cancelled by the positive energy of the rhythm:

---

27 *HV Works*, p. 82.
28 Simmonds, *Masques of God*, pp. 49, 52, 58.

> O what strange wonders could thee move
> To slight thy precious bloud, and breath!
> Sure it was *Love*, my Lord; for *Love*
> Is only stronger far than death.[29]

In the opening quatrain of 'The Ornament', the enjambement of the last two lines and the placing of the caesura after the second syllable of the fourth line enacts metrically the 'proud haste' of the rich as they scramble across the line-ending; and the closing rhyme (together with the internal rhyme 'poor/adore') completes the vision of a materialistic world in which the rich acquire and the poor worship the 'glittering store' on display:

> The lucky world shewd me one day
> Her gorgeous Mart and glittering store,
> Where with proud haste the rich made way
> To buy, the poor came to adore.[30]

By altering the length of lines in the structure of the quatrain, Vaughan was able to create further variations of verbal music. The contest between the corrupt pleasures of the idle verse he found attractive in his youth and the more austere demands of his mature religious aesthetic is played out not only in metaphors but also in the alternation of glibly flowing eight-syllable lines and more abrupt six-syllable lines (made more severe by the reversed foot at the start of the last line that throws the stress onto 'Wìnter'):

> Go, go, seek out some greener thing,
>   It snows, and freezeth here;
> Let Nightingales attend the spring,
>   Wìnter is àll my yèar.[31]

In contrast, the short last line in the 10–8–10–6 arrangement in one of the untitled elegies effects very different kinds of closure in adjacent stanzas, setting the mystery of the soul's habitation after death against a momentary glimpse of heaven:

---

29 *HV Works*, p. 78.
30 *HV Works*, p. 594.
31 'Idle Verse', *HV Works*, p. 111.

> He that hath found some fledg'd birds nest, may know
>   At first sight, if the bird be flown;
> But what fair Well, or Grove he sings in now,
>   That is to him unknown.
>
> And yet, as Angels in some brighter dreams
>   Call to the soul, when man doth sleep:
> So some strange thoughts transcend our wonted theams,
>   And into glory peep.[32]

The mystery and the wonder of the short final lines that follow the long sweep of an unbroken iambic pentameter are enhanced by the musical variations of rhythm within the first two lines of each quatrain, which result from enjambement and the careful placing of caesuras, so that the first lines are split eight–two and two–eight and the second lines balance three–five and four–four respectively.

III

Lyte's charge that Vaughan's rhymes are often 'defective' needs to be addressed before considering his management of the more complex stanzaic forms he adopted for some of the finest lyric performances in *Silex Scintillans*. It is certainly undeniable that his verses contain an abundance of what Martz describes as 'off-rhyme, or partial rhyme'.[33] One early poem supplies the following examples: sledge/*bridge*, *tricks*/*Picts*, drawn/*Fetter-lane*, secure/showre, *Stone*/one, upon/loome, Muse/abuse (noun). The same poem yields several instances of Vaughan's ubiquitous habit of rhyming (and off-rhyming) a monosyllabic with a polysyllabic word – necessity/by, I/*Micro-cosmo-graphie*, fear/*Conjurer*, be/*Anatomie*, e're/*Westminster*, knee/symmetrie, I/Courtesie – which sometimes achieves the satirical bite of his rebuke to the victorious opponents of the king in one of the *Thalia* poems: 'For shame desist, why should'st thou seek my fall? / It cannot make thee more Monarchical'; or the ring of vindicated faith in the couplet that ends the last poem in *Silex Scintillans*: 'With prostrate souls adoring thee, / Who turn'd our sad

---

32 'They are all gone into the world of light!', *HV Works*, p. 568.
33 Martz, 'Vaughan and Rembrandt', p. 236.

captivity.'[34] The 'modern reader may raise an eyebrow' at apparently imperfect matches or lazy disregard of artistic propriety, as Stevie Davies does at the 'loose and bathetic feminine rhyme' that brings 'Corruption' to what should be a stirring apocalyptic climax:

> All's in deep sleep, and night; Thick darknes lyes
>   And hatcheth o'r thy people;
> But hark! what trumpets that? what Angel cries
>   *Arise! Thrust in thy sickle.*[35]

And if modern readers raise an eyebrow at such infelicities, Vaughan's contemporaries must have looked askance at some of his choices of rhyme words, according to Joseph Summers' assessment of their aesthetic expectations: 'It is difficult to imagine that an English poet who had attended Westminster School or had been resident longer or nearer to the universities and the Court and London would have settled for so many oddly unrhymed lines, lines so twisted to achieve their rhymes, such imperfect rhymes, such awkward shifts in stanzaic and rhetorical constructions, so many sudden (and sometimes even bathetic) poetic descents.'[36]

Various explanations have been given for Vaughan's deviation from norms set by the poetic predecessors he sought to emulate, whether Jonson and the Tribe of Ben or George Herbert. Helen White put it down to his weak 'command of the possibilities of sound and rhythm'; Martz saw it 'as an aspect of his baroque fluidity: he is too much in a swirling rush to bother with perfect rhymes'; and Philip West regarded 'staccato, unsatisfying rhymes' as one of the formal devices that helped to create a 'poetry of disorder'.[37] Some of

---

34 See 'Upon a Cloke lent him by Mr. J .Ridsley', 'The Importunate Fortune', and 'L'Envoy', *HV Works*, pp. 187–89, 740, 632. Examples of Vaughan's imperfect rhyming and his habit of pairing a monosyllabic word with a longer one from across the range of Vaughan's work include *Amoret*/affect, lockes/drops, sport/art, exclaim/raign, house/loose, dust/huske, phlegm/dream, forgotten/broken; and he/destinie, be/Calamity, by/antiquity, thee/sympathie, see/immortality, thus/miraculous.

35 See *HV Works*, p. 104 and Stevie Davies, *Henry Vaughan*, Border Lines Series (Bridgend: Seren, Poetry of Wales Press, 1995), p. 162.

36 Joseph H. Summers, *The Heirs of Donne and Jonson* (London: Chatto & Windus, 1970), pp. 122–23.

37 Helen C. White, *The Metaphysical Poets: A Study in Religious Experience*

the so-called defects in his rhymes, however, may simply be the result of his native accent. Hutchinson explains that Welsh speakers do not naturally distinguish between *s* and *z* sounds (both pronounced *ss*) or between *s* and *sh*, which accounts for such rhymes as doses/closes, squeeze/piece, price/cries, voice/joys, wish'd/miss'd, and undress/fresh. Inherited from Welsh poetry was the 'consonantal chime', a pattern of sounds called *proest*, where 'the consonants echo while the vowel changes', permitting Vaughan to rhyme 'sport' and 'art', 'flesh' and 'crush', 'priest' and 'oppress'd'. Other features of Welsh poetry common in Vaughan's work are conspicuous alliteration and the toleration of 'almost any degree of assonance', licensing Vaughan's frequent rhyming of *n* and *m* sounds: sins/limbs, come/sun, since/glimpse, dawn/name; and the even more 'defective' weep/seek, locks/drops, dust/husk, forgotten/broken.[38] Sean McDowell has recently demonstrated in more detail that Vaughan deliberately uses the *proest* technique to unify the first two stanzas of 'The Bird', which rhyme night/wing/sto**rm**/bo**rm**/be**d**/hea**d** with light/sing/a**rm**/wa**rm**/ha**d**/ma**d**e, overlaying the orthodox rhymes with consonantal 'chimes' on *rm* and *d*. A number of Vaughan's other poems are shown to contain 'localized instances of *proest*-rhyme, which strike the modern ear more as off-rhymes or near rhymes, perhaps even lapses in inventiveness, as opposed to nods toward a venerable poetic practice'. Particularly effective is Vaughan's adoption of this Welsh device to reinforce a regular abab scheme and so bring a poem to a resonant close: the concluding stanza of 'The Daughter of Herodias' rhymes bre**d**/goo**d**/sprea**d**/bloo**d**; and 'The Obsequies' 'moves more gradually into a terminal note' with shed/bra**ve**/head/gra**ve**/ mo**ve**/Hi**ve**/lo**ve**/ali**ve**. Rather than instances of carelessness or ineptitude, such examples are evidence that Vaughan's ear was 'attuned to this native music'.[39]

Glyn Pursglove takes a more complex approach to Vaughan's exploitation of the 'complementary and competitive' energies of

---

[1936] (London and New York: Collier-Macmillan, 1962), p. 288; Martz, *From Renaissance to Baroque*, p. 236; Philip West, *Henry Vaughan's* Silex Scintillans: *Scripture Uses* (Oxford: Oxford University Press, 2001), p. 115.

38 *Life*, pp. 159–62.

39 Sean McDowell, 'The Sounds of Henry Vaughan's Welsh Bird' (a paper given at the 'Marcher Metaphysicals Conference' held at Gregynog Hall, Powys, in October 2015). For the examples, see *HV Works*, pp. 582, 590, 626.

rhyme. The 'relative force of the two kinds of energy' will differ in a particular instance according to 'the presence or otherwise of what one might call a semantic or conceptual rhyme between the two words which are phonological rhymes'. If there is a semantic and aural similarity between the two words, Pursglove uses the term 'synonymic'; where 'a difference in semantic force works against the phonetic rhyme', he uses the term 'antonymic'. He argues that Vaughan would have seen rhymes with 'light' – 'one of the key polarities' in his symbolic world – 'as more than merely decorative'.[40] As examples of synonymic rhyme, he quotes a couplet from 'L'Envoy' – 'The seers of whose sacred light / Shall all be drest in shining white' – and a quatrain from 'The Queer':

> Whose Eastern traffique deals in bright
> And boundless Empyrean themes,
> Mountains of spice, Day-stars and light,
> Green trees of life, and living streams?[41]

The contrasting antonymic force of the light/night rhyme is felt in 'Abels blood', where he pleads with the 'Almighty Judge' that he may 'duly pay' the heart he has vowed 'To thy bright arm, which was my light / And leader through thick death and night!'[42] The power that 'light' has over death and night is reinforced by the internal synonymic rhyme on 'bright' and the alliteration that connects 'light' and 'leader'. A striking example of antonymic rhyme occurs in 'Peace':

---

40 Glyn Pursglove, 'Henry Vaughan and the Energies of Rhyme', *Scintilla*, 1 (1997), 146–47. The rest of this paragraph is heavily indebted to Pursglove's article. Vaughan's frequent rhyming of 'light' with 'night' led Geoffrey Hill to wonder whether these 'basic mechanics' of verse 'assume ontological dimensions' in Vaughan's poetry ('A Pharisee to Pharisees: Reflections on Vaughan's "The Night"', *English*, 38 (1989), 103–05); and Sophie Read, noting that heart/part rhymes occur with 'almost the same frequency' as the light/night pairing, argues that they contribute to a synecdochic pattern in Vaughan's poetry that connects the heart with 'the salvific grace of the eucharist' (*Eucharist and the Poetic Imagination in Early Modern England* (Cambridge: Cambridge University Press, 2013), pp. 158–64).
41 *HV Works*, pp. 631, 628.
42 *HV Works*, p. 612.

> There above noise and danger
> > Sweet peace sits crown'd with smiles,
> And one born in a Manger
> > Commands the Beauteous files.[43]

Here the startling linkage of 'danger' and 'Manger' 'holds phonetic similarity and semantic dissimilarity in perfect equipoise'.[44] One final example illustrates how Vaughan could manipulate the contrasting energies of rhyme for both structural and expressive purposes. It occurs as part of the virtuoso performance that is 'The Bird':

> But as these Birds of light make a land glad,
> Chirping their solemn Matins on each tree:
> So in the shades of night some dark fowls be,
> Whose heavy notes make all that hear them, sad.[45]

Enclosed by the antonymic rhyming of 'glad' and 'sad', the quatrain also carefully sets the 'Birds of light' against the 'shades of night' by the internal antonymic rhyme on the sixth syllables of lines one and three. As Pursglove comments – and it is an insight that applies widely to Vaughan's management of rhyme in his poetry – 'there is nothing merely fortuitous about this carefully constructed scheme'.[46]

What has become clear as Vaughan's management of rhyme has been investigated from different angles is that its contribution to the structural integrity and distinctive sound of his verse – although he, like Homer, may nod from time to time – is the result of neither incompetence nor a defective ear.

IV

Although he foregrounds couplets and quatrains in his analysis of Vaughan's formal achievements, Simmonds acknowledges that some of the finest poems in *Silex Scintillans* are in more elaborate stanzaic forms that exploit 'the flexible interdependence of lines of varying

---

43 *HV Works*, p. 93.
44 Pursglove, 'Henry Vaughan and the Energies of Rhyme', 154.
45 *HV Works*, p. 583.
46 Pursglove, 'Henry Vaughan and the Energies of Rhyme', 152.

length' and 'the organic linking of regular patterns of rhyme'. Several of these were adopted directly from Herbert, from whom – as Mary Ellen Rickey was among the first to recognize – he 'derived a significant part of his conception of form'. Indeed, Post considers that it was in rising to the challenge of 'his master's skill with form' that he learned to 'chisel out' his own configurations of metre and rhyme.[47] Vaughan's earliest experiments with complex formal patterns in the Amoret poems can be illustrated by the opening stanza of 'To Amoret, of the difference 'twixt him, and other Lovers, and what true Love is', in which the last four syllables of the second line are drawn into rhythmic symmetry as well as rhyming harmony with the short third and fourth and the pairing of 'wings' with 'brings' is kept back until the very end:

> Marke, when the Evenings cooler **wings**
> Fanne the afflicted ayre, how the faint Sunne,
> Leaving undone,
> What he begunne,
> Those spurious flames suckt up from slime, and earth
> To their first low birth,
> Resignes, and **brings**.[48]

More indicative of Vaughan's later practice is the complex weaving of syntax across the formal unit, as the subject ('the faint Sunne') – already delayed by the opening imperative and the 'when' clause – is not united with its verbs ('Resignes, and brings') until after the object (the 'spurious flames') has been identified; and even then the verbs are placed after the prepositional phrase – 'To their first low birth' – that completes their function in the sentence. To add to the formal complexity, only one of the ensuing stanzas in this poem repeats the rhyme-scheme set up here and the others are different from one another.

The embryonic artistry glimpsed in some of the Amoret poems became a 'sudden burgeoning of stanzaic forms' once Vaughan had

---

47 Simmonds, *Masques of God*, p. 61; Mary Ellen Rickey, 'Vaughan, *The Temple*, and Poetic Form', *Studies in Philology*, 59 (1962), 162–63; Jonathan F.S. Post, *Henry Vaughan: The Unfolding Vision* (Princeton, NJ: Princeton University Press, 1982), pp. 84–85.
48 *HV Works*, p. 22.

fallen under 'Herbert's illuminating presence', giving rise – according to Post's calculations – to fifty-eight different verse forms in the 1650 *Silex Scintillans* alone, of which 'forty-five were used once only'.[49] As well as adopting and adapting stanza forms from *The Temple*, Vaughan played some of his master's 'tricks with rhymes', as Rickey has demonstrated.[50] For example, after supplying no rhymes for the fifth and final lines of the first three stanzas of 'Disorder and frailty', he imitates Herbert's device in 'Deniall' and mends the rhyme in the concluding stanza – ababcddeeffggdc; and the word that clinches the rhyme with 'perverse' (in line 5) crowns the theme of disorder in spiritual life that prevents the writing of 'a true hymn': 'tune to thy will / My heart, my verse'.[51] Another 'Herbertian trick' is to change formal direction altogether within a poem, as when Vaughan switches from quatrains to couplets in 'Repentance' or marks 'two different strains of adoration' by using 'two different stanza forms' in 'Praise'.[52]

The impact of poetry on the eye as well as on the ear is highlighted in Stevie Davies's comparison of *Silex Scintillans* with the visual experience provided by three of Vaughan's contemporaries:

> Opening *Paradise Lost*, we encounter facing blocks of text, massive and weighty, like twin pillars. Marvell's lyrics are classically elegant; Herbert's pages intricately patterned. But as we leaf through Vaughan's pages, the poems swirl between long and short lines, playing tricks on the eyes to produce a visual effect of fluctuating motion and emotion on the page.[53]

The strategic placing of caesuras, the interplay of lines of eight, six, and four syllables, the running over of line-endings, and the partial rhyme of 'in' and 'spring' combine to render the stanza devised for 'Regeneration' a perfect vehicle for the narrative of the

---

49 Post, *The Unfolding Vision*, p. 80.
50 Rickey, 'Vaughan, *The Temple*, and Poetic Form', 163.
51 *HV Works*, pp. 108–10.
52 Rickey, 'Vaughan, *The Temple*, and Poetic Form', 166–67. Rickey notes that the use of contrasting verse forms within a single poem 'was not common' in Vaughan's day and 'seems to have been popularized in English by Herbert' (p. 167).
53 Davies, *Henry Vaughan*, p. 105.

disorienting experiences of conversion that entrance and bewilder in equal measure:

> Here, I repos'd; but scarse well set,
>   A grove descryed
> Of stately height, whose branches met
>   And mixt on every side;
>   I entred, and once in
>   (Amaz'd to see't,)
> Found all was chang'd, and a new spring
>   Did all my senses greet.[54]

'The Proffer', Vaughan's indignant diatribe against Puritan officials who tried to entice him into collaboration with the new regime, furnishes another example of the expressive variety that can be achieved through the dynamic interplay of form and content:

>   O poys'nous subtile fowls!
>   The flyes of hell
> That buz in every ear, and blow on souls
>   Until they smell
> And rot, descend not here, nor think to stay,
>   I've read, who 'twas, drove you away.[55]

A single burst of anger and contempt rushes past markers of form, absorbing short lines into longer ones to create units of meaning that are at odds with the shaping devices of rhyme and metre – 'The flyes of hell / That buz in every ear'; 'Until they smell / And rot' – and yet the eye and ear register the underlying pattern, which is repeated from previous stanzas.

Among the most moving examples of short lines set against longer is the form devised for the second of the untitled elegies.[56] The three stanzas rhyme consistently and each has at its centre a couplet rhyming with the repeated imperative with which the poem begins. Metrically, the first line of this pivotal couplet is a single spondaic foot, which slows the pace to a dead stop before the stanza expands

---

54 *HV Works*, p. 58.
55 *HV Works*, p. 571.
56 *HV Works*, pp. 82–83.

into laconic dimeters. The first stanza contrives to articulate the intolerable burden of despair by formal means, not the least of which is the desolate isolation of the last line:

> Come, come, what doe I here?
>   Since he is gone
> Each day is grown a dozen year,
>   And each houre, one;
>   Come, come!
> Cut off the sum,
> By these soil'd teares!
> (Which only thou
> Know'st to be true,)
> Dayes are my feares.

The other two stanzas have trimeters in the first and third lines; but here, the third is stretched into a tetrameter to enact the slow passing of time for a soul in deep mourning. In the final stanza, the despairing drum-like beat of the repeated central imperative is followed not by a second imperative, as in the preceding stanzas – 'Cut off the sum'; 'Strike these lips dumb' – but by a moment of transforming self-awareness – 'Such thoughts benum' – which begins the process of recognizing that the death he longs for may be a prelude to resurrection and reunion rather than merely an escape from life:

>   Come, come!
> Such thoughts benum;
> But I would be
> With him I weep
> A bed, and sleep
> To wake in thee.

Almost the same form, with tetrameters consistently instead of trimeters for the longer first and third lines and minus the drum-beat of despair at the centre, is used to achieve something quite different in the next elegy.[57] The upbeat opening, with its metrical stresses on 'Joy', 'life', 'still', and 'Love' – 'Joy of my life! while left me here,

---

57 *HV Works*, pp. 85–86.

/ And still my Love!' – is based on the perception that the absent loved one continues to 'steere' the bereft speaker 'from above'; and this generates a series of analogies for the consoling belief that the positive influence of a 'well lead' life 'never ends': 'Stars are of mighty use'; 'Gods Saints are shining lights'; 'They are (indeed,) our Pillar-fires'. The astonishing contrast in tone between the two elegies is partly due to Vaughan's management of form. Instead of slowing the pulse of the verse with staccato self-contained lines and repeated imperatives, a more fluid and confident movement is created by masking the rhymes and line-endings, as the third stanza illustrates:

> Gods Saints are shining lights: who stays
>   Here long must passe
> O're dark hills, swift streames, and steep ways
>   As smooth as glasse;
>   But these all night
>   Like Candles, shed
>   Their beams, and light
>   Us into Bed.

The first four lines use the second tetrameter to evoke the many hardships and dangers that face those who – unlike young William Vaughan – must take a long time on their journey through life; the last four compress into fluent dimeters the poet's newly acquired faith that the light of the holy dead never ceases to guide the living towards death, which opens the way to 'that Cities shining spires / We travell too' in the final stanza.

Post suggests that Vaughan owed to his 'rekindled interest' in stanzaic poetry the development of 'the spectacular conclusions for which his devotional verse has always been famous'. Alongside the celebrated examples that he cites – the closing moments of 'Regeneration', 'Christs Nativity', 'The Proffer', 'Cock-crowing', and 'The Night' – there are other endings that are just as 'certainly fashioned by an immediate concern for verbal effects'.[58] The steady lengthening of lines from three to four to eight syllables in each stanza creates the soaring movement invoked by the title of 'Ascension-Hymn', but never more powerfully than in the last:

58 Post, *The Unfolding Vision*, p. 91.

> Hee alone
> And none else can
> Bring bone to bone
> And rebuild man,
> And by his all subduing might
> Make clay ascend more quick then light.⁵⁹

The rhythmic effect is reinforced by an artful harking back to the reminder at the start of the first stanza that 'Dust and clay' are 'Mans antient wear', which is left behind at death until God rebuilds the body at the Resurrection. In 'The Showre (I)', two short lines and a pentameter bring the poem to a close on a poignant note of yearning for the peace that only true repentance can bring and with a sense of rhythmic release from constriction:

> Perhaps at last
> (Some such showres past,)
> My God would give a Sun-shine after raine.⁶⁰

A similar rhythmic effect is achieved by the abrupt movement from short lines to an expansive final line at the end of 'Retirement (I)', which is perfectly adapted to the dramatic climax of God's peremptory command and the speaker's immediate act of submission: 'Up then, and keep / Within those doors, (my doors) dost hear? *I will.*'

And finally, after completing three six-line stanzas, Vaughan abandons 'Anguish' two lines into a fourth stanza as the agony of trying to compose 'true, unfeigned verse' overwhelms him: 'O my God, hear my cry; / Or let me dye! —'⁶¹

V

A third commonplace of later Vaughan criticism, and perhaps the most damaging, was articulated in Beeching's observation that 'Vaughan is very much the poet of fine lines and stanzas', many of whose poems 'begin finely' but fail to sustain the 'high level of

---

59 *HV Works*, pp. 566–67.
60 *HV Works*, pp. 74–75.
61 See *HV Works*, pp. 127–28; 614–15.

writing' that is found in his best work.⁶² Hutchinson made the same charge in a comparison with Herbert:

> In the matter of form, Vaughan failed to learn what Herbert had to teach. He knows less well than Herbert when to stop, and, after beginning with lines of such intensity as Herbert could never have written, he is apt to lose his way and forfeit the interest of his readers.⁶³

This had already become something of a mantra by the 1930s: Williamson – 'the poet of supreme lines and images'; Bennett – 'a selection of the best from Vaughan would include some single stanzas, lines, or even half-lines'; and White – 'that flashing quality that affords many brilliant beginnings and not a few brilliant endings, but that very seldom yields a fully sustained piece'.⁶⁴ And it continued to echo through the criticism of the twentieth century. For one commentator, 'Vaughan is generally good only in short bursts'; for another, 'all too often' a poem 'has no way of sustaining' the 'impassioned cadences' of the 'taut lyric pattern' with which it begins.⁶⁵ Simmonds accepts that there are enough 'lapses in power' to justify Vaughan's 'reputation for unevenness', but rejects the common implication that a failure 'to sustain a unified poetic structure' in some of his poorer performances was symptomatic of a fatal flaw that also damaged 'his most admired poems'.⁶⁶

In his study of *Silex Scintillans*, Pettet had made a useful distinction between Vaughan's earlier and later verse. Whereas the secular poems had been 'much more consciously organised, much more dependent on logical and argumentative forms of structure', many of the devotional lyrics 'evolve not so much through the logical connected

---

62 *Poems of Henry Vaughan Silurist*, ed. E.K. Chambers, 2 vols., The Muses' Library (London: George Routledge & Sons, 1896), Vol. I, p. xlviii.

63 F.E. Hutchinson, 'The Sacred Poets', in *The Cambridge History of English Literature*, Vol. 7, ed. A.W. Ward and A.R. Waller (Cambridge: Cambridge University Press, 1911), p. 40.

64 Williamson, *The Donne Tradition*, p. 133; Bennett, *Five Metaphysical Poets*, pp. 71, 85; White, *The Metaphysical Poets*, p. 286.

65 H.J. Oliver, 'The Mysticism of Henry Vaughan: A Reply', *Journal of English and Germanic Philology*, 53 (1954), 359; A.J. Smith, 'Appraising the World', *Poetry Wales*, 11 (1975), 57.

66 Simmonds, *Masques of God*, p. 43.

development from thought to thought as by way of association, sometimes rather oblique in nature, and by the spontaneous proliferating of some unifying complex of imagery'.[67] Martz's reading of Vaughan as a baroque poet offers a similar view of the sacred verse: 'Vaughan's best poems are *formed* but hardly *built*: they have a current movement, an elastic mode of action, a sense of moving along under the impulse of an inspiration or a goal not clearly defined, but dimly glimpsed.'[68] With these distinctions in mind, this section will consider three poems that were 'built' upon logical principles – one secular and two devotional – and the next will turn to some that were 'formed' in more idiosyncratic and challenging ways.

'To his retired friend, an Invitation to *Brecknock*', written in the latter stages of the Civil War, is clearly organized on the page into three paragraphs; and each of these divides into two contrasting phases: the first chides the retired friend for his prolonged absence from the provincial centre and then describes the changes that have taken place since he was last there; the second speculates about the reasons for his absence and warns that he is slipping from local memory; and the third ridicules the local traders, who are too dull to be inspired to wit or poetry by the wine that is wasted on them, and urges the friend to come and participate in an act of private resistance.[69] The first section, which contains light-hearted banter about the condition of the friend's horse, comes to a climax with a wry pun on the word 'sober':

> Or taught by thee (like *Pythagoras's Oxe*)
> Is then his master grown more *Orthodox*?
> What ever 'tis, a sober cause't must be
> That thus long bars us of thy Companie. (ll. 7–10)

Four lines then glide cleverly from the town's distress at being neglected by the friend to the distress that the friend will experience when he sees for himself the consequences of its political capitulation: 'Thou'ldst swear (like *Rome*) her foule, polluted walls / Were sackt by *Brennus*, and the salvage *Gaules*' (ll. 13–14). Classical allusions and assured couplets – balancing free-flowing and interrupted lines in

---

67 Pettet, *Of Paradise and Light*, p. 24.
68 Martz, *From Renaissance to Baroque*, p 238.
69 See *HV Works*, pp. 180–82.

Vaughan's familiar manner – give way to enjambements and metrical irregularities that disturb the formal integrity of the couplets and even slice in half a hyphenated noun, while a tumbling list of urban sights and sounds reinforces a harsh impression of contemporary disorder:

> here's noise
> Of bàng'd Mòrtars, blèw Àprons, and Bòyes,
> Pìgs, Dògs, and Drums, with the hòarse hèllish notes
> Of politickly-dèafe Ùsurers thròats ...
> Mìdst thèse the *Crosse* looks sad, and in the *Shire-*
> *Hàll fùrs* of an òld *Sàxon Fox* appear,
> With brotherly Ruffs, and Beards ... (ll. 15–23)

This formally orchestrated contest between Cavalier culture and Puritan 'noise' is continued through the rest of the poem.

In the second paragraph, a good-humoured enquiry into the motives of the absent friend (laced with knowing classical references to the hen-pecked Hercules and the mad emperor Domitian) leads into a bitter jest about the short memories of the 'Drawers' in the tavern, who 'have not seen thee here since *Charles* his raign' (a king who, not yet disposed of, had been deprived of effective authority). The final paragraph begins with a punning invitation to 'leave this sullen state' (both personal and political) and take part in a defiant celebration of civilized values. In two four-line movements, the metrical disturbance created by run-on lines and strong caesuras enacts the aesthetic disgust and class outrage felt by a royalist at the flagrant abuse of wine by the uncultivated usurpers:

> Shall the dull *Market-land-lord* with his *Rout*
> Of sneaking Tenants durtily swill out
> This harmlesse liquor? shall they knock and beat
> For Sack, only to talk of *Rye*, and *Wheat*?
> O let not such prepost'rous tipling be
> In our *Metropolis*, may I ne'r see
> Such *Tavern-sacrilege*, nor lend a line
> To weep the *Rapes* and *Tragedy* of wine! (ll. 57–64)

A promise that he has reserved 'a Cup' that will raise up the dormant Muse of his friend effects a transition to the second half of the paragraph, which is introduced by a more urgent summons and the proposal for a private demonstration of opposition in a brilliant evocation of the resources that will help them endure the Cavalier winter:

> Come then! and while the slow Isicle hangs
> At the stiffe thatch, and Winters frosty pangs
> Benumme the year, blith (as of old) let us
> 'Midst noise and War, of Peace, and mirth discusse.
> [. . . . .]
> Let's sit then at this *fire*, and while wee steal
> A Revell in the Town, let others seal,
> Purchase or Cheat, and who can, let them pay,
> Till those black deeds bring on the darksome day;
> Innocent spenders wee! a better use
> Shall wear out our short Lease, and leave th'obtuse
> Rout to their *husks*; They and their bags at best
> Have cares in *earnest*, wee care for a *Jest*. (ll. 73–88)

But the earlier self-contained and balanced couplets are not reinstated in this closing section. Both the gross materialism of the citizens – 'let others seal, / Purchase or Cheat' – and the defiant *carpe diem* philosophy of the beleaguered comrades – 'a better use / Shall wear out our short Lease' – break up the regularity of the verse-form; and contempt for their uncultured opponents occasions one last disruption – 'leave th'obtuse / Rout to their husks' – before the truncated couplet ends the poem on a note of uneasy jocularity that cannot quite dispel a sense of frustrated impotence. The only gestures of resistance open to these defeated royalists are to 'steal / A Revell in the Town' and utter threats about the 'darksome day' that will one day punish the 'black deeds' of the victorious party. A sure mastery of the verse medium and different levels of diction combine in a structure that allows the argument to develop steadily towards its conclusion, moving skilfully from banter to satire, from teasing speculation and acerbic mockery to defiant nostalgia for a lost past. This outstanding example of the epistolary poem not only holds the reader's interest throughout by its striking imagery and its metrical variety, but also captures a particular moment in royalist experience as powerfully as any item in the Cavalier canon.

When Francis Palgrave added 'The World' to later editions of *The Golden Treasury*, he printed only the first seven lines:

> I saw Eternity the other night
> Like a great *Ring* of pure and endless light,
>   All calm, as it was bright,
> And round beneath it, Time in hours, days, years
>   Driv'n by the spheres
> Like a vast shadow mov'd, In which the world
>   And all her train were hurl'd ...[70]

This not only helped to establish the passage as a prime example of Vaughan's visionary powers but also reinforced the widespread opinion that he could not sustain such a level of poetic intensity through the length of a poem. Helen White could claim confidently that 'every student of Vaughan's poetry has been struck by the curious tameness and flatness of what follows that breathtaking opening'.[71]

Simmonds was among the first to challenge this common response to 'The World' by arguing that 'the poem has a comprehensive unity of thought, image, and manner far more remarkable than the supposed disunity upon which critics have constantly harped'. He found the key to that unity in 'a dramatic technique' that enables Vaughan to fuse the various elements of the poem in 'a coherent, unified, allegorical exposition' of the contrast between the transient lusts of this world and the stable realm of eternity that is summarized in the epigraph from the second chapter of St John's Gospel. White and others have misread the nature and function of the image in the opening seven lines as the record of a mystical experience rather than a poetic device for setting before the reader a 'comprehensive vision' of the cosmic contest between the temporal and the eternal.[72] The time-bound devotees of the world are presented in emblematic portraits that occupy the remainder of stanza 1 and stanzas 2 and 3: the 'doting Lover', the 'darksome States-man', and the 'fearfull miser', together with the 'thousands' who 'plac'd heav'n in sense' and the 'weaker sort' who were enslaved to 'slight, triviall wares'. The consequences for those who are content to join the world's 'train' are made clear in the fourth stanza:

---

70 For the text of 'The World', see *HV Works*, pp. 131–33.
71 White, *The Metaphysical Poets*, p. 286.
72 James D. Simmonds, 'Vaughan's Masterpiece and Its Critics: "The World" Revaluated', *Studies in English Literature*, 2 (1962), 81, 82, 83–84, 85.

> Yet some, who all this while did weep and sing,
> And sing, and weep, soar'd up into the *Ring*,
>   But most would use no wing.
> O fools (said I,) thus to prefer dark night
>   Before true light,
> To live in grots, and caves, and hate the day
>   Because it shews the way,
> The way which from this dead and dark abode
>   Leads up to God,
> A way where you might tread the Sun, and be
>   More bright than he.
> But as I did their madnes so discusse
>   One whisper'd thus,
> *This Ring the Bride-groome did for none provide*
>   *But for his bride.*

The return to the opening image of eternity as a ring of light in the second line of this stanza merges in the final couplet with an allusion to the Song of Songs, which was traditionally interpreted as a hymn for the marriage between Christ and the Church or Christ and the individual soul, so that the ring now becomes the seal of immortality granted to those who turn away from the world with penitent tears and soar upwards into everlasting light. The whispered words that suddenly interrupt the speaker's earnest exhortation to the 'fools' who 'prefer the night' express what Simmonds calls 'the final authoritative explanation of the baffling phenomenon of grace'.[73] They not only resolve the thematic issue of the separateness of the dimensions of time and eternity, but also provide an effectively dramatic conclusion to the poem as a unified work of art.

A less controversial instance of the constructive skills on display in *Silex Scintillans* is 'The Dawning', which has been lauded for its economy, coherence, and undemonstrative craftsmanship: 'Concise, beautifully integrated in image and thought, and with a great clarity of vision [...] at one level extremely artful, at another level direct

---

[73] Simmonds, 'Vaughan's Masterpiece', 93. For other defences of the artistic integrity of 'The World', see Paul A. Olson, 'Vaughan's "The World": The Pattern of Meaning and the Tradition', *Comparative Literature*, 13 (1961), 26–32; Leland H. Chambers, 'Vaughan's "The World": The Limits of Extrinsic Criticism', *Studies in English Literature*, 8 (1968), 137–50.

and simple, and very moving.'[74] In content, the poem is divided into two equal parts, which explore a theological issue that was highly topical in the 1650s, and then present the poet's intensely personal engagement with it. The first twenty-four lines address the desperate questions posed at the outset: 'Ah! What time wilt thou come? when shall that crie / The *Bridegroome's Comming*! fil the sky?'[75] Unlike most of the contemporary apocalyptic preachers, Vaughan's concern is not with the timing of the Messiah's intervention into history but with the precise hour within the twenty-four-hour framework of Earth's day–night cycle that he will choose to descend in glory to claim the Church as his bride:

> Shall it in the Evening run
> When our words and works are done?
> Or wil thy all-surprizing light
>   Break at midnight?

The traditional view was based on the biblical verse alluded to in the opening lines – 'And at midnight there was a cry made, Behold, the bridegrome commeth' (Matthew 25:6) – but Vaughan was drawn instinctively to an alternative to that dismal hour, when 'mad man' is possessed by 'either sleep, or some dark pleasure':

> Or shal these early, fragrant hours
>   Unlock thy bowres?
> And with their blush of light descry
> Thy locks crown'd with eternitie.

The sense of urgency in the first half of the poem derives in part from the short lines that punctuate with further questions the octosyllabic couplets flowing down from the single pentameter at the beginning. Vaughan's own answer to this accumulation of questions – 'Indeed it is the only time / That with thy glory doth best chime' – receives immediate endorsement from the natural world that is waking up around him:

---

74 Noel Kennedy Thomas, *Henry Vaughan: Poet of Revelation* (Worthing: Churchman Publishing, 1986), p. 153.

75 For the text of the poem, see *HV Works*, pp. 116–17.

> All now are stirring, ev'ry field
>   Ful hymns doth yield,
> The whole Creation shakes off night,
> And for thy shadow looks the light,
> Stars now vanish without number,
> Sleepie Planets set, and slumber,
> The pursie Clouds disband, and scatter,
> All expect some sudden matter,
> Not one beam triumphs, but from far
>   That morning star.

The short lines now express wonder rather than uncertainty, and the last of them – positioned further to the right on the page than the other three to emphasize its crucial semantic and structural functions – brings the first half of the poem to a stunning and carefully calculated climax, in which the morning star rising above the Usk valley is a natural type of that other 'bright and morning starre' in the Book of Revelation, who announces himself as 'the roote and the offspring of Dauid' and foretells his return in words that hark back to the poem's opening allusion: 'And the Spirit and the Bride say, Come' (Revelation 22:16–17).

The second set of twenty-four lines – a number that has an obvious significance for this particular enquiry into the intersection of eternity with time – opens with a skilful transition from the objective meditation on the hour of the Second Coming to the subjective concerns of the sinful poet, who will have to face judgement whenever it is:

> O at what time soever thou
> (Unknown to us,) the heavens wilt bow,
> And, with thy Angels in the *Van*,
> Descend to Judge poor careless man,
> Grant, I may not like puddle lie
> In a Corrupt securitie.

Not until the fifth line, following the delayed optative verb 'Grant', does the speaker begin to contemplate the personal implications of what the descent of Christ will mean for humankind in general. Over the next fourteen lines, he prays that he – like the stream that runs and sings beside him on the Breconshire hillside – will remain 'untainted' by the material world, with which he admits he must have some 'Commerce', and will have the steadfastness to maintain his 'chief acquaintance' with the realm 'above' that of 'poor dust'. No short lines interrupt the octosyllabic couplets that move tentatively forward, with frequent pauses and an occasional enjambement, in imitation of the 'busie age' he must endure 'while here'. At the end, there is a magnificent rhythmical release from the 'vile, and low' prison of 'flesh' into that final sunrise that will also be the return of the Son who was longed for at the start:

> So when that day, and hour shal come
> In which thy self wil be the Sun,
> Thou'lt find me drest and on my way,
> Watching the Break of thy great day.

This is surely one of those 'brilliant endings' that Helen White admired in his poetry, but it is also the crowning glory of the kind of 'fully sustained piece' that she considered rare in *Silex Scintillans*.

VI

Some of the most striking and adventurous of the religious poems eschew the structured framework of traditional couplets and repeated stanzas for a freer kind of form. An extreme case is 'Distraction', described by Post as the 'most visually chaotic lyric in all of Vaughan', which looks on the page 'as if it should be divided into stanzas but offers no convenient place to do so'.[76] West is critical of the 'unhappily irregular rhythms, ever-changing line-lengths, and staccato unsatisfying rhymes', although he acknowledges the imitative function of techniques that 'hurl Vaughan's Man around like the voices of the world, while he desires order, but can possess none'.[77] Anne Cluysenaar takes a different approach to the formal aspects of a poem that 'makes an immediate visceral impact' and demands to be read 'as an event unfolding through time'. Likening it to the methods of Augustinian meditation, she highlights the 'mixing and metamorphosis of metaphor' – an 'inconsistency' that must be 'not only

---

76 Post, *The Unfolding Vision*, pp. 176–77.
77 West, *Scripture Uses*, p. 115.

tolerated but savoured' – and the intensifying of 'emotional impact' achieved by changes in the 'inter-relations of metre and syntax'. Together, the combination of unsettling imagery and unpredictable rhythm creates a poem that 'can be read as "organized" in the true sense of the word, if not indeed pre-planned: its form is "organic"'.[78]

Throughout 'Distraction', lines rhyme in pairs, but lengths vary in no discernible or predetermined pattern.[79] This unpredictability is reinforced by many caesuras and enjambements, so that metrical and syntactical units are continuously at odds with each other. For example, because of the pause after 'dust' and the runover of syntax into the second line, the first four lines might be heard rhythmically as three iambic tetrameters terminated abruptly by a dimeter, except for the rhyme on 'heape/cheape' that creates the counterpoint of ten syllables in line 1 against six in line 2:

> O knit me, that am crumbled dust! the heape
>   Is all dispers'd, and cheape;
>   Give for a handful, but a thought
>   And it is bought.

The sense of disintegration expressed in the words 'crumbled' and 'dispers'd' is conveyed by similar means throughout the rest of the poem. But what begins as the appeal of a disorientated individual to his Creator suddenly veers from a forlorn contemplation of his present state – 'But now / I finde my selfe the lesse, the more I grow' – into a general commentary on the condition of his entire species:

>   The world
> Is full of voices; Man is call'd, and hurl'd
>   By each, he answers all,
>   Knows ev'ry note, and call,
>   Hence, still
> Fresh dotage tempts, or old usurps his will.

Just as unexpectedly, the poet reverts to the personal alienation that would have caused him to spurn any intervention made

---

78 Anne Cluysenaar, 'Rereading Henry Vaughan's "Distraction"', *Scintilla*, 1 (1997), 98, 99–100, 103–05.
79 *HV Works*, p. 75.

by his Maker to save 'that light, which freely thou / Didst then bestow'. This admission extorts from him a cry of self-loathing – 'I grieve, my God! that thou hast made me such' – and this in turn awakens the certainty that his cry is heard: 'I grieve? / O, yes! thou know'st I doe.' This leads to a revision of the opening prayer for the dispersed 'heape' of his 'crumbled dust' to be 'knit' into a unified 'selfe'. Only God can 'keepe downe' the rebellious 'dust' that would blind him to the light and only God can drown out the multitude of 'voices' that will continue to tempt him towards the loud claims of 'the world':

> Come, and relieve
> And tame, and keepe downe with thy light
> Dust that would rise, and dimme my sight,
> Lest left alone too long
> Amidst the noise, and throng,
> Oppressed I
> Striving to save the whole, by parcells dye.

As Anne Cluysenaar puts it, 'Distraction' concludes with the will's arousal, which is the objective of Augustinian meditation: 'Vaughan has moved on from the notion that the whole of him may somehow be "knit" together and has realised that what he must do is let go of all but the one vital "handfull".'[80] The poem's unique form enacts rather than contains the spiritual experience of being distracted by worldly priorities, unfolding the process line by fractured line rather than pouring an already completed drama into a predetermined poetic mould.

'Affliction (I)' is another example of such 'organic' development, in which – to use Thomas Calhoun's formulation – the 'capacities of lyric forms are expanded to contain a wide range of associations'. In this instance, within the compass of forty lines, the poet mobilizes 'five analogous ways' of illustrating his argument about the health-giving effects of affliction: 'psychological, natural, aesthetic, political, and celestial'.[81] Sporting a title employed five times by George Herbert, the poem begins by rejecting its negative connotations:

---

80 Cluysenaar, 'Rereading Henry Vaughan's "Distraction"', 105.
81 Thomas O. Calhoun, *Henry Vaughan: The Achievement of Silex Scintillans* (Newark, DE: University of Delaware Press, 1981), p. 128.

> Peace, peace; It is not so. Thou doest miscall
>   Thy Physick; Pils that change
> Thy sick Accessions into setled health,
> This is the great *Elixir* that turns gall
> To wine, and sweetness; Poverty to wealth,
>   And brings man home, when he doth range.[82]

With no detectable pattern in its distribution of rhymes and line-lengths, this opening sentence sets up a 'norm' of metrical irregularity that will later supply a comparison with the natural world, where, but for God's use of 'his rod' to bring about 'fruitfull Change', 'weeds, and thistles' would grow 'more wild than is thy verse'. With many mid-line pauses and run-overs, the rest of the poem moves forward in groups of unequal lines loosely bound together by paired or interlaced rhyme. The 'Crosses' that curb the behaviour of 'the mule, unruly man' culminate in a six-line sentence, in which the insertion of a lopsided couplet delays the rhyme for 'stirrs' that completes the quatrain apparently set up in the first three lines:

>   Vicissitude plaies all the game,
>   Nothing that stirrs,
>   Or hath a name,
>   But waits upon this wheel,
> Kingdomes too have their Physick, and for steel,
>   Exchange their peace and furs.

The poem is then brought to a conclusion with an image that sums up the part played by affliction in the divine art of imposing order upon the chaos of human nature:

>   Thus doth God *Key* disorder'd man
>   (Which none else can,)
>   Tuning his brest to rise, or fall;
>   And by a sacred, needfull art
>   Like strings, stretch ev'ry part
>   Making the whole most Musicall.

---

82 For the text of the poem, see *HV Works*, pp. 124–25.

The harmony that the poet seeks to impose on the verse, however, reflects the aesthetic principle enunciated as part of his foregoing argument: 'that's best / Which is not fixt, but flies, and flowes'. The music of the closing movement results from a tension between two possible structures: either a couplet and a quatrain (aa|bccb) or two three-line units, like the sestet of a sonnet (aab|ccb). Complete regularity is denied to both of these options by the shorter second and fifth lines, four and six syllables respectively, which disturb the 'fixt' orderly march of the tetrameters towards closure.

This survey of Vaughan's practice of the poetic art may fittingly conclude with a widely acknowledged masterpiece that Joan Bennett considered 'perhaps the most perfect whole' among his poems.[83] 'The Morning-watch', laid out on the page as an unbroken stretch of verse like 'Distraction' and 'Affliction (I)', was described by Martz as 'an undivided ode in its appearance'.[84] In fact, as Calhoun observes, it is constructed from an 'incredibly challenging' eight-line form – a pattern that 'seems to form itself from within', as if 'Vaughan found his measure after an initial improvisation and then repeated it to sustain the poem'. In fact, the distribution of rhymes and line-lengths in the first eight lines is repeated precisely only once, in lines 24 to 31, the fourth of these units; and when read aloud, the 'continuous syntax and pulsing cadence' override the visual form 'so completely that the poem appears to have no line or rhyme scheme and no stanzaic divisions at all'.[85] This is because the rhymes so rarely mark syntactical and metrical boundaries, as the opening movement exemplifies:

> O Joyes! Infinite sweetnes! with what flowres,
> And shoots of glory, my soul breakes, and buds!
>   All the long houres
>   Of night, and Rest
>   Through the still shrouds
>   Of sleep, and Clouds,
>   This Dew fell on my Breast;
>   O how it *Blouds*,
> And *Spirits* all my Earth! heark! In what Rings,

---

83 Bennett, *Five Metaphysical Poets*, p. 83.
84 Martz, *From Renaissance to Baroque*, p. 237.
85 Calhoun, *The Achievement of Silex Scintillans*, p. 96.

>   And *Hymning Circulations* the quick world
>   Awakes, and sings ...⁸⁶

The forward thrust of the rhythm impels sense and syntax over the formal boundary at the end of the eighth line: 'O how it *Blouds*, / And *Spirits* all my Earth!' To contrive effective closure, the short line that ends the final group of eight lines combines with two pentameter lines, which – unlike the other pairs of decasyllabic lines that begin each rhyming group – creates a rhymed couplet to round off the poem:

>   So in my Bed,
>   That Curtain'd grave, though sleep, like ashes, hide
>   My lamp, and life, both shall in thee abide.

Even Pettet, for whom 'The Morning-watch' is 'by no means flawless', admits that the product of such energy and formal ingenuity is 'most firmly organised, with wholeness, balance, and continuity'.⁸⁷

This chapter will have served its purpose if it has reinforced the work of Simmonds and others in challenging the long-lived critical tradition that Vaughan is the 'poet of supreme lines and images', who rarely perfected 'a fully sustained piece'. He was, in fact, a skilled craftsman with words and images, whether he was stamping his individual mark on Jonsonian couplets or the intricate stanzas of Herbert – or forging his own organic forms in what Stevie Davies calls an 'expressionist' mode in order to figure forth 'the irregular rhythms and cross-currents of inner experience'.⁸⁸ He was undoubtedly prone, as Simmonds admits, to composing couplets that 'evince a kind of flaccid sprawl'; and his management of stanzas may lack the 'distanced, secure, and quiet' perfection that gave the lyrics of *The Temple* a texture 'as smooth as an aged altar-stone'.⁸⁹

---

86 *HV Works*, p. 87.
87 Pettet, *Of Paradise and Light*, pp. 125, 126. The flaws he mentions are 'a loss of tension in the lines on prayer (ll. 18–22)', the redundancy in the phrasing of 'the second night-description (ll. 24–31)', and 'the much overworked *cloud-shroud* rhyme'.
88 Davies, *Henry Vaughan*, p. 105.
89 Simmonds, *Masques of God*, pp. 49–50; Durr, *On the Mystical Poetry of Henry Vaughan*, p. 11.

But at his not infrequent best and in a variety of poetic forms, he created sustained works of art that 'move with the unpredictability of spontaneous gesture' and express 'Life ebullient, dynamic, unfixed, unformulated, "imperfect"'.[90]

---

[90] Durr, *On the Mystical Poetry of Henry Vaughan*, p. 11.

Epilogue

When I retired as a full-time academic in 2007, I began to read through everything I had written about Henry Vaughan (going back to the chapter on his poetry in my Ph.D. thesis in 1972 and my first published article in 1974) with a view to assembling a collection of essays.[1] I was struck by the preponderance of items intent upon placing his work in various historical contexts that had prompted or could be illuminated by it: biographical, literary, religious, political. It soon became apparent that the book I now had in mind would need to balance this approach with a more adequate treatment of the aesthetic dimension of Vaughan's poetry.[2] The trawl through past publications had brought to light a conference paper in which I had already tentatively tackled the complex matter of Vaughan's absorption into his own poetic idiom of conceits, imagery, and phrases from George Herbert's *The Temple*.[3] There would clearly have to be a more extensive chapter on this feature of Vaughan's art and that suggested another chapter on the use of imitation and allusion in his secular poems.[4] Slowly, the shape and strategy of the book emerged:

1 See *The Use of Natural Details in English Poetry: 1645–1668*, 2 vols. (Ph.D. thesis, Shakespeare Institute, University of Birmingham, 1972), Vol. II, pp. 115–70; 'Daphnis. An Elegiac Eclogue by Henry Vaughan', *Durham University Journal*, new series, 36 (1974), 25–40.
2 As part of the preparation for this book, I traced the evolution of Vaughan's attitudes towards the art of poetry as they can be abstracted from his poetry and prose. See 'Henry Vaughan's *Ars Poetica*', *Scintilla*, 21 (2018), 35–51.
3 '"The present times are not / To snudge in": Henry Vaughan, *The Temple*, and the Pressure of History', in *George Herbert: Sacred and Profane*, ed. Helen Wilcox and Richard Todd (Amsterdam: VU University Press, 1995), pp. 185–94.
4 This was originally written as a chapter for this book, but it was published at the request of the editor of the annual publication of the former Usk Valley

not a collection of self-sufficient and unconnected essays, but a series of carefully ordered chapters on the historical contexts and verbal artistry of Vaughan's literary endeavours. The first half of the book would open up significant aspects of the life and experiences of Henry Vaughan, as a mid-seventeenth-century member of the Welsh gentry: where he lived, his education, his relationship with his twin brother, the origin and development of those ideas about God and Nature that are fundamental to his finest work, the political events he lived through, and the impact of the Root and Branch reform of the Church on his own spiritual life and that of his South Wales community. The second half, on Henry Vaughan the craftsman with words, would need to explore in detail his creative use of the work of other writers, George Herbert in particular; his incorporation of phrases and images from the Scriptures; the various ways in which his poetry processed both previous literary treatments of the natural world and his own observations of the countryside in which he lived; and finally, his management of the technical features of the poet's art – imagery, rhyme, metre, poetic form.

Obviously, life and art cannot be segregated from each other as neatly as this binary arrangement suggests. The English and Latin verses can be scoured for evidence of the man's familiarity with the sights and sounds of the Usk valley; the success with which the poet communicates a vision of earthly transience and the promise of eternal life in describing the spectacle of a waterfall can be judged by paying close attention to his management of words and poetic form; but the poet who writes is dependent upon the man who observes and feels and reads.[5] A verse invitation to a former comrade-in-arms may be one among several poems that serve to reveal the Welsh royalist's contempt for the new Parliamentary authorities in Brecon; the same poem may be exhibited as an example of careful structure, striking imagery, metrical variety, and masterful modulation of tone; but it is the combination of political engagement and poetic technique that makes it one of the masterpieces of Cavalier art.[6] The man who longed for the release of death from the burden of

---

Vaughan Association (now, simply the Vaughan Association). See 'Henry Vaughan's Borrowings: Plagiarism, Imitation, Allusion', *Scintilla*, 17 (2013), 11–27.

5 See 'The Water-fall', *HV Works*, pp. 626–27.
6 See 'To his retired friend, an Invitation to Brecknock', *HV Works*, pp. 180–82.

bereavement and political defeat is also the poet who artfully adapted Herbert's poem about the resurrection of Christ into a call to himself and his fellow-sufferers to 'awake' from despair and 'disperse' the mists of Puritan oppression 'that would usurp' the celebration of Easter.[7] While the biographer or historian may light eagerly upon passages that bear witness to the desperate conflict experienced by a seventeenth-century royalist between Christian meekness and the desire for revenge, the reader of poetry will be interested in the weaving of images and words from the Bible into the poet's own language in such a way that the moral challenges of Israel's slavery in Egypt and Cain's murderous deed still resonate today.[8] The social and natural surroundings in which Henry Vaughan passed his daily life, the tumultuous politics that turned his world upside down, and the books that influenced the way he processed and expressed his experiences all fed into the verbal artefacts he created in his role as poet. It is hoped, therefore, that the two halves of this volume have proved to be mutually supportive: that the various kinds of historical detail provided to illuminate the genesis, meaning, and purpose of Vaughan's texts in Part One have also provided the necessary contextual groundwork for the more literary critical investigations in Part Two.

The author of the biography that marked the tercentenary of Vaughan's death observed that '[a]ll the stress of the riven mid-century seems crowded into his poetry'.[9] It was this stress that turned the literary ambition of a belated Son of Ben into the religious vocation of a disciple of George Herbert, but not without the 'quarrel' with God so powerfully recorded in 'Misery', which stood in the way of creating the harmonious 'Musick' that was the goal of a Herbertian poetic art:

> Thousands of wild and waste Infusions
> Like waves beat on my resolutions,
> As flames about their fuel run
> And work, and wind til all be done,
> So my fierce soul bustles about

---

7 See 'Easter-day', *HV Works*, p. 121.
8 See 'The Mutinie' and 'Abels blood', *HV Works*, pp. 133–34, 612–13.
9 Stevie Davies, *Henry Vaughan*, Border Lines Series (Bridgend: Seren, Poetry of Wales Press, 1995), p. 172.

> And never rests til all be out.
> Thus wilded by a peevish heart
> Which in thy Musick bears no part,
> I storm at thee ...[10]

Vaughan was not unique in thus crying out 'with the bloud of all [his] soul' in the process of remaking himself as a poet under painful pressure from internal and external events. Loss of eyesight and the failure of the Good Old Cause were among the necessary conditions for the composition of the major works published by Milton after the Restoration; Wilfred Owen was transformed as man and artist by the calamity that overwhelmed his world – 'My subject is War, and the pity of War'; and a catalyst for the twentieth-century masterpieces of one of the self-confessed 'last romantics' of the nineteenth century was pithily summed up by his elegist – 'mad Ireland hurt you into poetry'.[11] Milton and Yeats battled on as poets into old age; Owen did not survive the fires that had forged his new poetic voice; Henry Vaughan abandoned the art of poetry for that of the physician less than half way through a long life. By 1655, the deep despair, the anger, the yearning faith, and the spiritual unrest that had driven his literary activities forward after 1648, seem to have run their course. Perhaps the intolerable hurt had eased with time; perhaps his quarrel had been resolved into a calmer acceptance of God's will; perhaps he felt that he had fulfilled his bargain with Herbert in the second edition of *Silex Scintillans*. It may also have been that the interest in the healing of bodies evident in his last two translations was pulling him ever more strongly towards a new vocation, which he could pursue on the same principles that had impelled him towards the poetic goal of writing 'a true Hymn'. Those principles had been formulated in *Hermetical Physick* (1655) in the title of the first subsection under 'How a Physician ought to be qualified': '*Every*

---

10 *HV Works*, pp. 138–40.

11 See *Samson Agonistes* and *Paradise Lost*; the preface to a projected volume of poetry found among Owen's papers after his death, in *The Poems of Wilfred Owen*, ed. Edmund Blunden (London: Chatto & Windus, 1963), p. 40; 'Coole Park and Ballylee, 1931', in *The Collected Poems of W.B. Yeats* (London: Macmillan, 1963), p, 276; and Auden's 'In Memory of W.B. Yeats', in *W.H. Auden: Selected Poems*, ed. Edward Mendelson (London: Faber & Faber, 2009), p. 89.

Physician that desires to cure sick persons well and happily, must be a sound Christian, and truly religious and holy.'[12] Whatever psychological, spiritual, and contextual imperatives were at work, he seems to have been content to spend the rest of his days in the domestic and social roles he had been born to play – head of a growing family and respected member of a rural community – as he continued his journey in quiet confidence towards 'that Cities shining spires / We travell too'.[13]

12 *HV Works*, p. 677. See also *The Chymists Key* (1657). Already in *Olor Iscanus* (1651), he had published translations of two medical works, *Of the Diseases of the Mind and Body* by Plutarch and *Of the Diseases of the Mind, &c.* by Maximus of Tyre.
13 'Joy of my life!', *HV Works*, p. 85.

Bibliography

Editions of Henry Vaughan

Silex Scintillans: Sacred Poems and Private Ejaculations by Henry Vaughan, ed. Rev. H.F. Lyte (London: Pickering, 1847)

The Works in Verse and Prose Complete of Henry Vaughan, Silurist, ed. Alexander B. Grosart, 4 vols., The Fuller Worthies' Library (Blackburn, 1871)

Silex Scintillans. Being a facsimile of the First Edition, published in 1650, with an introduction by the Rev. William Clare (London: Elliot Stock, 1885)

Poems of Henry Vaughan Silurist, ed. E.K. Chambers with an introduction by Canon Beeching, 2 vols., The Muses' Library (London: George Routledge & Sons, 1896)

The Mount of Olives and Primitive Holiness set forth in the Life of Paulinus Bishop of Nola, ed. L.I. Guiney (London: Henry Frowde, 1902)

Silex Scintillans by Henry Vaughan, Silurist, intro. W.A. Lewis Bettany (London: Gresham Publishing, 1905)

The Works of Henry Vaughan, ed. Leonard Cyril Martin, 2 vols. (Oxford: Clarendon Press, 1914)

The Works of Henry Vaughan, ed. L.C. Martin, 2nd edn. (Oxford: Clarendon Press, 1957)

The Secular Poems of Henry Vaughan, ed. E.L. Marilla (Uppsala: A.-B. Lundequistska Bokhandeln, 1958)

The Complete Poetry of Henry Vaughan, ed. French Fogle (New York: New York University Press, 1965)

A Selection from Henry Vaughan, ed. Christopher Dixon (London: Longman, 1967)

Henry Vaughan: The Complete Poems, ed. Alan Rudrum (Harmondsworth: Penguin Books, 1976, revised 1983)

George Herbert and Henry Vaughan, ed. Louis L. Martz, The Oxford Authors (Oxford: Oxford University Press, 1986)

The Works of Henry Vaughan, ed. Donald R. Dickson, Alan Rudrum, and Robert Wilcher, 3 vols. (Oxford: Oxford University Press, 2018)

Primary Sources

Aubrey, John, *Aubrey's Brief Lives*, ed. Oliver Lawson Dick (Harmondsworth: Penguin Books, 1972)
Auden, W.H., *W.H. Auden: Selected Poems*, ed. Edward Mendelson (London: Faber & Faber, 2009)
Authorized Version, Bible, *The Holy Bible: King James Version/Authorized Version: 400th Anniversary Edition*, ed. Gordon Campbell (Oxford: Oxford University Press, 2010)
Bacon, Francis, *The Works of Francis Bacon*, ed. James Spedding and Douglas Denon Heath (London: Longman, Green, Longman, and Roberts, 1861)
Barnes, William, *The Poems of William Barnes*, ed. Bernard Jones, 2 vols. (Carbondale, IL: Southern Illinois University Press, 1962)
Book of Common Prayer, *The Book of Common Prayer: The Texts of 1549, 1559, and 1662*, ed. Brian Cummings (Oxford: Oxford University Press, 2011)
Carew, Thomas, *Poems* (London, 1640)
Cleveland, John, *The Poems of John Cleveland*, ed. Brian Morris and Eleanor Withington (Oxford: Clarendon Press, 1967)
Corbet, John, *An Historicall Relation of the Military Government of Gloucester* (London, 1645)
Cosin, John, *John Cosin: A Collection of Private Devotions*, ed. P.G. Stanwood (Oxford: Clarendon Press, 1967)
Cowper, William, *The Poetical Works of William Cowper*, ed. William Benham (London: Macmillan, 1879)
Donne, John, *John Donne: The Complete English Poems*, ed. A.J. Smith (Harmondsworth: Penguin Books, 1971)
Eikon Basilike with Selections from Eikonoklastes, ed. Jim Daems and Holly Faith Nelson (Peterborough, Ontario and New York: Broadway Press, 2006)
Finch, Anne, Countess of Winchilsea, in *Minor Poets of the Eighteenth Century*, ed. Hugh I'A. Fausset (London: Dent, 1930)
Geneva Bible, *The Geneva Bible: A Facsimile of the 1560 Edition* (Urbana: University of Wisconsin Press, 1969; repr. Peabody, MA: Hendrikson Publishers Inc., 2007)
Habington, William, *The Poems of William Habington*, ed. Kenneth Allott (Liverpool: Liverpool University Press, 1969)
Hall, Joseph, *A Plaine and Familiar Explication of All the Hard Texts of the Whole Divine Scripture of the Old and New Testament* (London, 1633)
Hall, Joseph, *The Holy Order: Or, Fraternity of Mourners in Sion* (London, 1654)
Herbert, George, *Herbert's Remains*, ed. Barnabas Oley (London, 1652)

Herbert, George, *The Works of George Herbert*, ed. F.E. Hutchinson (Oxford: Clarendon Press, 1941)
Herbert, George, *The English Poems of George Herbert*, ed. Helen Wilcox (Cambridge: Cambridge University Press, 2007)
Hooker, Richard, *Of the Laws of Ecclesiastical Polity*, 2 vols., Everyman's Library (London: Dent, 1907)
Hopkins, Gerard Manley, *The Poems of Gerard Manley Hopkins*, ed. W.H. Gardner and N.H. MacKenzie, 4th edn. (London, Oxford, New York: Oxford University Press, 1970)
Hyde, Edward, Earl of Clarendon, *The History of the Rebellion and Civil Wars in England*, ed. W. Dunn Macray, 6 vols. (Oxford: Clarendon Press, 1888)
Jonson, Ben, *Ben Jonson: The Complete Poems*, ed. George Parfitt (Harmondsworth: Penguin Books, 1975)
Juvenal, *Juvenal and Persius*, trans. G.G. Ramsay, Loeb Classical Library, rev. edn. (Cambridge, MA: Harvard University Press, 1940)
Lanyer, Aemilia, 'The Description of Cook-ham', in *Kissing the Rod: An Anthology of Seventeenth-Century Women's Poetry*, ed. Germaine Greer, Susan Hastings, Jeslyn Medoff, and Melinda Sansone (London: Virago Press, 1988), pp. 44–53
Marvell, Andrew, *The Poems of Andrew Marvell*, ed. Nigel Smith, Longman Annotated English Poets, rev. edn. (London and New York: Pearson Education, 2007)
Mercurius Cambro-Britannicus (1652)
Milton, John, *John Milton*, ed. Stephen Orgel and Jonathan Goldberg, The Oxford Authors (Oxford: Oxford University Press, 1990)
Nicholson, William, *An Exposition of the Catechism of the Church of England* (1655)
Ovid, *Ovid: Tristia and Ex Ponto*, trans. Arthur Leslie Wheeler, Loeb Classical Library (London: William Heinemann, 1924)
Owen, Wilfred, *The Poems of Wilfred Owen*, ed. Edmund Blunden (London: Chatto & Windus, 1963)
Philips, Edward, *Theatrum Poetarum* (1675)
Randolph, Thomas, *The Poems of Thomas Randolph*, ed. G. Thorn-Drury (London: Frederick Etchells and Hugh Macdonald, 1929)
Reed, John Curtis, 'Humphrey Moseley, Publisher', *Oxford Bibliographical Society Proceedings and Papers*, II (1927–30), 59–142
Shakespeare, William, *The Complete Works: Compact Edition*, ed. Stanley Wells and Gary Taylor, The Oxford Shakespeare (Oxford: Clarendon Press, 1988)
Spenser, Edmund, *Edmund Spenser: The Fairie Queene*, ed. A.C. Hamilton, Longman Annotated English Poets (London and New York: Longman, 1977, corr. 1980)

Symonds, Richard, *Richard Symonds's Diary of the Marches of the Royal Army*, ed. C.E. Long, Camden Classic Reprints 3 (Cambridge: Cambridge University Press, 1997)

Taylor, Jeremy, *The Golden Grove, Or, A Manuall of Daily Prayers and Letanies, Fitted to the Dayes of the Week* (London, 1655)

Taylor, Jeremy, *Jeremy Taylor: Holy Living and Holy Dying*, ed. P.G. Stanwood, 2 vols. (Oxford: Clarendon Press, 1989)

Vaughan, Thomas, *Works of Thomas Vaughan*, ed. Arthur Edward Waite [1919] (Kessinger Publishing's Rare Mystical Reprints, n.d.)

Vaughan, Thomas, *The Works of Thomas Vaughan*, ed. Alan Rudrum (Oxford: Clarendon Press, 1984)

Vaughan, Thomas, *Thomas and Rebecca Vaughan's* Aqua Vitae: Non Vitis, ed. and trans. Donald R. Dickson, Medieval and Renaissance Texts and Studies, Vol. 217 (Tempe, AZ: Arizona Center for Medieval and Renaissance Studies, 2001)

Waller, Edmund, *Poems, &c.* (London, 1645)

Winstanley, William, *The Lives of the Most Famous English Poets* (London, 1687)

Wood, Anthony, *Historia et Antiquitates Universitatis Oxoniensis*, 2 vols. (Oxford, 1674)

Wood, Anthony, *Athenae Oxonienses* [1691–92], ed. Philip Bliss, 3rd edn., 4 vols. (London: F.C. and J. Rivington, 1813–20)

Wordsworth, William, *The Poetical Works of William Wordsworth*, 5 vols.: Vol. II, ed. Ernest de Selincourt, 2nd edn. (Oxford: Clarendon Press, 1952); Vol. V, ed. Ernest de Selincourt and Helen Darbishire (Oxford: Clarendon Press, 1949)

Yeats, William Butler, *The Collected Poems of W.B. Yeats* (London: Macmillan, 1963)

Secondary Sources

Abrams, M.H., *A Glossary of Literary Terms*, 5th edn. (New York: Holt, Rinehart and Winston, 1985)

Achinstein, Sharon, 'Reading George Herbert in the Restoration', *English Literary Renaissance*, 36 (2006), 430–65

Allen, Brigid, 'The Vaughans at Jesus College, Oxford, 1638–48', *Scintilla*, 4 (2000), 68–78

Allen, Don Cameron, 'Vaughan's "Cock-Crowing" and the Tradition', *English Literary History*, 21 (1954), 94–106; repr. in Rudrum, *Essential Articles*

Alvarez, A., *The School of Donne* [1961] (New York and Toronto: Mentor Books, The New Amercian Library, 1967)

Anonymous, 'Olor Iscanus', *The Retrospective Review*, 3:2 (1821), 336–54

Ashton, Helen, *The Swan of Usk: A Historical Novel* (London: Collins, 1940)
Ashton, Robert, *Counter-Revolution: The Second Civil War and its Origins, 1646–8* (New Haven, CT and London: Yale University Press, 1994)
Bennett, Joan, *Five Metaphysical Poets* [originally *Four Metaphysical Poets*, 1934], 3rd edn. (Cambridge: Cambridge University Press, 1964)
Bethel, S.L., 'The Theology of Henry and Thomas Vaughan', *Theology*, 56 (1953), 137–43
Bird, Michael, 'Nowhere but in the Dark: On the Poetry of Henry Vaughan', *English*, 33 (1984), 1–20; repr. in Rudrum, *Essential Articles*
Bloom, Harold, *The Anxiety of Influence: A Theory of Poetry* (Oxford: Oxford University Press, 1975)
Blunden, Edmund, *On the Poems of Henry Vaughan: Characteristics and Intimations* (London: Richard Cobden-Sanderson, 1927)
Brann, Noel L., 'The Conflict between Reason and Magic in Seventeenth-Century England: A Case Study of the More–Vaughan Debate', *Huntington Library Quarterly*, 43 (1979–80), 103–26
Brooks, Cleanth, 'Henry Vaughan: Quietism and Mysticism', in *Essays in Honor of Esmond Linworth Marilla*, ed. Thomas Austin Kirby and William John Olive (Baton Rouge, LA: Louisiana State University Press, 1970), pp. 15–23
Brown, Eluned, 'Henry Vaughan's Biblical Landscape', *Essays and Studies*, new series, 30 (1977), 50–60
Brown, John, *Horae Subsecivae*, new edition in 3 vols. (London: Adam and Charles Black, 1900)
Burnham, Frederic B., 'The More–Vaughan Controversy: The Revolt Against Philosophical Enthusiasm', *Journal of the History of Ideas*, 35 (1974), 33–49
Bush, Douglas, *English Literature in the Earlier Seventeenth Century 1600–1660*, The Oxford History of English Literature, 2nd edn., revised (Oxford: Clarendon Press, 1962)
Calhoun, Thomas O., *Henry Vaughan: The Achievement of Silex Scintillans* (Newark, DE: University of Delaware Press, 1981)
Campbell, Thomas, *Specimens of the British Poets*, 7 vols. (London: John Murray, 1819)
Carlton, Charles, *Charles I: The Personal Monarch* (London: Ark Paperbacks, Routledge & Kegan Paul, 1984)
Cattermole, Richard, *Sacred Poetry of the Seventeenth Century*, 2 vols. (London: John Hatchard and Son, 1836)
Chambers, Leland H., 'Henry Vaughan's Allusive Technique: Biblical Allusions in "The Night"', *Modern Language Quarterly*, 27 (1966), 371–87
Chambers, Leland H., 'Vaughan's "The World": The Limits of Extrinsic Criticism', *Studies in English Literature*, 8 (1968), 137–50

Chapman, A.U., 'Henry Vaughan and Magnetic Philosophy', *Southern Review (Adelaide)*, 4 (1971), 215–26; repr. in Rudrum, *Essential Articles*
Cheek, Philip Macon, 'The Latin Element in Henry Vaughan', *Studies in Philology*, 44 (1947), 69–88
Cluysenaar, Anne, 'Rereading Henry Vaughan's "Distraction"', *Scintilla*, 1 (1997), 93–108
Coffey, John, 'Religion', in *The Oxford Handbook of Literature and the English Revolution*, ed. Laura Lunger Knoppers (Oxford: Oxford University Press, 2012), pp. 98–117
Coiro, Ann Baynes, 'Milton and Class Identity: The Publication of *Areopagitica* and the 1645 *Poems*', *Journal of Medieval and Renaissance Studies*, 22 (1992), 261–89
Corns, Thomas N., 'Thomas Carew, Sir John Suckling, and Richard Lovelace', in *The Cambridge Companion to English Poetry: Donne to Marvell*, ed. Thomas N. Corns (Cambridge: Cambridge University Press, 1993), pp. 200–20
Crawshaw, Eluned, 'The Relationship between the Works of Thomas and Henry Vaughan', *Poetry Wales*, 11 (1975), 73–97
Cross, Claire, 'The Church in England 1646–1660', in *The Interregnum: The Quest for Settlement 1646–1660*, ed. G.E. Aylmer (London and Basingstoke: Macmillan, 1974), 99–120
Dale, James, 'Biblical Allusions in Vaughan's "The World"', *English Studies*, 51 (1970), 336–39
Davies, John, *A History of Wales* (Harmondsworth: Penguin Books, 1994)
Davies, Stevie, *Henry Vaughan*, Border Lines Series (Bridgend: Seren, Poetry Wales Press, 1995)
Davis, Paul, *Translation and the Poet's Life: The Ethics of Translating in English Culture, 1646–1726* (Oxford: Oxford University Press, 2008)
Day, Hilary M., 'Bayly's *The Practice of Piety*: A New Source for Henry Vaughan's *The Mount of Olives*', *Notes and Queries*, 233 (1988), 163–65
Dickson, Donald R., *The Fountain of Living Waters: The Typology of the Waters of Life in Herbert, Vaughan, and Traherne* (Columbia, MO: University of Missouri Press, 1987)
Dickson, Donald R., 'The Alchemistical Wife: The Identity of Thomas Vaughan's "Rebecca"', *The Seventeenth Century*, 13 (1998), 36–49
Dickson, Donald R., *The Tessera of Antilia: Utopian Brotherhoods & Secret Societies in the Early Seventeenth Century* (Leiden: Brill, 1998)
Dickson, Donald R., 'Thomas Vaughan and the Iatrochemical Revolution', *The Seventeenth Century*, 15 (2000), 18–31
Dickson, Donald R., '*The Mount of Olives*: Vaughan's Book of Private Prayer', in Dickson and Nelson, ed., *Of Paradise and Light*, pp. 202–17
Dickson, Donald R., 'Henry Vaughan's Medical Library', *Scintilla*, 9 (2005), 189–209

Dickson, Donald R. and Holly Faith Nelson, ed. *Of Paradise and Light: Essays on Henry Vaughan and John Milton in Honor of Alan Rudrum* (Newark, DE: University of Delaware Press, 2004)

Dodd, A.H., *Studies in Stuart Wales*, 2nd edn. (Cardiff: University of Wales Press, 1971)

Durr, R.A., *On the Mystical Poetry of Henry Vaughan* (Cambridge, MA: Harvard University Press, 1962)

Duvall, Robert, 'The Biblical Character of Henry Vaughan's *Silex Scintillans*', *Pacific Coast Philology*, 6 (1971), 13–19

Eales, Jacqueline, 'Religion in Times of War and Republic, 1642–60', in *The Oxford Handbook of Early Modern English Literature and Religion*, ed. Andrew Hiscock and Helen Wilcox (Oxford: Oxford University Press, 2017), pp. 84–101

Eliot, T.S., 'The Metaphysical Poets', in *Selected Essays*, 3rd edn. (London: Faber & Faber, 1951), pp. 281–91

Ellis, George, *Specimens of the Early English Poets*, 3 vols. (London: G. & W. Nicol and J. Wright, 1801)

Enright, D.J., 'George Herbert and the Devotional Poets', in *The Pelican Guide to English Literature, Volume 3: From Donne to Marvell*, ed. Boris Ford (Harmondsworth: Penguin Books, 1956), pp. 142–59

Fallon, Stephen M., *Milton among the Philosophers: Poetry and Materialism in Seventeenth-Century England* (Ithaca, NY and London: Cornell University Press, 1991)

Farnham, Fern, 'The Imagery of Henry Vaughan's "The Night"', *Philological Quarterly*, 38 (1959), 425–35

Farr, Edward, *Gems of Sacred Poetry*, 2 vols. (London: J. W. Parker, 1841?)

Feingold, Mordechai, 'The Mathematical Sciences and New Philosophies', in *The History of the University of Oxford: Volume IV*, ed. Nicholas Tyacke (Oxford: Clarendon Press, 1997), pp. 359–448

Fissel, Mark Charles, *The Bishops' Wars: Charles I's Campaigns against Scotland, 1638–1640* (Cambridge: Cambridge University Press, 1994)

Fitter, Chris, 'Henry Vaughan's Landscapes of Military Occupation', *Essays in Criticism*, 42 (1992), 123–47

Fletcher, Anthony, *The Outbreak of the English Civil War* (London: Edward Arnold, 1981, corr. 1985)

Forey, Madeleine, 'Poetry as Apocalypse: Henry Vaughan's *Silex Scintillans*', *The Seventeenth Century*, 11 (1996), 161–86

Freeman, Rosemary, *English Emblem Books* (London: Chatto & Windus, 1948)

Friedenreich, Kenneth, *Henry Vaughan*, Twayne's English Authors (Boston, MA: G.K. Hall, 1978)

Galdon, Joseph A., S.J., *Typology and Seventeenth-Century Literature* (The Hague and Paris: Mouton, 1975)

Garner, Ross, *Henry Vaughan: Experience and the Tradition* (Chicago, IL and London: University of Chicago Press, 1959)

Gaunt, Peter, *A Nation Under Siege: The Civil War in Wales 1642–48*, Cadw Welsh Historic Monuments (London: HMSO, 1991)

Gottlieb, Sidney, 'A Royalist Rewriting of George Herbert: *His Majesties Complaint to his Subjects* (1647)', *Modern Philology*, 89 (1991), 211–24

Green, I.M., 'The Persecution of "Scandalous" and "Malignant" Parish Clergy during the English Civil War', *English Historical Review*, 94 (1979), 507–31

Green, Ian, *Print and Protestantism in Early Modern England* (Oxford: Oxford University Press, 2000)

Guiney, Louise Imogen, 'Henry Vaughan', in *A Little English Gallery* (New York: Harper & Brothers, 1894)

Guiney, Louise Imogen, 'Henry Vaughan the Silurist', *The Atlantic Monthly*, 73 (May 1894), 681–92

Guiney, Louise Imogen, 'Milton and Vaughan', *The Quarterly Review*, 220 (1914), 353–64

Guinsberg, Arlene Miller, 'Henry More, Thomas Vaughan and the Late Renaissance Magical Tradition', *Ambix*, 21:7 (1980), 36–58

Halley, Janet E., 'Versions of the Self and the Politics of Privacy in *Silex Scintillans*', *George Herbert Journal*, 7 (1983–84), 51–71

Hammond, Gerald, '"Poor dust should lie still low": George Herbert and Henry Vaughan', *English*, 35 (1986), 1–22

Hill, Christopher, *Change and Continuity in Seventeenth-Century England* (London: Weidenfeld and Nicolson, 1974)

Hill, Christopher, *The Collected Essays of Christopher Hill: Volume One: Writing and Revolution in 17th-Century England* (Brighton: Harvester Press, 1985)

Hill, Christopher, *The English Bible and the Seventeenth-Century Revolution* (London: Allen Lane, The Penguin Press, 1993)

Hill, Geoffrey, 'A Pharisee to Pharisees: Reflections on Vaughan's "The Night"', *English*, 38 (1989), 97–113

Hiltner, Ken, *Milton and Ecology* (Cambridge: Cambridge University Press, 2003)

Hollander, John, *The Figure of Echo: A Mode of Allusion in Milton and After* (Berkeley, CA, Los Angeles, CA, and London: University of California Press, 1981)

Holmes, Elizabeth, *Henry Vaughan and the Hermetic Philosophy* (Oxford: Basil Blackwell, 1932)

Hooker, Jeremy, 'Henry Vaughan: Image-Maker, Iconoclast', *The Swansea Review*, 15 (1995), 22–32

Hooker, Jeremy, 'For Roland Mathias: Tribute and Apology', *Scintilla*, 13 (2009), 95–100
Hooker, Jeremy, '"Pure and endless light": Henry Vaughan in his Landscape', in Siberry and Wilcher, ed., *Henry Vaughan and the Usk Valley*, pp. 1–16
Hughes, Helen Sard, 'Night in the Poetry of Henry Vaughan', *Modern Language Notes*, 28 (1913), 208–11
Humfrey, Belinda, 'Vaughan and Vegetables', *Scintilla*, 3 (1999), 137–49
Hutchinson, F.E., 'The Sacred Poets', in *The Cambridge History of English Literature*, Vol. 7, ed. A.W. Ward and A.R. Waller (Cambridge: Cambridge University Press, 1911), pp. 37–42
Hutchinson, F.E., *Henry Vaughan: A Life and Interpretation* (Oxford: Clarendon Press, 1947)
Irwin, William, 'What is an Allusion?', *The Journal of Aesthetics and Art Criticism*, 59 (2001), 287–97
Jaeckle, Daniel, 'From Witty History to Typology: John Cleveland's "The Kings Disguise"', in *The English Civil Wars in the Literary Imagination*, ed. Claude J. Summers and Ted-Larry Pebworth (Columbia, MO and London: University of Missouri Press, 1999), pp. 71–80
Jenkins, Philip, 'Welsh Anglicans and the Interregnum', *Journal of the Historical Society of the Church in Wales*, 27 (1990), 51–59
Jenkins, Philip, *A History of Modern Wales 1536–1990* (London and New York: Longman, 1992)
Johnson, A.M., 'Wales during the Commonwealth and Protectorate', in *Puritans and Revolutionaries: Essays in Seventeenth-Century History Presented to Christopher Hill*, ed. Donald Pennington and Keith Thomas (Oxford: Clarendon Press, 1978), pp. 233–56
Johnson, Samuel, 'The Life of Cowley', in *The Lives of the English Poets*, 2 vols., Everyman's Library [1925] (London: Dent, 1961), Vol. I, pp. 1–45
Jones, R. Tudor, 'Religion in Post-Restoration Brecknockshire 1660–1688', *Brycheiniog*, 8 (1962), 11–65
Jones, S.R. and J.T. Smith, 'The Houses of Breconshire: Part III. The Brecon District', *Brycheiniog*, 11 (1965), 1–149
Jones, Theophilus, *A History of the County of Brecknock in Two Volumes*, reprinted from the edition of 1805–09 (Brecon: Edwin Davies, 1898)
Judson, A.C., 'The Source of Henry Vaughan's Ideas Concerning God in Nature', *Studies in Philology*, 24 (1927), 592–606
Kenyon, J.P., ed., *The Stuart Constitution 1603–1688: Documents and Commentary* (Cambridge: Cambridge University Press, 1966)
Kermode, Frank, 'The Private Imagery of Henry Vaughan', *Review of English Studies*, new series, 1 (1950), 206–25
Kerrigan, John, *Archipelagic English: Literature, History, and Politics 1603–1707* (Oxford: Oxford University Press, 2008)

Lewalski, Barbara K., 'Typology and Poetry: A Consideration of Herbert, Vaughan, and Marvell', in *Illustrious Evidence: Approaches to English Literature of the Early Seventeenth Century*, ed. Earl Miner (Berkeley, CA and London: University of California Press, 1975), pp. 41–69

Lewalski, Barbara Kiefer, *Protestant Poetics and the Seventeenth-Century Religious Lyric* (Princeton, NJ: Princeton University Press, 1979)

Llewellyn-Williams, Hilary, '"As Above, So Below": Reflections of the Hermetic Philosophy', *Scintilla*, 1 (1997), 69–76

Loxley, James, *Royalism and Poetry in the English Civil Wars: The Drawn Sword* (Houndmills, Basingstoke: Macmillan, 1997)

MacDonald, George, *England's Antiphon* (London: Macmillan & Co., 1874)

Mahood, M.M., 'Vaughan: The Symphony of Nature', in *Poetry and Humanism* (London: Jonathan Cape, 1950), pp. 252–95; repr. in Rudrum, *Essential Articles*

Maltby, Judith, *Prayer Book and People in Elizabethan and Early Stuart England*, Cambridge Studies in Early Modern British History (Cambridge: Cambridge University Press, 1998)

Marilla, E.L., 'Henry Vaughan and the Civil War', *Journal of English and Germanic Philology*, 41 (1942), 514–26

Marilla, E.L., 'The Significance of Henry Vaughan's Literary Reputation', *Modern Language Quarterly*, 5 (1944), 155–62

Marilla, E.L., '"The Publisher to the Reader" of *Olor Iscanus*', *Review of English Studies*, 24 (1948), 36–41

Marotti, Arthur F., *Manuscript, Print, and the English Renaissance Lyric* (Ithaca, NY: Cornell University Press, 1995)

Martz, Louis L., 'Vaughan and Rembrandt: The Protestant Baroque', in *From Renaissance to Baroque: Essays on Literature and Art* (Columbia, MO and London: University of Missouri Press, 1991), pp. 218–45

Matar, Nabil I., 'George Herbert, Henry Vaughan, and the Conversion of the Jews', *Studies in English Literature*, 30 (1990), 79–92

Mathias, Roland, 'Man on those Hills of Myrrh and Flowres', *Dock Leaves*, 3:7 (1952), 20–31

Mathias, Roland, 'The Silurist Re-examined', *Scintilla*, 2 (1998), 62–77

Mathias, Roland, 'The Making of a Royalist', *Scintilla*, 3 (1999), 107–120

Mathias, Roland, 'Reasons, Reasons', *Scintilla*, 4 (2000), 109–24

Mathias, Roland, 'The Midlands: Introductions and Identifications', *Scintilla*, 5 (2001), 93–103

McColley, Diane Kelsey, *Milton's Eve* (Urbana, IL: University of Illinois Press, 1983)

McColley, Diane Kelsey, *A Gust for Paradise: Milton's Eden and the Visual Arts* (Urbana, IL: University of Illinois Press, 1993)

McColley, Diane Kelsey, 'Water, Wood, and Stone: The Living Earth in Poems of Vaughan and Milton', in Dickson and Nelson, ed., *Of Paradise and Light*, pp. 269–91

McColley, Diane Kelsey, *Poetry and Ecology in the Age of Milton and Marvell* (Aldershot: Ashgate, 2007)

McDowell, Sean H., 'Herbert as *Barrd* in the Imagination of Henry Vaughan', *George Herbert Journal*, 34 (2010–11), 102–18

McDowell, Sean, 'The Sounds of Henry Vaughan's Welsh Bird' (a paper given at the Marcher Metaphysicals Conference held at Gregynog Hall, Powys, in October 2015)

McMaster, Helen N., 'Vaughan and Wordsworth', *Review of English Studies*, 11 (1935), 313–25

Mendelsohn, J. Andrew, 'Alchemy and Politics in England 1649–1665', *Past and Present*, 135 (1992), 30–78

Milton, Anthony, 'Introduction', in *The Oxford History of Anglicanism, Volume 1: Reformation and Identity c. 1520–1662*, ed. Anthony Milton (Oxford: Oxford University Press, 2017), pp. 1–27

Miner, Earl, *The Cavalier Mode: From Jonson to Cotton* (Princeton, NJ: Princeton University Press, 1971)

Mitford, John, *Sacred Specimens Selected from the Early English Poets* (London: Baldwin, Cradock, and Joy, 1827)

Monta, Susannah, 'Vaughan's Life of Paulinus: Recharting the Royalist Journey', in *Renaissance Tropologies: The Cultural Imagination of Early Modern England*, ed. Jeanne Shami (Pittsburgh, PA: Duquesne University Press, 2008), pp. 121–41

Moore Smith, G.C., 'Review of *The Works of Henry Vaughan* ed. L.C. Martin', *Modern Language Review*, 11 (1916), 245–47

Morrill, John, 'The Church in England, 1642–9', in *Reactions to the English Civil War 1642–1649*, ed. John Morrill (Houndmills, Basingstoke: Macmillan, 1982), pp. 89–114

Morrill, John, 'The Attack on the Church of England in the Long Parliament', in *The Nature of the English Revolution: Essays by John Morrill* (London: Longman, 1993), pp. 69–90

Nauman, Jonathan, 'Toward a Herbertian Poetic: Vaughan's Rigorism and "The Publisher to the Reader" of *Olor Iscanus*', *George Herbert Journal*, 23 (1999), 80–104

Nauman, Jonathan, 'F.E. Hutchinson, Louise Guiney, and Henry Vaughan', *Scintilla*, 6 (2002), 135–47

Nauman, Jonathan, 'Classicism and Conversion: The Role of the Poems and Letters of St. Paulinus of Nola in Henry Vaughan's *Silex Scintillans*', *Scintilla*, 18 (2015), 13–26

Nauman, Jonathan, '"The truth and light of things": Henry Vaughan and Nature', in Siberry and Wilcher, ed., *Henry Vaughan and the Usk Valley*, pp. 61–78

Nauman, Jonathan, 'Louise Imogen Guiney and Henry Vaughan', *Brycheiniog*, 48 (2017), 98–121

Oliver, H.J., 'The Mysticism of Henry Vaughan: A Reply', *Journal of English and Germanic Philology*, 53 (1954), 352–60

Olson, Paul A., 'Vaughan's "The World": The Pattern of Meaning and the Tradition', *Comparative Literature*, 13 (1961), 26–32

Oxford Dictionary of National Biography (Oxford: Oxford University Press, 2004)

Packer, John W., *The Transformation of Anglicanism 1643–1660* (Manchester: Manchester University Press, 1969)

Palgrave, Francis T., *Landscape in Poetry from Homer to Tennyson* (London: Macmillan, 1897)

Parker, William R., 'Henry Vaughan and His Publishers', *The Library*, 4th series, 20 (1940), 401–11

Parker, William Riley, *Milton: A Biography*, 2 vols. (Oxford: Clarendon Press, 1986)

Parry, Edward, 'Charles I in South Wales, July to September 1645', *Brycheiniog*, 29 (1996–97), 39–46

Parry, Graham, *Glory, Laud and Honour: The Arts of the Anglican Counter-Reformation* (Woodbridge: The Boydell Press, 2006)

Parry, Graham, 'Vaughan and Laudianism', *Scintilla*, 13 (2009), 185–96

Patrides, C.A., ed., *George Herbert: The Critical Heritage* (London: Routledge and Kegan Paul, 1983)

Perri, Carmela, 'On Alluding', *Poetics*, 7 (1978), 289–307

Pettet, E.C., *Of Paradise and Light: A Study of Vaughan's* Silex Scintillans (Cambridge: Cambridge University Press, 1960)

Poppy, Ithiel Vaughan, 'The Homes of the Vaughans: Part II', *Brycheiniog*, 19 (1980–81), 96–104

Porter, Harry Boone, *Jeremy Taylor Liturgist (1613–1667)* (London: Alcuin Club/ S.P.C.K., 1979)

Post, Jonathan F.S., 'Spitting out the Phlegm: The Conflict of Voices in Vaughan's *Silex Scintillans*', *Philological Quarterly*, 59 (1980), 165–86; repr. in Rudrum, *Essential Articles*

Post, Jonathan F.S., *Henry Vaughan: The Unfolding Vision* (Princeton, NJ: Princeton University Press, 1982)

Post, Jonathan F.S., 'Walking with Vaughan in *Silex Scintillans*', *Scintilla*, 22 (2019), 11–28

Pursglove, Glyn, 'Henry Vaughan and the Energies of Rhyme', *Scintilla*, 1 (1997), 143–57

Pursglove, Glyn, '"Winged and free": Henry Vaughan's Birds', in Dickson and Nelson, ed., *Of Paradise and Light*, pp. 250–68

Radford, C.A. Ralegh, 'Tretower: The Castle and Court', *Brycheiniog*, 6 (1960), 22–50

Ray, Robert H., 'Herbert's Seventeenth-Century Reputation: A Summary and New Considerations', *George Herbert Journal*, 9:2 (1986), 1–15

Ray, Robert H., 'The Herbert Allusion Book: Allusions to George Herbert in the Seventeenth Century', *Studies in Philology*, 83:4 (1986)

Read, Sophie, *Eucharist and the Poetic Imagination in Early Modern England* (Cambridge: Cambridge University Press, 2013)

Rees, Sir Frederick, 'Breconshire during the Civil War', *Brycheiniog*, 8 (1962), 1–9

Reid, David, *The Metaphysical Poets* (Harlow: Longman/Pearson Education, 2000)

Rickey, Mary Ellen, 'Vaughan, *The Temple*, and Poetic Form', *Studies in Philology*, 59 (1962), 162–70

Ricks, Christopher, *Allusion to the Poets* (Oxford: Oxford University Press, 2002)

Robertson, Jean, 'The Use Made of Owen Felltham's "Resolves": A Study in Plagiarism', *Modern Language Review*, 39 (1944), 108–15

Rogers, John, *The Matter of Revolution: Science, Poetry, and Politics in the Age of Milton* (Ithaca, NY and London: Cornell University Press, 1996)

Rothberg, Michael, 'An Emblematic Ideology: Images and Additions in Two Editions of Henry Vaughan's *Silex Scintillans*', *English Literary Renaissance*, 22 (1992), 80–94

Rudrum, A.W., 'Henry Vaughan's "The Book": A Hermetic Poem', *AUMLA: Journal of the Australasian Universities Language and Literature Association*, 16 (1961), 161–66

Rudrum, Alan, 'The Influence of Alchemy in the Poems of Henry Vaughan', *Philological Quarterly*, 49 (1970), 469–80

Rudrum, Alan, 'Thomas Vaughan's *Lumen de Lumine*: An Interpretation of Thalia', in *Literature and the Occult: Essays in Comparative Literature*, ed. Luanne Frank (Arlington, TX: The University of Texas at Arlington, 1977), pp. 234–43

Rudrum, Alan, *Henry Vaughan*, Writers of Wales (Cardiff: University of Wales Press on behalf of the Welsh Arts Council, 1981)

Rudrum, Alan, 'Henry Vaughan, the Liberation of the Creatures, and Seventeenth-Century English Calvinism', *The Seventeenth Century*, 4 (1989), 33–54

Rudrum, Alan, 'Paradoxical Persona: Henry Vaughan's Self-Fashioning', *Huntington Library Quarterly*, 62 (1999), 351–67

Rudrum, Alan, 'Resistance, Collaboration, and Silence: Henry Vaughan and Breconshire Royalism', in *The English Civil Wars in the Literary Imagination*, ed. Claude J. Summers and Ted-Larry Pebworth (Columbia, MO: University of Missouri Press, 1999), pp. 102–18

Rudrum, Alan, 'For then the Earth shall be all Paradise: Milton, Vaughan and the Neo-Calvinists on the Ecology of the Hereafter', *Scintilla*, 4 (2000), 39–52

Rudrum, Alan, 'Henry Vaughan's Poems of Mourning', in Dickson and Nelson, ed., *Of Paradise and Light*, pp. 309–28

Rudrum, Alan, ed., *Essential Articles for the Study of Henry Vaughan* (Hamden, CT: Archon Books, 1987)

Sencourt, Robert, *Outflying Philosophy: A Literary Study of the Religious Element in the Poems and Letters of John Donne and in the Works of Sir Thomas Browne and of Henry Vaughan the Silurist* (London: Simpkin, Marshall, 1925)

Sharpe, Kevin, *The Personal Rule of Charles I* (New Haven, CT and London: Yale University Press, 1992)

Shawcross, John T, 'Vaughan's "Amoret" Poems: A Jonsonian Sequence', in *Classic and Cavalier: Essays on Jonson and the Sons of Ben*, ed. Claude J. Summers and Ted-Larry Pebworth (Pittsburgh, PA: University of Pittsburgh Press, 1982), pp. 193–214

Siberry, Elizabeth and Robert Wilcher, ed., *Henry Vaughan and the Usk Valley* (Little Logaston Woonton Almeley: Logaston Press, 2016)

Simmonds, James, 'The Date of Henry Vaughan's *Silex Scintillans*', *Notes and Queries*, 205 (1960), 64–65

Simmonds, James D., 'Vaughan's Masterpiece and Its Critics: "The World" Revaluated', *Studies in English Literature*, 2 (1962), 77–93

Simmonds, James D., *Masques of God: Form and Theme in the Poetry of Henry Vaughan* (Pittsburgh, PA: University of Pittsburgh Press, 1972)

Smith, A.J., 'Appraising the World', *Poetry Wales*, 11:2 (1975), 55–72; repr. in Rudrum, *Essential Articles*

Spink, Ian, *Henry Lawes: Cavalier Songwriter* (Oxford: Oxford University Press, 2000)

Spitz, Leona, 'Process and Stasis: Aspects of Nature in Vaughan and Marvell', *Huntington Library Quarterly*, 32 (1968–69), 135–47

Spurr, John, *The Restoration Church of England, 1646–1689* (New Haven, CT and London: Yale University Press, 1991)

Srigley, Michael, 'Ritual Entries: Some Approaches to Henry Vaughan's *Silex Scintillans*', *Scintilla*, 3 (1999), 43–59

Srigley, Michael, 'Thomas Vaughan, the Hartlib Circle and the Rosicrucians', *Scintilla*, 6 (2002), 31–54

Sterrett, Joe, 'The Dynamic of Despair: Evolving Toleration for Cain in Herbert and Vaughan', *Scintilla*, 16 (2012), 81–91

Sturrock, June, '"Cock-Crowing"', *Scintilla*, 5 (2001), 152–58

Summers, Claude J., 'Herrick, Vaughan, and the Poetry of Anglican Survivalism', in *New Perspectives on the Seventeenth-Century English Religious Lyric*, ed. John R. Roberts (Columbia, MO and London: University of Missouri Press, 1994), pp. 46–74

Summers, Claude J. and Ted-Larry Pebworth, 'Vaughan's Temple in Nature and the Context of "Regeneration"', *Journal of English and Germanic Philology*, 74 (1975), 351–60; repr. in Rudrum, *Essential Articles*

Summers, Claude J. and Ted-Larry Pebworth, 'Herbert, Vaughan, and Public Concerns in Private Modes', *George Herbert Journal*, 3 (1979–80), 1–21

Summers, Claude J. and Ted-Larry Pebworth, 'The Politics of *The Temple*: "The British Church" and "The Familie"', *George Herbert Journal*, 8 (1984), 1–15

Summers, Joseph H., *The Heirs of Donne and Jonson* (London: Chatto & Windus, 1970)

Thomas, Hugh, *A History of Wales 1485–1660* (Cardiff: University of Wales Press, 1972)

Thomas, Keith, *Man and the Natural World: Changing Attitudes in England 1500–1800* (London: Penguin Books, 1984)

Thomas, M. Wynn, *Morgan Llwyd*, Writers of Wales (Cardiff: University of Wales Press on behalf of the Welsh Arts Council, 1984)

Thomas, M. Wynn, '"No Englishman": Wales's Henry Vaughan', *The Swansea Review*, 15 (1995), 1–19

Thomas, M. Wynn, '"In Occidentem & tenebras": Putting Henry Vaughan on the Map of Wales', *Scintilla*, 2 (1998), 7–24

Thomas, Noel Kennedy, *Henry Vaughan: Poet of Revelation* (Worthing: Churchman Publishing, 1986)

Thomas, P.W., *Sir John Berkenhead 1617–1679: A Royalist Career in Politics and Polemics* (Oxford: Clarendon Press, 1969)

Thomas, Peter, 'Henry Vaughan, Orpheus, and the Empowerment of Poetry', in Dickson and Nelson, ed., *Of Paradise and Light*, pp. 218–49

Thomas, Peter, 'The "Desert Sanctified": Henry Vaughan's Church in the Wilderness', in *Sacred Text–Sacred Space: Architectural, Spiritual and Literary Convergences in England and Wales*, ed. Joseph Sterrett and Peter Thomas (Leiden and Boston, MA: Brill, 2011), pp. 163–91

Thomas, Peter W., 'The Language of Light: Henry Vaughan and the Puritans', *Scintilla*, 3 (1999), 9–29

Trickett, Rachel, 'Henry Vaughan and the Poetry of Vision', *Essays and Studies*, new series, 34 (1981), 88–104; repr. in Rudrum, *Essential Articles*

Vaughan, J., 'Henry Vaughan, Silurist', *The Nineteenth Century and After*, 67 (1910), 492–504

Wall, John N., *Transformations of the Word: Spenser, Herbert, Vaughan* (Athens, GA: University of Georgia Press, 1988)

Walley, Harold R., 'The Strange Case of *Olor Iscanus*', *Review of English Studies*, 18 (1942), 17–37

Walters, Richard H., 'Henry Vaughan and the Alchemists', *Review of English Studies*, 23 (1947), 107–22

Wanamaker, Melissa Cynthia, '*Discordia Concors*: The Metaphysical Wit of Henry Vaughan's *Silex Scintillans*', *Texas Studies in Literature and Language*, 16 (1974–75), 463–77

Wardle, Ralph, 'Thomas Vaughan's Influence upon the Poetry of Henry Vaughan', *Publications of the Modern Language Association*, 51 (1936), 936–52

Watson, Graeme J., 'Two New Sources for Henry Vaughan's *The Mount of Olives*', *Notes and Queries*, 230 (1985), 168–70

Watson, Graeme J., 'Political Change and Continuity of Vision in Henry Vaughan's "Daphnis. An Elegiac Eclogue"', *Studies in Philology*, 83 (1986), 158–81

Watson, Graeme J., 'The Temple in "The Night": Henry Vaughan and the Collapse of the Established Church', *Modern Philology*, 84 (1986), 144–61

Watson, Robert N., *Back to Nature: The Green and the Real in the Late Renaissance* (Philadelphia, PA: University of Pennsylvania Press, 2006)

Wedgwood, C.V., *The King's Peace 1637–1641* [1955] (London: Collins Fontana Library, 1966)

Wedgwood, C.V., *The King's War 1641–1647* [1958] (London: Collins Fontana Library, 1966)

Wedgwood, C.V., *Thomas Wentworth: First Earl of Strafford 1593–1641: A Revaluation* [1961] (London: Phoenix Press, 2000)

West, Philip, *Henry Vaughan's* Silex Scintillans: *Scripture Uses* (Oxford: Oxford University Press, 2001)

White, Helen C., *The Metaphysical Poets: A Study in Religious Experience* [1936] (London: Collier-Macmillan, 1962)

Wilcher, Robert, *The Use of Natural Details in English Poetry 1645–1668*, 2 vols. (Ph.D. thesis, Shakespeare Institute, University of Birmingham, 1972)

Wilcher, Robert, '"Daphnis. An Elegiac Eclogue" by Henry Vaughan', *Durham University Journal*, new series, 36 (1974), 25–40

Wilcher, Robert, '"Then keep the ancient way": A Study of Henry Vaughan's *Silex Scintillans*', *Durham University Journal*, new series, 45 (1983), 11–24

Wilcher, Robert, 'What was the King's Book for?: The Evolution of *Eikon Basilike*', *The Yearbook of English Studies*, 21 (1991), 218–28

Wilcher, Robert, '"The present times are not / To snudge in": Henry Vaughan, *The Temple*, and the Pressure of History', in *George Herbert: Sacred and Profane*, ed. Helen Wilcox and Richard Todd (Amsterdam: VU University Press, 1995), pp. 185–94

Wilcher, Robert, 'Henry Vaughan and the Church', *Scintilla*, 2 (1998), 90–104

Wilcher, Robert, '"Feathering some slower hours": Henry Vaughan's Verse Translations', *Scintilla*, 4 (2000), 142–61

Wilcher, Robert, *The Writing of Royalism 1628–1660* (Cambridge: Cambridge University Press, 2001)

Wilcher, Robert, 'The "true, practic piety" of "holy writing": Henry Vaughan, Richard Crashaw, Christopher Harvey, and *The Temple*', in Dickson and Nelson, ed., *Of Paradise and Light*, pp. 50–70

Wilcher, Robert, 'The Darkened Scribe and the Blessed Man: Changing Uses of Allusion in the Work of Henry Vaughan', *Scintilla*, 9 (2005), 38–52

Wilcher, Robert, 'Henry Vaughan, Jeremy Taylor, Edward Sparke, and the Preservation of the Anglican Communion', *Scintilla*, 12 (2008), 141–59

Wilcher, Robert, 'Henry Vaughan and the Poetry of Trees', *Scintilla*, 14 (2010), 28–50

Wilcher, Robert, 'Exile in Breconshire: The Double Displacement of Henry Vaughan', *Scintilla*, 15 (2011), 119–28

Wilcher, Robert, '*Eikon Basilike*: The Printing, Composition, Strategy, and Impact of "The King's Book"', in *The Oxford Handbook of Literature and the English Revolution*, ed. Laura Lunger Knoppers (Oxford: Oxford University Press, 2012), pp. 289–308

Wilcher, Robert, '"Thalia" and the "Father of Lights": Nature and God in the Works of Henry Vaughan and Thomas Vaughan', *Scintilla*, 16 (2012), 9–36

Wilcher, Robert, 'Henry Vaughan's Borrowings: Plagiarism, Imitation, Allusion', *Scintilla*, 17 (2013), 11–27

Wilcher, Robert, 'Lucy Hutchinson', in *The Oxford Handbook of Early Modern English Literature and Religion*, ed. Andrew Hiscock and Helen Wilcox (Oxford: Oxford University Press, 2017), pp. 360–73

Wilcher, Robert, 'Henry Vaughan's *Ars Poetica*', *Scintilla*, 21 (2018), 35–51

Wilcher, Robert, 'Henry Vaughan's Use of Biblical Epigraphs in *Silex Scintillans*', *Scintilla*, 24 (2021)

Wilcox, Allan, 'Nicodemus and "The Night"', *Scintilla*, 15 (2011), 141–55

Wilcox, Allan and Helen, 'Matter and Spirit Conjoined: Sacred Places in the Poetry of George Herbert, Henry Vaughan, R.S. Thomas and Rowan Williams', *Scintilla*, 11 (2007), 133–52

Wilcox, Helen, '"Scribling under so faire a Coppy": The Presence of Herbert in the Poetry of Vaughan's Contemporaries', *Scintilla*, 7 (2003), 185–200

Wilcox, Helen, 'In the *Temple* Precincts: George Herbert and Seventeenth-Century Community-Making', in *Studies in Community-Making and Cultural Memory 1558–1689*, ed. Roger D. Bell and Anthony W. Johnson (Farnham, Surrey: Ashgate, 2009), pp. 253–71

Wilkinson, Ronald Sterne, 'The Hartlib Papers and Seventeenth-Century Chemistry', *Ambix*, 17:2 (1970), 85–110

Willard, Thomas, 'The Publisher of *Olor Iscanus*', *Bibliographical Society of America, Papers*, 75 (1981), 174–79; repr. in Rudrum, *Essential Articles*

Williams, G., 'Hugh Price, Founder of Jesus College, Oxford', *Brycheiniog*, 25 (1992–93), 57–66

Williams, W.R., ed., *Old Wales: A Monthly Magazine of Antiquities for Wales and the Borders*, Vol. 1 ("Old Wales" Office Talybont, Breconshire: Privately Printed for Subscribers, 1905)

Williamson, George, *The Donne Tradition: A Study in English Poetry from Donne to the Death of Cowley* [1930] (New York: Noonday Press, 1958)

Woolrych, Austin, *Britain in Revolution 1625–1660* (Oxford: Oxford University Press, 2002)

Index of Vaughan's Works

(Arranged in chronological order of volumes)

Poems, with the tenth Satyre of Iuvenal Englished (1646) 19, 25, 42, 46, 51, 96, 101, 123, 173
the 'Amoret' poems 46, 264, 306
'An Elegy' 173
'Juvenal's Tenth Satire translated' 85–89, 172
'A Rhapsodie' 16, 82–84
'A Song to Amoret' 184
'To all Ingenious Lovers of Poesie' 19, 85, 96, 182–83, 198
'To Amoret gone from him' 53–54, 175
'To Amoret, of the difference 'twixt him and other Lovers, and what true Love is' 175–77, 185, 187, 264, 291–92, 306
'To Amoret, Walking in a Starry Evening' 53, 291
'To Amoret Weeping' 173, 185
'To my Ingenuous Friend, R.W.' 49, 174, 181, 184, 275, 296–97
'Upon the Priorie Grove, His usuall Retyrement' 25, 26, 54, 185, 275
Silex Scintillans (augmented edition 1655) 4, 5, 6, 31, 32, 43, 46, 51, 58, 104, 105, 126, 127, 139, 142, 157, 165, 193, 194, 198, 202, 204, 212, 223, 225, 230, 232, 241, 246, 247, 257, 280, 282, 294, 295–96, 299, 301, 305, 307, 312, 330
differences between Part I and Part II 105, 128, 197, 221, 295–96
Silex Scintillans Part I (1650) 43, 103, 105, 111, 118, 121, 128, 152, 155, 156, 185, 194, 200, 218, 221, 222, 307
poems in Part I
'Affliction (I)' 74, 113, 322–24, 324
'And do they so?' 65–66, 232–33, 282, 295–96
'Begging (I)' 118
'The Brittish Church' 107–09, 129, 145, 166
'Buriall' 107
'The Call' 106
'Christs Nativity' 111, 310
'Come, come, what doe I here?' 106–07, 308–09
'The Constellation' 114–16, 117, 145, 219, 220, 226, 245, 270
'Corruption' 110, 247, 302
'The Dawning' 69, 109–10, 317–20
'Day of Judgement' 106, 107, 245

Silex Scintillans Part I, poems in continued
  'Death. A Dialogue' 106
  'Disorder and frailty' 69, 233–34, 268, 307
  'Distraction' 320–22, 324
  'Dressing' 74, 111, 161
  'Easter-day' 111–12, 161, 208–10, 329
  'Easter Hymn' 112, 161
  'Faith' 244
  'The Holy Communion' 112, 161
  'H. Scriptures' 234, 246–47, 251, 295
  'Idle Verse' 110–11, 300
  'The Incarnation, and Passion' 206–07, 299–300
  'Isaacs Marriage' 233
  'I Walkt the other day' 69–70, 118, 156, 244
  'Joy of my life! while left me here' 244, 309–10, 331
  'The Lampe' 106
  'The Law, and the Gospel' 230, 236–37
  'Man' 118, 293–94
  'Mans fall, and Recovery' 106, 107, 233
  'The Match' 110, 111, 127, 200
  'Midnight' 204, 257
  'Misery' 116–17, 135, 204, 212–20, 247, 264, 329–30
  'The Morning-watch' 63–64, 281, 324–25
  'Mount of Olives (I)' 118
  'The Mutinie' 114, 116, 117, 218, 219, 238–39, 329
  'The Passion' 205–06
  'Peace' 304–05
  'The Pilgrimage' 113, 133, 230, 274
  'Praise' 210–11
  'Psalm 121' 112–13, 161
  'Regeneration' 106, 113, 127, 155–56, 243–44, 247, 257, 265–66, 307–08, 310
  'Religion' 238, 280–81
  'Repentance' 202, 244, 307
  'The Resolve' 201–02
  'Resurrection and Immortality' 106, 230
  'Retirement (I)' 156–57, 310
  'The Retreate' 5, 6, 107, 228, 298–99
  'Rules and Lessons' 64, 110, 111, 241, 269, 281
  'The Sap' 118
  'The Search' 107, 298
  'The Shepheards' 116, 117, 185, 220
  'The Showre (I)' 207, 273, 278, 311
  'Silence, and stealth of dayes!' 107
  'Son-dayes' 210, 244, 294
  'The Storm' 208, 272–73
  'The Tempest' 67, 270
  'Thou that know'st for whom I mourne' 106
  'Unprofitablenes' 110–11, 268
  'Vanity of Spirit' 32, 61–63, 296
  'The World (I)' 113, 202–03, 315–17
Olors Iscanus (1651) 3, 4, 5, 11, 19, 24, 25, 27, 28, 30, 42, 48, 51, 58, 91, 92, 93, 95, 103, 120, 121, 124, 126, 127, 142, 152, 172, 173, 179, 275, 289, 294, 331
  '*Ad Echum*' 29
  '*Ad Fluvium Iscam*' 29
  '*Ad Posteros*' 11, 91–92, 120–21
  Boethius (translations from) 30, 58, 104–05, 124, 269–70, 275
  Casimir (translations from) 30, 58–60

'The Charnel-house' 4–5, 28, 142–43, 161, 174, 179, 295
'An Elegie on the death of Mr. R. Hall, slain at Pontefract, 1648' 49, 99–100, 173, 179
'An Elegie on the death of Mr. R.W. slain in the late unfortunate differences at Routon Heath, neer Chester, 1645' 49, 92, 173–74, 179, 275
'An Epitaph upon the Lady Elizabeth, Second Daughter of his late Majestie' 122–23
'Monsieur Gombauld' 174
Ovid (translations from) 19–23, 28–29
'To his Friend—' 49, 296
'To his retired friend, an Invitation to Brecknock' 24–25, 28, 93–94, 94, 96, 143, 313–15, 328
'To my worthy friend Master T. Lewes' 49, 123–24, 181
'To Sir William D'avenant, upon his *Gondibert*' 122
'To the best, and most accomplish'd Couple—' 4, 48, 267
'To the most Excellently accomplish'd, Mrs. K. Philips' 17, 174
'To the River Isca' 4, 27, 54, 174, 181–82, 185, 186–87
'Upon a Cloke lent him by Mr. J. Ridsley' 28, 92–93, 94, 96, 294, 301–02
'Upon Mr. Fletcher's Playes, published, 1647' 28, 98–99, 122
'Upon the Poems and Playes of the ever memorable Mr. William Cartwright' 16, 28, 121–22
'*Venerabili viro, præceptori suo olim & semper Colendissimo* M^{ro} *Mathæo Herbert*' 29

The Mount of Olives: Or, Solitary Devotions (1652) 43, 100–01, 104, 126, 127, 137, 158–62, 177, 198, 221, 222, 232, 241
  'Man in Darkness, Or, A Discourse of Death' 125, 221–22, 222
  'The Mount of Olives: Or, Solitary Devotions' 125, 241
  'The Praise and Happinesse of the Countrie-Life' 152–53
  'To the Peaceful, humble, and pious Reader' 158–59, 161
Flores Solitudinis (1654) 43, 126, 222, 223
  'Of Life and Death' 126
  'Primitive Holiness, Set forth in the Life of blessed Paulinus' 222–23
Silex Scintillans Part II (1655) 70, 120, 128, 163, 188
  poems in Part II
    'Abels Blood' 137–38, 247–51, 304, 329
    'The Agreement' 188, 238
    'Anguish' 136, 310
    'Ascension-day' 70, 130, 163, 226, 232, 237, 245
    'Ascension-Hymn' 70, 72, 130, 163, 244, 310–11
    'As time one day by me did pass' 46, 136
    'The Authors Preface to the Following Hymns' 60, 103, 129, 172, 188–90, 193, 198–99, 223, 255–56, 258
    'Begging (II)' 244
    'The Bird' 64–65, 134, 266, 303, 305
    'The Book' 68, 282, 284
    'Childe-hood' 136
    'Cock-crowing' 38, 67, 70, 205, 310
    'The Daughter of Herodias' 303
    'The day of Judgement' 67

Silex Scintillans Part II, poems in
    continued
        'Fair and yong light!' 46, 136,
            242, 274
        'The Feast' 74
        'Jacobs Pillow, and Pillar' 165,
            239–41
        'The Jews' 68, 134–35, 244, 281,
            282
        'Joy' 295
        'L'Envoy' 68, 138–39, 166–67,
            246, 257, 301–02, 304
        'The Men of War' 136–37
        'The Night' 227, 228, 251–55,
            267, 281, 295, 310
        'The Obsequies' 303
        'The Ornament' 300
        'Palm-Sunday' 267, 281
        'The Palm-tree' 133, 263–65,
            284–85
        'The Proffer' 131–33, 137, 203,
            308, 310
        'Providence' 133
        'Psalme 104' 281
        'The Queer' 304
        'The Rain-bow' 5, 205
        'St. Mary Magdalen' 133–34, 226
        'The Seed growing secretly'
            135–36, 242
        'The Starre' 270
        'They are all gone into the
            world of light!' 74, 130,
            264–65, 274, 300–01
        'The Timber' 5, 284, 285–87
        'To the Holy Bible' 257–58
        'Trinity-Sunday' 163, 237
        'The Water-fall' 242, 265,
            271–72, 273, 278, 328
        'White Sunday' 130–31, 163,
            226, 231–32, 237–38, 241–42,
            245–46
        'The Wreath' 5
Hermetical Physick (1655) 43, 330–31

The Chymist's Key (1657) 43, 51, 331
Thalia Rediviva (1678) 1, 5, 13, 33, 37,
    50, 97, 127, 153, 276
    'Daphnis. An Elegiac Eclogue'
        5, 13, 32, 49, 52, 185, 187–88,
        275–78, 280
    'De Salmone' 33
    'The Eagle' 274
    'Fida: Or, The Country-beauty: To
        Lysimachus' 17
    'The importunate Fortune, written
        to Doctor Powel of Cantre' 61,
        297–98, 301–02
    'The King Disguis'd' 97–99
    'The old man of Verona out of
        Claudian' 33–34
    'Retirement (II)' 153, 295
    'To Etesia (for Timander,) the first
        Sight' 271
    'To his Books' 295
    'To his Learned Friend and Loyal
        Fellow-Prisoner, Thomas Powel
        of Cant. Doctor of Divinity'
        49, 267, 292–93
    'To Lysimachus, the Author being
        with him in London' 16–17
    'To the Editor of the matchless
        Orinda' 17
    'To the pious memorie of
        C.W. Esquire who finished
        his Course here, and made his
        Entrance into Immortality
        upon the 13 of September, in
        the year of Redemption 1653' 49
Letters
    Letter 2 (15 June 1673) 1–2, 18, 43,
        48–49, 50
    Letter 3 (7 July 1673) 49
    Letter 4 (9 December 1675) 2
    Letter 5 (28 June 1680) 33
    Letter 6 (25 March 1689) 2, 50–51
    Letter 7 (25 April 1689) 50–51
    Letter 8 (14 September 1693) 47

General Index

Abel 248, 250
Abercynrig 17, 24, 90
Abergavenny 90
Abraham 153, 244, 281
Abrams, M.H. 179
Achinstein, Sharon 223
Act for the Better Propagation and Preaching of the Gospel in Wales 31, 119, 128, 129, 130, 149–50, 156, 165
Adam 233
Agincourt 79
Agrippa, Cornelius 71
Ainsworth, Henry 257
Alanus de Insulis 38
Albury 47, 49
alchemy 7
Allen, Brigid 15
Allen, Don Cameron 67
Allt yr Esgair 12, 31
allusions 181–83, 199–200
    defined 180–81
Alvarez, A. 197, 287
Ambrose 256
Amoret 25, 26
Andrewes, Lancelot 142, 230
Anon. (1821) 289, 295
approvers 119, 161–62
Aquinas, Thomas 234, 260
Archer, Rebecca (wife of Thomas Vaughan) 44–45
Arden, Goditha 25

Aristotle 55
Ark of the Covenant 253
Ashburnham, John 94
Ashmolean Museum 33
Ashton, Helen 18, 39
Ashton, Robert 99
Askew, Egeon 257
Astley, Sir Jacob 94
Aubrey, John 1, 2, 16, 18–19, 33, 39, 41, 43, 44
Auden, W.H. 330
Augustine 234, 241, 256
Authorized Version of the Bible 225, 229, 230, 232, 233, 234, 243
    books
        Acts 163, 232, 243
        Amos 239
        2 Chronicles 251, 253, 254
        Colossians 244–45, 250, 251, 255
        1 Corinthians 73, 241
        Daniel 106
        Deuteronomy 238
        Ephesians 253
        Exodus 238, 239, 241, 244, 251, 253, 254
        Ezekiel 242, 245
        Galatians 235
        Genesis 154, 238, 239, 241, 243, 244, 247, 251, 256, 291
        Hebrews 235, 237, 250, 251, 252–53, 253, 254
        Hosea 234

Isaiah 111, 236, 251, 256
James 38, 244
Jeremiah 244
Job 106, 245, 256, 269
Joel 250
1 John 251
John 108, 226, 228, 235, 240, 243, 244, 251, 252, 316
Jonah 244
Judges 226, 245
1 Kings 251, 255
Luke 136, 137, 226, 232, 235, 244, 250–51, 251, 253, 254
Malachi 228, 232, 251, 254
Mark 226, 228, 251, 253
Matthew 226, 244, 245, 253, 257, 318
Numbers 130, 226, 236, 239, 251, 253
Obadiah 239
1 Peter 107, 244
Psalms 157, 246, 248–49, 251, 253
Revelation 109, 136, 228, 232, 242, 245, 249, 251, 255, 319
Romans 66, 232, 233, 235, 245, 286
Song of Solomon 108, 109, 228, 251, 255, 257, 317
Wisdom of Solomon 243–44
translated into Welsh 229
Babylon 246
Bacchus 20, 21
Bacon, Francis 260
Badger, George 51
Balaam 130, 226
Barnes, William 279
Bauthumley, Jacob 283
Bayly, Lewis 160
Beaumont, Francis 177
Beeching, H.C. 193, 311–12
Beeston Castle 18, 24, 29, 41, 92, 94, 294

Bemerton 193, 223
Bennett, Joan 171–72, 191, 290, 312, 324
Berkenhead, John 17
Berwick, Pacification of 80
Bethel 154, 155, 243
Bethell, S.L. 60, 72
Bettany, W.A. Lewis 194, 195
Beza, Theodore 65, 229, 230, 232
Bird, Michael 173
Bishops' Wars 80–81
Black Mountains 79
Black Sea 19
Bloom, Harold 197
Blunden, Edmund 7, 31, 51, 266, 295, 296
Blunden, Humphrey 51
Boethius 30, 31, 58, 104–05, 124, 172, 269–70, 275–76
the Book of Common Prayer 74, 111, 125, 134, 141, 142, 148, 156, 157, 158, 159, 160, 161, 230, 256
banned by Long Parliament 144, 221
the Book of Homilies 141
the Book of Nature 269, 270
Boyle, Robert 43, 44
Brann, Noel L. 42
Brecon Beacons 13, 31, 91
Brecon (Brecknock) 1, 3, 12, 24, 25, 33, 80, 90, 93, 128, 142, 328
Breconshire (Brecknockshire) 23, 27, 31, 33, 41, 48, 79, 84, 90, 91, 131, 149, 150, 153, 272, 280, 319
Bristol 91
Bristol, John Digby, Earl of 82
Brooks, Cleanth 228
Brown, Eluned 32, 228, 280
Brown, John 263–64
Browne, William 26, 177, 183
Bruce, Robert 257
Buckingham, Duke of 142
Buckland 14, 17–18
Bucklersbury 17

Burnham, Frederic B. 42
Bush, Douglas 226
Bwlch 12, 13

Caesar, Julius 83
Cain 247, 249, 251, 329
Calhoun, Thomas O. 8, 74, 178–79, 198, 322, 324
Caligula 83
Calvin, John 256, 257
Cambria 28
Cambridge, University of 142
Campbell, Thomas 5, 289
Cantref 118, 119
Cardiff 79
Carew, Thomas 95, 177, 186
Carisbrooke, Castle 122
Carlton, Charles 94
Carmarthen 150
Cartwright, William 2, 16, 17, 177, 186
Cattermole, Revd. Richard 5
Catullus 177, 275
Cavalier winter 124, 135, 315
Cefnyllis 80
Chambers, E.K. 6, 225–26
Chambers, Leland H. 227, 317
Chapman, A.U. 292
Charles I 23, 24, 31, 40, 77, 78, 80, 91, 104, 109, 113, 116, 121, 123, 142, 147, 164, 187, 199, 277
    assented to Bill to execute Strafford 82, 89
    attempt to arrest Five Members 83–84
    flight from Oxford 94, 98
    recruiting in South Wales 90–91
Charles II 47, 109, 132, 135
Chaucer, Geoffrey 38, 260
Cheek, Philip Macon 177–78
Chepstow Castle 151
Cheshire 89, 91
Chester 18, 24, 41, 77, 92, 94
Child, Dr Robert 43

Chirk 91
Church of England 94, 103–04, 108, 125, 141, 164, 165
    dismantled and outlawed by Long Parliament 142, 143–45, 167, 183
    ejection of orthodox clergy 80, 149–50
    Laudian reforms 141–42
    liturgical calendar 162–63
    puritan persecution of 115, 217
    significance of George Herbert for 222
    survivalist movement 147–48
    use of King James bible 229–30
Chymical Club (Christian Learned Society) 43
Cicero 178
Civil Wars 3, 18, 40, 77, 89, 313
    in the Marches and South Wales 77–80, 89–91, 104
Clare, Revd. William 194
Cleveland, John 96–98, 177
Cluysenaar, Anne 320–21, 322
Cobbet, Thomas 148
Coffey, John 146
Coiro, Ann Baynes 95–96
Coleshill Manor 25, 26
Commissions of Array 89, 90
Committee of Compounding 149
Corbet, J. 78
Cornwall 89
Cosin, John 142, 160–61
Cowper, William 279
Cradock, Walter 79, 119, 163
Cranmer, Thomas 141, 158, 160
Crawshaw, Eluned 61
Crickhowell 11, 13, 33, 80
Cromwell, Oliver 90, 113, 120, 129, 166
Cross, Claire 149

Dale, James 228
Davenant, Sir William 177
Davies, John 82

Davies, Stevie 7, 12, 13, 39, 45, 46, 47, 48, 50, 191, 196–97, 221, 225, 276, 278, 286, 302, 307, 325, 329
Davis, Paul 20, 50
Day, Hilary M. 160
Day, John 160
Democritus 86
Denham, Sir John 177
Descartes, René 75, 283
Dickson, Donald R. 41, 42, 43, 44, 158, 231, 241, 242, 257, 283, 290–91
Digby, George 25, 81–82
Digby, Lord Kildare 26
Diodati, John 257
the Directory of Public Worship 144, 156, 159
Dixon, Christopher 226–27
Dodd, A.H. 90, 119
Doncaster 91
Donne, John 95, 171, 178, 266, 290
 allusions to 174–77, 183–85
Dorchester 94
Drayton, Michael 177
Dryden, John 296
Durr, R.A. 8, 115, 132, 225, 269, 290, 326
Duvall, Robert 228, 242–43
dyfalu 210, 255, 295

Eales, Jacqueline 142–43
Earle, John 294
Edgehill, Battle of 18, 24, 77
Egypt 218, 246, 329
Eikon Basilike 116, 137, 164
Elias 281
Elijah 255
Eliot, T.S. 293
Elizabeth, Princess 122–23
Elizabeth, Queen 15, 89
Elizabethan Settlement 141
Ellis, George 4, 289
emblem poetry 271–74
Enright, D.J. 195

Erbury, William 79, 128, 134, 135
Esau 241
Eugenius Philalethes (Thomas Vaughan's pseudonym) 3, 37, 51, 61

Fairfax, Sir Thomas 90, 91
Fallon, Stephen 283, 284
Farnham, Fern 227, 251
Farr, Edward 5
Fawkes, Guy 143
Feingold, Mordechai 44, 75
Felltham, Owen 172, 173, 177
Finch, Anne, Countess of Winchilsea 279
Fissel, Mark Charles 80–81
Fitter, Chris 117
Fleet Street 16, 83
Fletcher, Anthony 89, 90
Fogle, French 8
Forey, Madeleine 128–29, 247
Fowler, John 17
Freeman, Rosemary 163–64, 271
Frewin, Accepted (Bishop of Lichfield) 151
Friedenreich, Kenneth 8, 185, 228
Fychan, Sir Roger, of Bredwardine 79

Galdon S.J., Jospeh A. 239–40, 256
Galilee 254
Gam, Dafydd 78–79
Gam, Gwladys 79
Games, Edward 24
Games, Elizabeth 14
Games, Meredith 14
Garner, Ross 8, 283
Gassendi, Pierre 75
Gatford, Lionel 148
Gaunt, Peter 90
Geneva Bible 229, 230, 232, 233, 234, 257
 Genesis 233
 Hosea 234
 Romans 233

Gifford, George 257
Gilbert, William 292
Glamorgan 33, 99, 150
Glendower, Owen 78
Globe Tavern 16, 82, 83
Golden Grove 151
Gottlieb, Sidney 199
Grand Remonstrance 122
Green, Ian M. 149, 160
Grosart, Revd. Alexander B. 6, 194, 225–26
Guevara, Antonio de 153
Guiney, Louise Imogen 4, 6, 7, 13, 14, 83, 194, 195, 266, 289–90, 295
    on Vaughan's borrowings from Herbert 194–95
    on Vaughan's use of Milton 185–89
Guinsberg, Arlene Miller 43
Gunter, John (of Tredomen) 150
Gylston Manor 25

Habington, William 171, 178, 185, 186, 242
    Vaughan's borrowings from 174, 176–77, 181–83
Hall, Joseph (Bishop of Exeter) 148, 149, 154–55, 159, 256
Hall, R. 99–100
Halley, Janet E. 146
Hammond, Gerald 197, 201, 203, 204, 242
Hammond, Henry 147, 148, 151, 159, 161
Hampden, John 79
Hampton Court 84
Harris, Robert 257
Hartlib, Samuel 43
Harvard College 43
Hazlitt, Carew 4
Henry IV 78
Henry V 78
Henshaw, Thomas 42–43, 44

Herbert, George 60, 101, 111, 141, 145, 152, 156, 158, 167, 171, 172, 173, 289, 290, 302, 306, 307, 312, 322, 328, 329
    changing nature of Vaughan's allusions to 221–23
    critical views on Vaughan's debt to 171–72, 173, 193–98
    Herbert's Remains 223
    A Priest to the Temple, Or, The Country Parson 223
    The Temple 95, 194, 195, 196, 198, 200, 207, 208, 212, 213, 222, 242, 307, 325, 327
    poems figuring in Vaughan's texts
        'Aaron' 111, 202
        'Affliction (I)' 201
        'The Agonie' 205–06
        'The Altar' 155
        'The Bag' 206–07
        'The British church' 108, 145, 219
        'The bunch of grapes' 235–36, 237
        'The Church-floor' 155
        'Church-lock and Key' 155
        'The Church Militant' 222
        'Church-monuments' 155, 212
        'Church-musick' 222
        'The Church-porch' 212, 213–14, 221, 222
        'Church-rents and schismes' 108, 219, 222
        'The Collar' 212, 216–17
        'Complaining' 203
        'Confession' 202–03
        'Content' 222
        'The Dawning' 208–10
        'Death' 222
        'Deniall' 207, 307
        'Dulnesse' 202
        'The Familie' 218–19
        'Giddiness' 212, 216
        'The Glance' 205, 212

Herbert, George, poems figuring in
    Vaughan's texts, *continued*
        'The Glimpse' 212, 214
        'Good Friday' 205
        'The H. Scriptures (II)' 231
        'Jordan (II)' 204, 212
        'Life' 222
        'Love (II)' 212
        'Love Unknown' 165
        'Miserie' 212–16
        'Mortification' 212, 215
        'Nature' 212, 217
        'Obedience' 110, 200
        'An Offering' 211
        'Praise (II)' 210–11
        'Prayer (I)' 202, 210, 295
        'Prayer (II)' 207
        'The Priesthood' 221, 222
        'Providence' 204
        'The Reprisall' 201, 202
        'Sighs and Groans' 212
        'Sion' 155, 164, 212
        'The Starre' 212
        'The Storm' 208
        'Sundays' 295
        'Vanitie (II)' 222
        'The Windows' 155
Herbert, Revd. Matthew 3, 11, 13, 14, 15, 29, 39, 52, 53, 79–80, 178, 185, 276, 277
Hereford 19, 91
Hermetism 38, 43, 52–53, 56
Herrick, Robert 186
Hertford, Marquess of 24
Hill, Christopher 78, 103, 226, 230
Hill, Geoffrey 228, 251, 252, 305
Hiltner, Ken 284
Hobbes, Thomas 283
Hollander, John 204
Holly Bank Cottage 33
Holmes, Elizabeth 7, 61, 266–67
Hooker, Jeremy 7, 264, 269
Hooker, Richard 154, 155, 158

Hopkins, Gerard Manley 279–80
Horace 178, 181
Horeb 241
House of Commons 81, 82, 83, 88
House of Lords 82, 144
Hudson, Michael 94
Hughes, Helen Sard 227, 274
Humfrey, Belinda 274
Hutchinson, F.E. 1, 6, 14, 17, 42, 48, 79, 93, 123, 145, 185, 189, 274–75, 276, 303, 312
    composition of *Life and Interpretation* 6–7
Hutchinson, Colonel John 75
Hyde, Edward, Earl of Clarendon 88

imitation 178
interregnum 139, 241
Irwin, William 181
Isca *see* Usk, River

Jacob 154, 155, 156, 239, 240, 241, 243, 257, 281
Jaeckle, Daniel 97
James I and VI 142, 145
Jeffreys, John (of Abercynrig) 17–18, 24, 90, 93, 119
Jenkins, Philip 77, 151
Jerome 256
Jerusalem 165, 236, 254
Jesus College 3, 15, 40–41, 42, 48, 80, 151
    Laudian reforms in chapel 141–42
Johnson, A.M. 119, 149
Johnson, Samuel 293
Jones, Edmund 119
Jones, Jenkin (of Landetty) 79, 119–20, 124
Jones, R. Tudor 150
Jones, S.R. 12
Jones, Theophilus 4, 5, 12, 32, 34,
    A History of the County of Brecknock 4, 13–14

Jones, William 14
Jonson, Ben 177, 178, 181, 183, 210, 275, 278, 295, 302
Joseph of Arimathæa 252
Judson, A.C. 60–61
Junius–Tremellius Bible 229, 230
Juvenal 85, 86, 87, 91, 178

Kermode, Frank 172–73, 191, 193–94
Kerrigan, John 34, 108, 143, 145
King James Bible *see* Authorized Version of the Bible
King's Lynn 94

Lancashire 89
Lanyer, Aemilia 278–79
Laud, William (Archbishop of Canterbury) 17, 81, 142, 144, 230
Laugharne, Rowland 93
Lawes, Henry 95, 186
Lewalski, Barbara Kiefer 235–36, 246, 256, 257
Lewes, Thomas 118–19, 120, 181
Littleton, Adam 257
Livy 178
Llanafan Fawr 150
Llandaff 31
Llanfigan 118, 119, 181
Llanfihangel-Aberythych 151
Llangattock 11, 13, 14, 15, 39, 52, 80, 178, 276, 277
Llangorse 12
Llanhamlach 15, 32, 90
Llansantffraed 3, 4, 13, 15, 43, 47, 73, 143, 150
 the old church 13–14
Llantrithyd 151
Llaworth y Ty 12
Llewellyn-Williams, Hilary 57–58, 75
Lloyd, Judge Sir Marmaduke 18–19, 25, 41, 85, 91, 93
Llwyd, Morgan 107, 134, 163

London 3, 16, 23, 27, 41, 42, 47, 48, 51, 57, 81, 82, 83, 84, 85, 94, 113, 150, 267, 302
Long Parliament 81, 82, 83, 86, 124, 143, 147, 156, 163
 arrangements for governing Wales 118–20
Lovelace, Richard 26, 186
Loxley, James 97, 100
Lucan 178
Ludgate 83
Lyte, Revd. Henry F. 5–6, 193–94, 289–90, 295, 296, 301

MacDonald, George 263
Mahood, M.M. 103, 191, 225, 283, 285–86, 290
Mainwaring, Bishop 41
Maltby, Judith 146
Mandiham 151
Mansell, Dr Francis 15, 142, 150–51
Marilla, E.L. 4, 5, 8, 17, 91, 92, 99, 120–21, 122–23
Marlarat, Augustin 257
Marotti, Arthur 95
Marshall, William 164
Marston Moor, Battle of 90, 91
Martin, L.C. 6, 7, 172, 173, 195, 225
Martz, Louis L. 295–96, 301, 302, 313, 324
Marvell, Andrew 278, 307
Mary, Queen 229–30
Matar, Nabil I. 134–35
Mathias, Roland 7, 14, 17, 18, 24, 25, 26, 45, 79–80, 92, 100
McColley, Diane Kelsey 75, 284, 286
McDowell, Sean 197–98, 210, 303
McMaster, Helen N. 5
Mendelsohn, J. Andrew 43
Mercurius Pragmaticus 99
Militia Ordinance 89
millenarianism 128
Milton, Anthony 146

Milton, John 198, 221, 284, 307, 330
　Vaughan's allusions to 185–90
Miner, Earl 124
Mitford, Revd. John 5, 283
monarchy 103, 123
Monmouthshire 89, 118, 149
Montah, Susannah 126
Montrose, Earl of 91
Moore Smith, G.C. 83
Moray, Sir Robert 47
More, Henry 42
Moreiddig Warwyn 34
Morgan, Gwenllian E.F. 6, 7, 14, 18, 42, 83, 266
Morgan, John (of Wenallt) 32
Morgan, William 229
Morgan, William (M.P. for Brecon) 90
Morrice, Captain John 99
Morrill, John 144, 147
Moseley, Humphrey 51, 95–96
Moses 236, 241
Mount of Olives 158
Mount Sinai 236, 250, 253
Mount Sion 236, 250

Naseby, Battle of 24, 90, 91
Nauman, Jonathan 6, 51, 67, 126
Neile, Richard (Bishop of Durham) 142
Newark 95, 96
Newburn 81
Newcastle-upon-Tyne 94
New Model Army 90, 108, 118, 124
Newport 79
New Testament 112, 231, 235, 236, 240, 247, 248, 249, 250, 251, 254
Newton, Sir Isaac 44
Newton Hall 151
Newton (Vaughan's birthplace) 3, 4, 5, 11, 13, 14, 17, 33, 79, 118, 150, 155, 276, 277
　description of 11–12
Newtown 91

Nicholson, William 150–52
Nicodemas 243, 251, 252, 254
Noah 239
Nottingham 23, 77, 88

Old Testament 134, 152, 228, 229, 231, 235, 238, 239, 240, 241, 245, 247, 248, 249, 250, 251, 253, 254, 280
Oley, Barnabas 223
Oliver, H.J. 312
Olson, Paul A. 317
Origen 256
Ovid 16, 30, 172, 178, 260
　Vaughan's translations from 19–23, 39–40, 49–50
Owen, Wilfred 330
Owthorpe 75
Oxford, City of 2, 40, 42, 44, 49, 51, 57, 94, 96, 98, 186
Oxford, University of 1, 11, 41, 48, 55, 75, 80, 142, 178
Oxford Dictionary of National Biography 7, 16
Oxford English Dictionary 179, 264, 274

Pacification of Berwick 80
Packer, John W. 148
Palgrave, Francis T. 6, 263, 315
　The Golden Treasury 6, 315
Paracelsus 75
Parker, William Riley 51, 188
Parry, Edward 91
Parry, Graham 142
Paulinus, Bishop of Nola 126
Pebworth, Ted-Larry 104, 109, 146, 155, 218–19
Pembrokeshire 77, 93
Penpont 79
Pentecost 163, 231, 243, 245
Perri, Carmela 79
Persius 178
Petronius 177

Pettet, E.C. 8, 31, 127, 204, 208, 210, 227–28, 242, 269, 285–86, 290
  on Vaughan's borrowings from Herbert 195–96, 221, 312–13, 325
Pharisees 252, 254
Philiphaugh, Battle of 91
Philips, Edward 4
Philips, James 17
Philips, Katherine (née Fowler) 17, 174, 179
Philolethes, Eugenius *see* Vaughan, Thomas (junior)
Pilate 252
plagiarism 172–73, 178
Plautus 178
Pliny 178
Plot, Dr Robert 33
Pontefract Castle 99
Pontywal 12
Pope, Alexander 296
Poppy, Ithiel Vaughan 14
Porter, Harry Boone 151
Post, Jonathan F.S. 8, 28, 54, 104, 123, 127–28, 146, 185, 200, 212, 221, 238, 247, 255, 269, 306, 306–07
  on Vaughan's borrowings from Herbert 195–97
Powell, Thomas 33, 38, 51, 118–19, 120, 292
Powell, Vavasor 79, 119, 128, 135, 163
Powicke Bridge 24
Prayer Book *see* Book of Common Prayer
Price, Colonel Sir Herbert 18, 24, 25, 26, 41, 90, 91, 92, 93
  member of Short and Long Parliaments 81–82
Price, Hugh 15
the Priory 24, 25, 26, 275
Priory Church (Brecon) 143
the Priory Grove 25, 277
proest rhyme 303

Propagation Act *see* Act for the Better Preaching and Propagation of the Gospel in Wales
Protectorate 129, 136, 166
Protestation Oath 86, 87
Prynne, William 189
Puritanism 77, 86, 104, 115, 121, 132, 138, 230
puritans 25, 86, 104, 115, 121, 132, 138, 230
  appropriation of the Scriptures 232
  claim to divine inspiration 128, 130, 163
  disrupters of the Caroline church 219
  extemporary prayer 159–60
  military victory 104
  millenarianism 128
  oppressive power 129, 152, 165, 329
  political activities in Long Parliament 86
  political regime in South Wales 79, 119, 203
  reforming of the national church 143–44, 146, 147, 157
Pursglove, Glyn 266, 274, 303–05
Pym, John 81, 82, 83, 88, 113

Radford, C.A. Ralegh 15
Radnorshire 91
Raglan Castle 24, 77, 78, 90, 94
Randolph, Robert 174, 178
Randolph, Thomas 177, 178, 181, 183, 242
  Vaughan's borrowings from 173–75, 179
Ray, Robert H. 199
Read, Sophie 74–75, 161, 304
Reed, John Curtis 95
Rees, Sir Frederick 90, 91, 93, 119
Reid, David 195–96
Rhys, John David 2
Rickey, Mary Ellen 195, 211, 306, 307
Ricks, Christopher 181, 199–200, 200, 202, 211–12

Robarts, Foulke 154
Robertson, Jean 172
Rogers, John 75, 282–83, 284
Rome 19, 20, 22, 83, 85
Root and Branch Bill 144
Rosicrucian Brotherhood 71
Rothberg, Michael 129
Rowton Heath, Battle of 18, 24, 29, 41, 91
Royal Society 44, 47
Rudrum, Alan 7, 8, 16, 31, 37–38, 46–47, 65, 68, 70, 105, 121, 123, 127, 138, 195, 227, 232, 233, 268, 284
Rupert, Prince 91

St Alban's 94
St Bridget's *see* Llansantffraed
St David's 142
St Fagan's, Battle of 31, 100
St Francis 266
St John 251
St Paul 241, 250, 251, 253, 255, 281
St Paul's Cathedral 81
Sanderson, Robert 148
Sarbiewski, Casimire 30, 31, 58
Scethrog 11, 32
Scethrog House 14
Scottish Covenanters 80, 86, 91
Second Civil War 99, 152
Second Coming of Christ 132, 135–36 237, 254, 282, 319
    Vaughan's longing for 107–10, 132–33, 134
Sejanus 85
    see also Strafford, Earl of
Sencourt, Robert 61
separatists 230
sequestration 133, 149–50
Seth 294
Severn, River 182, 186
Shakespeare, William 177
Sharpe, Kevin 79
Shawcross, John T. 183–84

Sheldon, Gilbert 148, 151
Ship Money 79
Short Parliament 81
Shrewsbury 23, 24, 77, 79
Sidney, Sir Philip 183
Simmonds, James D. 8, 83, 85, 104, 105, 132, 183, 295–96, 296, 298, 305–06, 312, 316, 325
Smith, A.J. 127, 312
Smith, J.T. 12
Somersets, Earls of Worcester 5, 38, 78, 90
Speed, John 294
Spenser, Edmund 25, 141, 259–60, 262, 276, 277, 285
Spink, Ian 186
Spitz, Leona 267, 269
Spurr, John 147, 149, 150, 151
Srigley, Michael 37, 47, 75
Starkey, George 43
Stationers' Register 96, 103
Sterrett, Joseph 251
Stow-on-the-Wold 94
Strafford, Earl of 81, 82, 84, 86, 87, 88, 96
    likened to Sejanus 87–89
the Strand 16, 83
Sturrock, June 67
Suckling, Sir John 96, 177, 186
Sulla 83, 84
Summers, Claude J. 104, 109, 146, 147, 155, 218–19
Summers, Joseph H. 265, 302
Symonds, Richard 92, 93

Talybont Forest 13
Taylor, Jeremy 148, 151, 159, 160
Tertullian 256
Tewkesbury 24
Thalia 37, 73
Thame, River 49
Thames, River 22, 49
Thomas, Hugh 77, 90, 119
Thomas, Keith 259, 260, 275, 287

Thomas, M. Wynn 107, 119, 163
Thomas, Noel Kennedy 8, 130, 146,
    150, 228–29, 254, 317–18
Thomas, Peter W. 15, 16, 27–28, 29, 30,
    32, 34, 129, 139, 148, 149
Thomas, William (of Brecon) 150
Tower Hill 82
Tower of Babel 238
Tower Wharf 16, 83
Trephilip 12
Tretower Court 5, 14–15, 32
    Vaughans of 79, 80
Trevers, Judge Arthur 32
Trickett, Rachel 264
Tweed, River 81
Ty Illtid 32
Ty Mawr 14
Tyndale, William 229
typology 234–42

Usk, River 3, 11, 12, 22, 27, 28–29, 266,
    273
Usk valley 12, 18, 27, 28, 31, 40, 52, 54,
    79, 91, 155, 156, 181, 267, 276, 319, 328

Vaughan Association 7
Vaughan, Catherine *see* Wise,
    Catherine
Vaughan, Charles 14
Vaughan, Elizabeth *see* Wise,
    Elizabeth
Vaughan, Sir George 41
Vaughan, Henry
    as country doctor 43, 44, 330–31
    belief in ascent to heaven 69–72
    belief in restitution of nature 67–68
    changing nature of allusions to
        Herbert 221–23
    childhood and adolescence 52–55
    Christian orthodoxy 72–76
    coat-of-arms 34
    courtship and marriage 25–26,
        45–47
    death and burial 3, 34–35, 47
    education 11, 15–16, 41
    gravestone 34–35
    influence of Herbert analysed
        199–220
    influence of Herbert discussed
        171–72, 173, 193–98
    influence of Hermetism 58–73
    in London 16–17
    interregnum prose 124–27
    military service 24, 41, 92–92
    poetic treatment of trees 274–87
    recovery of life and works from
        oblivion 4–7
    relationship with twin brother
        47–52
    twinship 39–40, 47
    use of biblical allusions 242–46
    use of biblical commentaries 255–57
    use of biblical epigraphs 232–34
    use of complex stanza forms 305–11
    use of conceits and images 289–95
    use of couplets and quatrains
        295–301
    use of organic form 320–26
    use of poetic metre 295–301
    use of rhyme 301–05
    use of vitalist ideas 63–66
Vaughan, J. 289–90
Vaughan, Rebecca *see* Archer, Rebecca
Vaughan, Richard, second Earl of
    Carbery 151
Vaughan, Thomas (junior) 1, 5, 11
    alchemical research 42–43, 44, 48
    childhood and adolescence 52–55
    death and burial 47
    education 16, 40–41, 42
    ejected from living 43, 150
    hermetic beliefs 55–58
    heterodoxy 72–76
    marriage 44–45
    military service 41, 92
    ordained 41

Vaughan, Thomas (junior) *continued*
   twinship and relationship with
      Henry Vaughan 39–40, 47–52
   works
      Anima Magica Abscondita 38,
         42, 54–55, 57, 61, 71–72
      Anthroposophia Theomagica
         42, 51, 55–57, 70–71, 73
      Aqua Vitae: Non Vitis 45,
         52–53, 73–74, 276
      Aula Lucis 42, 53, 63
      Coelum Terrae 42
      Euphrates, or, The Waters of
         the East 42, 53, 67–68
      Lumen de Lumine 37, 42, 45,
         51, 53, 73
      Magia Adamica 42, 51, 53, 63,
         66, 67
      The Man–Mouse Taken in a
         Trap 42
      The Second Wash: or, The Moor
         Scour'd Once More 42
Vaughan, Thomas (senior) 11, 29, 79, 92, 120
Vaughan, William (younger brother of twins) 31, 42, 49, 52, 100, 104, 117
Virgil 16, 28, 37, 178, 275
the 'Vitalist Moment' 75–76, 282–83
the Vulgate 229, 230, 260

Waite, Arthur Edward 71–72
Walbeoffe, Charles 1, 15, 90
Wall, John N. 141, 147, 160, 161, 242
Waller, Edmund 26, 95, 186
Waller, Sir William 90
Walley, Harold R. 19, 58
Walters, Richard H. 63
Wannamaker, Melissa Cynthia 294–95
Ward, Richard 257
Wardle, Ralph M. 66
Warwickshire 33
Watson, Graeme J. 146, 160, 187–88

Watson, Robert N. 284
Wedgwood, C.V. 81, 82, 84, 88
Westminster 31, 118
Westminster Assembly of Divines 144
Westminster School 302
West, Philip 8, 152, 153, 154, 155–56, 227, 229, 231, 232, 235, 241, 245–46, 256, 302–03, 320
Whitehall 47
White, Helen C. 172, 302–03, 312, 316, 320
Wiehe, Edwin 125
Wilcher, Robert 20, 89, 104, 116, 146, 161, 164, 187, 223, 230, 327–28
Wilcox, Allan 156, 252
Wilcox, Helen 145, 156, 199, 220
Wilkins, John 44
Wilkinson, Robert Sterne 43
Willard, Thomas 51
Williams, G. 15
Williams, John 38
Williams, W.R. 80
Williamson, George 171, 290, 312
Willmott, Robert 5
Winstanley, William 4
Wise, Catherine 25, 26, 45, 46, 275
Wise, Elizabeth 45, 47
Wood, Anthony 1, 2, 3, 4, 5, 50
   Athenae Oxonienses 2–3, 5, 41
   Historia et Antiquitates
      Universitatis Oxoniensis 2, 51
Woolrych, Austin 84
Worcester 24
Worcester, Earls of *see* Somersets, Earls of Worcester
Wordsworth, William 261–63, 269, 272, 276, 277, 278, 285
Wren, Matthew (Bishop of Norwich and Ely) 142
Wrexham 79, 91

Yeats, William Butler 330
York 90

Printed and bound by CPI Group (UK) Ltd, Croydon, CR0 4YY
16/10/2024

14575015-0004